FROM WOLF
TO SUPERMUTT

FROM WOLF TO SUPERMUTT
and everything in between

Erika K. Gősi

Copyright © 2022 Erika K. Gősi

The moral right of the author has been asserted.

Apart from any fair dealing for the purposes of research or private study, or criticism or review, as permitted under the Copyright, Designs and Patents Act 1988, this publication may only be reproduced, stored or transmitted, in any form or by any means, with the prior permission in writing of the publishers, or in the case of reprographic reproduction in accordance with the terms of licences issued by the Copyright Licensing Agency. Enquiries concerning reproduction outside those terms should be sent to the publishers.

"The author acknowledges the trademarked status and Embark Veterinary's ("Embark") ownership of trademarks for the wordmarks "Supermutt", as well as certain passages of material appearing on pages 107-109 and appreciates Embark's permission to use such terms and passages in this work."

Matador
Unit E2 Airfield Business Park,
Harrison Road, Market Harborough,
Leicestershire. LE16 7UL
Tel: 0116 2792299
Email: books@troubador.co.uk
Web: www.troubador.co.uk/matador
Twitter: @matadorbooks

ISBN 978 1803131 788

British Library Cataloguing in Publication Data.
A catalogue record for this book is available from the British Library.

Printed and bound by CPI Group (UK) Ltd, Croydon, CR0 4YY
Typeset in 11pt Minion Pro by Troubador Publishing Ltd, Leicester, UK

Matador is an imprint of Troubador Publishing Ltd

CONTENTS

Introduction xi

Acknowledgements xv

Chapter 1. To Return or Not to Return Smelly Dog 1
Adoption * Smelly dog * Demodex * House-soiling * Carpet-chewing * Stress * Stomach issues * Adoption pitfalls

Chapter 2. Lulu 18
Lulu * Italian greyhound characteristics * Lulu's tail * Lulu's death * Hemangiosarcoma * Franky's bowel obstruction

Chapter 3. Urine Lakes, Poop Mountains and the Hungarian Dog Whisperer 37
Anxiety * Unwillingness to play * Basic obedience * Reactive issues * Hungarian dog whisperer * Zoli's assessment * Appeasement behaviour * Obedience course

Chapter 4. Training with Zoli and the Canine Evolutionary Path 54
Canine evolutionary path * Divergence from wolf * Domestication events * Ancient wolves * Artificial selection * Modern wolf * Fox project * Natural selection * Disruptive selection * Bonobos and Chimps * Gene-regulatory mechanism * Hunter-Gatherers' influence

Chapter 5. Training with Zoli Continues   **71**
and We Explore Dog Domestication
Clicker * Mila superstar * Dog first domestic animal * Horse/zorse/hebra * Changes in gene pool, famine, illness, geographical areas * Human selection * Evidence of dog domestication * Ancient canine fossils * Dogs in ancient civilisations * Pedigrees * Emergence of modern breeds

Chapter 6. Shedding, Guarding and   **91**
Protection, Prey Drive, Conformation
Mila's itching * Hypoallergenic food * Mila's shedding * Obedience work * Guard and protection training * Hedgehog * Soft mouth * Dachshunds as hunters * Mice * Ancient predatory sequence * Prey drive * Physical conformation * DNA test

Chapter 7. Dominance Theory   **112**
Dominance theory * Nincompoop owners * Cesar Millan * Alpha dog behaviours * Wolf behaviour * Konrad Lorenz * Konrad Most * Dominance aggression * Dominance theory hierarchy * David Mech * Free-Ranging Dog Society

Chapter 8. Ongoing Training with Zoli and Pack Theory   **129**
Pack theory * Mila's reactivity * Aversive training methods * Pack rules * Free-ranging wolves

Chapter 9. How Dogs Learn and Classical Conditioning   **141**
How dogs learn * Classical conditioning * Mila's reactivity * Reaction to various dogs * Counterconditioning * Reactive issues * Dog socialisation * Pavlov * Watson * Limbic system * Phobias * Little Albert * Little Peter * Thunder desensitisation * Flooding

Chapter 10. Operant Conditioning   **161**
Operant conditioning * Skinner * Thorndike * Reinforcement, punishment, positive, negative * Treat-based training * Extinction * John and Dog * Mila's reactive training * Lego & Co

Chapter 11. Neonatal-Sensitive Period — 182
Puppy purchasing * Dachshund breeder * Neonatal period 0-12 days * Transitional period 13-21 days * Socialisation period to dogs 4-6 weeks * Socialisation period to humans 4-16 weeks

Chapter 12. Ongoing Early Learning — 205
Importance of breeders * Fear response * Socialisation with other dogs * Imprinting * Behaviour problems due to lack of socialisation * Habituation * Importance of ongoing socialisation * Bite inhibition * Puppy socialisation checklist

Chapter 13. Choosing the Right Breed — 228
Canine intelligence * Importance of canine characteristics * Power breeds * Managing canine physical and mental needs * Choosing the right breed

Chapter 14. Punishment — 252
Portrayal of dogs * Canine communication signals * Punishment in all its guises * Aversive training * Prong collars and choke chains * Electronic devices

Chapter 15. Aggression — 276
Owner-directed aggression * Anthropomorphising dogs * Lack of discipline * Factors contributing to aggression * Food aggression * Idiopathic aggression * Inter-dog aggression * Red-zone dogs

Chapter 16. Reactivity, Agility, Foxes, Gastritis — 301
Reasons to leash dogs on walks * Dogs' greeting signals * Benefits of walking dogs * Reason dogs sniff * Reason dogs chew * Day care * Agility * Vulpine visitors * Mila's gastritis

Chapter 17. Our Relationship with Dogs — 327
Ancient civilisations and dogs * Consuming dogs * Dogs in laboratory research facilities * Laika the cosmonaut dog * Canine heat exhaustion

* German bomb dogs * Anti-German-dog feelings in USA, WWI * Euthanising pets in UK, WWII * War dogs * Wuhan coronavirus dogs * Post-Covid dogs * Sterilising pets * How dogs serve us

Chapter 18. Behaviour Analysis   355
Importance of veterinary support * Mila's continuing gastritis * Functional analysis * Behavioural diagnostics * How human personality influences dogs * Case study: Vee * Case study: Elle

Chapter 19. Addressing Common Behaviour Problems   381
Recall * Fireworks anxiety * Food aggression * Inter-dog household aggression * Housetraining * Rescue dogs * Coprophagy * Roaming in dogs * Separation anxiety

Chapter 20. Finale   417

References   431

INTRODUCTION

After we adopted our rescue dog, Mila, I realised that some of her problems, including leash reactivity and general anxiety, were beyond my scope of expertise. While obedience training helped up to a certain point, beyond that I needed more specialised assistance. Unable to find a canine behaviourist, I started researching these problems for myself. My exploration into all things canine resulted in an avalanche of fascinating and practical information. The more I researched, the more interested I became, which motivated me to rejoin academia and study canine behaviour, where I eventually qualified as a canine behaviourist.

Based on my studies, experience with previous dogs and interactions with Mila, I recognised that many canine behaviour problems exist solely because the general public does not understand how their dogs think, why these problems occur or how to address them. For example, why do dogs chew the furniture? How can we avoid separation-related disorders? Why is early and ongoing canine socialisation so vital? What is the importance of choosing the right breed? Why should we not hit our dogs? In addition, unsuspecting owners often rely on outdated beliefs about dog training, including the dominance, alpha dog and pack theories, without realising that these archaic misconceptions are harmful to dogs and can lead to a host of behaviour issues.

To truly understand all things canine, I have explored their ancestry, evolutionary path, artificial and natural selection, and the domestication processes that reshaped wolves into canines. These processes dictate how dogs behave and include, but are not limited to, genetics, breeding, early learning, ongoing socialisation and owner interactions. When we understand the theory of what drives dogs and their behaviour, whether hardwired primaeval responses, reflexive learning, associative learning or a combination of various elements, we can successfully train the behaviours we want. This knowledge also allows us to shape our dogs' behaviour and overcome many undesirable traits. For example, if we understand the reasons for canine aggression and can predict what reactions our actions are likely to generate, we can avoid many pitfalls.

While this book is not a training manual, it will assist readers in understanding their dogs' cognitive processes, what motivates them and why they behave in a certain way. Knowing the source of canine behaviour problems, whether anxiety, aggression, boredom, prey drive or inadequate training, we can circumvent them before they develop. In addition, this will provide an insight into the numerous physical and environmental elements that also influence canine behaviour.

Dogs are not born instinctively knowing our rules. However, with an awareness and a basic comprehension of classical and operant conditioning, dog owners will better understand the science behind successfully training dogs with positive reinforcement and how to pre-empt or solve common behavioural issues, including food aggression, wandering, housetraining and separation-related disorders.

Our relationship with dogs stretches back to ancient civilisations, and, sadly, we have not always been kind to our canine companions. Additionally, while urbanisation continues, many household dogs can no longer adapt to the stresses and restrictions humans impose on them, especially in cities. As the trade-offs between their needs and the constraints of urbanisation clash, our dogs often end up at a disadvantage, undermining their inherent instincts, behaviour and health.

With a better understanding of their needs, readers will also gain an accurate picture of what responsible dog ownership entails, which is vital in creating happy, healthy dogs and strengthening the human–canine bond. Furthermore, this knowledge will help ensure that the human–canine relationship will flourish for many more millennia to come.

ACKNOWLEDGEMENTS

Writing a book doesn't magically happen overnight; it certainly didn't for me. Initially, the idea for this undertaking was planted by Freundy many years ago. Whether her encouragement was meant as a pipe dream or something to spur me on, it was the original catalyst that motivated me to realise this project, for which I will always be thankful. Of great assistance were Hope, Faith and Patience, all of whom are alive and well.

Once the idea of the book began to germinate, all my actions seemed to take on a self-fulfilling role that guided me in a preordained direction. Unbeknown to me, the dominos were already neatly stacked in place, and it was the death of our little Italian greyhound, Lulu, that began the chain reaction. Fortuitously, that devastating tragedy led us to Mila, who is my inspiration for all things canine. Her influence propelled me to qualify as a canine behaviourist and encouraged me on this journey of discovery. So many sensational people influenced me along the way, who unwittingly helped me over the hurdles and kept the wheels in motion.

A special mention to Jáni, who pushed me to take the first step, and unbeknown to him, unleashed my interest in dog behaviour. Without this progression, I'd still be at the start line. Noémi supported all my endeavours and lent me her ear when required, for which she has my sincere gratitude. Additionally, I offer my most profound appreciation to Judy, who came into my life at the darkest hour and has constantly brightened it ever since. Not only did she unobtrusively, and relentlessly, keep whispering to me about the book (no pressure), she also sent me energy transmissions that kept me going.

Another driving force in my life was my dearest mother, who encouraged me and propelled me along. I appreciate her less-than-gentle nudges and demands to hurry up and finish the book, which frequently helped me over the deep ravines and insurmountable cliffs.

Not least of all, I am greatly indebted to my husband, Rezső, who stoically participated in this venture with me. Day after day, he enthusiastically endured my discourses on a plethora of topics ranging from dogs, foxes, chimps and bonobos, contingent on the subject of the day. During this project, he was my greatest comfort, who also accepted my histrionics when I hit a brick wall and always spurred me on when my resolve faltered.

I treasure the support of my children, Tammy and Lance, which came in different packages. Lance helped me persevere by encouraging my tenacity. On the other hand, Tammy, who has a keen instinct for survival, diplomatically agreed with everything I said. My limited presence for the past three years has been a challenge to my family.

Furthermore, none of this would have been possible without the hundreds of experts whose combined body of works I was able to study and draw upon as my sources. I am also extremely grateful to the readers; I hope you enjoy this book as much as I have enjoyed writing it.

Last but not least, thank you to Ed.

CHAPTER 1
TO RETURN OR NOT TO RETURN SMELLY DOG

"I want to give her back."

The horrified look on my husband's face spoke volumes. Judging by his expression, I knew that I had suddenly sprouted a pair of horns.

"We can't give her back," was his emphatic response.

With hunched shoulders, I mulled over his comments and sipped my after-lunch coffee. Through the tall, elegant French doors of our dining room, I gazed at the maple trees in the front garden, displaying their seasonal finery in tones of gold, russet and claret while gentle sunbeams danced between the ageing leaves. The autumn scene was in complete contrast to the arid African landscape and the lush tropical Australian setting of our previous abodes. While Botswana on the edge of the Kalahari Desert is hot, dry and savagely beautiful, the verdant humidity of Queensland is spectacularly flamboyant. Conversely, the Hungarian vistas have an aristocratic gracefulness bound with intrinsic complexities. Our son's comment shattered my fleeting tranquillity.

"Mother, you cannot give her back," said Lance, who only addressed me by this term when he was displeased with me.

United by their outrage, I was outnumbered and had to bear my feelings of remorse and guilt alone. Genetically I am programmed never to lose an argument, and I had no intention of losing this one. While my fingers played with the now empty coffee cup, I persisted against their critical convictions.

"Look at her. She hates me, she is not happy, and I'm certainly not feeling her either. If something doesn't change, it might be better if we gave her back as I have no idea what to do with her, and I can't carry on like this forever."

"How would it look if you gave her back? What would people think? You cannot just give dogs back. Consider the poor animal, hasn't she been traumatised enough?" parried my husband, Rezső. Despite the silver hair, his youthful good looks were still evident under the furrowed lines of consternation, marring his normally untroubled expression.

"I do feel very sorry for her," I admitted, "but I'd rather she went to a home where she will be content than stay with us and be miserable for the rest of her life. The rescue centre won't have any difficulty finding her a new home."

At the time, I didn't realise the rescue centre's negative sentiments, with good reason, towards individuals who returned dogs. I felt like the monster my family believed I was. What kind of person gives back a rescue dog?

"I don't suggest we give her back straight away, we need to give each other some time and see how things develop in a few weeks. I'd just like to know that I have other options in case it doesn't work out."

Considering that my initial idea to adopt a dog was with the best intentions, the idea seemed to be backfiring on me spectacularly. Amidst our disheartening discussion, the subject of our debate, tightly curled in a ball on the carpet under the table, glanced up at us, a miserable little wretch displaying the whites of her eyes. A clear sign that she was anxious and uncomfortable.

In the past, we had bought all our previous puppies from breeders, but we had never considered rehoming a rescue dog. The thought had never occurred to us, simply because there were no dog shelters where we lived in Africa. Additionally, we were also guilty of being judgemental, and, for some reason, we always considered mixed-breed dogs disadvantaged in some way. Yes, we were guilty of canine breed snobbism.

Although, this all changed the weeks after our little Italian greyhound, Lulu, died. At the time, I scrutinised websites and found several Italian greyhound breeders; unfortunately, none had available puppies, and they all had a waiting list of at least one to two years. Purely by chance, I visited a few online rescue organisations based in Budapest, where we currently lived, and scrolled through a multitude of homeless dogs. The sight of those wretched stray dogs began to germinate thoughts of adoption, and, shortly afterwards, I came across Mila on a dachshund rescue site. Not wanting to rush into anything on a whim, I had taken a few days to consider the matter before presenting the idea to Rezső.

The emaciated little creature with an elongated body, abnormally long legs, and severely protruding hip bones was my first unforgettable image of Mila. Each rib was clearly defined and visible under her dusty coat. Dejectedly, her head hung down as if she'd already given up hope of a better future. This dismal picture touched my soul, and I knew we had to adopt her. Despite regulations, she had neither a name tag nor a microchip, and nobody knew where she came from, hence her background remained a mystery. From her appearance, it was conspicuously evident that she was starving and had wandered the streets alone for some time.

Following Lulu's death, Rezső and I both resolutely agreed that we would not have any more dogs. The ache of losing a cherished family member was far too intense. Therefore, with campaign-like precision, I prepared for a great deal of pleading and cajoling to win Rezső over. Surprisingly, he didn't require much persuasion, and as soon as I showed him the photo of the pitiful little dog, he agreed with my suggestion.

Bearing in mind that all our dogs in the past gave us so much joy, we both concurred that we wanted to give something back to a homeless dog. This alternative would also fulfil my need for instant gratification, and we wouldn't have to wait two years for a puppy. Unconditional love and living happily ever after were at my fingertips.

Lulu had been a little princess, as only Italian greyhounds know how to be. Despite her small, delicate appearance, she was no shrinking violet. With an exceptional personality that filled every corner of our home and hearts, she was affection personified. Over the years, I learnt that we could never replace a departed pet, but following Lulu's death, the void was intolerable. One of my favourite mantras is that 'a house is not a home without a canine companion'.

We were destined to fill the emptiness and make our home whole again. Considering my sorrow over Lulu, I felt unable to face the challenges of training a young dog; therefore, bringing home an adult dog seemed the perfect solution. Although I usually prefer moulding a new puppy, I was emotionally and physically far too exhausted following Lulu's death to face the intense needs of a new puppy. Housetraining a puppy is not difficult but does require almost constant attention. Additionally, the pressures of adequately socialising a puppy before they reach the peak socialisation period seemed far too daunting at the time.

Before our final decision, we visited Mila, the little black and tan dachshund cross, at one of the carers where the rescue centre housed their adoptee dogs. After our arrival on the appointed day, we waited in the parking area for the carer to bring Mila to us.

Bundled in extra layers, we took in the tranquil autumnal scene, reminiscent of a Constable painting. The only sound that disturbed the peace was the barking of dogs from behind the ageing farmhouse, where the kennels were. Maria, a short, slightly rounded amiable lady who lived on the smallholding, invited us to take Mila out for a short walk. On the winding dirt road bordering fields stripped of their summer produce, we had few environmental stimuli to contend with other than chirping birds. During the brief time we spent with Mila, there were no indications that she had any health or behaviour issues. On the contrary, even though she seemed unsure of us, she cooperated and behaved well during the walk, which was picturesque and uneventful.

Prior to our departure, Maria appraised us of Mila's reasonably straightforward assessment. There were no complicated issues to consider except that Mila was afraid of large dogs, which we did not perceive as a problem, considering we had no large dogs. Mila was housetrained, which we were glad to hear, as the lack of housetraining would have been a deal-breaker. Additionally, we were delighted to hear that Mila could use a doggy door and that she was unafraid of fireworks. On the negative side, Mila was infested with demodectic mange, which gave me pause for thought. However, Maria reassured me that it was not a complicated condition to treat. All dogs carry demodex mites, which the mother passes to her pups in their first few days of life. Unlike sarcoptic mange, demodectic mange is not contagious to other dogs or humans. While sarcoptic mange mites live just under the skin's surface and cause intense itching, demodex mites live in hair follicles and seldom cause any problems. Maria advised that a daily bath with a special medicated shampoo and a course of Bravecto tablets would quickly clear up the condition.

Taking my uncertainty into consideration, Maria gave me the option to leave Mila with her until the demodex had completely cleared up, for which I was grateful. However, I assured her that a daily shampoo would not be an immense problem. After all, how hard can it be? Therefore, even though Maria was dedicated to all of her many charges, I believed that Mila would be better off in a warm house with my undivided attention and opted to continue Mila's treatment at home. Based on Maria's evaluation and information, I did not foresee any further problems regarding Mila's care, and we decided to adopt her.

Within a few days following our decision, volunteers from the centre delivered Mila to us and, as we clustered in the front garden and watched her reactions, Mila seemed oblivious to everything and preferred to stay by our side.

Prior to their departure, the volunteers and I signed the adoption contract with instructions for an annual update from us. Naturally, we were thrilled to have Mila at home with us, although the joy faded slightly after one whiff of her. Even at the rescue home, I noticed her powerful doggy odour and assumed it was nothing that a bath couldn't resolve.

Before we went inside our renovated, turn-of-the-century family villa, nestled amongst ancient trees, I encouraged Mila to take a tour of the front garden, now ankle-deep in rustling multi-coloured leaves that she ignored. Disconcertingly she made a beeline towards the only thing that interested her: the now-closed gate where she saw the volunteers leave and knew the exit and escape lay. With this gloves-off gesture, Mila clearly indicated that she would not hesitate to use it if she ever found the gate open. The realisation that Mila wanted to leave unnerved me, but it was early days, and as an eternal optimist, I hoped that in time we would grow on her.

Once we made our way inside, my first task was to bathe her. Following a thorough cleansing, she still stank. Rank neglected dog odour. She smelt like a filthy abandoned outdoor dog with wet fur that no one had ever bathed.

I gave Mila a tour of her new residence, during which she wafted and spread her unique stench to every room while I trailed air freshener in our wake. Fortunately, when I introduced Mila to the doggy door in the laundry room, just off the large bright kitchen, she used it with practised ease. Happily, things were looking up. Just before feeding time, I also showed Mila her night-time bed in the laundry room, a selection of toys, as well as the water and food bowl, although she almost broke my arm in her boundless enthusiasm to attack her dinner. After I released her, the food barely lasted a few seconds. Mila had an excellent appetite, which was a marvellous sign, although I needed to work on her impulse control. With the introductions over, we let her settle into her new home at her own pace, although she chose to follow me around from room to room, and so did her odour.

Before Lance left to go home that evening, we converged in the TV room for a family conference. While Mila rested on one of her day beds (courtesy of our previous dogs, Franky and Lulu we had an abundance of dog beds, one for every room), we decided on her name. Within minutes, we unanimously agreed to keep the name she was given by the rescue centre, as we could think of nothing more suitable, and we all liked 'Mila'. Several weeks later, a friend with Polish roots told me that Mila is a Slavic female name originating from Eastern Europe, and as a form of endearment, it can also mean 'dear'.

The following morning, I walked barefoot and luxuriated in the warmth seeping from the beige stone floors. In the high-ceilinged room with large picture windows that kept watch over the garden, an overpowering stench assaulted my olfactory senses. And then I spotted the enormous yellow lake with a massive brown mound incongruously unloaded in the middle of the otherwise elegant room. On reflection, I decided that I should be grateful. What if she had deposited her revolting offering on a Persian rug? Thankfully with great deference, she aimed her contribution onto the stone floor.

Often dogs that are not properly housetrained use carpeting as a grass substitute when they relieve themselves indoors. However, despite Mila's thoughtfulness, my mood sank. Would this be the rest of my life? To further avoid such offerings, I demonstrated how to use the dog door, and once again, Mila used it without any hesitation. The enigma was perplexing. Mila's behaviour contradicted what Maria had told us. My sentiments had not changed in this matter, and an untrained adult dog that regularly relieved herself in the house was a deal-breaker. However, it could have been worse, and I should have been ecstatic considering that Mila had one out of the two requirements. At least she could use the doggy door, even if she relieved herself in the house.

Later, when I filled Lance in on Skype regarding Mila's abomination, he pleaded with me not to give her back. Even though I had agreed to give Mila a several-week trial period, Lance was concerned that I had changed my mind after this latest *faux pas* and would return her immediately.

"She is just a poor little dog." I couldn't help wonder how benevolent Lance would be if he had to clean up the mess. "If you do not want her, I'll take her." Although I appreciated Lance's offer, I felt that it was easy for him and my husband to feel charitable when the responsibility of Mila and her problems had landed squarely on my shoulders.

In my ignorance, I did not expect adoption to be so difficult. Despite the circumstances, the object was not to abandon Mila but to secure a placement where she would be content and able to reach her full potential. Moreover, Lance worked all day; he was not the solution for a dog that needed a great deal of everything. At the time, I had no clue what 'everything' was, but, obviously, whatever I was offering at the moment was not enough.

On my hands and knees, wearing rubber gloves and armed with cloths, disinfectant, bucket, mop and paper towels, I cleaned up the stinking mess. The task was unpleasant, but someone had to do it, and, strangely, there were not many volunteers.

Taking advantage of my cleaning mode, I also bathed the repulsive-smelling dog with the medicated shampoo, but first, I donned suitable waterproof garments from head to toe. A wetsuit would have been more appropriate. And goggles; perhaps even a snorkel or full scuba gear.

Mila and I both came to loath the daily baths, which had become a battle of wills, as she'd try to jump out of the laundry basin in a fearful panic, splashing water all over the walls, floor and on me. I tried to restrain her, even though she seemed determined to squirm out of my hands and drown me. Have you ever tried to hold a torpedo-shaped wet dog who is single-mindedly intent on escaping? Cooperation was not in her vocabulary.

Furthermore, the situation proved even more difficult, as the instructions advised leaving the shampoo on Mila for several minutes, while she stood there shivering. Despite my frustration, I sympathised with her aversion to these daily conflicts and tried to make these events as pleasant as possible. While I talked to her, I stroked her side as she shivered and wished me in hell. A further spanner in the works was Mila's reaction to the hairdryer, which she fled from in a panic, and wouldn't allow it anywhere near her. Even though she had short hair, it took several hours for it to dry completely.

Unfortunately, despite the baths, Mila's odious stench still perplexed me. None of my previous dogs ever had a problem with doggy odours. On the contrary, both Lulu and Franky were entirely odourless. I realise that I have not stopped alluding to her less-than-pleasing fragrance, but believe me, it was terrible. Even if we didn't know where Mila was, all we had to do was follow the acrid fumes if we needed to locate her.

Could the demodex be causing the smell?

Despite the possibility of returning Mila, we had to live with her and her smell for several weeks, and I decided to see if I could find an explanation, more for our benefit than hers. I doubt the stench bothered her. According to my research, all healthy dogs have the parasitic mites that live in their hair follicles and are responsible for demodectic mange, or demodex. Healthy dogs usually don't have any problems with mites. Infestations that develop into mange are frequently a symptom of a compromised immune system that is unable to control the rapid increase of the skin mites, which a vet can diagnose with a skin scraping. Even though this type of mange is not contagious, visually it can look quite frightful when the dog loses hair in patches all over its body.

Moreover, the effect of stress in canines is well documented and is like that experienced by humans. When the body releases adrenaline and cortisol, these chemicals cause heart rate and respiration to increase, contributing to the fight or flight mode in canines. However, when stress is ongoing, and the body does not have a chance to recover from high cortisol levels, the immune system can become compromised, whereby dogs are unable to fight off diseases and infections.

Without any details of her past, we could only speculate why Mila was roaming the streets. Possibly, she found an open gate and decided to go for a walk, or was frightened by other dogs and, panic-stricken, ran off and lost her way. Contrary to the belief that dogs have a strong homing instinct, most dogs who escape never find their way home. Judging by her emaciated state, Mila had probably wandered alone for some time, as she was in deplorable physical condition. Additionally, her digestive system was severely compromised, and even the vet was dubious about her continued existence if he couldn't stabilise the terrible diarrhoea.

Mila needed to put, and keep, weight on to survive.

At the rescue centre, Maria and the vet battled for days to normalise Mila with a plethora of medication, drugs, potions and concoctions, anything they could think of, but nothing helped control the loose bowels. Eventually, at her wits' end, and seriously afraid of losing Mila, a friend advised Maria to try the universal cure for an upset stomach, which was nothing more than Coca-Cola. Surprisingly, or not, it worked. As soon as the digestive issues improved, Mila started to put on weight.

At the time, Mila had also undergone sterilisation surgery, which is mandatory by the rescue organisation before rehoming. However, dogs often develop a stress response from this kind of operation. During her homeless period on the streets, it is safe to assume that Mila experienced extreme mental and physical anxiety, which significantly compromised her health. Even though a depressed immune system can cause a demodex infestation, there was no indication that demodex can cause unsavoury odours. Although, if generalised, and the mange affects large areas of skin or the entire body, it can become itchy if there are secondary bacterial infections, which can cause foul-smelling skin. Fortunately, in Mila's case, the mange was localised to a few small areas, and there was no bacterial infection that could cause any offensive odours.

Even though returning Mila was still on the cards, in the interim we had to live with her smell, and, unwilling to rest on my laurels, I resorted to reading everything I could find on the fascinating subject of dog odours. I navigated through a multitude of information from hormonal imbalances to fungal infections, parasites and localised inflammations. Nothing seemed to explain the reason for Mila's smelly condition. Even before she came to us, despite her weak immune system and poor physical condition, the rescue centre vet could not find any chronic health issues other than the demodex mites.

More research followed, with further suggestions from urinary tract problems to tooth and gum infections and the lack of grooming. Without a doubt, I could rule out the latter, as I still bathed Mila every day. Further articles followed with many recommendations on neutralising the smell of malodorous dogs, including adding essential oils or herbs such as crushed parsley, ground cinnamon and cloves to a dog's diet. Interestingly, I also discovered that several independent tests on various dog food brands established that mediocre-quality pet food, with substandard ingredients loaded with corn and wheat, including unidentified additives, can also cause an unpleasant smell in some pets.

Initially, I excluded the idea that the high-quality dog food I was feeding her caused the smell. As Mila arrived in tandem with her odour, she obviously developed the revolting aroma before coming to us. However, as I had no idea what food the rescue centre used, on reflection, I could not rule out the dog food hypothesis.

Further reading established that some dog breeds tend to be naturally smelly, which is most often caused by gland secretions that are heavier in some types and naturally carry a dreadful odour. I was hoping that Mila was exempt from this group.

Whenever we bring home a new pet, it is always an excellent idea to have a thorough health evaluation, so a few days after we adopted Mila, I scheduled a visit with our family vet. As it was his day off, Lance decided to accompany us. Mila reacted like a banshee as soon as we arrived. She barked and screamed at a poor dog that sat quietly and patiently with its owner in the small waiting area. Lance and I were shocked by this unexpected and unwarranted behaviour, which really disturbed me. To avert any further disturbances, our vet, Dr Réka, hastily called us into the examination room and gave

Mila a thorough check-up but found nothing out of the ordinary.

"What do you think can be causing the smell?" I enquired.

"Smell? What smell?" My question surprised Dr Réka, an attractive lady who was smelling Mila's back. "I can't smell anything."

Astonished, I looked up at Lance, who towered above me, only to see the same sentiments reflected on his face. Unaccustomed to Mila's smell, Dr Réka couldn't have developed nose blindness so quickly. Could it be?

As we headed out to the car, both Lance and I sniffed Mila, and we both agreed that the unbearable odour seemed to have diminished. Was it fading?

Although Buddhism teaches that we should not become overly attracted to material objects, I readily admit that I have a great attachment to my Persian rugs. Apparently, so did Mila, as she happily chewed on one of my favourite silk carpets in the living room, later that day. I despaired from this latest development. Generally, canines chew for several reasons, including pleasure and to displace tension. Anxious dogs often chew more than stable pets, and owners should provide them with satisfying outlets. Well-cultivated Zen feelings vanished when I realised that Mila found the silk rug immeasurably more satisfying than the many suitable chew toys I scattered around the house for her sole pleasure. Discarded and ignored, the boxes of toys inherited from Franky and Lulu in every room didn't seem to interest Mila.

Even though I tried to engage her in some games, my overtures failed miserably as she looked at me blankly and made no move to join in. Unsure of her history, I didn't know if Mila knew how to play, or whether she was unwilling to play, or just hated me. I placed my bet on the latter, although I realised that she might need more time to earn our trust. Until I read about a study undertaken at Bristol University, I did not realise the significance of play for dogs. Their research revealed the importance of playing with our dogs and confirmed that increased playful interactions lead to fewer behaviour issues, such as anxiety. Additionally, playing with our dogs helps strengthen bonds and is vital for their emotional and mental wellbeing. Engaging in a game of tug and allowing them to win is another excellent way to boost their self-confidence; it is also physically and mentally challenging. Scientists are beginning to agree that play is the key to a dog's happiness and an excellent rehabilitation tool.

Up to that point, I was not doing well with either Mila's rehabilitation or her happiness and felt entirely out of my depth. The idea of a rescue dog seemed an easy option, perfect at the time. Optimistic visions of a trained adult dog who would slip effortlessly into our lives to love us instantly and unconditionally did not live up to the reality of the situation.

Unfortunately, like most people, I was unprepared for the hazards of adopting a rescue dog, which is why many owners return them, hence my similar dilemma. My preconceived notions only prepared me for a few emotional issues, which an abundance of love and attention would solve. Or so I thought. Although I had successfully housetrained puppies, an adult dog seemed more challenging, as did the chewing and the reactive issues that I had never previously encountered.

Before we adopted Mila, I had no way to predict that I might wish to return her. These radical thoughts did not endear me to those nearest and dearest to me; there was no solidarity in the ranks. Not only did the full power of my family's disapproval come crashing down on me, but I also had to grapple with my disturbing lack of experience regarding canine behaviour problems.

Although I did not know this at the time, I have since learnt that it is almost universal to feel that you have made a mistake after bringing home a rescue dog. It happens to the best of us, even experienced dog trainers. Self-doubts surface, and you wonder if you will ever love this dog. Usually, the penny drops after the third day, when the cracks in the perfect bundle of fur begin to develop, and surprisingly it starts to act like a dog. On the contrary, I had no illusions about Mila being a perfect bundle of fur. She acted like a dog from the first day she came to us.

Not willing to make a hasty decision, I intended to give my relationship with Mila at least four weeks. At that point, only time would tell.

CHAPTER 2
LULU

My first impression of Mameli Lady Phoenix was not entirely flattering. Furthermore, the eight-week-old fawn and white puppy that resembled an amusing cartoon version of a mouse on stilts certainly did not suit her registered name. At the time, Lulu seemed more appropriate and matched her slightly quirky appearance and character. Her abnormally long legs looked comical, although as Italian greyhounds are a miniature version of their larger counterparts, they grow into very slender, fluid dogs.

We lived in Botswana when we acquired Francesca, aka Franky, our red dachshund, a year earlier. Shortly afterwards, we decided that she should have a companion and, accordingly, I researched numerous breeds based on specific criteria, including affection, fur type and size. My eventual shortlist included the Italian greyhound, which were virtually unknown at the time. However, their popularity became more widespread after the film *Good Boy* launched them into stardom, and the breed became more popular, which is when this fragile breed caught my attention. Dubbed as a miniature greyhound, the elegant, graceful IG would be the perfect foil for our long and low dachshund. During our daily walks in subsequent years, we certainly attracted countless inquisitive glances and delighted comments.

Due to their scarcity, I had to wait on a breeders' list for a year before a puppy became available. But the wait was worthwhile, and during the years we had her, Lulu did not disappoint us. Despite breed characteristics, housetraining was not difficult, although I imagine this is a lot less challenging to achieve in temperate climates, such as Africa and Australia. However, the sub-zero temperatures of a European winter proved more testing when Lulu was less inclined to venture outside, especially when she no longer had Franky to guide her. Fiercely determined, her competitive nature drove her to imitate whatever Franky did. When Franky used the doggy door to go outside, so did Lulu. When Franky played with a toy, Lulu wanted the same toy, and when Franky raced to lay claim to my lap, so did Lulu. Although when it came to a race, Lulu far outstripped Franky.

Italian greyhounds can attain sprinting speeds of up to twenty-five miles per hour, and because of their high prey drive, they will chase anything that moves. Notwithstanding their reputation for being highly strung, Lulu was unexpectedly stable and took everything in her stride. However, fireworks proved to be her nemesis and unfailingly launched her into sheer panic. Unfortunately, sleepy, rural Botswana didn't present many opportunities to habituate our dogs to urban living and diverse stimuli during the socialisation period, and some fears stayed with them for life. Interestingly, Italian greyhounds are very catlike in their grooming habits, and Lulu was no exception. She would lick her already clean paws obsessively for what seemed like hours until she was satisfied.

By virtue of their fearless attitude to heights, Italian greyhounds believe they can fly and leap from elevated vantage points, repeatedly putting their thin legs in jeopardy. Lulu habitually propelled herself across the living room from one piece of furniture to another. It was imperative to monitor these acrobatic feats, as their fragile limbs can fracture from hapless landings.

Like most Italian greyhounds, Lulu was a very high-spirited and affectionate lapdog who loved nothing more than to snuggle with us when she was not in motion. She was the epitome of a Velcro dog, who was always at my heels and who the whole family adored.

As much as Lulu loved company and attention, equally, she detested the cold. Even in the height of summer, we'd often discover Lulu sleeping in her bed, burrowed under a chunky sheepskin, waiting in vain for us to light a fire in the fireplace. There were times when Lulu would vanish, and invariably I'd find her luxuriating under still warm, freshly washed laundry straight out of the dryer. She had a very hedonistic nature like felines and had a penchant for concealing herself under down duvets or cashmere blankets. We always had to watch where we sat. Fighting the urge not to smile, we'd often discover Lulu stretched out dead to the world in the garden, basking in the noonday sun, and although she was no mad dog, she often challenged the boundaries of our sense of humour, but we wouldn't have had it any other way.

While we were fortunate that Lulu was a happy, healthy dog, full of energy, and seldom required veterinary care other than annual inoculations, she did need attention for a specific problem many years ago.

Australia was our home at the time when Lulu was around three years old. There were no indications of what caused it, but one day her tail was straight, and the next day, she developed a slight kink in it, near the tip. When they navigate around corners at full speed, Italian greyhounds use their tail as a rudder, and I suspected that she might have whipped it forcefully against a wall or door and dislocated it. So, without further delay, we headed to our local animal surgery, which had nothing to set it apart from all the other veterinary clinics we had visited in the past. As soon as we went into the examination room, the vet came straight to the point.

"The best plan of action would be to cut it off immediately," advised the vet, after a brief look at the tail.

"Cut what off?"

Comprehension deserted me, and I wasn't sure I understood what she was alluding to and needed to clarify the matter to ensure there were no misunderstandings. When faced with an unexpected grim realisation in any given situation, my mind, having already imagined a pre-planned scenario, refuses to comprehend new developments. Additionally, this vet had a disconcerting effect on me with her no-nonsense attitude. After all, I expected further diagnostic exploration, perhaps an X-ray, at least some discussion, or a spot of small talk about the weather, and not such a perfunctory conclusion.

"We ought to cut off the tail. If this small lump is a tumour, it would be best to remove it." The vet showed me the little bump at the point where the tail kinked that was causing her concern.

"Don't you think Lulu might just have dislocated it? That would account for the small lump at the point of the injury. Can't you take an X-ray? Frankly, if possible, I'd rather keep the tail, after all, Lulu is very attached to it."

From her impassive expression, I had an intense suspicion that my attempt at humour went over her head. The more I pondered on the matter, the more astonished I was that the vet hadn't even proposed taking additional diagnostic tests, which I pointed out.

"Yes, I could take an X-ray, but they are inconclusive, and they're not very clear. Alternatively, I can give her a steroid injection, and we can monitor the situation for a week or two and take it from there."

I was relieved that the tail had been given a stay of execution, for the time being at least, and we weren't obliged to chop it off without examining other options. Two weeks later, the kink and the small lump remained the same size. Consequently, the vet no longer saw any cause to truncate the appendage, and it remained unchanged throughout Lulu's life, without anyone even noticing it. As with all matters, I like to be as proactive as possible, and, fortunately, this tail had a happy ending.

Other than minor issues, Lulu was in good health, although after she turned eleven, she had two unidentified episodes about two months before she died. By then, we'd already been living in Budapest for a few years. Both incidents happened in the blink of an eye. The first time, Lulu was supervising me in the kitchen one morning after breakfast. And while she looked out the French doors onto the garden, a vantage point for watching squirrels that were daily visitors on the century-old ash tree just off the kitchen terrace, she fell over onto her side. Even though she was conscious throughout, she seemed a bit bewildered after she stood up. The second incident, a few weeks later, was identical to the first. One moment Lulu was standing, and the next, she was on her side.

For my peace of mind, after the second fainting spell, I asked our vet to check out Lulu. After Dr Réka concluded the physical examination, the blood tests also revealed nothing out of the ordinary. However, she advised that we should investigate more thoroughly and look at possible cardiac issues if the incident reoccurred. It didn't happen again, and I gave no further thought to the matter.

Lulu started coughing sporadically about two months later, and even though she seemed a bit tired, I assumed that perhaps age was catching up with her. She was her usual self in all other aspects, and I wasn't too concerned, although I decided to err on the side of caution, and I took Lulu to see our family vet a week later. During the examination, Dr Réka discovered that Lulu's heart sounds appeared abnormal, and she took Lulu for an X-ray.

When Dr Réka returned with Lulu and the images, her sombre expression testified to the graveness of the situation. The X-rays distinctly revealed that Lulu's chest cavity was full of fluid and identified what looked like a mass near the heart. Without even hazarding a diagnosis,

Dr Réka referred us to a cardiac specialist that same evening.

Naturally, by then, I was apprehensive and felt the gravity of the situation; however, I remained optimistic and surmised that whatever the malady, we'd be able to cure it with medication or surgery. Up till that point, Lulu hadn't had any significant illnesses or symptoms of any serious ailments. Even though I comprehended the severity of the matter, I was still relatively hopeful.

While we lived in the forestry area of the Buda Hills, the specialist clinic was on the other side of the Danube in Pest. Although the sweeping river vistas and the magnificence of the neo-Gothic parliament building never fail to enthral us, that Thursday evening, as Rezső drove across the iconic Chain Bridge, we were blind to the charms of the city. Driving down the wide tree-lined boulevards flanked on either side by spectacular Art Nouveau villas and palaces, we noticed nothing of their aristocratic finery as Lulu lay in a ball on my lap.

We didn't have long to wait in the slightly outdated reception area on our arrival at the veterinary centre. The cardiac specialist who, to this day, remains faceless attended to us without delay. After an examination, he took Lulu for a subsequent ultrasound examination while Rezső and I took a seat in the waiting room. Did we talk to each other, try and reassure each other? I have no idea. Anxiety clouded my recollection of the evening's events that took on a surreal aspect.

In due course, the specialist called us into his office.

"Lulu has fluid in her pericardium, and my suggestion is that we put her to sleep immediately. A tumour is bleeding into the heart-sac, which is disrupting cardiac function and, additionally, the extra fluid is compressing the lungs and compromising her breathing. She won't survive for very long."

Paralysis overwhelmed our cognitive functions, and we found it impossible to process the information. Mentally, I was debating whether I had heard the vet correctly. Was he joking? He looked dead serious. I imagine our faces mirrored our feelings of disbelief and confusion as both Rezső and I stood there stunned and speechless.

Possibly as a measure to soften the blow, the vet offered a compromise.

"As a temporary measure, I can draw out the fluid from the heart-sac; however, this will only be a short-term solution, as the pericardium will fill up again. I cannot predict when this will occur – possibly immediately, or in a week or a month; however, when it does happen, I advise that we euthanise Lulu immediately. There is nothing we can do for her; I am unable to prescribe any medication as there is no cure for this condition. Lulu will not recover."

From having a healthy little dog at the beginning of the day to facing the probability of losing her, possibly in hours or days, was an impossible transition to make in a few short minutes.

Predictably, we agreed to the pericardiocentesis, but when we saw the massive needle the specialist was going to insert through Lulu's chest wall into the heart-sac, we opted to withdraw to the waiting area while he carried out the procedure.

We didn't have long to wait; it was over quickly. When the veterinary cardiologist summoned us back into the examining room, he showed us a beaker full of brown blood that he had tapped from Lulu's pericardium. Nevertheless, Lulu had visibly perked up and was curiously exploring her surroundings. It was immediately evident that her lungs were functioning more efficiently without the fluid pressing on them. At the time, we had no idea how long the reprieve would last, and we agreed to take Lulu back on Tuesday for a check-up, and continue to monitor her condition in the meantime.

There was nothing more to do but go home and trust that we would have some additional time with Lulu – weeks rather than days. We realised that our little treasure was already living on borrowed time.

I tossed and turned as sleep eluded me that night, and my first thought in the morning was whether Lulu had survived to live another day. She had.

During that Friday, everything seemed under control. Because Lulu didn't have much appetite and didn't eat her dry dog food, I cooked chicken and rice for her, which she consumed with great gusto.

We couldn't visualise our lives without Lulu, and we clung to the possibility that perhaps we'd have several more months rather than weeks with her. Facing the unknown is harrowing, and it distressed us to watch our terminally ill pet, unable to predict the length of time we still had.

Ordinarily, Lulu slept in the laundry room at night, but that evening, for some reason, the door wasn't closed, and when the coast was clear, she came upstairs to the bedroom and snuggled up to me, where she stayed the entire night.

On Saturday morning, when Lulu jumped off the bed, she yelped in pain, and I noticed that she appeared tired. As the morning progressed, she became even more drained, and Rezső realised that Lulu had reached the end of the road, but I was not ready to accept that and held out for more.

By early afternoon as I sat on the lawn under the canopy of trees dominated by the ancient ash tree that stood guard over us, I stroked Lulu lying beside me. From her laboured breathing, I knew we had run out of time. As hard as it was, I had to accept that Lulu was dying. It would be kinder to ease her to sleep than watch her suffer as the fluid pressing on her lungs squeezed the life out of her.

Usually, Lulu was very attentive to what was happening around her. However, on that day, she just slept curled up on my lap, barely even lifting her head as we drove over the Chain Bridge to the veterinary centre.

On the drive over, I phoned the cardiologist, who was not on duty, but he alerted his colleague of our imminent arrival. Eventually, the on-duty vet who was expecting us at the clinic ushered us in and took Lulu for the ultrasound. Regretfully the vet confirmed our worst fears: Lulu's pericardium had once again filled up, and each laboured breath was a struggle to stay alive.

We had done all we could, and it was time to let Lulu go.

The vet explained the euthanasia process and suggested that we leave Lulu after the primary injection, but Rezső and I opted to remain with Lulu till the end. We stroked her fine silky fur and comforted her during the process as we said our goodbyes.

While we watched, the vet administered a fast-acting sedative to put Lulu to sleep, and within seconds we lay her down on the cold, sterile aluminium examining table as she closed her eyes for the last time. The final stage of the procedure was also over quickly after the vet injected pentobarbital to slow and stop Lulu's heart and life. Listening with her stethoscope, the vet confirmed that there were no longer any heart sounds and that Lulu had gone.

She expressed her condolences at our loss as an assistant brought out a small black body bag, but hung back when he saw us still there. The only other formality that remained was arranging Lulu's cremation. We tried to linger, but it was time to leave her. Before we did, I removed Lulu's collar, which I strapped to my handbag, where it has remained ever since.

Outside, the day had died in solidarity with Lulu. Too overwrought, Rczső and I needed time to collect ourselves before driving home, so we sat down on a bench under the only tree near the parking area and tried to comfort each other.

Looking back on that day, I am still unable to articulate our emotions. To state that we were devastated, inconsolable and that the pain was intolerable seems far from adequate. The waterfall of tears sliding down my face on the wordless drive home remains vivid in my mind; the rest is just a blur of streetlights as darkness had taken over the world. Our usually bright, inviting home felt monochromatic and unwelcoming. Void of all warmth and joy, as Lulu's toys, beds, water and food bowl were a sad reminder of her permanent absence.

That evening, through the paralysing haze and wrapped in silence, Rezső and I watched TV with vacant expressions, apathetically plunged in our grief, unable to grasp or process the content of what we were viewing. One thing that remains clear is the film's title, which was *The American Sniper*. The funeral scene, with the haunting tones of the trumpet solo, which has always had a profound effect on me, was a poignant reminder that we were also burying our little Lulu by proxy.

The experience of losing a beloved pet is distressing, and, unfortunately, most people did not understand the extent of our grief, which made it so much more difficult. A constant shadow, Lulu had been my faithful little companion for eleven years, and I missed her presence.

Over the years, we had so many adventures together and relocated from Africa to Australia and Europe – three different countries on three different continents. Generally, the life expectancy of Italian greyhounds is between thirteen to fifteen years, so, naturally, we hadn't expected Lulu to die so soon, and not from one day to the next.

Rezső, like me, was in deep mourning, both of us mindlessly trying to fill the empty days. In all honesty, I can say that a zombie has more life than I felt at the time. Even though I instinctively went through the motions, the cavernous chasm I had fallen into left me devoid of emotions, scarcely functioning. While we tried to comfort each other, the dark plains of our suffering were impassable.

Eventually, out of sheer desperation, I joined a pet loss forum. This action had no precedents, as I'd never participated in online chat rooms in the past. The heartbreak and the outpouring of anguish by men and women from all over the world were tangible and comforting as I realised that I was not alone. Thankfully, I was not losing my mind but was going through a natural grieving process. The intensity of our collective grief, which was on a par with losing a close family member, disorientated us. I absorbed their pain, and I posted my own.

Judy replied to my message.

Several weeks earlier, she had also lost her little Italian greyhound, and we found solidarity in our desolation and tried to reassure each other as best we could. In due course, Judy became very supportive of my dilemma regarding whether to return Mila or not and managed to put herself in my shoes regarding my relationship with Mila. Undeniably, Judy was one of the few people who supported any decision that I decided to make, and I appreciated her non-judgemental compassion and her down-to-earth counsel. Without pandering to my whims or expectations, she was, and till this day remains, the pragmatic voice of reason when needed. Even though Judy lives in the States, and we have never met, I am grateful that she is still in my life over five years later.

When Lulu died, I was too numb to focus on the implications of her condition, and I hadn't even heard the medical name for what killed her. Months later, when I researched various canine cancers, I came across a word that jumped out at me. Hemangiosarcoma (HSA). A highly malignant incurable cluster of cells that line the internal surface of blood vessels precipitates this condition, and most commonly affects the spleen, less often the liver and the heart. This form of hemangiosarcoma is potentially fatal because these tumours grow internally and develop very slowly with no warning signs or symptoms until the advanced stages, leaving little time to make decisions or research treatment options. These malignancies leak blood into the surrounding areas, and, eventually, the tumours rupture without warning, manifesting acute symptoms, including difficulty breathing, increased respiratory and heart rates, and collapse. Unfortunately, by the time owners register the severity of the problem, it is often too late, and their much-beloved pooches frequently die of internal bleeding. Severe symptoms that may appear in the advanced stages include lethargy, weight loss, fainting, weakness, lack of coordination, coughing, nosebleeds, seizures, abdominal swelling, partial paralysis.

Sadly, most dogs diagnosed with HSA of the internal organs will die within one to two weeks of the diagnosis. If diagnosed in time, surgery, chemotherapy and radiotherapy can be effective for all locations, except those involving the heart. Although, in most cases, due to life-threatening haemorrhage and a gloomy prognosis, it is difficult to decide whether to pursue emergency surgery. Even with surgery and chemotherapy, the disease will progress, creating masses throughout the body, which may haemorrhage from each cancer site, resulting in shock and collapse. Depending on the type of tumour, chemotherapy and radiation, post-surgery survival rates vary between one and eight months. Italian greyhounds and whippets are prone to developing HSA, as are vizsla, German shepherds, golden retrievers and Labradors, just a few of the breeds that are genetically more disposed to succumb to this deadly form of cancer.

Additionally, UV light exposure can trigger the dermal form of hemangiosarcoma in dogs who love to bask in the sun, including Italian greyhounds, whippets and all thin-haired dogs. These skin tumours form lesions, dark purple or red spots, becoming larger and raised over time. Fortunately, they rarely metastasise if eradicated in time; therefore, it is imperative to remove the skin tumours before they invade the deeper tissue cells and spread throughout the body. In addition, keeping thinly haired dogs protected from UV radiation by applying a pet-safe sunscreen, having them wear a shirt, or keeping them indoors during the most vulnerable hours, can help minimise the risk of dermal HSA.

Naturally, after Lulu's death, I frequently questioned whether we had overlooked other alternatives in our ignorance of the condition and speculated whether we could have done more. Unfortunately, the final events overtook us so rapidly, and we had no time to really consider other options or even question the prognosis. Perhaps if Dr Réka had picked up an abnormality after Lulu's fainting spells, we could have been more pre-emptive and aggressive with the treatment. Although at the time, Lulu's heart sounds did not present with any irregularities, nor did her blood work.

Tragically, the prognosis for dogs with tumours in the heart and liver are more life-threatening than those located in the spleen. Indisputably, cardiac surgery on its own is very demanding. However, with the added complication of vascular tumours, the procedure can prove to be an insurmountable obstacle, which is why vets usually decide to euthanise pets with HSA in the liver and the heart. Furthermore, considering the fragility of an Italian greyhound, I recognise that major cardiac surgery with very little chance of long-term survival would not have been in Lulu's best interest, even if we had detected it earlier.

Canine statistics are rather alarming, and up to 50% of dogs who live beyond the age of ten develop some form of cancer. Some of these are easily curable or treatable. Even though hemangiosarcoma in dogs is a grave diagnosis, some researchers believe that they have discovered a test to determine if a dog has HSA at the cellular level and are working on a treatment to achieve successful results if the disease is diagnosed at the emerging stage.

At the time, Rezső and I decided we wouldn't have any more dogs.

Although they bring us immeasurable joy, on the other hand, losing them is devastating. Moreover, we were desolate following the death of Franky, our dachshund, a few years earlier. We had recently moved to Budapest, and, as newbies, everything was new and unfamiliar. With winter approaching, I had to buy doggy coats for Franky and Lulu, and at the same time, I asked the pet shop owner if he could recommend a vet in case of need. Based on the feedback of his clients, he was happy to oblige.

When Franky suddenly developed an acute onset of profuse vomiting overnight, we rushed her to the recommended veterinary surgery the following morning. Although the reception area looked in dire need of modernisation, I did not hold that against them.

To pre-empt a possible misdiagnosis and trying to be helpful, I even took a sample of Franky's vomit with us.

With barely a glance, the vet dismissed it and diagnosed a non-specific canine virus, which causes vomiting and a runny tummy. Even though I pointed out that the vomiting was copious, and there was no diarrhoea, the vet did not order any additional tests, no blood work, ultrasound or radiographs, but requested that we return the next day for a follow-up antibiotic treatment. As head of the clinic, he recorded his diagnosis on the computer.

During subsequent daily visits, I pointed out that Franky could not keep anything down; as soon as she drank or ate, she vomited it all up, nor had she had any bowel movements. While subordinate staff members who attended to us agreed that Franky had a distended and painful stomach, regrettably, no one disputed the head vet's diagnosis.

Under normal circumstances, the internet is an incredible diagnostic tool that I frequent daily for solutions on many subjects that attract my attention at any given moment. Unfortunately, during Franky's illness, it was impossible to confirm the vet's diagnosis. I had to trust in his expertise and wisdom, which is the reason we seek professional assistance.

At the time, we'd recently moved from Australia to Hungary, and the enormous container filled with our household items had arrived the previous day. The stacked packing boxes formed high-walled canyons leading from room to room, and, as yet, we had no internet connection either, so I was unable to verify the veracity of the vet's conclusion.

Despite taking Franky for daily evaluations, antibiotic and pain injections, her condition deteriorated. Finally, the last vet who treated her suggested that we leave her overnight so she could do a contrast test of her intestines. Unfortunately, Franky died alone that night, without her family, in a wire cage at the clinic. Tragically, she succumbed to a gastrointestinal obstruction which the vet incorrectly diagnosed as a non-specific canine virus.

During the necropsy, the vet discovered a bowel obstruction and a perforated intestine. Initially, when we first rushed Franky to the clinic, had the vet ordered the necessary diagnostic test, including radiography, ultrasound or even a Barium series, the chances are that they would have made the correct diagnosis. It is indisputable that if a dog receives immediate treatment for an intestinal obstruction and there are no complications, there is a strong possibility it will recover well. With immediate surgery, Franky would have had an excellent chance of survival. Unfortunately, in her case, as the blood supply to the affected area was compromised, her bowel perforated, which led to septic peritonitis and agonising death.

In the past, we erroneously believed that dogs do not feel pain. However, since the dark ages, researchers have confirmed that dogs, as part of their evolutionary legacy, instinctively hide their pain as a matter of survival. As a result, they cannot show weakness, or they become vulnerable to attack. Consequently, I had no idea how much Franky was suffering. Although she snapped at me on the last day when I placed her in the car, she must have been in unbelievable pain to show even momentary aggression.

Franky's death left us disconsolate for weeks, but we still had Lulu, who did her utmost to heal our broken hearts and fill the void where Franky had been. Consequently, after we euthanised Lulu, there was only a deep dark hole. At the time, it felt like we'd never recover and had no wish to go through such anguish again. Therefore, we were unanimous and unshakable in our conviction that we wouldn't have any more dogs.

And yet, six weeks later, there was a little moth-eaten creature, thumping her stump of a tail at my feet.

CHAPTER 3
URINE LAKES, POOP MOUNTAINS AND THE HUNGARIAN DOG WHISPERER

To circumvent the urine lakes and mountains of excrement, I accompanied Mila outside several times a day for the next few days, so that she could relieve herself in a more appropriate location than the middle of my living room.

While we were in the garden, she took advantage of every second to explore her surroundings and investigate every unique odour on the lawn and in the undergrowth as her nose diligently tracked the trails of squirrels, martens and cats. Whenever I called her, she hurtled over to me, and I was delighted that she was so responsive, although it took a while for me to discover that she feared being left alone in an alien environment. I had not appreciated just how anxious Mila was. As she scrutinised her new domain and sniffed each blade of grass, she flinched in alarm at the slightest rustle or unfamiliar sound.

That was a genuine light-bulb moment when I stumbled on the explanation for the indoor lakes and poop peaks. Simply put, Mila was scared to be in the garden on her own.

When we decided to adopt, I stipulated that we would only consider a housetrained dog. Alas, after we got Mila, she didn't seem to have the attributes I requested, which is why her long-term presence with us was in jeopardy. However, when Mila demonstrated that she had specific reasons for the house-soiling, and was very well housetrained, the biggest obstacle to keeping her vanished. Although there was still the matter of the carpet chewing, and the jury was still out on Mila's fate, I started warming to her.

When I realised her behaviour was based on fear, I experienced an upwelling of empathy towards Mila and a touch of remorse for not identifying her difficulties sooner. How easy it is to misunderstand another species. Although I had no preconceived theory for her obstinate practice of using the house as a potty, I was aware that others thought she was acting dominant and vengeful, so I was glad to have proven them wrong. On the contrary, Mila was not purposefully problematic, and, in all likelihood, she did not detest me, although that was open to debate. Under the circumstances, it was evident that she was just very anxious and fearful of her surroundings.

On a more positive note, Mila's stench had faded away within a few days of her arrival. With each positive milestone, I felt a warm and fuzzy feeling sneaking up on me, generating even more affinity for her. Considering all the evidence, I attributed the unusual odour since her arrival to the quality of dog food at the rescue centre. As soon as it had cleared from her system, the smell vanished, never to return.

Run by volunteers, who rely exclusively on generous contributions, the charity organisation's financial constraints dictate its budget. Rescued dogs often require expensive medical treatment and undergo mandatory microchipping and sterilisation before they are rehomed. The centre does not charge new owners for these services; however, they gratefully accept all monetary and in-kind donations. Despite this, I imagine that these funds do not cover the rehabilitation and the daily expenses of the numerous unfortunate pooches who frequently remain at the centre for months or even years. Consequently, the rescue centre relies heavily on its patrons' generosity and is restricted to quantity over quality in purchasing consumables, including dog food. Although, I have not discounted the possibility that Mila was sensitive to specific ingredients or additives in the dog food at the kennels, which manifested as an unpleasant epidermal emission.

Within days, we were making progress in other areas as well, and Mila was less fearful when going into the garden on her own and no longer used the living room for her convenience. Similarly, the medicated bathing had decreased to once a week, making both our lives immensely easier. Imperceptibly, I warmed to Mila more and more despite the enduring carpet chewing.

Regardless of the initial complications, Mila was very polite. Although we did not forbid it, she never attempted to jump on the sofa, unlike our previous pooches, who were permanently resident couch potatoes. Even when we did invite her to join us, Mila didn't overstay her welcome and only tarried for a minute or two before jumping off and going back to her bed. Similarly, each time I went upstairs, she followed me to the bottom of the staircase from where she looked at me questioningly, waiting for my guidance, and when I instructed her to stay, she did. Even when I was not in evidence, she never attempted to use the stairs unless so requested.

Although Mila had overcome some of her distress, she was still very submissive, and when we spoke to her, she invariably threw herself on her back, which dogs habitually do when they are frightened or stressed. Mila's deep-seated anxieties troubled me. Dachshunds can be somewhat sensitive as a breed, and, coupled with her fears, we had to tread lightly. I wished for Mila to obey us because she wanted to and trusted us and not out of terror. Bearing that in mind, I now had a goal, which was to earn Mila's trust.

Even after our brief but favourable interactions, it was impossible not to become emotionally involved as compassion began to stir in my heart, which was an unanticipated development. In all honesty, based on my initial reactions, I was astonished that I was already developing feelings for Mila. As each obstacle to my acceptance of her faded, so did my resistance. Considering my preliminary uncertainty regarding the lack of compassion for Mila, I did not believe we would ever overcome the chasm that divided us. However, as soon as I recognised how receptive she was and evaluated her emotional needs, I acknowledged that with considerable effort and patience on my part, Mila would ultimately thrive. From that point on, everything seemed to follow a predetermined pattern.

There was no doubt that Mila needed to learn a few basic manners, and the first lesson I taught her was not to dislocate my shoulder when she attacked her food but to sit and wait politely. Undoubtedly, our mannerisms and behavioural characteristics make us who we are. I hoped that eventually, with the proper guidance, we would make Mila the hound that we aspired for her to be. In record time, she learnt to sit and wait in front of her bowl until I allowed her to eat.

Bearing in mind Mila's fast uptake, I unearthed a doggy doorbell that I bought a year or so before Lulu died. Just for fun, I taught Lulu how to use it, which she mastered in several weeks. Astonishingly, when I demonstrated its use to Mila, she was happily ringing the bell, on-demand, within a few days. Her quick mind and eagerness to learn encouraged me, although the abundance of treats I shoved down her throat may have also contributed to her enthusiasm.

Generally, I still tried to encourage Mila to play, but with very little success. Fortunately, I found that when she determinedly headed towards the oriental carpet, I could distract her with an antler, which was one of the items in the selection of appropriate chewable objects at her disposal. Considering all our recent successes, I also started to teach her basic obedience, sit, stay and spin around.

During my work with Mila, I discovered that I harboured various misconceptions. In the past, I wrongly assumed that dogs over twelve months old were challenging to train and would take considerably longer to understand diverse tasks. Although we were unsure of Mila's age, a veterinary examination placed her around two years old, and I was amazed at how swiftly she mastered all my instructions. After I realised that I could elicit a constructive response from her, our progress was rapid. Her fervour warmed her to me, and, gradually, her tension also eased.

The more eager and receptive Mila was, the more she inspired me to discover and learn about what influences her behaviour, which is when I commenced my adventure of discovery on all things canine. The sheer volume of documentation was overwhelming, but I unearthed a substantial number of fallacies, as well as a confounding quantity of fascinating and, at times, unusual facts. For example, amongst the abundance of data, I stumbled upon a noteworthy item regarding Mila's unwillingness to play.

Apparently, a fearful dog will act on what is most familiar to provide comfort, such as following obedience commands, which furnish a sense of stability and possibly treats. On the other hand, because play is less structured and requires high energy, it puts dogs in a more vulnerable position. We can compare this to a person who may feel comfortable sitting down and chatting but would feel ill at ease if asked to get up and dance.

This awareness certainly explained why Mila was reluctant to play, yet eager to learn. I also believe that, initially, Mila had been presenting avoidance or displacement behaviour. Generally, when stressed, the brain has difficulty processing information. Bearing in mind everything Mila had gone through, it was not surprising that she struggled to make sense of everything new and unfamiliar and could not deal with, or take in, everything we required.

Naturally, I realised that, to a great extent, her recent willingness to cooperate stemmed from the fact that I found her motivation. Food. By offering her copious amounts of treats, I spoke her language, which opened the door to all our channels of communication. Additionally, as soon as I gave her a purpose, she stopped chewing the carpets. Bingo.

That was the turning point when I realised that I was making a difference and I could help Mila; subsequently, her future with us was guaranteed. Although, this was not a sudden awareness, rather a realisation that gradually unfurled over the course of two weeks. After that there was no further mention of taking her back to the rescue centre.

On the contrary, I patted myself on the back for my progress with Mila as I assessed my success. In a relatively short time, I had not only established a rapport with her, but I contributed significantly to curing the demodex infestation, and I had inadvertently played a part in eliminating the horrid smell. More importantly, I had established the reason for the house-soiling incidents, and I had also put an end to the carpet chewing. My pride knew no bounds.

Although, in reality, as soon as I stopped to observe Mila and pay attention to her and her needs, it was relatively easy to decipher what she was trying to communicate to me: that she was a very anxious little dog. Unexpectedly, Mila was already teaching me vital lessons.

Not all rescue dogs have healthy minds in healthy bodies, and I now realise the depths of despair some rescue dogs may experience.

They need time to settle into a foreign environment, to get used to the people, the smells, the sounds, unfamiliar routines and a strange diet. An adult dog may already have fixed habits that are not easy to change. Therefore, consistency and patience are essential. We cannot assume that they know everything we'd like them to, so it is our responsibility to teach them how we would like them to behave, building trust with copious amounts of affection and praise. Subsequently, it is also crucial to discover what motivates the dog, whether it is food, praise, play, which will help build a solid foundation and is an integral part of the remedial process. Once we understand each dog's needs, whether they are shy, anxious, fearful of particular stimuli, people or animals, we can gradually and systematically work on remediation positively and confidently to rebuild their trust.

Rescue dog adoption can be a most challenging undertaking but also an enriching experience.

Mila and I were not out of the woods yet, although as I regained my confidence, I sensed that we were on the right track. Long walks were always part of our daily ritual with our previous dogs, so Rezső and I were looking forward to the same with Mila. The Buda Hills where we lived is home to forestry and recreational areas that offer a selection of walking trails and quiet tree-lined neighbourhoods, ideal for hiking, jogging or leisurely strolls. However, the first day we tried to take Mila out, her behaviour stunned us. We'd barely made it out of the gate when, sight unseen, Mila heard a dog barking in the distance, and she went into complete meltdown, to the extent that no amount of coaxing would convince her to walk on, or even accept a very high-value hotdog treat from me. Her high-pitched screams echoed throughout the neighbourhood; she sounded as if someone was skinning her alive. From a dog who virtually broke my arm the first couple of nights to get to her dinner, this complete disregard of food was disconcerting.

When Maria at the rescue centre initially advised us that Mila feared large dogs, we had no idea of the implications and were unprepared for her reaction. Mila's absolute and unanticipated panic unnerved me, especially as I'd never experienced a reactive dog before, and, alas, our much-anticipated outing turned into a complete disaster. I can only assume how very traumatised she must have been by dogs in the past. Although, a study at the University of Illinois found that "excessive noise in shelters can physically stress dogs and lead to behavioural, physiological and anatomical responses". Undoubtedly, the shelter situation may also have contributed to Mila's state of mind.

We persevered and attempted to take Mila out several times, however to no avail, and going for a walk, quite obviously, stressed Mila more than it benefited her. Being low to the ground, she didn't always spot other hounds in the distance, but when we arrived in an area where another pooch had walked a few minutes earlier, she screamed in fear, even though she had not physically seen the other dog. If Mila actually saw a dog, she turned into a lunging, barking, screaming banshee, while I nonchalantly tried to pretend that I was just an innocent bystander and not her owner attached to the other end of the leash. Mila pulled the leash so vehemently, she gasped and gagged in between her screams, even in a harness. I could barely hold her, and all I could do was stand still until the other dog moved away.

Even though I tried to distract her with treats, I soon learnt that an anxious and overstressed dog is not interested in food. Initially, I tried to walk away in the opposite direction, but that usually proved futile, as Mila would not budge until the other dog had gone. But hard as it is to imagine, that was the least of my worries when faced with off-leash dogs that added to our frustration and proved to be a recipe for disaster when they bounded over to a hysterical and fearful Mila.

I studied everything I found on the subject and decided that the problem was more significant than I could handle alone, so I searched for professional help. In countries such as the UK and the USA, the solution would have been relatively straightforward but proved quite impossible in Hungary. At the time, canine specialists experienced in dog behaviour did not exist in Hungary, only dog trainers who did not have the essential expertise I required.

The most accomplished person I came across professed to be the 'Hungarian Dog Whisperer'. Although he had no formal training, he'd studied and read all the books and videos from his idol Cesar Millan. Very modestly, he also claimed to be an expert in dog behaviour issues. Glowing reviews filled his online home page. Even though I had never used a dog trainer or behaviourist in the past, I did recognise that if someone professed to be a dog whisperer and had no real qualifications, I should run a mile. Admittedly, I was also biased, as I was not a Cesar Millan fan.

Nevertheless, I was desperate. I would have engaged the Devil if he could help, so I decided to give him – the whisperer, not the Devil – the benefit of the doubt.

I phoned the dog whisperer and explicitly detailed the problem, explaining that we inherited Mila with a highly reactive disorder, making it impossible to walk her. Without a doubt, the dog whisperer was unbelievable. He exceeded all my expectations. In the absence of an individual consultation with us or a behavioural assessment of Mila, he diagnosed the problem over the phone. He informed me that I was to blame for Mila's reactivity. That stunned me, as I'd distinctly told him that we inherited Mila with this issue, and we'd hardly even had time to walk Mila since we got her. I was also surprised when he instructed me to use a collar on Mila and not a harness.

Knowing what forces reactive dogs can generate on their neck and delicate spine when they pull, collars are not recommended, especially for dogs with elongated backs. I never used collars for any of my dogs, especially not for dachshunds, known for their fragile backs. Furthermore, harnesses offered additional security, knowing the impossibility of wriggling out of them. All I can say is that the dog whisperer was genuinely gifted. Naturally, much to his disappointment, I declined to engage his services.

Just as hairdressers often become our confidants, when I required an unbiased opinion, I'd invariably unburden myself to Noemi, my Pilates instructor, who also supported me in my quandary over whether to return Mila to the rescue centre or not.

Since we had adopted Mila, my workout classes at the studio routinely included a saga of Mila and her ongoing difficulties. Bearing in mind the latest development, Noemi suggested that I contact an acquaintance of hers, who worked with dogs. Perhaps he'd be able to help or recommend someone. What did I have to lose? Anticipating a resolution to the matter, I wrote to Zoltán (Zoli) detailing the scope of the problem and asked him to recommend someone if he was unable to assist me. The efficiency of his response was encouraging, so was his offer to help, so we duly arranged a mutually suitable time for an appointment at his home to assess Mila.

In the past, I found that sharing unique experiences is always more congenial than doing them solo, and when Lance offered to accompany me on his day off, I gladly accepted.

Zoli's home was in nearby Budakeszi, a small town that has recently become part of the Budapest agglomeration where many commuters now reside. Yet, off the busy main road, driving down the sleepy tree-lined narrow side streets, we stepped back in time to a typical Hungarian settlement of a hundred years ago. The long narrow properties housed equally long traditional village houses with porches extending the length of the structure. Adjacent to the buildings, long thin yards widened to gardens at the bottom of the house, where fruit trees and a kitchen garden provided for the family living there.

As we stepped out of the car, Mila heard dogs barking in the distance and transformed into meltdown mode, shattering the peaceful Saturday afternoon with her bloodcurdling screams. No doubt Zoli and the whole neighbourhood heard us coming from a mile away.

Zoli, who I judged to be in his late thirties, a loose-limbed man wearing his height effortlessly, greeted us at the gate. Mila was far too stressed to cope with the pack of hounds that were lazing in his sparse yard and had to be locked in the house before we could enter. Once we were safely on the premises and introductions were over, Zoli removed Mila's leash and allowed her to sniff around the yard for a while. While he observed Mila, Zoli periodically responded to someone inside the house.

"Don't be like that, Svetlana, just be patient, I'm coming in soon."

"Do you think he is talking to his wife?" Lance asked *sotto voce*.

There was no time to wonder about anything, as Zoli let out one of his dogs, which I guessed was a German shepherd. As expected, Mila lunged and scream-barked at the poor hound and retreated to repeat the whole process several times, while Zoli once again conversed with Svetlana through the closed door. Lance stared at me.

Zoli released another similar breed of dog, making Mila worse as she now had two dogs to attack front and back. Each time one of the dogs tried to get a bit closer to sniff Mila, she went into assault mode. She shrieked like a demented animal and whirled around between dogs, although she never actually attacked either dog and withdrew each time. Thankfully, both dogs showed enormous restraint and seemed more interested than disturbed by Mila's behaviour and made no effort to reciprocate in kind.

I wasn't sure what kind of impression Mila had made during this frenzied performance. Eventually, Zoli suggested we go inside to discuss the matter and called his dogs as he carried Mila into the house. Weak winter light penetrated the interior, where we made out two additional large hounds who sat waiting for us, one of which was Svetlana. So much for the wife theory. Lance and I exchanged amused glances. The imposing wall of four large, very well-mannered dogs sat in a row, while Mila, a snarling, barking bundle of hostility, retreated to the farthest corner of the small room.

From there, she made aggressive forays towards the barrier of large hounds who quizzically observed this insignificant mass of fury while we sat at a dining table in the middle of the room. Gradually, almost imperceptibly, a chocolate Labrador broke away from other dogs and crawled under the table and our chairs, inching along on its belly, closer and closer to Mila, a clear example of appeasement behaviour.

Interestingly, I hadn't realised until then that dogs could feel empathy and respond to signs of stress in other dogs. Moreover, in recent studies, a team from the University of Vienna confirmed these findings. Dogs listening to recordings of their canine partners in distress reacted to the sounds with signs of stress and insecurity, including licking lips, low body posture, tail between legs, whining and shaking. However, after being united with their partners, they showed comfort-offering behaviours.

The ensuing submissive gesture of friendship from the Labrador did restore a modicum of Mila's equilibrium, even though she was still exceedingly stressed, but the screaming had stopped. These overtures by the Labrador clearly illustrate that dogs have the capability of appeasement gestures and, if required, will adopt a submissive attitude to make another fearful dog feel more confident. The Labrador's behaviour to reassure an anxious dog was instinctive.

Zoli's lean features, exaggerated by the muted light, remained inscrutable under his buzz cut as he assessed the situation. Eventually, he suggested we undertake a private twenty-hour obedience course with Mila. Based on Mila's reaction towards the Labrador's overtures, Zoli believed that we could help her, although his suggestion was not the behaviour modification programme I expected. Naturally, I was sceptical and questioned how obedience training would alleviate reactivity issues. Zoli explained that it would help Mila build confidence and, bowing to his expertise, and for the lack of more appropriate strategies, I consented to give it a try. Additionally, as Mila came to us in mid-October and by then it was early December, I didn't wish to delay Mila's rehabilitation any further.

We would start our gruelling schedule of two lessons a week over ten weeks, during the height of winter. The endeavour didn't seem like an insurmountable undertaking until I registered the reality that Zoli did not have any indoor space, not even a shed or a garage, and the training would take place outside in his yard. I was already dubious about the effectiveness of Zoli's suggestion, and with this final realisation, I began to seriously doubt my sanity.

Twice a week, suitably bundled up in the face of subzero temperatures, Mila and I ran the gauntlet of fog, sleet or snow, and tackled the half-hour drive to Zoli's house. The elements, in turn, transformed his sparse unloved yard into a wonderland each time we went. From sparkling glimmering frost to shiny mirror expanses of ice and the magic of freshly fallen snow covering all traces of weeds and the lack of gardening skills. Although, frostbite usually distracted me from noticing anything other than the cold.

At the start of each lesson, Zoli allowed Mila a ten-minute sniffing session, as she was very distracted and overwhelmed by the abundance of odours left by previous dogs in the yard and needed the time to settle down.

Following this initial period, Zoli always showed me the new exercises of the day, which Mila and I emulated to make sure that we understood them, and we'd have till the next lesson to practise them at home. Subsequently, Mila and I demonstrated the perfected exercises from the previous week's session and proudly showed off our incredible abilities, and I say this with a complete lack of modesty. Mila was a superstar, who mastered new tasks with blistering velocity and only required a modicum of burnishing to sparkle and emerge as a precious gem.

Mila's intelligence and our rapid progress astounded Zoli, who frequently referred to us as his star pupils. Of further benefit was the exceptional rapport and bond that Mila and I quickly established. At the end of each lesson, Zoli would let out one or other or all of his dogs to give Mila a chance to socialise. Initially, this went predictably dismally, but in time Mila accepted the dogs without comment. Obviously, socialising with other dogs was also helping her. She was a particular favourite of Zoli's eight-month-old Caucasian shepherd bitch, Svetlana, who always tried to pick Mila up by her winter coat and carry her around.

Caucasians were initially bred as livestock guardians to defend flocks against wild predators and have earned a reputation as wolf killers. Additionally, they can be stubborn and demanding to train, with a natural mistrust of strangers and other animals, leading to aggressive tendencies. As a result, the Russian military and prisons often utilise them as guard dogs. This breed will fiercely protect whomever it believes is family, children, dogs, even cats, but will attack anyone else. However, with an experienced, patient owner, consistent training, and socialisation, these dogs can become excellent lifelong family members.

At eight months old, Svetlana was already a gorgeous bear of a dog, but each time she had her formidable jaws and teeth around Mila's back or neck, trying to pick her up, my heart was in my throat. From Mila's tight expression and rigid carriage, I could tell that she was uneasy about these overtures; however, as a form of self-preservation, she did not object to Svetlana's behaviour and thus lived to see another day.

CHAPTER 4
TRAINING WITH ZOLI AND THE CANINE EVOLUTIONARY PATH

During our first lesson, Zoli advised me that dogs originated from wolves, and to know dogs, one has to know wolves. I'd always been sceptical of this theory; somehow, I couldn't equate a poodle with a wolf or justify the difference in appearance and size between a Great Dane and a Chihuahua. However, regardless of the myths and assumptions, technically, this was the beginning of my ventures into dogdom. During that grey, frigid winter, my desire to understand all things canine germinated in Zoli's arctic backyard, which is where my research and studies on dog behaviour began.

Fundamentally I am an inquisitive person and seldom take anything at face value until I have investigated the topic on hand. My curiosity into all things canine was no different. Each new revelation opened an Aladdin's cave of treasures waiting to be inspected and investigated. It began with my research into finding solutions for Mila's needs, which activated a domino effect. Additionally, as

Mila responded more and more to my training, it ignited a profound fascination and a need to study the subject of canine behaviour in depth.

Believe it or not, our story does, in fact, start with the wolf, *Canis lupus*, but not with the modern wolf. The actual ancestors of dogs have long been extinct.

After years of research and a plethora of studies, the one constant that most scientists agree on is that all dogs are the domesticated descendants of ancient wild wolves. Conversely, there seems to be no consensus regarding dog domestication's precise time and location, which has proved elusive and remains a hotly debated and controversial subject due to the seemingly insufficient and conflicting evidence.

Based on molecular DNA sequencing research, Vilá *et al.* suggested that divergence between the wolf and domestic dog occurred around 135,000 years ago, which is considerably older than the 13,000 to 17,000 years ago supported by archaeological evidence available at present.

Many scientists disagree with the Vilá *et al.* suggestion, which would place the start of the domestication event around the *Homo neanderthalensis* era. Furthermore, some researchers suggest that it seems unlikely that the nomadic *Homo neanderthalensis* would have had the necessary communication skills, social abilities or abstract thought processes to have a role in dog domestication.

Based on their own studies, Holt and Driscoll challenged the findings of Vilá *et al.* and believe that this early date for divergence is inaccurate. Since the Vilá *et al.* publication, many experts have seriously questioned the reliability of mitochondrial DNA as an evolutionary clock.

Conversely, other researchers hypothesise that dog domestication occurred 30,000 years ago, citing the canine skull found in the Altai Mountains of Siberia, dated to 33,000 YBP (Years Before Present). These remains seem to be the earliest fossil evidence of domestic dogs; however, numerous experts argue that the evidence is not conclusive. Additionally, they have suggested that the skull is not canine but belongs to an ancient wolf. Even though the DNA tests seem irrefutable, the debate still rages.

Additionally, various skull fossils believed to be canine, found in Belgium and at Lake Baikal in Russia, dated to 30,000 and 31,000 YBP, are wolf skulls and not domesticated dogs. Although, more recent research by Botigué *et al.* estimated the dog-wolf divergence period to be 36,900–41,500 years ago. While dog domestication has been the subject of many studies, it often produces conflicting findings. Even though some researchers have concluded that dogs evolved from two different wolf populations, one in Europe and one in Asia, others have contradicted the double domestication hypothesis.

In 2017, researchers Botigué *et al.* examined the DNA of ancient dogs from available fossils. By including the complete genomes of a hundred modern dogs and the DNA from modern wolves, they managed to trace the mutation rate in the dog genome. This technique created a 'molecular clock', which suggests dogs diverged from wolves in one domesticating event, 36,900–41,500 years ago. Although the research could not determine where the split happened, all indications are that some 20,000 years later, dogs divided into the European and the Asian groups.

Moreover, the Oetjens, Matthew T. *et al.* 2018 study of the canid Y-chromosome phylogeny, using short-read sequencing data based on paternal yDNA, revealed the presence of distinct haplogroups among Neolithic European dogs. A haplogroup is a genetic population group related to a single descent line that shares a common ancestor on either their paternal or maternal line. Examples of human haplogroups are well-known ancestral groups such as the Vikings, Aboriginal Australians and the Celts. Consequently, based on the conclusions of the 2018 study, researchers estimate that the wolf and the dog genetically diverged from a common ancestor between 68,000 and 151,100 YBP. Moreover, the Y-chromosome data shows that at least two Y-chromosome haplogroups were present among European dogs during the Neolithic era.

Despite existing evidence, archaeologists suggest one theory, while geneticists propose another. As palaeogeneticist Krishna Veeramah, a 2017 and 2018 research group member, points out, "everyone has a distinct idea where and when dogs originated". Similarly, Cornell University geneticist Adam Boyko, who is also Chief Science Officer at Embark Dog DNA, also agrees that there is a need for additional diverse DNA samples from all over the world, from all periods. Hopefully, this will one day solve the mystery of dog domestication.

Unfortunately, despite the ongoing work of researchers, geneticists, evolutionists, biologists, archaeologists, anthropologists, to date, there is no conclusive proof regarding the origin of domestic dogs.

Interestingly, genetic studies have revealed the wolves that initially gave rise to dogs are now extinct; therefore, sequencing modern wolves is inconclusive. Indeed, the behaviour of modern wolves is unlikely to shed any light on understanding the behaviour of either ancestral wolves or dogs.

Oxford evolutionary biologist Greger Larson claims that because dog domestication occurred so long ago, with profuse and frequent crossbreeding between dogs and wolves, their genes are like "a completely homogenous bowl of soup", almost impossible to distinguish from each other. Similarly, some scientists believe that all canids are so closely related genetically they are all the same species, and maintain that a wolf is a dog, is a coyote, is a dingo. To shed more light on the subject, geneticists have compared sequences from DNA found in ancient dog bones to modern dogs. These comparison studies will enable scientists to build a family tree and reveal the relationship between various canids that will hopefully fill in the gaps of the puzzle.

Although opinions vary, there is less discord regarding how dogs were domesticated rather than when and where it occurred. One theory regarding the domestication process of wolves to dogs suggests artificial selection. This process is a selection by people rather than the changing environment, whereby humans raised rescued orphan wolf cubs. People would select animals that possessed a behavioural trait they wanted to keep – perhaps the animal was especially docile – and ensure that this animal was the parent of future offspring. When these domestically reared cubs reached maturity, they may have mated with other domesticated wolves, and each successive generation became tamer.

The theory supports evidence collected by the Siberian fox project that Russian geneticist Dmitry Belyaev started in the 1950s. At the time, Russia had banned all genetic research; therefore, initially, the circumstances forced Belyaev to work in secrecy under the veil of the government fox farm. However, over time he formulated an audacious plan to realise his long-term dream to imitate the evolution of the wolf into a dog. After much contemplation, Belyaev chose the fox for his research subject, since the fox is a close genetic cousin of the wolf. Consequently, it was feasible to assume that whatever genes were involved in the evolution of wolves to dogs were also shared by the silver fox. Even though the odds seemed good, Belyaev was aware that genetic closeness was no assurance that his experiment would work. Inevitably, the scientific community consider this decades-long project to breed domesticated foxes as the most extraordinary and unique breeding project ever undertaken.

Initially, Belyaev and his assistant, Lyudmila Trut, started the project with thirty of the calmest males and one hundred vixens, taken from a fur farm in Estonia, where they had been captive-bred for over fifty years. In the early 1900s, Russian fur farms imported their stock from Canada, and even though the foxes had been bred in captivity for decades, they were not tame.

In 1991, Lyudmila, who took over the project following Belyaev's death, stated that "after forty years of breeding 45,000 foxes they managed to breed a group of animals that were as tame, and as eager to please as a dog." By this time, some of the foxes had many other doglike features, including floppy ears, curly tails, shorter, rounder snouts, mottled coats and extended reproductive seasons. Interestingly, they even lost their musky fox smell. As of 1999, 70–80% of the selectively bred foxes were in the elite category, assigned to only the friendliest foxes.

One significant difference between domesticated dogs and foxes is the ability of dogs to socialise with humans, which does not disrupt a dog's natural social relationship with other dogs. In contrast, foxes socialised to humans lose interest in their own species. Thus, even though many questions remain unresolved, the project provided significant insight into all aspects of domestication, including physiological, morphological and psychological changes. More importantly, it has furnished us with a conceptualisation of the initial separation of wild wolves and those friendly enough to remain near humans.

Notwithstanding the project's significance, it has its opponents, who feel that because foxes are generally more social towards humans than wolves, the results are not unequivocal. Even though the silver fox is a breed of red fox that is not antagonistic in the wild, in captivity, most are highly aggressive and ferocious, even after several decades of captive breeding. Despite a great deal of data, many experts are doubtful that selective breeding was responsible for creating dogs from wolves.

Furthermore, experts like the late Raymond Coppinger, professor emeritus of biology at Hampshire College who spent years studying dog evolution and behaviour, do not accept the artificial selection theory. Understanding the biology and behaviour of wild wolves, Coppinger affirmed that the artificial selection theory is based on vague assumptions, as there is no conclusive evidence. Furthermore, he does not accept that there is even a ghost of a chance that people tamed and trained wild wolves and turned them into dogs.

To a certain degree, we can account for this by the different time frames of the critical or sensitive period for socialisation in wolves and dogs. Puppies of both species only have a limited time to develop positive associations within their environment, after which they become increasingly cautious about things and situations they have not previously encountered. This genetically inherited trait ensures that these animals are alert to dangers and treat anything unfamiliar as potentially hazardous. Fear is not only a threshold response but also an avoidance of anything unknown. Before the onset of fear response, pups are unafraid of unusual shapes or sounds and find everything novel and exciting. Canines explore the world around them with great curiosity; however, they approach unfamiliar forms and sounds with intense caution, or even fearfully avoid them after the onset of the fear response.

For wolves, this critical period for socialisation begins earlier and is shorter than in dogs; consequently, attempting to socialise captive wolf pups after they have reached nineteen days results in failure. Humans can only socialise wolves successfully if they separate the cubs from their mothers before their eyes open, and socialisation begins before day ten.

Similarly, Klinghammer and Goodmann (1987) support this idea. During their studies, they observed that, for adequate socialisation with humans, wolves must be removed from their mother between ten and fourteen days of age and raised with a twenty-four-hour human caregiver until three to four months of age. Conversely, the socialisation window for dogs only closes at around twelve weeks of age, depending on breed.

Interestingly, the sensitive period for the social development of wild foxes is short, ending before forty-five days. At this time, the onset of fear responses decreases exploratory behaviour, and young fox pups approach new stimuli apprehensively or even fearfully avoid them. However, by generations twenty-eight to thirty, the socialisation window of the experimentally domesticated foxes had increased to twelve weeks of age, making their timeline of social development more comparable to that of domestic dogs.

Ethologists at the Wolf Park in Indiana, USA, have been socialising wolves from the age of eight to ten days for twenty-five years, generation after generation. Despite this, they have not turned wolves into dogs. Admittedly, their work revolved around socialisation and not selecting for tameness. During his lifetime, professor of animal behaviour Erich Klinghammer, an expert in taming wolves, detailed the laborious process involved in hand-rearing, training and socialising wolf puppies, which takes a great deal of time and dedication. Considering the above, one would find it challenging to imagine Stone Age villagers undertaking wolf domestication, devoting numerous hours each day to hand-rearing puppies from eight days old and performing socialisation processes.

On the other hand, a research project conducted by Kubinyi *et al.* found that when they hand-reared their wolves identically to dogs, their wolves were just as manageable as dogs in many ways, with some individual differences. During the study, it appeared that intensive early handling proved to be an effective means of socialising wolves to a level comparable to dogs. However, the research ended before the wolves reached full maturity at two years old. Therefore, the findings may not be conclusive. Even though many young, wild animals can become quite approachable, they will revert to wild instincts and behaviour on maturity. Wolf cubs, unlike puppies, are unable to adopt a dual identity and will never be able to socialise with humans as effortlessly as dogs. Genetically, no matter how tractable they may seem, it is impossible for tamed wolves to pass their tameness onto their offspring and they will never give birth to genetically tame puppies. At this point, there is no substantial evidence that people domesticated wolves by artificial selection.

However, we should also bear in mind that the above comparisons and studies refer to modern wolves. Even though they had a common ancestry, there is no evidence to suggest that we can even remotely consider that today's wolves are the ancestors of domestic dogs. Based on the behaviour of modern wolves, it seems more likely that they are descendants of a very wild wolf, whereas dogs are more likely to have evolved from a much friendlier wolf.

Unfortunately, the comparison between modern wolves and dogs continues. Yet, no wolf alive today can successfully help us understand dogs and how they think or behave. Bearing in mind that the wolf ancestors of domestic dogs are extinct, it would be ludicrous even to attempt to replicate domestication by taking modern wolves out of the wild.

The second theory is that the domestication of dogs was unintentional, and dogs evolved by natural selection.

John Bradshaw, director of the Anthrozoology Institute at Bristol University's Vet School, believes that the alliance between man and wolf developed spontaneously, in different locations, over thousands of years, long before fossil records document any dogs that were distinct from wolves.

The first archaeological evidence of dogs as a separate species from wolves dates to around the end of the last Ice Age, 15,000–20,000 years ago, coinciding with the first human settlements. While many scientists believe this period to be the start of domestication, others feel that this identifies the end of the initial phase, when dogs became physically separate from wolves. However, we must not forget that the transition from the wolf to the dog did not happen overnight. Consequently, the subsequent sudden emergence of dogs worldwide at a similar time around 15,000 years ago is compatible with the theory that there were several domestication events in the preceding millennia, as ancient wolves evolved into proto-dogs and gradually into modern dogs.

Over time, wild animals can become habituated to environmental factors and learn to ignore elements that are not dangerous. For example, many wild animals, including lions, leopards, elephants, visit or pass through safari camps or human habitations in Africa, especially at night. Subsequently, it is entirely within reason to believe that bold and curious wolves learnt to approach ancient settlements to feed on human waste. Even today, humans often see and photograph wild wolves feeding on refuse dumps. However, due to centuries of persecution from people, they remain nervous and naturally shy of people and quickly bolt when disturbed.

According to Raymond Coppinger, how shy the animal is, is a measure of a species' 'flight distance', categorised by how close you can get to an animal before it flees and what distance it runs. Wild wolves have a long flight distance. They run instantly and far, hence require more food energy. The first wolves had to be less nervous, and instead of running away, they would have stayed for extended periods and eaten more. Subsequently, they wouldn't have used as much energy running away. Coppinger's hypothesis for self-domestication of dogs by natural selection lies in the one trait: flight distance.

As wolves began to split into different populations, one group remained nervous, maintaining long flight distances. At the same time, the steady supply of food encouraged the less reserved wolves to stay near the camps, which no modern wolf can manage. As these ancient wolves lost their fear of humans, they gradually moved closer to the settlements, forming a mutually beneficial bond, and initiating the domestication process.

In nature, there is intense competition for food, and even a stable wolf population will lose 70–90% of its puppies due to starvation. Consequently, it seems plausible to believe the theory that wolves began to exploit a new niche close to human settlements to access a renewable food source, in the form of waste, bones, carcasses, seeds, grains, as well as the end products of human digestion.

This domestication wave continued for several thousand years in various parts of the world, possibly across Asia, the Middle East and Europe, where different proto-dogs evolved in isolation. As human settlements developed, they provided a new environmental niche for natural selection to take place.

Additionally, Dmitry Belyaev's theory regarding dog domestication rests on disruptive selection, a form of natural selection. Usually, it takes place in a large population, which creates considerable pressure on individuals to find another niche, as they compete with each other for food to survive.

Natural selection can select for diverse traits on the opposite ends of the spectrum, each having an advantage within their specialisations. In the case of wolves, the environment favoured extreme characteristics in the population and selected against average individuals, thereby splitting the group into two or more subpopulations. One population remained wild predators and continued successfully as wolves. At the same time, the other group became less timid and could utilise the food sources so readily available in villages and became proto-dogs. This hypothesis has opened the doors to various theories regarding the domestication of other animals, including humans.

Similarly, environmental pressure conceivably caused the division between the chimpanzee and the bonobo when the Congo River formed in Africa about two million years ago and split their common ancestor into two groups. In an area to the south of the Congo River, one group had less competition for higher quality food, enjoyed a more relaxed lifestyle with plenty of time for play, and evolved into a peaceful, gentle bonobo. On the other hand, the group to the north of the river had to contend with gorillas that were a threat and competition for food, and evolved into the more hostile chimpanzees. Chimps are infamous for their aggressive tendencies and resolve conflicts with war, while bonobos prefer sex to reconcile arguments. Subsequently, it seems evident that bonobos must have written the '60s slogan 'Make love, not war'.

Compared to dogs and wolves that share 99.9% of their DNA, bonobos and chimpanzees share 99.6%. However, their ancestral spilt took place much earlier than the split between the wolf and dog. Bearing in mind that the ancestors of humans split with the common ancestor of the bonobo and the chimp over four million years ago, it is interesting to note that we still share approximately 98.8% of our DNA with both of these species.

Even though two groups that have split, such as the bonobo and the chimp, or the wolf and the dog, may share many identical DNA, their gene regulatory mechanism can turn gene activity up or down; therefore, they often use them differently. The same genes are expressed in the same brain regions but in differing amounts, affecting brain development and function. The gene regulatory mechanism explains why, out of two or more groups with a common ancestor that share similar values of DNA, one species may be brighter or have a larger brain and can use it differently.

The variation in any population of animals ensures that some will gain a slight advantage in a changing environment, becoming more efficient than others. They, in turn, will pass these traits to their offspring, who will, subsequently, pass them on to future generations.

Genetically, as these wolves became tamer, they started evolving towards a new species.

Intense selection for one characteristic causes others to transform into a new form spontaneously. Consequently, wolves that specialise in hunting large prey need large bodies with large brains, which cost many calories to grow and maintain. However, as they evolved, physiologically and physically, their heads and teeth became proportionally smaller, as did their bodies, while the smaller brains severely modified their wolf qualities.

As a result, the smaller incipient dog had a selective advantage and adapted well to its new niche, scavenging on the dump. Moreover, because it no longer required a large brain, it consequently expended less energy and survived better than the powerfully built nervous hunters.

Additionally, the calmer proto-dogs went through a cyclic reaction of accelerated maturation, resulting in increased reproductivity, producing smaller-sized, younger parents, with a tendency for more petite puppies but larger litter sizes. With their scaled-down brains, they no longer had the same thought processes as wolves, nor did they behave like them.

By living on the fringes of human settlements, this new species was drawn to people and responded to human voices and gestures. Furthermore, it is plausible to believe that humans must have tolerated these wolves close to their settlements, and perhaps even encouraged them. However, we can assume that villagers only accepted wolves that did not present any danger and would have killed others that threatened to injure humans. If this is the case, then humans may have actively contributed to artificial selection, thus encouraging the breeding of only friendly wolves.

Although the scavenger theory may have been a catalyst for wolves to move closer to human settlements, it is unfeasible to believe that wolves requiring over 2,000 calories a day could survive solely on human by-products. Additionally, it seems unlikely that hunter-gatherers could regularly produce enough surplus food – around 1kg per day – to keep a wolf well fed for long enough to produce offspring. Even though wolves are not strictly carnivores and can survive on a diet of plants with odd scraps of meat and bone, it is difficult to believe that scavenging would have sustained even a pair of wolves well enough for them to be able to breed.

A more plausible theory by John Bradshaw is that hunter-gatherers may have intentionally fed these wolves. He based this idea on modern hunter-gatherer populations, such as the Penan of Borneo and the Huaorani of the Amazon rainforest. These populations have diverse pet-keeping habits and often adopt various birds, mammals and even reptiles. Other societies such as the Guaja of Amazonia keep monkeys as pets and suckle the infants at their breasts just as they would their children. Similarly, Polynesians and Melanesians also keep puppies in this manner.

Additionally, Aboriginal Australians are also known to take dingo puppies from the wild and keep them as pets. However, as the dingos become a nuisance on maturity, the Aborigines eventually chase them away. Clearly, maintaining pets depletes resources. Yet, the practice has flourished for hundreds if not thousands of years and it therefore seems likely that ancient hunter-gatherers may have also embraced similar customs and kept wolf puppies as pets.

Bradshaw believes that for domestication to have taken place, the wolf ancestor of our dogs needed to have been raised by humans from a cub to ensure that it stayed near humans by choice. He also suggests that the ability to socialise with humans is not the consequence of domestication. On the contrary, it is the prerequisite behaviour that opened the door to domestication in the first place.

Whether we accept the artificial or natural selection theories, there seems to be no doubt that humans had a role in dog domestication, either directly or indirectly.

CHAPTER 5

TRAINING WITH ZOLI CONTINUES AND WE EXPLORE DOG DOMESTICATION

As I waded through a ton of research, enough to fill countless books, and travelled the evolutionary path from wolf to dog, I was still busy fine-tuning Mila, and our lessons with Zoli continued under extreme conditions. On days when the yard turned into an ice-skating rink and daytime temperatures remained at -10°C, Zoli cancelled our lessons, for which I was grateful.

The winter madness was one of the most difficult challenges I've ever had to undertake, and sadly I realised that I had no aptitude for arctic exploration. Despite the elements, I enjoyed our lessons, even through chattering teeth, as Zoli was easy going with a good sense of humour, and I also liked his teaching methods. Unlike many experts, he did not lecture but demonstrated practical techniques for me to learn so that I could train Mila effectively. Based on the affection that all dogs showered on Zoli, and vice versa, it was apparent that he adored dogs.

As instructed, I arrived for lessons armed with a

notebook, pencil and suitable rewards. When Zoli asked to see the treats during our first lesson, I showed him Mila's dry dog food that I had cut into small, quarter-sized pieces, nestling unobtrusively in the brand new, neon pink treat bag. Judging by Zoli's expression, I failed the treat test miserably. He tried to explain that the higher value the treat, the better the dog performs, but I assured him that Mila was happy with her dog food, which worked very well. I was a hard nut to crack. During each subsequent lesson, Zoli drilled into me the importance of high-value treats and suggested a few canine culinary delicacies such as cheese, frankfurters and raw liver.

I was horrified. Being especially vigilant of Mila's waistline, fattening cheese was undoubtedly not on the menu. As for frankfurters, perish the thought. With artificial additives and preservatives, I was certainly not going to consider them for Mila. I had never fed my dogs raw meat in the past, so, needless to say, the uncooked liver didn't appeal to me either. But eventually I relented. Against my better judgement, I introduced low-fat cheese, tiny pieces of hot dog sausage and small slivers of cooked liver. I also learnt to adjust Mila's food intake at mealtimes to compensate for the extra calories.

Initially, Zoli set out to teach Mila to spin around and sit, both of which I'd already taught her, which I duly pointed out.

"But can she spin in both directions?" Zoli countered with a grin. "And does Mila have a solid sit?"

I admitted that Mila had only recently become proficient at spinning in one direction, and I had not yet taught her the other way.

In the past, when I taught Franky the same exercise, I only demonstrated the other direction when she was proficient in the first, which avoided any confusion on her part. Consequently, I did not wish to rush Mila, as her training had only just begun and was still a work in progress. I also confirmed that her 'sit' was rock solid for about two seconds. According to Zoli, two seconds did not qualify. What a hard taskmaster he was. Taking the above into account, we had no choice but to return to basics. In due course, Zoli showed me how to achieve a reliable sit and stay, but first, he introduced me to the clicker.

My previous experience with this gadget amounted to watching professional animal trainers on television, expertly wielding this magical device. The clicker was a novel experience for me, which I loved, and quickly mastered. First, I had to acquaint Mila with the training aid, and for the next week, I fed her breakfast and dinner by hand, clicking, feeding, clicking and feeding, until she was able to associate that the click sound meant food. When the circumstances involved tasty edibles, she was always a quick study. Initially, I was a bit clumsy, but with practice, I was soon clicking away.

Such a small device packed a massive punch and precisely marked the exact behaviour that I wanted, and Mila responded superbly. As a tool for teaching new actions, it is impressive. I was delighted to use the clicker, and I only wished that I'd known about it sooner. Mila was spinning in both directions in record time, and I felt like a professional trainer, making our sessions effortless and a great pleasure.

Furthermore, we managed to achieve a very credible sit, down and stay, providing no squirrels or other animals of interest ambushed her attention; then all bets were off. Previously, I hadn't realised the extent of Mila's intelligence or her eagerness to please. Although, technically, dogs are unable to formulate thoughts of pleasing. All their actions revolve around primaeval urges, food being one of them, so her eagerness was not to please but to get the next treat. To me, it didn't matter. Of prime importance was that she was focused on learning and less anxious. Mila had good eye contact with me, which demonstrated her trust in our evolving relationship. Both humans and dogs avoid looking at things that make them uneasy, and direct eye contact indicates a feeling of security and confidence in their owners. During our daily practice sessions, I could almost see her smiling in satisfaction as she gained confidence and swiftly mastered each task and pirouetted from one exercise to another.

Training and teaching our dogs' various behaviours and skills, with the aid of rewards and positive reinforcement, helps shift their focus to something constructive, which can boost an anxious dog's self-esteem.

Our training sessions also built trust between us, which helped Mila feel more secure in her environment. There was no doubt, Mila was even looking like a different dog. She had filled out nicely, the demodex had completely cleared up, and she received numerous compliments regarding her super glossy coat. However, Mila's ancestry still intrigued us, which proved to be quite an enigma. Generally, she looked like a dachshund, albeit with slightly longer legs. Even though she had a distinctly Jack Russell skull from a certain angle, she had a very puppyish-looking profile. Unsurprisingly her appetite was comparable to a dachshund's; yet several other characteristics were very distinct.

One quite noticeable and endearing dachshund trait she lacked was that she didn't burrow under covers. On the other hand, I could never locate Franky. She and Lulu were always under duvets, blankets, dressing gowns, or freshly washed laundry. Even though dachshunds are intelligent, they are not especially easy to train, and although Franky was also clever, Mila was in a league of her own. In all fairness, Franky had potential, but she didn't have the benefit of all my newfound knowledge, and instead of high-value treats, I expected her to work for a pat on the head. With high-value treats, I'm sure she'd also have gone far.

Zoli frequently commented on Mila's incredible aptitude and regularly mentioned that we were his star pupils. I don't believe in false modesty, and therefore I wholeheartedly agreed with his sentiments. Although, in all honesty, Mila was the superstar, she made me look good. I just basked in her reflected glory.

A further mystery was Mila's short tail, which we suspected had been docked sometime in her past. Additionally, much to my displeasure, she was a little yo-yo, continually jumping up like a Jack Russell. With so many modern dog breeds to choose from, it was impossible to speculate on Mila's family tree or even visualise a wolf on the top. At times I tried to glean clues about her mysterious background. I routinely studied her features, but I found it impossible to discover any hints about her ancestry or detect any lupine characteristics or attributes.

The evolutionary process is a mind-boggling wonder of nature, with infinite possible combinations and the potential to create innumerable outcomes. Over the millennia, it is incredible to envision the journey our domesticated dog must have taken to reach its present-day appearance and status.

To clarify a point, domestication refers to the process whereby the genetic and morphological features of a breeding population are changed and heritable by offspring. Moreover, we should not confuse this process with taming, which is the habituation of individual animals that become accustomed to human presence. For example, wild wolves can become tame but not domesticated.

The earliest domestic animal was the dog, followed several millennia later by pigs, cows and horses, at around 7000 YBP. On the other hand, scores of animals have resisted human efforts to domesticate them, including the zebra, which is a close relative of the horse. Interestingly, it is possible to breed a horse and a zebra. The hybrid union of a male zebra and a female horse is known as a zorse, while the mating between a male horse and a female zebra produces a hebra.

Attempting to tame these striped, African mammals from the *Equus* species, the eccentric baron and British zoologist Lord Rothschild imported a team of zebras to London and trained them to pull a carriage he often used, even on a visit to Buckingham Palace in 1898. He often delighted Londoners with the sight of his tame zebras; however, they never became domesticated. Consequently, even though many animals are trainable, not all animals have the genetic variation for domestication.

Although domestication *per se* does not account for the variety of breeds, a feasible hypothesis to explain dogs' DNA diversity is that ancient wolves migrated all over Europe and Asia, where they developed into isolated proto-dog populations at human settlements. There they remained secluded for thousands of years. Depending on various geographical areas, the isolated pre-dogs would have developed distinct characteristics and unique features from other isolated populations. Diverse regions can impact the physical appearance of divergent breeds. For example, pre-dogs living in mountainous areas required a modified body structure and adeptness compared to dogs living in flat areas.

A great deal would also depend on the size and type of predators and prey in any given area, which would, over time, physically alter the dog's shape into smaller, quicker, or larger and more powerful animals. Additionally, parasites and parasitic infections may have decimated weaker dogs, as periodic epidemics were commonplace and only allowed the strong to survive. Over time, expanding populations, food shortages or diseases often wiped out all but a few of the total population, leaving only a handful of survivors.

In this way, the gene pool variation of any population can undergo a severe reduction, limiting the genetic diversity to pass on to future generations. This reduction will determine various hereditary characteristics, including eye colour, fur colour, muzzle and tail length, and body size, to name a few. When populations crash, the original mitochondrial DNA information is lost. As a result, the surviving dogs have diminished genetic information to pass on to future generations.

Consequently, changing environmental conditions and periodic population catastrophes can create distinctive breeds by natural selection.

Over thousands of years, any given population may have several crashes, and each time the gene pool loses valuable mtDNA information. Similarly, if two isolated dog populations merge, it will increase the genetic material's diversity and modify the original population's mtDNA, leading to broader variations in traits. The continually changing gene pool is why some scientists believe that basing research on the mitochondrial DNA clock is wildly inaccurate and may result in erroneous data. With the perpetually regenerating and evolving genetic information, no modern breed can be ancient. Over the millennia, gene sequences have not remained constant, and present-day dog breeds do not represent their ancient ancestors' gene frequency.

As the original dog evolved and formed long-lasting attachments within settlements, humans realised the advantages of keeping dogs, which may have provided an important food source during shortages. Moreover, their hide provided durable material for clothing. According to Eskimos, dog skin does not tear when sewn into garments and far outwears wolf skin, although puppy skin is preferred for children, as it is soft but durable.

Furthermore, while some dogs displayed a natural ability to guard or fight, others exhibited an aptitude for tracking and flushing out prey on hunts. In contrast, yet others made excellent companions around the home and provided warmth on cold nights. While guarding dogs had to be robust, courageous, intelligent, with an imposing and intimidating appearance, on the other hand, the prerequisite for hunting dogs was stamina, endurance, a good sense of smell, with a swift and quiet tread.

As a result, humans learnt to exploit the desirable traits and only kept the most promising offspring in each successive generation. Consequently, they eliminated undesirable dogs from the gene pool, limiting that particular population's genetic variation. For example, if a breed was required to venture into burrows to chase animals, such as rabbits, then a smaller size was preferable. With each generation, humans would choose the smallest offspring to mate, artificially 'selecting' for this smaller trait. Gradually, as domestication progressed and merchants opened vital trade routes, dogs also became a bartering commodity, allowing individuals from one population to meet and breed with, up until then, other isolated groups, thus increasing the gene pool's diversity.

Even though evidence of proto-dogs remains scarce, there is some archaeological authentication indicating that dogs became domesticated over 12,000 years ago. These rare discoveries include unearthed Palaeolithic dog remains, which possibly resembled Siberian huskies at Hohle Fels in Germany, dating between 40,000 and 31,700 YBP. Although the molar dimensions are consistent with wolves, scientists proposed it as a Palaeolithic dog based on the jaw fragment shape and structure. Similarly, scientists believe that dog remains uncovered in Belgium's Goyet Caves, dated to 36,500 YBP, also belong to a Palaeolithic dog. Although the Goyet dog has no descendants and does not match mtDNA of any living dogs or wolves, its genetic classification is inconclusive and possibly indicates a failed dog domestication event.

Based on the morphology and the mtDNA analysis of a dog-like skull and mandibles from the Altai Mountains in Russia, dated 33,500 YBP, scientists initially classified the fossil as a dog, although a later study found these results inconclusive. However, two prominent evolutionary biologists further reviewed the evidence and supported the original findings that the Altai bones are indeed from a dog whose lineage is now extinct. Additionally, experts proposed that the Voronezh jawbones in Russia from 33,500 to 25,500 YBP, and the Predmosti skulls in the Czech Republic from 31,000 YBP, are Palaeolithic dogs. Moreover, a canid skull from Yakutia in Siberia from 30,800 YBP remains unclassified.

One of the most famous discoveries is a fifty-metre trail of footprints made by a young child walking beside a canine, which archaeologists uncovered in the Chauvet Cave in southern France, dating from 26,000 YBP. The initial examinations revealed the canid to be a dog. However, more recently, geometric morphometric analysis indicates they are wolf tracks. Frequently, following initial testing, researchers may later challenge a fossil's classification when further studies often uncover additional information.

In addition, the taxonomy of several other fossil discoveries from varied locations, including Siberia, Germany and Switzerland, from 16,900 to 15,770 YBP, remains uncertain. On the other hand, researchers have classified at least nine fossil discoveries dating between 15,000 and 12,000 YBP in Siberia, France and Germany as Palaeolithic dogs.

A further rare find is a Natufian grave in what is now northern Israel of an older man buried with his hand on a puppy, both dating to 12,000 YBP. The puppy's teeth size indicates that it was not a wolf and must have originated from a domesticated animal. However, both the domestic dog's physical features and the unquestionable close relationship with the human suggest that neither could have evolved overnight. The preceding evidence is, ultimately, too flimsy to give us a firm idea of when or where the domestication of the wolf began. Nevertheless, this process does appear to have been repeated several times, in various locations in Europe and Asia, over many thousands of years. Interestingly, experts rejected North America as a location for proto-dog migrations because North American wolves' DNA differs from domestic dogs.

More recently, archaeologists unearthed a virtually intact two-month-old puppy in the Siberian permafrost, which has been radiocarbon dated to 18,000 years old. Unfortunately, the first round of genetic testing was inconclusive; therefore, scientists cannot be sure whether it is an early modern wolf or a proto-dog and are still working on the remains. Regardless of the animal's species, it is still extraordinary to find such a well-preserved animal with fur after 18,000 years.

As we have seen, scientists do not always agree on the taxonomy of the archaeological evidence, and it is often impossible to differentiate between a wolf and an early dog. Hopefully, in time, with fresh evidence and newer testing methods, scientists will uncover additional pieces of the canine puzzle.

Ancient artefacts have also recorded significant visual confirmation portraying the extent and types of dogs in evidence, such as the Neolithic rock art paintings from Shuwaymis and Jubbah along the Ha'il region of Saudi Arabia. Scientists believe these to be the largest body of surviving Neolithic petroglyphs, possibly aged between 6,000 and 9,000 years old, though they may be younger. One particular panel illustrates a hunter with thirteen dogs, several of which appear to have a leash around their neck, the other end tethered to the hunter's waist. Without a doubt, these depictions are distinctly canine, similar in appearance to modern Canaan dog, with pricked ears, short snouts and curly tails. Moreover, the Neolithic petroglyphs are the oldest documentation of dog restraints, suggesting that people were already training and controlling dogs at that time.

Presuming that the Shuwaymis petroglyph dates are correct, they may pre-date the 8,000-year-old Iranian painted dogs, previously thought to be the oldest portrayal of canines. These images of dogs adorn pottery vessels from various regions in Khuzistan, Iran. They portray the omnipresent guard dogs with short snouts and curly tails reminiscent of modern Canaan dogs.

In contrast to the above, dog presence became more abundant around 4,000 years ago, although very little breed differentiation is evident at that time. Even though the reconstruction of a 4,500-year-old dog skull, found at Cuween Hill in the Orkney Islands, shows distinctly European grey wolf features, Neolithic dogs seem to have resembled modern-day feral or village dogs, similar to breeds like dingoes and Canaan dogs. Interestingly, the Canaan dog, whose ancestors have been part of the Middle Eastern landscape for thousands of years, ranks as one of the earliest domestic dog breeds. Drawings from the tombs at Beni-Hassan, dated to 2200–2000 YBP, feature canines used as herding and guard dogs by ancient Israelites resembling today's Canaan dog.

From the many depictions of dogs on works of art, including paintings and amulets, we can detect that dogs also featured prominently in the daily lives of ancient civilisations from Mesopotamia to China. Portrayals of saluki-type dogs on pottery objects from the Susa settlement in Persia, dating to 4200–3900 YBP, attest to the high esteem in which Mesopotamians held their dogs. Although dogs were still scavengers and roamed freely in the villages, they had masters who cared for them. At the time, there seem to be several unidentifiable sub-breeds in the Middle East; however, the two main breeds were a muscular mastiff-type dog used to protect herds and large greyhound-type dogs used for hunting. Moreover, although Muslim cultures generally prohibit handling dogs, even the Koran mentions and approves dogs as hunting aids. Dogs also filled the role of companion dogs and protectors of the home.

During the nineteenth and twentieth centuries, archaeologists and researchers excavated numerous dog artefacts, including amulets, inlaid plaques, carved stones and sculptures, in Nimrud and Nineveh, ancient Assyrian cities located in Upper Mesopotamia. While individuals wore talismans for personal protection, Mesopotamian citizens regularly placed figurines cast in clay or bronze under their homes' thresholds as protective entities against devils and demons. Located under the North Palace's doorway, the clay counterparts of real mastiff dogs of Nineveh in ancient Assyria are excellent examples. Similarly, archaeologists uncovered many other canine artefacts in various parts of Mesopotamia, including the famous Nimrud clay figurines discovered in Kalhu, also known as Nimrud.

Moreover, the earliest portrayal of dog collars comes from the Sumerians of ancient Mesopotamia, credited as the first civilisation to introduce dog collars. Many depictions of dogs from that era include a golden pendant of a saluki from 3300 YBP that wears a wide collar to protect the animal's neck, which probably evolved from plaited rope to leather.

At the time, dogs were hunters and companions to Egyptians, who used papyrus rope or leather restraints extensively, as evidenced by tomb paintings from ancient Egypt dated 3500 YBP that illustrate a man walking his dog on a leash.

The most popular breeds in Egypt were basenji-type dogs used for small-game hunting and greyhound-type dogs, as depicted on the Victory Stele of Ramesses II from 1279 BCE, that hunted in open areas for bigger game. Dogs similar in appearance to the Ibizan hound are also much in evidence and appear most often in Egyptian art. Additionally, there is some artefactual evidence on Itef II's tomb, from 2181 BCE, of a dog that resembles a Pharaoh hound, often portrayed in hunting scenes. One of the most popular breeds in the region believed to have been first bred by the Sumerians is a saluki-type dog, which is recognisable on artwork and amulets as both hunting dogs and companions.

Additionally, Molossian dogs from Greece were also popular as hunters, guard and police dogs. In contrast, whippet-type dogs, possibly from breeding greyhounds and basenji-type dogs, proved helpful as small, fast hunters. Moreover, the general assumption is that the ancient ancestors of the basenji inspired the image of Anubis.

On the other hand, even though the ancient Chinese highly respected their dogs, they were primarily regarded as working animals and not companions. Nevertheless, dogs of the era fulfilled a functional role and were bred for several purposes, including herding, hunting, guarding, and were also utilised as draught animals and as a source of clothing and food. Furthermore, dogs also carried out the role of ratcatcher, as there were no domesticated cats at the time. Based on canine fossil finds in Neolithic middens, archaeological evidence suggests that the Chinese kept dogs more than 7,000 years ago. More recently, there is mention of hunting dogs that resembled lean, long-legged saluki-type hounds during the Han dynasty. During the Qing dynasty, lasting between 1644 and 1912, the Imperial Court favoured keeping Pekingese as lapdogs which became very fashionable.

Unlike ancient Chinese, dogs were of considerable significance to the Greeks, not just as hunters and protectors but also as beloved companions, valued for their faithfulness and courage. Omnipresent in Greek literature, Plato also mentions dogs in *Republic* as well as in *Book II, 376b*, where Socrates refers to dogs as true philosophers because they can "distinguish the face of a friend and of an enemy only by the criterion of knowing and not knowing". The most famous dog in Greek literature is probably Argos, King Odysseus's loyal friend, who recognises his master after an absence of twenty years and rises with tail wagging to greet him. In disguise to conceal his appearance, Odysseus cannot acknowledge the old dog that he ignores, whereby Argos lies back down and dies (Book 17, Homer's *Odyssey*).

The visual arts is a rich chronicle of canine representations often featuring dogs on ceramics, frequently with the goddess Artemis. Similarly, Cerberus, a three-headed dog that guards the gates of Hades, is also a well-known figure in Greek mythology.

Among the ancient Greeks' valued canine breeds was the Molossian hound, famed throughout the ancient world for its size and aggression. The Molossians, an ancient Greek tribe, held their dogs in such high esteem that they issued silver coins with a Molossus image as their emblem. They kept two types of dog: one a hunting dog with a broad snout, which is sometimes considered the ancestor to the modern mastiff-type dogs, and a large livestock-guarding dog, renowned for its ferocity in the face of wild animals.

On the other hand, the Laconian hound was a fast and agile dog, probably used for shepherding work with a reputation as an excellent scenthound and hunter, able to pursue game over all terrains. Argos, from Homer's *Odyssey*, may well have been a Laconian. Another dog favoured by ancient Greeks was the agile Cretan hound which originated from Crete over 3,000 years ago and hunted small animals.

The most prolific miniature dog in ancient Greek artistic depictions and literary sources seems to be the Melitan. This dog originated from the island of Melité, a name given to two distinct locations in the ancient world, one of which is modern Malta, and the other is the island now known as Mljet in Croatia. Due to the vast body of illustrations from around 450 BCE, we know that the Melitan was a small, fluffy, spitz-type dog, with a sharply pointed nose and triangular pointed ears, very fox-like in appearance. However, the most poignant artefact from 340 BCE shows the relief carving on the gravestone of a young girl named Melisto, playing with her Melitan puppy.

Additionally, classical writers like Aristotle mention the alopekis, which is Greek for fox-like or small fox, referring to its appearance. We can find depictions of alopekis-type dogs on pottery, carvings, sculptures and other archaeological finds, including an engraved terra cotta vase from Thessaly, dated to circa 3000 BCE. Furthermore, researchers believe that the alopekis originated during the Pelasgians' Neolithic culture, an ancient people pre-dating the ancient Greeks from around 3000–4000 BCE. These people used the highly adaptable multipurpose little dogs as watchdogs, pets and livestock-herding dogs, which were very efficient ratcatchers. While some consider the alopekis to be an ancient dog breed, others feel that it is a dog category that describes a typical street dog and is not an actual breed.

Similar to the ancient Greeks, many ancient Roman friezes, mosaics and sculptures depict massive brutes with spiked collars, dainty hounds and even small lapdogs. Not least of all, the famous Pompeii mosaic which cautions, '*Cave Canem*' – Beware of the dog. Ancient Romans also held their dogs in high regard. They utilised all six of the specific dog types existing at the time according to their abilities comparable to all the various ancient cultures.

During the ongoing excavation of the Pompeii ruins in 1874, archaeologists found the petrified remains of a dog tied to a post in an atrium. Unable to flee the eruptions, it was buried alive. Indications are that the dog was a *Canes villatici*, a house or watchdog.

Additionally, the role of the *Pastorales pecuarri* was critical to the agricultural Roman Empire; therefore, sheepdogs were in abundance, as were sporting dogs *Canes venatici*, the dog most likely used for entertainment purposes at the Colosseum. Romans also used the Molossus as herding dogs but supposedly fed them a vegetarian diet to prevent them from developing a taste for the animals they were protecting.

Feared for their large war dogs, *Canes pugnaces* and *Canes bellicosi*, the Roman Army trained them to run in formation under the stomach of enemy horses, thus disembowelling them with their spiked coats. Privileged classes have always enjoyed hunting. The Romans were no exception and often used scenthounds (*Nares sageces*) to track game animals, and sighthounds (*Pedibus celeres*) for coursing and hunting.

Perhaps the reason our ancestors were so captivated by dogs is that dogs were the first, and for thousands of years remained the only, wild animal to have become domesticated. Having lived together so closely for centuries, through many environmental changes, we have adapted similarly to complex genetic transformations such as the ability to eat starchy food, including wheat, barley and rice. On the other hand, wolves lack the complex genetic system and have fewer copies of the alpha-amylase enzyme responsible for breaking down starch molecules, and cannot eat these grains.

Over the past 100–200 years, humans have artificially created the many breeds in existence today. Subsequently, it is fascinating to remember that all dogs, from tiny teacup dogs to the massive wolfhounds, are the successors of one single type of dog, the descendant of ancient wolves.

Considering these breed differences, it might seem logical to assume that we can determine a dog's breed using DNA sequencing. Unfortunately, this is not true. All dogs belong to the same species; therefore, they have the same genetic make-up. The morphological differences between modern breeds result from artificial selection by humans. These differences were not caused by natural selection, which takes hundreds of thousands of years, allowing for chance DNA mutation and the evolution of a new species. Therefore, dog DNA from a few hundred years ago is still the same as the DNA dogs have today. Even though we have altered their appearance, the DNA sequencing remains the same for all dogs, regardless of breed. Therefore, Chihuahua DNA is the same as Great Dane DNA, which is *Canis familiaris* in both cases.

Consequently, pedigrees are a fallacy of the nineteenth century, even though breeders make a concerted effort to keep various breeds pure and separate from others to emphasise specific breed characteristics. Unfortunately, by limiting the population, there is less gene diversity, leading to the emergence of particular weaknesses and health issues that breeders cannot remedy in certain breeds. Additionally, with a limited gene pool, there is also a higher risk of interbreeding. If allowed to reproduce freely, the different breeds would soon disappear, and all dogs would look very similar to street dogs worldwide.

During the height of our ancient civilisations, there were six or seven types of dogs in existence. By 1800, when natural history illustrator Sydenham Edwards produced the encyclopaedia of British dog breeds, *Cynographica Britannica*, seventy years before the British Kennel Club's founding, he only managed to identify fifteen permanent breeds, one of which was the shepherd's dog, *Canis pastoralis*. However, by 1900 there were more than sixty, while today, over 400 breeds exist worldwide.

With the current pet explosions, this trend is increasing daily, especially while there is a considerable demand for designer dogs. Additionally, many dog breeds are transitioning from working dogs to companion dogs, often to their detriment.

CHAPTER 6
SHEDDING, GUARD AND PROTECTION, PREY DRIVE, CONFORMATION

All was well on the home front, although I was concerned when Mila started to compulsively scratch her sides, lick and bite her foot, which became quite raw. Naturally, I worried that the demodex infestation had returned, even though demodex is not itchy.

Once again, off to the vet we went, to, Budakeszi, near Zoli's home. After Franky died, I had to find a new vet, and, courtesy of a Google search, I stumbled on Klapka Animal Clinic. Although there were vets closer to us, I didn't mind the twenty-minute drive along the partially wooded road, and due to its semi-village location, parking was always assured. Additionally, I like the team at Klapka, and, more importantly, Mila likes them, as did Lulu while she was alive.

Dr Réka always seemed pleased to see Mila, and as gently as she could, took a skin scraping to eliminate possible ailments, such as fungal and bacterial infections. Naturally, Mila loathed the experience, although she did try to be as accommodating as possible. Despite the sometimes painful and invasive procedures, she never bears a grudge, and the vets never fail to praise her. Bearing in mind Mila's uncontrollable skin irritation, Dr Réka gave us a few Apoquel tablets that soothe itching and reduce inflammation without the inherent side effects associated with steroids. They worked like a charm and gave Mila instant relief.

Within a few days, Dr Réka received the laboratory test results for the skin scraping, which was negative for everything, including demodex, fungal and bacterial infections. Nevertheless, as a precaution, she consulted with her colleague at the clinic, Dr Anna, a canine dermatologist, who suggested that we try hypoallergenic dog food to see if it made a difference.

As I was feeding the highly regarded Acana Lamb to Mila, I did not think the hypoallergenic food would make a difference, but, miraculously, it did. Shortly after introducing Mila to the new dog food, with limited ingredients, the itching stopped, Mila's raw paw healed quickly, and she was soon back to her usual self.

Although our vet recommended Trovet, a Dutch dog food brand prominent for products catering to various health problems in dogs and cats, I also had to find suitable hypoallergenic treats, which provided an additional headache. My online search was limited to within the EU to avoid paying taxes and duties on imported goods from the rest of the world. While I found a good selection for large dogs, not many companies cater for mini canines. Fortunately, Mila was an enthusiastic guinea pig and eagerly accepted all the treats I decided to try. The freeze-dried liver got her attention, but it crumbled when I tried to cut it, so I quickly discarded it. We also loved the German liver pâté that Mila could lick directly from the squeeze tubes. The no mess, no fuss product was great when we were out on training walks. Additive and preservative-free, once opened, it only kept in the refrigerator for a few days, so we had to finish them quickly, which we never did. Unfortunately, more often than not, I had to throw out half-used tubes of pâté, which were not suitable for freezing.

The search continued for the perfect training treats. One of our favourites from the UK is the small fish and sweet potato delicacies produced by Bounce and Bella. They are hypoallergenic with no additives, preservatives, flavourings, sugars and absolutely no grain. We also tried various dried single-source protein treats such as 100% goat, horse, kangaroo by JR Pet Products from the UK, albeit they are too large for small dogs as training treats, so I had to cut them into smaller sizes.

From the same company, I discovered their natural 100% single-source protein pure salmon or meat pâté for dogs, which are also hypoallergenic, grain, gluten and preservative-free and are firm enough to cut into small pieces but soft enough for dogs to swallow during training. According to Mila, the pâté is delicious and our favourite for recall work, or used as a Kong stuffing, and it can also be cut into slices and frozen. Another staple in our treat cupboard, also from a UK company, Barker and Barker, who offer a selection of treats according to dog size, including small dogs, and are ideal for training. Additionally, they make their products from the highest-quality human-grade ingredients with no corn, wheat, potatoes, rice, oats, GMO, artificial additives, preservatives, flavourings or colouring.

Another firm favourite in our treat pantry is from the award-winning European company the Pet Farm Family, offering various organic dog foods and freeze-dried treats, none of which contain preservatives, soy, fillers or useless ingredients. Their selection also caters for dogs with food sensitivities and includes single-source protein treats with no other ingredients.

In contrast to all the above that are limited to a few components, Zuke's Naturals from the USA has many ingredients not ideal for allergic dogs. However, their Mini Naturals are perfect for training, as they are small and soft. According to the company, they manufacture their products using the Earth's best ingredients. Every recipe is made without corn, wheat or soy, and free of fillers, by-products and artificial colours or flavours. Additionally, their quality control and safety standards exceed the Association of American Feed Control Officials (AAFCO) standards for pet food and meet stringent US quality standards. A further endorsement is that Mila loved them. Unfortunately, shortly after I purchased them, the company issued a product alert, and they voluntarily removed the Zuke's Mini Naturals from retail stores due to quality issues. Disappointingly, I had to dispose of our order of Zuke's Mini Naturals.

Even though I managed to find an excellent selection of treats, I usually mix small pieces of dry dog food into the assortment of rewards for daily training so Mila does not become complacent. Each tidbit remains a surprise, and she never knows what I will give her. On the other hand, when we learn new skills, I take out the big guns and only use her favourites, such as freeze-dried salmon or salmon pâté.

Zoli's lessons on the importance of high-value treats were not in vain, and I realise how crucial incentives are. Mila is incredibly food motivated, and, in her case, there would be no learning or training without treats. She would never have gone through the agility poles or up the seesaw or excelled at obedience without treats. Playing tug with her as a reward, patting her, or telling her what a good girl she is would only inspire a vacant expression. Love and respect for me would not drive her. Naturally, as soon as she becomes proficient in a particular exercise, I can cut back or phase out the treats and reward her with praise and a tummy scratch, with only intermittent treats.

Another issue was Mila's shedding, which remained heavy from the very first day we got her. Actually, it surprised us that she was not already bald. Had I collected the handfuls of shed fur over the past few years, I could have made a beautiful and unique black and tan pashMila. Regarding the shedding, unfortunately, our vet had no insight or remedies to offer.

Nevertheless, I resisted defeat and tried salmon oil, which did not help, while the results with hemp seed oil were equally disappointing. I ran the gamut from herbal remedies, various seed oils, brush gloves, but nothing made a difference. Mila's short black hair blanketed our off-white stone tiles, and I swept up piles of dark doggy fur daily. Invariably after we stroked her or scratched her neck, the floor was covered, and so were our clothes.

Consequently, in desperation, I bought a robot vacuum cleaner that we christened 'Slave'. Although Slave didn't stop the shedding, she certainly cleaned up all the short black hairs, for which I was grateful.

In the meantime, our lessons with Zoli were still ongoing. Did I mention that it was a long course? Without wasting any time, Zoli introduced us to obedience work, which Mila aced. Even though we practised the new exercises daily, and we put in a great deal of effort to reap the rewards, it was evident that Mila had a natural aptitude for the activity. Bearing this in mind, Zoli suggested that we sign Mila up for an advanced course with an acquaintance of his, who is an obedience competition trainer.

At the time, I remained unconvinced that Mila had the composed temperament or the discipline for competition work, as we'd only been training with Zoli for a few weeks. Additionally, her reactive issues were an ongoing problem, and as training was in groups, I did not want to set her up for failure at this early date. Furthermore, odours and smells of any kind distracted Mila. She was overwhelmed by the environment and took an eternity to settle down to lessons, as she had to investigate every blade of grass in Zoli's yard before we could begin our sessions. Fortunately, Zoli had a small yard. Nevertheless, Mila required much more ongoing training before I could let her loose in a high-distraction environment. Moreover, Mila had no impulse control and no reliable recall, both of which are requirements for competition dogs.

As part of our training, Zoli also wanted to include some personal guard/protection work. Surprisingly, I thought this was somewhat optimistic on his part, and I reminded him, if it was not apparent by Mila's short legs and low-slung body, that Mila is a dachshund. One would not usually equate dachshunds with personal protection. Unperturbed, Zoli assured me it would do her good, as the exercises generate self-confidence and promote a well-balanced dog. Nevertheless, Zoli's assurances did not convince me, and I pointed out that Mila is a nose dog; she'd be far better suited to scent work, which would also promote confidence.

To strengthen my case, I reminded Zoli about the hedgehog incident. Shortly after Mila came to us, we found a hedgehog in the garden and put it in a cardboard box on the terrace. The plan was to relocate it to the nearby forest the following day; however, by morning, it had escaped. At the time, I wondered if Mila had the olfactory skills to locate the AWOL creature. I gave Mila the empty hedgehog box to sniff, and I let her loose to follow her nose. Without delay, Mila found and followed an invisible track, to the millimetre, along the terrace, down the steps, into the garden, where she found the errant hedgehog fast asleep under a thick pile of dry leaves.

Similarly, from the kitchen with its large French doors overlooking the back garden, Rezső and I often saw resident squirrels hop-hopping over the length of our lawn under the canopy of mature oak, hornbeam and ash trees that were home to the little rodents. Long after a squirrel disappeared, Mila would pick up its scent and follow it like a line drawn on the ground and didn't deviate an inch from the squirrel's route.

Unfortunately, Zoli had no training in scent work. However, because he was already working with a few dogs on personal protection, it was a natural progression after basic training and obedience work. Although, based on the fact that most personal protection dog trainers specify that only suitable breeds should apply, I did wonder if Zoli was in full possession of all his mental faculties. Despite this, I agreed to try it. After all, it was something new, and Mila might enjoy the experience.

Until then, Mila had performed fabulously on basic training and obedience work, but she failed miserably on her first attempt at personal protection. Initially, she had to grab and latch onto a training dummy and not let go, but she did. Let go. Time and time again, she let go. No matter what we tried, she would not lock onto the dummy. I purchased 100% pure rabbit scent from a hunting supply store, which we sprayed on the lure. For even greater authenticity, I sourced genuine rabbit fur from a breeder that I substituted in lieu of a dummy, but all to no avail.

Usually, Mila likes to play tug, but with her very soft mouth, she pulls gently and seldom destroys any of her toys. However, try as we might, she was incapable of holding onto a lure. Conversely, hunters regard trained dachshunds as being very determined and able to pull burrowing animals from underground, which is why Zoli was perplexed by Mila's soft mouth and her inability to bring down, hold and kill prey. Nevertheless, we did not give up as yet.

While hunters consider dachshunds to be the smallest, most effective hunting dogs in Europe, many use them for blood tracking. Because of their natural ability to follow scent trails, they are adept at hunting down burrow-dwelling animals and flushing them out from their hiding place. Even though dachshunds are not trained to kill, they can immobilise their prey for long enough until the hunter gets there. Often hunters use larger dogs to bring down animals that the smaller dachshunds flush out of subterranean tunnels. So much for Zoli's idea that Mila should be able to hunt and kill her food. Mila can't even kill a mouse.

Last summer, Mila discovered a nest of mice hidden in the undergrowth of the tall Leyland cypress hedge bordering our garden. As the tiny adolescent youngsters were ready to leave the nest, Mila hunted them down one by one over several days.

As I have previously pointed out, she is an excellent tracker and has proved to be a competent hunter, but not a killer. Endearingly, she brought all her live trophies over to Rezső or me when we were in the garden, and on our request in exchange for a treat, she proudly dropped them at our feet. Moreover, she held each minute mouse ever so gently in her mouth with their tails hanging out between her teeth.

Disappointingly for Zoli, the grab-hold never developed, although he remained optimistic and continued to believe that we'd be able to train Mila within a few months. Consequently, he was already planning to register Mila for her first personal protection exams. To me, the idea was comparable to sending a shy, sensitive child to boot camp. Undoubtedly, Mila enjoyed the retrieving, but she was not the grab and hold kind of pooch, certainly not like a German shepherd or a Dobermann. Naturally, Zoli could have as many aspirations as he wanted, but Mila didn't seem cooperative or very interested in the whole personal protection matter. Usually, when a dog is enjoying itself, the body language says it all, but Mila looked bored and distant, and I learnt to recognise avoidance or displacement behaviour.

Zoli based his idea that Mila should hunt and kill prey on ancient canid motor patterns or predatory sequences as detailed by Raymond and Lorna Coppinger in *Dogs*. The full sequence of a basic ancestral motor pattern, whereby one reaction triggers the next is:

orient>eye>stalk>chase>grab-bite>
kill-bite>dissect>consume

These predatory sequences, also known as prey-drive, are primaeval, instinctive hunting urges, motivated by self-preservation to find, pursue and capture prey. When observing predators hunt, the sequence of events is quite clear, beginning with the search (see, hear, smell) followed by the stalk and chase, progressing to the grab-bite and kill-bite, culminating in the dissecting and consuming. However, not all dogs have a complete set of predatory motor patterns.

Even though dogs became domesticated thousands of years ago, we can often witness these behaviours in our dogs. For instance, Mila becomes wholly fixated on a squirrel sitting in a tree with such intense focus, daring the squirrel to come within reach and make her day. Additionally, she delights in chasing small animals and, at times, shakes her favourite toys to death. Then, of course, she also has her mice-hunting skill.

To a greater or lesser extent, this genetically inherited subconscious behaviour is definitely more pronounced in certain breeds. For instance, one day, much to my horror, Lulu, our little Italian greyhound, known for her gentleness and fondness of sleeping on the couch, launched herself into the air and caught a pigeon mid-flight. Not only did she kill the bird instantly, but she started to consume it with great gusto; although not all dogs progress past the kill stage, many are content with just the thrill of the chase/hunt, as is Mila.

Sighthounds, scenthounds and terrier breeds have relatively strong prey drives, which prospective owners should consider when choosing a pet. Generally, inexperienced owners should avoid dogs with a high prey drive such as the Akita, husky and malamute, which will challenge even experienced dog owners. Moreover, we cannot eliminate these drives. However, if we understand them, we can motivate and shape each dog using its inborn instincts to achieve positive training results and create more harmonious relationships. Additionally, if we recognise that dogs with a high prey drive and natural abilities to pursue and catch prey are the perfect choice for search and rescue and detection work, while Rottweilers, Dobermanns and German shepherds make better guard dogs because of their exceptional guarding instincts, we can customise these drives to our benefit.

Unfortunately, some owners stimulate their dog's innate instincts and train them to be aggressive, mistakenly believing that they can control the dog's aggression in all situations, which is not always the case, often with tragic consequences. A well-balanced dog is optimum; it serves no purpose to overstimulate or repress a dog's natural drives. We cannot eliminate them, and if we try to suppress these drives and urges, we will only succeed in making our dogs miserable. Consequently, if we do not allow dogs an outlet for these instincts, the lack of stimulation can cause frustration and stress, possibly leading to various canine behaviour problems, such as destructive chewing, digging, barking, which may even lead to aggression. Generally, these activities could include flyball and agility, which provide a physical and mental outlet for high prey drive dogs. Additionally, jogging and long walks can be just as satisfying for both dogs and owners and can effectively release unwanted energy and provide an outlet for instinctive behaviours.

Most importantly, before buying a puppy, would-be owners should research the various breeds and only buy a dog with suitable instincts and drives compatible with their circumstances. Fortunately, most dedicated breeders now insist on interviewing prospective buyers before allowing them to take a puppy and can ascertain whether the new home and lifestyle would suit that particular breed. Therefore, with some foresight, we can make sure that we have a happy and satisfying partnership with our trusted canine friends.

Interestingly, selective breeding practices have altered natural physical and behaviour conformations, resulting in a loss of ancient motor patterns and hunting sequences in many dogs. By rearranging the functional chain of a motor pattern, deleting some, weakening or strengthening others, connecting or disconnecting still others, we can create dogs specialised in certain activities.

In certain breeds, this sequence has been interrupted at crucial points. For instance, pointer breeds have an exaggerated stalking pattern, while the emphasis with sheepherders is on stalking and chasing. On the other hand, retrievers have a modified grab-bite which results in a soft mouth, as they would be useless if they dissected and ate the birds they were fetching. Conversely, vermin dogs follow the sequence all the way through: orient>eye>stalk>chase>grab-bite>kill-bite>dissect>consume. In this example, the first motor pattern triggers the second, while the second triggers the third, etc.

According to Namibian farmers, wild cheetahs seldom kill young calves because they don't run. A cheetah cannot perform the paw slap to bring down its prey unless it is chasing an animal. When cheetahs kill, they eat as much as possible before leaving the carcass, as they never return to a previous kill to feed. Without activating the chase>dissect>consume sequence, they are unable to eat a dead animal they have not chased and killed.

The sequence of a sheepherding border collie would be:

orient>EYE-STALK>CHASE   dissect>consume.

In this instance, the EYE-STALK>CHASE are exaggerated behaviours, and the sequence is interrupted before dissect>consume. Fortunately, it is unusual for the grab-bite or kill-bite to appear, or for border collies to injure or kill any sheep.

On the other hand, the predatory sequence of a pointer would be:

orient>EYE-stalk>   grab-bite>   consume.

In certain dogs, the grab-bite can trigger kill-bite and dissect, which are virtually impossible to eradicate out of a functional sequence as the behaviour is self-rewarding. Unfortunately, pointers that ate their prey would become useless as working dogs.

Over time, breeders can modify, or shorten, these sequences, just as the flush for the pointer is a modified grab-bite, which has been altered for certain retrievers to show a soft mouth, such as the English cocker spaniel. Accordingly, most herding, retrieving, pointing dogs have had the kill-bite>dissect>consume disconnected from their sequence. Even though the kill-bite>dissect>consume may still routinely reappear, that part of the pattern has usually become weak and non-functioning.

Selectively producing dogs ensures that they will remain functional in the environment they were bred for. For instance, we consider it normal behaviour when a collie herds sheep. However, when it decides to herd children, we regard this as abnormal behaviour.

Based on their behavioural shape, breeds like the border collie are selectively bred for a particular task. Each breed has uniquely wired brains with breed-specific behaviour conformations that predispose them to accomplish specific jobs they perform better than other breeds. As their brains mature, we can shape them by developing them in the appropriate environment. Hence, we have different breeds that are specialised for hunting, guarding, retrieving, herding, etc. Can we imagine a Great Dane herding sheep? Or a dachshund pulling a sled? Neither breed has the conformation to undertake these tasks with positive results.

Usually, working dogs are bred to a physical shape based on skeletal, musculature and metabolic abilities, which allows them to undertake the task we wish them to perform successfully. For instance, sled dogs require a specific conformation that enables them to run marathon distances, pulling a sled with stability, and not overheat in the process. A dog that is too large will overheat.

While greyhounds can sprint brilliantly, they do not have the stamina to run marathons, and their fast-running stride is unstable and unsuitable for pulling a sled. Similarly, they also have the wrong skeletal and musculature shape, nor do they have the right weight-to-size ratio.

On the other hand, malamutes have energy-efficient motion, based on all the essential physical factors, including size to weight, ratio, perfect skeleton, and musculature, which allows them to accomplish this task more efficiently than other breeds.

Nevertheless, physical conformation is not enough; the dog might have the right shape and size, but if the brain is not in unison with the body, the dog will always be limited to what its brain dictates. The brain also must adapt itself to harmonise with the body. Technically the brain must program itself to coordinate with the different physical features of each breed, including the range and flexibility of the spine, skeletal features and length of the legs. These various features determine not only the stride of the dog but whether it will be a sprinter or a marathon runner and whether it will be quick and agile or slow and bulky.

Many dog breeds often have two distinct bloodlines, one for working dogs and another for show dogs, which prioritises appearance over behaviour. For example, today, American show-line Labradors are shorter and fatter than twenty years ago, while Labradors from the English field lines are thinner and leggier. These dogs may not only look different but may also have different behaviour profiles. Generally, working lines retain more of the historical working trait than show lines and pet dogs.

Undoubtedly, dogs are happiest doing what breeding and genetics dictate. When the brain and body are perfectly coordinated for specific tasks, all functions are self-motivating and self-rewarding. A working dog loves nothing better than work; therefore, the behaviour is virtually impossible to extinguish.

No matter how I tried, I could not find either the physical or the behavioural conformation in Mila which predisposed her as a successful personal guard/protection dog.

More mystified than ever, I decided to try a canine DNA test, hoping it might shed light on Mila's background and explain some of her character anomalies that didn't seem to fit with the dachshund breed. Embark and Wisdom Panel were the two tests that I investigated, and both are available from Amazon UK.

Even though Wisdom Panel can test for over 350 dog breeds, they did not recommend their DNA test for Mila, as they have not extensively researched and collected samples to represent the unique gene pools of Hungary. Furthermore, during their test development, they observed that certain breeds sometimes have quite distinct genetic breed signatures in different geographical regions due to a phenomenon known as genetic drift. For this reason, their database may not represent some breed lines from Hungary. Therefore, the test would be unreported or misreported, as would be the case for samples from Germany, the Netherlands or Great Britain. Accordingly, they would be unable to guarantee the accuracy of the results and would advise against it.

Whereas at the time, Embark only tested for 250+ breeds, they had no similar issues. Additionally, what convinced me is that they screened for 170+ genetic and health conditions. Knowing Mila's genetic background and any health problems was very important for us. Since then, Embark has expanded its database to include 350+ unique dogs and over 200+ genetic health risks. Additionally, Embark is proactively committed to utilising their collected data for ongoing studies in canine health issues and is in partnership with Cornell University College of Veterinary Medicine, to further canine health research. My decision was, therefore, quite clear-cut.

After collecting Mila's DNA, we waited impatiently for approximately four weeks for the outcome.

How is DNA testing done? According to Embark:

DNA is inherited in pieces, called chromosomes, that are passed along from parent to offspring. Each generation, these chromosomes are broken up and shuffled a bit in a process known as recombination. So, the length of the segments your dog shares with her ancestors decreases with each generation above her: she shares longer segments with her mom than her grandma, longer segments with her grandma than her great-grandma, and so on.

HOW DOES EMBARK KNOW WHICH BREEDS ARE IN MILA?

We can use the length of segments MILA shares with our reference dogs to see how many generations it has been since they last shared an ancestor. Long segments of DNA that are identical to known purebred dogs tell Embark's scientists that MILA has, without a doubt, a relative from that breed. By testing over 200,000 genetic markers, we build up her genes one DNA segment at a time, to learn the ancestry with great certainty.

Dogs have 39 pairs of chromosomes, almost double humans who have 23. 38 of those pairs are the same for all dogs, while the 39th is the sex chromosomes – two X's for females and one X and one Y for males. One copy of each chromosome came from your dog's mother and one from your dog's father. Each copy contains between 24 million and 123 million bases, or letters of DNA code, for 2.5 billion total letters inherited from each parent. This chromosome illustration shows a representation of each of your dog's 38 pairs of chromosomes (excluding the X and Y sex chromosomes).

Because the members of a breed have similar stretches of DNA, we can use our 200,000+ genetic markers to determine what part of each chromosome in your dog came from what breed. For each pair of chromosomes, your dog's mom and dad each gave your dog one copy of that chromosome, for a grand total of 78 chromosomes. So if your dog's mom was a poodle and dad was a schnauzer, then the painting would show one complete poodle and one complete schnauzer chromosome for each pair. The more complex your dog's ancestry, the more complex the painting, as in each generation recombination (the splitting apart and "shuffling around" of genes between paired chromosomes) mixes up bits of chromosome from grandparents, great-grandparents, and beyond.

Each trait your dog exhibits, such as fur shedding, is based on the letter at one or more locations in your dog's genome. For example, the location determining if your dog sheds their fur is located on chromosome 1. Some other traits, like size, are complexly inherited from many locations, including ones on chromosomes 1, 3, 4, 7, 10, 15, and more. Your dog looks the way it does not because of averaging or blending the breeds that form it, but because specific traits were inherited from specific breeds. That's one reason your mix may look, act, and have certain health issues much more like one breed than another!

Mila's DNA results were unexpected, to say the least. Much as we assumed, her lineage showed that she is part dachshund, but only 21.9%. Not surprisingly, she also has 20.8% Jack Russell-type terrier, but what really knocked our socks off was that she is 20.8% English cocker spaniel and 9.9% cocker spaniel. Furthermore, the most endearing part of her is 26.6% Supermutt. We also discovered that Mila is a natural bobtail, courtesy of her Jack Russell-type dog heritage.

Additionally, the genetic study revealed that she is likely a heavy seasonal shedder. Bearing this in mind, Slave has a job for life. As extra insurance, I also invested in a special Furminator brush, as well as a T-shirt with the caption 'Rich people have brand labels on their clothes. Happy people have dog hair on their clothes'.

Mila also tested negative for over 160 genetic diseases. However, as a carrier for hyperuricosuria and hyperuricemia, she is unlikely to develop this condition, although she could pass it on to her offspring, possibly resulting in kidney and bladder stones. Additionally, the tests revealed that Mila also has one copy of a mutation associated with reduced ALT (alanine aminotransferase activity), the standard value in most blood chemistry panels, which technicians use to indicate liver health. Although a low ALT does not predict liver disease, Embark advised us to inform our vet of Mila's 'low normal' levels, so she can adjust the value of future blood panels to interpret them correctly.

Without a doubt, Mila has many dachshund traits; however, I surmise that she inherited her extreme aptitude for learning and easy trainability from the English/cocker spaniel family. Nevertheless, it would be interesting to find out what breeds she also represents within the 26.6% Supermutt. With over 400 modern dog breeds, there are numerous choices.

Based on her lineage, it is evident that Mila inherited superb hunting skills from all three of her ancestor breeds, including an exceptional sense of smell. Interestingly, the English/cocker spaniel is known for its very gentle mouth and can retrieve prey without so much as bruising it. This information certainly explained volumes about Mila's character. Knowing our dog's breed and selecting appropriate activities based on their physical and behavioural conformation, which shape a dog's skills and abilities, allows us to channel them towards activities predetermined by their genetics, setting them up for success and enjoyment.

Overviewing the situation, there seemed little reason to keep flogging a dead horse; therefore, much to Zoli's disappointment, I cancelled all further personal guard/protect lessons.

In conclusion, zoologist Kenth Svartberg from Stockholm University states that "the basic dimensions of dog behaviour can be changed when selection pressures change, and therefore, the domestication of dogs is still evolving. In dog breeding, there is a conscious and unconscious selection for wanted and against unwanted traits. Assuming that these traits have a genetic base, the dominant selection will decide the typical behaviour of the dogs in future generations."

CHAPTER 7
DOMINANCE THEORY

From the 1970s to the early 2000s we lived somewhat isolated lives in Botswana, unexposed to the latest trends and popular television shows. Streamed television only arrived in the mid-'80s from heavily sanctioned South Africa, and therefore popular TV shows were not in evidence at the time. It was a bit like living under a rock, and, consequently, I was ignorant about pack structure and the dominance theory. The foundations of both rest on misguided theories that unwanted behaviour in dogs develops because they want to be dominant and will be in constant aggressive competition with pack members to reach the top of the hierarchy, and alpha dog status.

Imagine my surprise when I first learnt that owners should not allow their dogs to sleep on the furniture, walk through doors ahead of them, or eat their meals before their owners, all of which I was guilty of allowing. According to Stephen Budiansky, American science and history writer, in his book *The Truth About Dogs*, I was either a nincompoop with naturally subordinate and compliant dogs, or possibly due to my passivity and wimpiness, I had created monsters.

Furthermore, Budiansky suggests that aggressively dominant dogs are often the product of lax and loving owners. Without realising, it seems that I had created monsters. Happily, my monsters were content and secure, with absolutely no signs of growling, biting, or any other behavioural or aggressive tendencies. I realise that ignorance is no excuse, but little did I know that I should treat my dogs as subordinates rather than as family members to avoid encouraging dominant behaviours.

Did previous generations of dog owners treat their dogs as subordinates? Or were they all nincompoops as well?

Following our relocation from arid Botswana to tropical Queensland in Australia, various television shows introduced me to 'The Dog Whisperer', Cesar Millan, and some of his theories, including the alpha dog concepts. However, by then, I concluded that we were already doomed, and therefore I didn't feel the need to fix what was not broken. Not to mention the fact that Mr Millan's methods did not win me over, as knowledgeable as he seemed to be. Even though his techniques appeared to have instant results, they just seemed too good to be true.

Several years later, we came to live in Budapest, Hungary, where my hands-on experience with the dominance concept started soon after adopting Mila. Amongst other things, Zoli introduced me to the wolf pack and dominance theory. I usually enjoyed our lessons with Zoli, who had worked in Africa in the past and had some amusing anecdotes that I could relate to. He was also well informed and had a good sense of humour. Therefore, during the many weeks of training, I was quite surprised by his 'alpha dog' ideas, which was the only bone of contention between us.

Zoli seriously believed in dominance-based training.

For example, to teach Mila to leave the room, I had to make myself look big and threatening and stare her down until she felt uncomfortable enough to leave the room, which also supposedly showed her that I was the 'alpha dog'. In another exercise, I had to growl above her food bowl when Mila approached and pretend to eat her food. This exercise was to teach Mila that I was dominant, and I had priority over all resources. As such, she was only allowed to eat when, and if, I gave her permission. Zoli also suggested that I should not feed Mila for two to three days to show her that I was in charge.

During one of our lessons, another client dropped off her corgi while Mila watched off-leash from the back of the yard. Despite his awareness of her reactive issues and her recent conduct with his own dogs, Zoli called Mila over, and she obligingly obeyed. However, when she got close, she lunged at the corgi. In response, Zoli smacked Mila on the nose and knelt above her and growled intimidatingly in her face several times, while Mila threw herself on her back in submission.

When I questioned this type of training, Zoli advised that he wouldn't tolerate confrontational behaviour in any of his dogs. But why was Mila hostile towards the corgi? Zoli was fully aware that Mila had issues in her past and was agitated and fearful of dogs; therefore, I felt that he should have handled the situation more appropriately. For example, he could have led Mila over gradually on a leash until she felt more confident about approaching a strange dog. Whereas hitting and growling at a fearful dog teaches them nothing positive, and only makes them more anxious.

Furthermore, one cannot cure aggression with aggression. Naturally, I shared my opinion with Zoli. Although he felt there was no need to dwell on Mila's past and her issues with other dogs, he did agree with my point of view that perhaps he could have dealt with the situation more positively. Of course, I did not agree with this assessment. Despite his dismissal of Mila's issues, the cornerstone of any remedial training involves in-depth functional analysis. If we recognise the problem behaviour and evaluate why the problem exists, we can help determine an appropriate solution. Although, I also understood that Zoli was not a canine behaviourist and, as a dog trainer, he was doing his best.

Additionally, Zoli's idea of training good manners when Mila pulled on her leash was to jerk her around by the collar. This practice puts an incredible amount of pressure on the dog's neck. It can cause severe trauma, including thyroid gland injuries, damage to the spinal cord and nerves, bruising of the oesophagus and crushing of the trachea. Innumerable veterinarians and other professionals have warned about the devastating number of physical injuries resulting from pulling and jerking a dog's collar. Unfortunately, many trainers still use this method to train leash control. Alas, I have seen first-hand that this method is not only dangerous, but it does not teach a dog anything. It may momentarily suppress a behaviour, but it certainly won't correct it.

A further difference of opinion arose when Zoli showed me how to teach Mila not to run through an open door/gate. First, he made himself look big and intimidating, and then he shoved Mila back from the opening. Each time Mila tried to go through the door, Zoli pushed her back while staring at her threateningly. If Mila refused to cooperate, probably because she didn't understand what Zoli required of her, he cornered and growled at her, coercing her to submit. Most of these 'alpha dog' behaviours did little more than make Mila nervous and unsure of what we required.

Under normal circumstances, she enjoyed learning and was very receptive and quick on the uptake if I showed her exactly what I wanted; she was happy to oblige. If I wanted her to leave the room, all I had to do was teach her to go out on command. There was no need to stare her down or engage in these so-called dominating behaviours. Before joining Zoli, the first exercise I taught Mila was to sit and wait for her food, which she learnt quickly. After completing the course with Zoli, I gradually taught Mila to sit and stay in front of an open door/gate until I released her. It is not rocket science, and all it takes is time, patience and positive reinforcement. I found that it was more straightforward and quicker to train her positively than to intimidate her, corner and growl at her. All that achieved was to shut her down.

I challenged all these less than humane ideas and methods. Fortunately, Zoli was receptive to my views, and the intimidation and the leash-jerking stopped. Although Mila remained very fond of Zoli – she loves everyone –

she was noticeably more hesitant whenever she had to approach him, which I believe was a consequence of the alpha dog exercises.

I certainly learnt a lot during the ten-week training programme, especially how not to treat my dog.

Once I started researching the topic, I realised there is a mind-boggling amount of information, theories, discussions, vigorous debates for both sides of the dominance theory, written by highly respected professionals. Yet, as a newcomer to these ideas, it was difficult to challenge what I believe are misguided concepts, especially as some experts have spent decades working with and studying dogs.

The foundations of the dominance theory rest on research, initially carried out by Rudolph Schenkel at Basel Zoo, on captive wolves in 1946. These wolves were unrelated strangers of different ages and genders, all originating from diverse locations, which does predispose a certain amount of social tension and aggression, especially at breeding time, when hostility and fights were frequent. This study based its theory on the idea that wolves fight within their packs to gain dominance, which gave rise to the belief in alpha wolves. Konrad Lorenz, the co-editor of the German Society for Animal Psychology's journal, further perpetuated the dominance myth. Even though his speciality was birds, he may have modelled his views of wolves on the strictly hierarchical and rigid structure of the Nazi Party. His reasoning possibly formed the basis of his ideas, not just about wolves, but also on dog behaviour, which he perpetuated in his book *Man Meets Dog*, published in 1949.

A further progenitor of 'compulsive inducements' was Colonel Konrad Most. Although he was undoubtedly thirty years ahead of his time in understanding operant conditioning principles, Colonel Konrad Most, who trained dogs for police work in the early 1900s, was a further advocate of coercive methods. Furthermore, he advocated the use of the switch, spiked collars and forced compliance, as published in a training manual, *Training Dogs*, which was translated into English in 1944.

Accordingly, in the past decades, owners generally accepted the idea that to really know a dog, you had to know wolves, and believed they are the same species. From this notion, it was a logical progression to assume that the dominance theory of wolves should apply equally to dogs.

I can't help wondering if all the individuals who use physical force to gain dominance over a dog and snarl into its face would be equally as brave and attempt that with a wolf.

On the other hand, does the dominance theory realistically apply to domestic dogs, even if it does apply to wolves?

Decades of artificial breeding has undoubtedly altered our dogs' behaviour, which now bears little resemblance to either wild wolves or free-ranging dogs. Moreover, it seems clear that even though wolves and dogs share very similar DNA and have the same number of chromosomes, dogs took a different evolutionary path to wolves at least 14,000 years ago, so why should we treat our dogs like wolves?

On the other hand, English zoologist Aubrey Manning, whose pioneering work on animal behaviour was published in 1972, believes that even 8,000 years of intense selection and domestication have not changed canines' ancestral patterns. In other words, he believes that evolution and artificial breeding practices have had virtually no effect on canine behaviour and states that no matter how we manipulate a dog, it will always be limited to its repertoire from the wolf.

Additionally, this also leads us to the controversy of whether we should classify dogs as *Canis familiaris*, a distinct species. Unfortunately, there is a vast difference of opinion on this matter. Some people believe that dogs and wolves are the same species, and we should classify them all as *Canis lupus familiaris* accordingly. Usually, scientists consider animals to be of the same species when the two animals can create fertile offspring.

Yet other animals are also interfertile and can produce viable offspring, including the polar bear and the brown bear, the bonobo and the chimpanzee, the roan antelope and the sable antelope, and domestic cattle and bison. Many bird species and several big cats are also interfertile, although, usually, only the male or female hybrid is fertile in the big cats. Yet, scientists have classified all of the above as different species.

Arguably, interbreeding between most of the above does not typically occur in the wild, as they are unlikely to encounter each other and inhabit different geographical areas. While it is true that wolves and dogs do occasionally breed on their own in the wild, this only happens rarely, due to their relative isolation from each other.

Even though the wolf and dog are very close genetically, we can gain additional insight and form a more precise picture if we examine the overall ecology of wolves and dogs and not just the sequencing of their nucleic acids.

One is a wild animal independent of humans; the other is a fully domesticated companion animal. The wolf is a hunter and carnivore, while the dog is a scavenger that lives off dead food sources; whether it is at the dump, or the commercial dog food we give them, dogs do not hunt for or kill their food. Wolves and dogs have entirely different survival strategies. Wolves stay away from humans, whereas dogs are dependent on them. Furthermore, they have different reproductive cycles and different early socialisation periods, and behaviourally they have almost nothing in common. When the canid tree split, wolves and dogs went along separate branches. While the wolf manifests specialised adaptations to the wilderness, the dog adapted to domestic life.

Some experts theorise that if we correctly interpret the 1977 research data of Vilá *et al.*, dogs appear to be more closely related to coyotes than wolves. Additionally, Charles Darwin himself suggested that hybridisation between wolves and jackals may have provided the necessary variation for the evolution of dogs.

Although this is not evidence that dogs evolved from coyotes or jackals, it does present compelling alternatives to the various evolutionary paths domestic dogs may have taken, other than the generally accepted theories. Considering their multiple studies, many experts find it ludicrous to classify the dog and the wolf as the same species. Based on mtDNA evidence, it is incontestable that dogs are related to wolves. However, based on evolutionary processes and human-made selective breeding, it should be just as evident that neither domestic nor free-ranging canines are wolves of any shape, size or form. Dogs do not have a wolf brain, and they do not think like wolves, nor do they behave like them. The all-encompassing, and insurmountable difference between wolf and dog, and why they will never be the same species, is revealed in the latter's Latin name: *Canis* = dog, *familiaris* = of, or pertaining to a household or family.

In light of the many canine studies over the past decades, including ongoing research by canine institutes globally, there is much more reliable information readily available regarding the behaviour of dogs. Therefore, it is preposterous to believe that we should dominate our dogs by pressing them into the ground and snarling into their faces. Despite this, specific individuals still maintain that there is nothing wrong with asserting dominance by lifting a dog by the scruff and staring at it or smacking it on the nose.

Some trainers even encourage this practice with puppies and advise owners to do it several times a day. Doubtless, there will always be individuals who doggedly believe that wolves and dogs are social climbers and are always looking for signs of weakness, hesitation or lack of confidence in their humans.

Nevertheless, it is no secret that dogs do not have large frontal brain lobes, and indeed scientists use this as proof that dogs cannot formulate complex thoughts. Consequently, they are not calculating and are incapable of premeditation. With the cognitive abilities of a two- to three-year-old child, they do not have the mental capacity for complex planning. If a dog has a 'theory of mind', it must have forethought and be aware of its motives and consequences; however, there doesn't seem to be any scientific evidence to support that a dog has any of these capabilities. Moreover, dogs live in the moment, so it is absurd to believe that they can hatch evil plans to become household dictators.

There are many arguments from both sides, including Cesar Millan and UK dog trainer Colin Tennant, who believe that because dogs have a genetic pack mentality, they always try to dominate other dogs and humans. If we do not pre-empt this behaviour by asserting leadership, our dogs may become unstable and aggressive. I can't help but wonder whether some so-called dominant characteristics in many pets may actually be behaviour problems caused by dominance-theory owners.

Generally, people tend to label dogs that resist their owners' efforts of control as dominant, when, in fact, the dog is merely behaving in a manner that conflicts with its owner's expectations. This lack of understanding may result in frustration on the dog's part and a lack of consistency on the owner's. Inevitably, dogs pull on their leash for a reason, perhaps because they lack impulse control. They also jump up on their owners for a reason, which owners may have unwittingly reinforced by giving their dogs attention at inappropriate times. However, they are certainly not scheming to take over the world or dominate their owners.

Contrary to Millan and Tennant, animal behaviourist and dog trainer Dr Ian Dunbar regards dominance theory as cruel, unnecessary and based on a complete misconception, which assumes that a dog's misbehaviour is motivated by the desire to have a high rank. Dunbar also confirms that our dogs perform certain unwanted behaviours simply because we have rewarded these behaviours many times in the past. Other experts also concur that any action our dog adopts will depend on its prior experience. Any successful strategy will reinforce this behaviour.

Similarly, author and animal behaviourist Alexander Semyonova points out that dogs with perceived dominant, aggressive behaviour problems are often treated with anti-anxiety medication and operant conditioning therapy. Yet, if we believe that dominance is instinctive behaviour, how is it possible to treat it with operant conditioning or medication? There are many examples demonstrating that so-called dominance is neither a natural canine behaviour nor a social status. On the contrary, it is usually a learnt behaviour, which we can successfully control or eliminate, with training and management techniques.

You may recall our dachshund, Franky, who usually loved going for walks; however, on certain days, she refused to leave the house. No matter how much I cajoled, she stubbornly resisted and did not budge. Was my dog rebelling? Was she acting dominant? Actually, she merely indicated that being such a low-slung sporty model, so close to the ground, the over 25°C degree temperatures were far too hot for her to contemplate a walk.

Similarly, when Mila initially relieved herself in the house (remember the lakes of urine and the mountains of poop?), well-meaning friends advised me that Mila was displaying dominant behaviours, and I should punish her. So often, what seem to be 'dominant' displays have a logical explanation; however, applying misguided dominance theory practices only serve to increase the dog's frustration and fears and exacerbate the problem.

Additionally, the terminology is often inconsistent, and the lines become blurred. Frequently, we interchange words and refer to a confident and bold dog as dominant and a fearful dog as aggressive, often equated with dominance. Seemingly, even experts are unable to agree on what dominance means.

A leading figure in the revolution of canine studies, Professor John Bradshaw concurs that we use the word 'dominance' extensively as an example of dog behaviour. Subsequently, we frequently misuse dominance aggression to explain a dog's personality. As Bradshaw points out, this is often just the behaviour of an unmanageable, untrained dog but says nothing about its relationship with other dogs or people.

When we apply the term correctly, Bradshaw advises that 'dominance' describes a relationship between two individuals at any particular time. It does not predict how the situation occurred, when it will end, or the personalities of those involved.

In this context, dominance takes on a fluid aspect, with various individuals taking leadership roles at different times under different social situations. Just as I might have a leadership role in my household, but I'd mostly defer to my boss at work, whereas, if he knows what is good for him, he will certainly defer to his mother-in-law. Dominance in dogs is not a hierarchy, nor is it a status.

According to *Encyclopaedia Britannica*, the dominance hierarchy is a "form of animal social structure in which a linear or nearly linear ranking exists, with each animal dominant over those below it and submissive to those above it in the hierarchy."

Norwegian zoologist Thorlief Schjelderup Ebbe first noted this biological concept in the early 1900s after he observed chickens and their social structure for years and identified what he called a 'pecking order'. In this process, each bird pecks another lower in the scale without fear of retaliation and submits to pecking by one of higher rank. The 'pecking order' concept and dominance hierarchy were subsequently applied to other social animal groups, including wolves.

Further fuel on the fire of the dominance theory came from American biologist L. David Mech, following the release of his book in the late 1960s, *The Wolf: Ecology and Behavior of an Endangered Species*, which popularised the alpha wolf and dominance theory. From the original premise that dogs are the same as wolves, naturally, the dominance hierarchy theory filtered down to include canines, and for decades it flourished. In 1999, Mech, the very person who propagated the dominance theory in wolves, ushered in the age of enlightenment.

In various articles, he corrected previously published misinformation. A further nail in the coffin of the wolf dominance theory was the new book *Wolves: Behavior, Ecology, and Conservation* edited by L. David Mech and Luigi Boitani. Eventually, Mech explained his about-face regarding the dominance theory in wolves and admitted that he based his previous views on the information available when he wrote his original book, referencing the 1944 study based on a random assortment of captive wolves.

After living with wild wolves on Ellesmere Island, Mech realised that the wolf pack was not an aggressive assortment of fiends competing with each other to take over leadership. On the contrary, wolf packs are family units built on cohesion and cooperation, not conflict and dominance. The parent wolves have a leadership role and guide the family, similar to a human family. Each year the parents produce a new litter of pups, which become the younger siblings of the previous litter. As in a human family unit, older brothers and sisters guide their younger siblings, but there is no battle to gain pack leadership. The family members stay voluntarily and are free to move away at any time. Older siblings usually leave the family to find mates and form their own packs when they are between one and two, or even up to three years of age.

In light of these studies, it certainly seems that we can lay the alpha myth and dominance theory in wolves to rest.

Numerous canine experts believe that dogs live in a social structure based on the principles of no aggression. In social interactions, each dog respects the other's personal space and are considerate of each other's preferences. There are no hierarchies, no dominance or submission, which are purely human projections. Generally, dogs that engage in aggression are not products of nature and result from human artificial manipulation.

When examining canine social structures, we can more logically describe them as deference hierarchies, whereby the group's unity relates to forming social and emotional bonds with others. Whenever possible, village dogs/pariah dogs avoid conflict and enjoy a relaxed social structure with no dominance; each dog respects the other's boundaries.

This behaviour is identical to what I observed in African village dogs and dogs in the rural Hungary of my childhood. Everyone in the village had a yard dog of no specific breed, and as their owners did not restrict them behind fences, they often came and went during the day as they pleased. Sometimes they explored alone, at other times they met up with friends. Even though these dogs were not genuinely free-ranging dogs – they all had owners who fed them – like free-ranging dogs, they liked to socialise and investigate their surroundings.

Similarly, the beach dogs of the Seychelles that are actual free-ranging dogs have an identically fluid social structure with no 'leader' or 'dominant' dog. Each dog comes and goes at will, sometimes alone, at other times with a companion or two, and they seem content to defer to one another. Additionally, the West Bengal pariah dog population regularly exchange, what appears to be, greeting signals with each other and coexist amicably even with neighbourhood groups of pariah dogs. These dogs seem to have no desire to dominate or displace their neighbours, even as occasional competitors for food.

Indeed, all successful social groups function precisely because of voluntary deference and not because of enforced dominance. Social, body language rituals exist in order to avoid conflict. Considering all the currently available information, it is not difficult to accept the idea that dominance, as a status, does not exist in dogs.

Even though the newer studies and viewpoints have been around for over a decade, it can take over twenty years for new concepts to filter down and for the general population to assimilate them.

Sadly, this is the reason why some people still believe in the dominance concept, which was initially based on a regrettable misconception. However, the latest studies indicate that dogs defer to each other and avoid confrontation, including any form of enforced dominance, although scientists and experts admit that they still don't have all the answers. We require further studies to establish precisely how canine social structures function; nevertheless, it is probably safe to assume that neither dominance nor conflict are elements of this intricate framework.

CHAPTER 8
ONGOING TRAINING WITH ZOLI AND PACK THEORY

As we neared the end of our ten-week course, we had not addressed the matter of Mila's reactivity, which was the reason I initially sought Zoli's help. I pointed out this omission to Zoli, who suggested that we take Mila out for a walk around his neighbourhood during our next training session. And so, we went for a walk. Honestly, it felt more like running the gauntlet.

Virtually every house we passed, dogs barked at us, restrained behind fences. Embarrassingly, Mila was in her element as she screamed at each dog, stressed and out of control. Furthermore, it was impossible to calm her; she ignored all her favourite treats, which is saying a lot considering that, usually, she lives for her stomach.

Once again, as expected, Zoli did his dominance thing and made himself look more commanding and in charge. Additionally, much to my annoyance, Zoli jerked and tugged on Mila's leash, and when she didn't respond, he poked her in the ribs and held her down on the ground while he growled into her face. These remedial training methods occurred before I had my chat with Zoli and pointed out my aversion to such practices. These methods that treat fear with fear might temporarily stop a behaviour, but they do not teach a dog anything long term other than to fear its owner or handler. So much for our leash-reactivity training.

Obviously, we were getting nowhere fast, and Zoli mentioned that he also offered a dog walking service. Each morning he took ten to fourteen dogs out for a run on the open meadows and suggested that Mila and I join him. As we had nothing to lose, we met Zoli at his house the following morning before collecting the other dogs in his panel van and made our way to the open fields, where he released the dogs to run around untethered. Once again, circumstances forced me to put my foot down, and I refused to let Mila run free. As we've established, she is a scenthound, and it would be natural for her to follow an animal trail to the ends of the earth. Doubtless, many animals used the meadow as their highway during the night – deer, fox, marten – so I was not in the mood to tempt fate or Mila's nose.

Additionally, although Zoli's dogs were there, including Svetlana, I was unsure how Mila would behave with so many large, unfamiliar dogs. If she became scared, she might take off, and we'd never see her again. Moreover, Vinnie was also there, the corgi that Mila had had an altercation with earlier, during our training. Although, I'm happy to report that when Mila is off-leash, she has never made any further aggressive moves towards another dog since the corgi incident and became friends with Vinnie. Optimistically, Zoli assured me that Mila would stay with the pack because dogs are pack animals, and she would not run away.

Furthermore, he also felt that I should have more faith in Mila and trust in our bond. Because I knew her well enough and realised that she has a high prey drive, I was not prepared to take any risks. Numerous warnings alert owners never to trust a dachshund off-leash. Because of their strong prey drive, it is not unusual for a dachshund to spot something interesting and take off in an instant and it will be oblivious to all attempts at recall. Even if they have been walking off-leash for many years, without any incidents, it doesn't mean that it can't happen; therefore, it is better to be safe than sorry.

Similar warnings caution cocker spaniel owners to keep their dogs leashed, even if they have a reliable recall. Throughout our long weeks of training, I was surprised that Zoli hadn't introduced any recall work, especially as, during our sessions, Mila often became distracted and suddenly developed selective hearing problems when she refused to acknowledge our calls. Naturally, we were both aware of Mila's recall limitations. Doubtless, a good recall can save a dog's life. Where there was no threat to life or limb, at home in our fenced garden, Mila performed brilliantly, but in any other high-stimulus environment, all bets were off, which is why I never allowed Mila off-leash.

Based on Mila's genetics, I stuck to my guns, so Zoli decided to humour me and attached her to a seven-metre-long leash. When we led Mila from the car on the long leash, the 'pack', as Zoli referred to them, were already frolicking in the open meadow, with woodland on the one side. When they spotted the newcomer, they all came bounding over for an introduction. Unexpectedly, Zoli dropped the end of the leash to the ground, and, not feeling restricted, Mila behaved very well. Even though she was tense and anxious, she didn't react, she didn't bark or scream, and after they all exchanged introductions, she gradually relaxed a little, but not enough to take any treats.

As the large dogs milled around, she remained on edge in the general mayhem as they encircled her, a piece of flotsam in a shoal of herrings; being the smallest, the other dogs herded her in various directions. Zoli did ask me to try a few recalls. However, an anxious dog will not respond well to training. In all fairness, Mila tried to get back to me; however, as soon as I called her name, the other dogs bounded over in anticipation of getting one of Mila's treats. With a wall of dogs packed tightly in front of me, Mila, being the smallest, could not get through the canine barrier. Under these conditions, I was unhappy about working on recall, as it just set Mila up for failure.

The dogs did not mind the heavy frost or the frozen earth under their feet and ran around the open field together, enjoying each other's company. Even though the untethered leash snaked perilously along the ground and unsettled me, I knew we could grab it quickly, as long as we were near the end. At one point, 'the pack' ran off into the distance and turned back along the tree line. All except one little short-legged hound who carried on running full speed ahead, straight towards freedom and the very distant horizon. The uninterrupted open vista was her open gate, and she was not going to miss the opportunity. Mentally, I could almost hear her shouting '*hasta la vista*' as she grew smaller and smaller in the distance. Alarmingly, we were nowhere near the end of the leash.

Zoli sprinted into action and took off after Mila, his long legs doing double time. Disappointed and hurt that Mila seemed so willing to abandon me, I looked on helplessly as Mila carried on running. Eventually, after what seemed like an eternity but was only a few minutes of flat-out sprinting, Zoli managed to grab the end of the leash and restored the little escape artist to me.

So much for Zoli's pack theory.

Closely related to the dominance theory is the pack structure, which believes that free-ranging dogs naturally live in a complex social group with precise ranking. As with dominance principles, pack theorists formulated the regrettable fallacy that dogs are like wolves that have a pecking order, with each wolf in the pack being dominant over the one below it. This hierarchy of status entails constant competition within the group. As each wolf attempts to gain dominance over the wolf above it, they will resort to aggression when necessary to increase their rank in the pack. In this scenario, the alpha pair are the leaders with exclusive rights to all resources, while the rest of the pack, depending on their ranking, would be in constant competition to increase their status.

Naturally, these misconceptions contaminated beliefs about our unfortunate canines, as pack theorists decided that domestic dogs spend their lives striving to increase their status within their human families. Accordingly, so-called experts warn owners, as pack leaders, to manage their dogs with a list of rules to ensure that their pets don't gain dominance. The most common pack rules include the following:

- Dogs should not lead on a walk but should walk just behind their owners.
- Owners should start and end all games with their dogs.
- No tug-of-war games.
- Owners should eat before their dogs.
- Dogs should not precede humans through doors.
- Humans should not lie on the floor with their dogs.
- Dogs should not be elevated higher than their owners, nor allowed to sit on beds or furniture.
- Always make a dog move out of your way; never step over it.
- Force your dog into an alpha roll.

This code of conduct is more than vaguely reminiscent of medieval serfdoms or the US slave codes of the late 1600s.

Geneticist J.P. Scott and biologist J.L. Fuller also agreed that these ideas are very similar to those once employed in human slavery. I can't help wondering who has delusions of grandeur, dogs or their humans? The pack rules dictate that owners must follow these rules to ensure their dominance and retain their position as the 'alpha leaders' within the pack. After all, a dog is much happier if it knows its place, and owners should ignore these guidelines at their peril.

Additionally, if we do not consistently administer regular psychological and physical intimidation, our dogs will become dominant, which will result in behaviour problems, particularly aggression. Yet, individuals pretending to be the alpha leader may intimidate their dog by growling at them, but these behaviours only teach fear.

Unfortunately, many people still believe the alpha pack rules. However, with ongoing studies, we now know that even free-ranging wolves have a much more relaxed family structure that bears no resemblance to a strict dominance hierarchy.

Consequently, the pack theory seems somewhat irrelevant if we understand that a pack is a social group of conspecific canids from the same family. Furthermore, dogs know that we are not dogs; therefore, they would never form a pack with humans. Fortunately, with ongoing research and studies on both free-ranging and pet dogs, it is evident that canines do not form packs, as they have neither the need nor the inclination. Additionally, canine pack behaviour is not genetic, and if dogs do not develop pack behaviour during the critical period, there is no sense in imitating pack leadership after this time.

Wolves, and indeed most predators, do forge packs as a matter of survival, as hunting and killing large prey is usually a cooperative activity, which solitary predators, with certain exceptions, are seldom able to achieve successfully on their own. In contrast to wolves, dogs do not need the assistance of other dogs to find food, nor do they have to travel long distances in search of prey. A further consideration is that domestic dogs do not have enemies; therefore, pack protection is unnecessary, just as group living has no reproductive advantages for dogs.

Additionally, with no large prey that requires communal hunting, dogs hardly need the social organisation of a pack to scavenge for chicken bones on a village dump. Furthermore, other dogs are a source of competition for food; thus, there is no motivation for dogs to form packs. Generally, most free-ranging dogs live alone or in small family groups. However, they search for food solo, not cooperatively. Similarly, the West Bengal pariah dogs have demonstrated dogs' natural social structure over many generations. Even though they may cluster in small family groups, they scavenge on their own.

Considering that free-ranging dogs do not organise their societies like wolves, it is probably safe to assume that domestic dogs wouldn't either. To examine this theory, leading canine expert John Bradshaw observed dogs at a shelter in Wiltshire and concluded that there was no evidence that pet dogs have any inclination to form packs when left to their own devices. Interestingly, his findings seem to support the scientific evidence that domestication has removed most wolf-like behaviours from our dogs. Now that researchers have established that dogs do not form packs, and there is no pecking order, the whole pack theory implodes like a house of cards.

Contrary to the above, the argument remains that certain breeds of dogs do form packs, such as foxhounds and beagles. Indeed, some owners socialise various hunting breeds to the 'pack' from an early age. However, this is an artificial arrangement for the hunter's benefit and has no survival or procreational advantages for dogs. Additionally, pack behaviour in dogs is not genetic; therefore, dogs cannot pass this function to future generations, and it would swiftly extinguish if left to nature.

Various studies on free-ranging dogs have conclusively documented how evolution in canines has extinguished wolf behaviour, and there are no advantages for dogs that wander freely to form packs. Conversely, writer Stephen Budiansky suggests that free-ranging canine society has fragmented from a group of fiefdoms to a world where each citizen is a delusional lordling. Additionally, he further compares their social order to a band of lunatics, all of whom believe they are Napoleon. Budiansky certainly paints a bizarre picture, although I am confident that as long as caring, wimpy, nincompoop owners oversee the insane asylum, the wannabe Napoleons will be a happy band of lunatics.

Not that I am advocating a canine free-for-all; despite possible indications to the contrary, we do need to provide leadership and guidance for our pets. Just as we don't allow our children to run rampant and out of control, we also have to teach our dogs acceptable behaviour. Unfortunately, when dogs are born, they have no intuitive knowledge of how to behave in human societies. They are dogs and only know how to act like dogs. Our pets don't instinctively become housetrained, nor do they realise that the appetising joint of roast on the kitchen counter is not an invitation for self-service. Furthermore, a couch is just a comfortable place to sleep, and if we don't want them to become couch potatoes, we have to teach them and show them alternative options.

Our job as parents is to manage and educate our children and be consistent in how we wish them to behave. Similarly, we are responsible for guiding and teaching our dogs the necessary social skills and acceptable behaviour that we expect from them without forcing them into a submissive relationship based on dominance or ignorance and inflicting long-term psychological damage.

Experts on dog behaviour Scott and Fuller commented on one of the apparent features of the human–canine bond: the striking resemblance to the parent–child relationship.

During one of our unsuccessful attempts to walk Mila, shortly after we got her, seeing us in the street, our neighbours from across the road, Malcolm and his slightly younger, pretty, blond wife, Suzie, came over to chat with us. As with all chance meetings, we exchanged a few pleasantries, and seeing their curiosity about our new dog, Rezső and I introduced Mila. I explained that she was a rescue dog with some anxiety issues. Trying to be helpful, Malcolm, in the manner of a seasoned authority, launched into a monologue about wolves, dogs, the dominance theory and pack rules. Furthermore, he advised us that as pack leaders, we should eat before our dog and walk through doors ahead of her. Naturally, I was astonished by his sage grasp of the subject, especially as I knew that Malcolm did not have a dog. Additionally, he had never shown any interest in canines and, judging by Malcolm's squeamish, finicky behaviour around Lulu before she died, I gained the impression that he didn't care for the species at all. However, I didn't have to wonder about his erudite manner for long, as he excitedly recounted his experiences at the Cesar Millan show he had attended several days earlier.

Touted as a dog behaviour specialist and professional dog psychologist, Hungarians flock to see their celebrity idol, who remains the hero of many trainers. Undoubtedly, Cesar is a consummate showman, who captivates his audiences, and entranced Malcolm and his wife. Celebrity trainers often communicate outdated ideas to unsuspecting and gullible fans who, enthralled by the stature of these canine experts, unquestioningly trust them and their theories. Once again, it was disheartening that with so much available information, only a few short years ago, Cesar was still promoting the dominance theory and pack rules to impressionable audiences.

Inevitably, I tried to dissuade Malcolm from these archaic beliefs, but what chance did I have against a world authority?

Furthermore, for decades Cesar Millan has been a household name. His numerous live shows, TV programmes, YouTube videos and tutorials, as well as books translated into many languages, including Hungarian, have flooded the markets and 'educated' dog trainers and owners alike. Moreover, Millan dominates the Hungarian dog training book market with five books translated into Hungarian and an equal number available in English.

Conversely, experts such as professor of animal ethics James Serpell, anthrozoologist John Bradshaw, professor of evolutionary anthropology Brian Hare and adjunct professor of zoology Patricia McConnell only have one Hungarian translation and two English language books available in Hungary between them.

Fortunately, thanks to Hungarian ethologist and author of *If Dogs Could Talk*, Csányi Vilmos, as well as head of the ethology department at Eötvös Loránd University in Budapest, Professor Ádám Miklósi, the tide in Hungary is gradually turning. Furthermore, Miklósi, author of the influential book *Dog Behaviour, Evolution, and Cognition*, is also head of the prestigious Family Dog Research Project. The project currently incorporates three institutions and many scientists. It is considered the world's formative research centre for dog cognition, where ongoing studies and research is generating a new understanding of the dog–human relationship.

Finally, in the absence of the pack theory, we are free to enjoy our dogs without continually having to second guess our actions. We no longer have to worry about whether we should play tug with our dogs or wonder if we should ignore them or not when we come home. Furthermore, we don't have to agonise over whether to sit, or not to sit on the floor with them, or live in constant fear of letting our guard down, on pain of ending up with egocentric dictators.

Dogs are social creatures, eager to please, and love being part of a human family. By recognising how our dogs communicate, accepting and meeting their canine needs, including early socialisation and providing them with ample opportunities to be dogs, but at the same time giving them boundaries, consistent leadership, guidance and love, we ensure a stable and enduring relationship based on mutual trust, respect and understanding.

CHAPTER 9
HOW DOGS LEARN CLASSICAL CONDITIONING

As much as I enjoyed training with Zoli, I was troubled that we had not addressed Mila's reactive issues, which was the principal reason I sought professional help. Possibly, another endearing genetic trait I suffer from is that I question everything, and I am unable to relax until I uncover all the answers. When in doubt, I invariably resort to research, and this was no exception, as I discovered a flood of practical advice on the topic.

Even though dog trainers often blame owners for their reactive dogs, most experts agree that there are various reasons for leash reactivity including fear, excitement, pain, owner tenseness, diet, age.

Many people confuse leash reactivity with general aggression, so how can we tell the difference?

Generally, reactive dogs only display lunging, barking behaviour when restrained and are usually very friendly off-leash, which is why reactivity is easily distinguishable from general aggression. Undoubtedly the typical leash-reactive behaviour applied to Mila, and since her initial altercations with Zoli's dogs, she learnt to relax and socialised well with his so-called pack when unrestrained by a leash. Similarly, when Mila first met Mignon, the little papillon from across the street, Mila wanted to exterminate him, yet when we allowed the little pooch into our yard to meet and greet Mila on her own terms, they became good friends. Since then, whenever Mignon comes to our front gate, the two of them always greet each other excitedly, with wagging tails.

Last year our neighbour obtained an Australian sheepdog puppy, and Mila made the acquaintance of Paws through the mesh fence behind our green hedge, where they see each other daily. Unfailingly, Paws always greets Mila with great enthusiasm, and neither dog has ever been aggressive towards the other. Unfortunately, because Paws is a persistent barker and yaps unceasingly at passing strangers, Mila has always been blasé about his friendship. Out of necessity, she puts up with him but rarely takes the time to acknowledge him.

A few months ago, as legal etiquette demands, a suitably harnessed Paws returned from a walk with his owners when Mila and I were practising obedience exercises in front of our house, which offered slightly more distractions than our garden. When I spotted Paws some distance away, I decided to take Mila over so that they could greet each other for the first time without a fence between them. Surprisingly, Mila went ballistic. Incredibly, it appears that she didn't recognise Paws from a distance.

In the past, most of our dogs displayed similar visual deficits when trying to identify us from afar. This is because the dominant sense in dogs is smell, followed by hearing, with vision ranking third in importance. Because a dog's brain has fewer neurons to process visual information and has fewer sensory cells in the retina, their visual acuity is not on a par with humans'. While in terms of human vision, 20/20 refers to normal acuity, under the same conditions, our dogs would only achieve 20/50 and would need glasses to drive a car. Under the circumstances, Mila does not drive, and her inability to identify Paws from a distance is understandable.

Unfortunately, we could not get close enough for Mila to identify our neighbour by smell, and the encounter turned into a huge fiasco when Paws also decided to yell back. Yet, they reverted to their usual relationship in the garden behind their respective fences and have never barked or threatened each other since.

Additionally, some time ago, my cousin adopted Skyler, a mix-breed herding-type hound, and brought him over to visit Mila. As we sat at the wrought iron table on the garden terrace, with our refreshments, we observed the two dogs as they made friends, quite relaxed in each other's company. After a while, Skyler started to bark in playful excitement at Mila, who ran over to us with her tail between her legs and whined softly in distress. Noticeably anxious, Mila was distressed by Skyler's barking. It was the first time I consciously realised the profound effect the barking of another dog has on Mila, even if the dog is a friend.

Maria from the rescue centre did warn us of Mila's fear of large dogs. However, at the time, we didn't comprehend the seriousness or the impact this would have on Mila's reactions and behaviours.

Once again, we can only surmise that Mila may have been undersocialised when she was young and never learnt to interact with other dogs when she was on a leash. My theory is that she may have had traumatic experiences with other canines in the past that generates a fear response when leashed and unable to run away.

Additionally, fear response can also be genetic, and some breeds are more disposed to develop leash reactivity, which is usually a defensive and emotional response to a distressing event. Because experts regard it as a psychological and behaviour issue, rehabilitation must not solely focus on the outward symptom, fear, but also the source of the problem.

After perusing an abundance of information, I found that canine behaviour experts recommend gradually introducing a leash-reactive dog to other dogs from a distance, making sure to stay far enough away so that our dog remains below its stress threshold and doesn't react. Once we have established the optimum range, whether it is one block or several blocks, we should gradually decrease the gap between the two while feeding our dog high-value treats. It is crucial to be patient and not rush this phase and ensure that our dog always stays under its stress limit, which could take days, or even weeks. The object is to keep our dog from reacting as it associates wonderful treats with a pooch in the distance.

Naturally, I mentioned this technique to Zoli, who dismissed it and advised me that it doesn't work because the reactive dog gets used to the one dog but will still react to other dogs. Although if we have the help of a trainer who has access to multiple dogs, he can alternate them daily. Once a hound learns to associate good things with a dog in the distance without rebelling, it is advisable to reinforce the behaviour with various dogs at different times and in multiple settings.

Unfortunately, many people believe that socialising dogs is the holy grail for all things canine and don't explore or have the knowledge to try other options. Admittedly, socialising Mila to the 'pack' off-leash did miraculously stabilise her conduct compared to her first introduction to Zoli's dogs, for which I was immensely grateful. Although, sadly, it did nothing to improve her reactivity when she was on a leash, which requires specific rehabilitation. Subsequently, I acknowledged that the scope of the problem was possibly beyond a dog trainer's expertise and looked further afield at dog behaviour specialists. Although, I found that every dog trainer in Budapest claims to be a dog behaviourist and consults YouTube tutorials when diagnosing behaviour issues. However, it is essential to note that there is a difference between the two.

A dog trainer can teach a range of tasks, including basic obedience, such as sit, down, stay, whereas a behaviourist is an expert in canine behaviour modification. Early on, I surmised that I needed a behaviourist; unfortunately, I found no one that filled the criterion. Experts in this field are sorely lacking in our part of the world.

Eventually, after much seeking, the only person whom I found with a semblance of canine behavioural training was a woman who had completed a dog psychology course. In my email, I outlined Mila's leash-reactivity issues and what steps I had taken concerning our ongoing training with Zoli. I also detailed my concerns about the lack of any specific behaviour therapy or progress to date and questioned the effectiveness of an obedience course in treating a reactive dog.

When it came, her response was less than encouraging. Ironically, she assured me that we were on the right track and should carry on as we were. Naturally, I wondered how learning to spin, sit and stay would help with Mila's reactive issues; after all, many highly trained dogs in obedience have a complete breakdown at the sight of another pooch.

Undaunted, I asked our vet, Dr Réka's, advice; although, in my experience, vets are experts in medical diagnostics, they are not well versed in canine behaviour issues. Once again, this became apparent when she suggested that I socialise Mila, which seems to be the universal cure for all canine behaviour problems. Obviously, I understand the importance of socialisation, and I've seen the benefits, but it cannot address specific behaviour issues. I can't begin to describe the frustration and helplessness, as I knew how to resolve the problem but could not find the help we needed.

The situation seemed like an insurmountable obstacle. Nevertheless, I tried not to be discouraged and disappointed by my inability to locate the right person with the necessary background in classical conditioning, which Mila required. Of course, there were many highly qualified professors at the forefront of canine research, none of whom offered behaviour modification programmes to the general public. Consequently, I imagine that some knowledge of classical and operant conditioning principles would be helpful in a dog trainer's palette, which would give them a better appreciation of how dogs learn.

During any exploration of canine behaviour, we will inevitably encounter Ivan Pavlov and his salivating dogs. While researching the physiology of digestion, Nobel Prize-winning scientist Ivan Pavlov (1849–1936) began to study the triggers that cause dogs to salivate. As expected, when the assistants gave the dogs their food, the dogs started to drool, which is a normal reflex reaction in preparation for digestion. Before long, Pavlov noticed that the dogs were salivating without the stimulus of food. He realised that the dogs reacted to the assistants' presence, who always wore white lab coats when they served the dogs their food. Even when the white-coated figures did not take food, the dogs had learnt to associate and react to them in anticipation of receiving food.

Pavlov experimented with various stimuli to act as triggers at mealtimes and found that the dogs soon became conditioned and would drool at the sound of the different triggers in anticipation of feeding, even when there was no food present. Pavlov defined classical conditioning, which involves automatic or reflexive response, and is not voluntary behaviour. Involuntary responses may include salivation, nausea, increased or decreased heart rate, pupil dilation or constriction, as well as reflexive motor responses, recoiling from pain, or fear.

A puff of air in our eyes will elicit a blink, while the taste of lemon juice will make our mouth water, and a clap of thunder might startle us. These are all involuntary responses. In the words of psychology professor and canine researcher Stanley Coren, "classical conditioning is the way we learn to attach emotional responses to things".

By chance, Pavlov stumbled on the foundations that paved the way for new behaviour modification theories when he discovered how to train animals to react in a prerequisite way after introducing a particular stimulus. Additional research confirmed that an unconditioned stimulus would elicit an unconditional response. For instance, when we provide an unconditioned stimulus such as food, salivation is the automatic response, which is an unconditional response. Therefore, classical conditioning can only occur if an association is formed with a neutral stimulus, such as a lab technician, which would provoke no reaction under normal circumstances.

However, after the technicians were repeatedly paired with the food, the dogs formed an association between them. At this point, because the technicians evoked an automatic response, they became a conditioned stimulus. Consequently, a conditioned stimulus, in this case a technician, can elicit a conditional response, such as drooling, even without the unconditioned stimulus, food, being present. In this way, Pavlov evoked an involuntary, reflexive response to a previously neutral stimulus.

A leash is a neutral stimulus, which will initially evoke no response. However, with regular exposure, the dog learns to associate a leash with going for a walk. Each time it sees the leash, it will exuberantly jump around in anticipation of an outing without actually going anywhere.

Furthermore, the first encounter with the vet is quite pleasant for most dogs and seldom leaves an adverse impression. However, if the dog experiences subsequent prodding, poking and pain, the mere sight of the surgery will become a cause of anxiety and stress for many dogs who learn to associate suffering and discomfort with the clinic.

How receptive are dogs to classical conditioning?

One bad experience is enough for some dogs. Years ago, back in Africa, Franky was stung by a bee, and from that day on, she had an overwhelming, uncontrollable terror of bees. To such an extent, she even avoided and feared other bee-like creatures and always rushed to me in a panic when she saw a fly in the house. On the other hand, Lulu was also stung by a bee, and from that day on, nothing changed. She continued to fearlessly sniff out the tiny buzzing insects and stick her nose into their 'beesness'.

Many of us have also become classically conditioned to fear the dentist, a neutral stimulus that may have caused us pain and elicited a fear response. In time, even if there was no pain, we still associate fear with the dentist. These automatic responses to stimuli are known as classical conditioning.

Renowned psychologist John B. Watson carried out one of the most controversial examples of classical conditioning, involving a nine-month-old child, known as Little Albert. The 1920s experiment took place at Johns Hopkins University in Baltimore. Initially, when they showed Little Albert a white rat (neutral stimulus), there was no response. However, after repeatedly pairing the white rat with a loud noise (unconditioned stimuli), Little Albert reacted reflexively in fear (unconditional response). Eventually, just the sight of the rat (conditioned stimulus) evoked extreme fear (conditional response) in the child.

This fear gradually generalised into a fear of all animals that were white and furry.

Connected to our emotions and reactions is the limbic system, which is a complex loop of neural structures that evolved as a response to danger or opportunities. The system generates instinctive emotions, including anxiety, fear, happiness, and provides an immediate response to these reactions. This complicated system plays a vital role in learning and memory. It is also responsible for the ambivalence between what dogs instinctively want to do, chase a squirrel, and what we want them to do, ignore the squirrel and come to us.

The limbic system incorporates:

- the amygdala, which manages fear and aggression
- the hippocampus, which is not an institute of higher learning for large herbivorous ungulates but is the organ responsible for memory
- the hypothalamus, which regulates the release of hormones into the body.

The limbic system is responsible for how a dog understands and responds to its experiences and the environment around him.

Can we influence the limbic system?

It is possible to override this system by offering high-value rewards for behaviour that we want and shift the focus from what they want to do. Through learning, the limbic system records how a dog feels in any situation and decides whether it is worth leaving whatever they are doing in favour of the reward we are offering. Interestingly, positive reward stimulates the part of the brain associated with positive emotions. For example, instinctive behaviour like chasing squirrels (prey drive) gives dogs considerable enjoyment. Therefore, we must reward them with something that will provide them with even greater pleasure if we want them to come to us rather than chase the squirrel.

If we wish to override the limbic system and instinctive behaviour, we must provide as many positive, feel-good experiences as possible from an early age, utilising whatever activities our dog enjoys. These may be a combination of play, positive training, walks, lots of tactile and verbal interaction, and high-value food rewards. The limbic system records these interactions as enjoyable, emotional experiences. Subsequently, when faced with a choice of following instinctive behaviour or obeying us, our dog is more likely to rule in our favour. With the appropriate rewards, we can override this system, allowing us to control our dog's behaviour.

Additionally, the olfactory bulb is the processing centre in the forward part of the dog's brain, responsible for analysing scent particles and odours. The olfactory system is extremely sensitive and efficient, relative to brain size, and is approximately forty times larger in dogs than in humans. No wonder the olfactory system in dogs acts like a well-organised conveyor belt. When dogs sniff the air or the ground, they inhale odours, which are captured by a mucus layer within the nasal cavity.

Subsequently, the sensory cells process these odours and are sent to the olfactory bulb by scent receptors. After the olfactory bulb receives the information, it sends it to different parts of the brain, including the limbic system, which processes emotion, memory and behaviour. Via its connection to the limbic system, a familiar scent can become a profusion of intricate messages, memories and emotions, which can elicit various responses in our dogs and can influence their behaviour through emotion. Just as smells and scents can evoke different feelings in us, either good or bad, and we react with happiness, sadness or anger, dogs with unexplained behaviour problems may associate a specific odour with a bad experience. In addition, the limbic system records any unfamiliar scents as a new experience and emotion.

The survival instinct teaches us to remember fearful and painful events for longer; therefore, it is a lengthier process to disassociate from a fearful stimulus than a positive one. Fearful and aggressive dogs were almost certainly exposed to negative experiences creating unpleasant associations; however, with classical conditioning, or associative learning, and positive emotional stimuli, it is possible to retrain unwanted behaviour.

Many fields incorporate Pavlovian training, including phobia treatment in adults. Behaviourists use the technique to considerable effect with fear-related conditions in dog training when they pair fears with something that evokes a reflexive positive response.

For example, if we condition emotional reactions in our dogs based on rewards, they will almost certainly evoke favourable emotions towards us. On the other hand, negative experiences based on fear or pain will result in withdrawal or even aggression. Thus, a trainer can classically condition a dog with behaviour modification to react to a specific stimulus differently to how it had before. Similarly, experts use counterconditioning to undo the effects of previous conditioning and it would have been an appropriate therapy to reverse Little Albert's fear conditioning.

Various aversion therapies also rely on the principles of classical conditioning. For example, shock collars and other similar concepts, including electric pet fences, all rely on delivering a mild shock to discourage certain behaviours in dogs. Additionally, there has been ongoing interest and research on taste aversion, which would help farmers and wildlife departments in Africa minimise predation on livestock.

Therapists often use associative conditioning to elicit the desired response from dogs, which subsequently learn to respond in a certain way. However, most behaviour modification techniques rely on classical conditioning, including desensitisation and counterconditioning, which therapists primarily utilise in treating fearful dogs.

The foundations of classical conditioning rely on forming a reflexive association between a previously neutral stimulus and an unconditioned stimulus. For example, Pavlov's dogs were involuntarily conditioned to associate the sight of the technicians with food, which elicited a conditioned response, salivating. If we no longer pair the conditioned stimulus with the unconditioned stimulus, the conditioned response decreases or disappears, and extinction occurs.

For instance, if the lab technicians stopped giving the dogs food, the dogs would gradually stop salivating at the sight of the technicians. Thus, the association between the technicians and the food would become extinct.

In 1924, Mary Cover Jones, known as 'the mother of behaviour therapy', became the first therapist to use counterconditioning to undo the effects of an earlier experience. This valuable strategy helps dogs change the way they feel about things that scare them.

After the Little Albert experiment, his mother removed him from the hospital, and Watson was unable to decondition the child. However, Mary wondered if she could use Watson's techniques to make children less fearful of a stimulus, in essence reversing his findings.

Some years later, Mary Cover Jones proved that it was possible to eradicate fear when she worked with a three-year-old boy known as Little Peter, who feared white rats and rabbits. In the laboratory, seated in a highchair, they gave Peter his favourite snacks, while, at the same time, they placed a white rabbit in a cage at a distance where it did not alarm the child. The following day they moved the rabbit a little closer while Peter was occupied with his nibbles. They subsequently repeated this process each day until Peter could calmly eat his snack with the rabbit right next to him. Eventually, Peter was even able to pat and play with the rabbit.

This form of behaviour modification is known as systematic desensitisation, which is a form of counterconditioning that reverses the effects of traumatic experiences.

Joseph Wolpe expanded the procedure in the 1950s to treat human behaviour problems, such as fears and phobias, which are excessive and unreasonable fears to non-threatening stimuli. Wolpe based his idea on the premise that much of our behaviour, both good and bad, is learnt; therefore, there is no reason why they cannot be unlearnt. Additionally, desensitisation has been adapted successfully to help dogs overcome various behaviour issues resulting from fears or phobias.

When we first got Mila, it was not apparent that she was such an anxious dog with various issues. Despite Maria's assurances at the rescue centre to the contrary, Mila is terrified of sudden loud noises, including thunder and fireworks. A while ago, I dropped an empty metal pot in the kitchen, which made a colossal clatter as it fell to the floor, resulting in a panicked exodus by Mila, who was overseeing my culinary activities at the time. Naturally, sudden noises may well startle most dogs, but she refused to go near the kitchen for days, while her tail remained between her legs each time she even looked towards the offending room. After a week of patient coaxing with liberal helpings of her favourite treats, she eventually returned to supervise my creative endeavours in the kitchen. Fear, a negative emotion, forced her to abandon the kitchen, but I overcame her fear by offering her positive experiences in the form of food.

Regrettably, the sound of rumbling thunder was not so simple to remedy, as Mila took off in a mindless panic, panting and drooling as she hurtled through the house full speed, totally out of control and oblivious to anything. Her instinct to flee what she fears dominated any rational thoughts, overwhelming her behaviour. In addition, the danger that Mila might hurt herself was alarming, as no amount of treats or obedience training could get through to her. Usually, Mila never uses the stairs. However, thunderstorms often induced her to run up and down the stairs in a panic, as she tried to hide from the source of her fear, the noise. After such episodes, we often found her cowering in the basement.

Dogs diagnosed with storm phobia react with extreme anxiety, and one study revealed a 207% increase in salivary cortisol levels after exposure to simulated sounds of a thunderstorm. Research has shown that persistent and recurrent noise anxiety causes immense distress and panic in animals. Various studies concluded that up to 40% of dogs suffer from noise sensitivity caused by thunderstorms and fireworks.

Recently scientists have indicated that our pets are not just frightened by the sheer volume of thunder but are also upset by the unpleasant feeling of static electricity, which causes a tingling sensation through their fur. During a thunderstorm, they may receive numerous shocks from the static electricity generated by the storm. This uncomfortable feeling can prompt our dogs to run around the house looking for a place to hide, especially basements and garages that are grounded. Porcelain bathtubs are also earthed and offer a secure spot for dogs to weather a thunderstorm.

Clinical studies on thunder shirts indicate that up to 80% of dogs respond positively to these pressure wraps, effectively calming and controlling dog anxiety. However, I found no noticeable change in Mila when she wore a wrap.

So the question remained, could I help Mila in some way?

I purchased a few thunder sound CDs. Once I started the therapy, I played these sounds 24/7 in my study, where we spent a lot of time during the day. Generally, Mila likes to hang out there even when I am busy in another part of the house. Although, when I initially turned on the thunder sounds, at a barely audible volume, she left the room, and even though she came back for short periods, at intervals, to make sure I was working, she didn't dally for long.

A week later, Mila returned to my study, although she did not linger on her own when I left the room. It took her another week to relax entirely and ignore the thunder at its barely audible volume. Happily, after that, I increased the thunder sounds by one notch every week, with no reaction from Mila. After several months, I ended the therapy when the thunder sounds were at an overpowering volume, and I found that Mila's behaviour in a real storm had improved noticeably. Although Mila remains nervous when she hears thunder, she can tolerate most thunderous events without reacting in a panic. As long as she has the security of our company she can relax enough to rest on her bed. If the thunder is particularly overwhelming, she prefers to spend the duration of the storm in our small, grounded, personal lift, where she feels less anxious and more secure.

When I initially researched desensitisation therapy using thunder sounds on CD, many reviews suggested it was a waste of time, and it does not work. Naturally, a CD cannot replicate the atmospheric conditions of an actual storm that negatively affect dogs, such as the dark skies, barometric pressure, static electricity, the sound of rain and flashes of lightning. Therefore, the audio desensitisation will not be 100% effective. However, even if the results are only 50%, it might mean the difference between a dog that is out of control and one that is able to manage its fear. The whole point is to condition a dog to the stimuli and make its reactions more manageable, as we cannot remove or cure fear.

Unfortunately, most people do not realise that desensitisation is a slow and systematic exposure to a fearful stimulus, gradually increasing in intensity until the dog becomes accustomed to it and no longer reacts. Additionally, various research indicates that the longer the technique takes, the more effective it is. However, results do not happen overnight. Furthermore, it is essential to remember that desensitisation can wear off. If dogs do not regularly experience the stimulus, such as thunder, the fear response will return at full strength, which is known as spontaneous recovery. Therapists should, therefore, expose the dog to the stimulus regularly.

Naturally, I realise that Mila will not become wholly desensitised to thunder. She will never ignore it completely; nevertheless, the technique works, and we can now maintain her anxiety at a controllable level. I am delighted at our progress over the months and pleased that Mila is no longer charging around the house in sheer terror.

A more intense form of fear treatment is flooding, which is the exact opposite of desensitisation. According to John Bradshaw, the technique of immersion therapy or flooding is the exposure to extreme intensities of unavoidable fear. This technique has been successful in treating phobias and fears in humans. Nevertheless, when using it on less rational species, flooding can cause overwhelming anxiety and stress and may traumatise dogs to the extent that they become aggressive and dangerous.

During flooding, the therapist restrains the dog so that it is unable to escape, and for a specific time, it is exposed to the feared stimulus at full strength, resulting in a fear response. Burch and Bailey explain that the theory behind the technique is that high levels of anxiety and fear are induced quickly, leading just as rapidly to the extinction of the fear reflex associated with that stimulus.

The idea is based on classical conditioning and established psychological theory. At the sign of a threat, the body goes into the 'alarm stage' or 'fight or flight' mode, which elicits various responses in the body. The heart beats faster, blood pressure rises and adrenaline is released into the blood. The body can only stay in the alarm stage for a certain period, and at some point, it must go back to a state of normalcy when the heartbeat returns to normal, breathing slows and adrenaline levels drop. At the end of the alarm phase, patients are emotionally drained but realise that despite still being exposed to the object of fear, they are no longer in a panic and learn to associate the feared stimulus with neutral emotions. The feared stimulus no longer produces a fearful conditioned response and goes back to being a neutral stimulus, and extinction occurs.

Thomas Stampfl developed the technique of flooding in the 1960s, which is successfully used to treat post-traumatic stress syndrome (PTSS) in humans and is still used in behaviour therapy today. Mott *et al.* (2013) conducted a study on the outcome of flooding on PTSS patients, and 85% of the participants confirmed their satisfaction with the results. This type of therapy may be helpful in humans who can reason, but not surprisingly, most dog experts consider flooding cruel and inhumane.

The controversial Dog Whisperer, Cesar Millan, is a great proponent of flooding, which is one of his main techniques. Following flooding sessions, many dogs stop struggling, not because Millan has cured them, but because of a phenomenon known as 'learnt helplessness'. This situation occurs when a therapist repeatedly exposes a dog to aversive stimuli, and it learns that there is no escape.

Experts warn that flooding is unethical in treating dogs. It is not only unhealthy and traumatic for dogs but also extremely dangerous for handlers. If we force an animal into an aggressive state, it will make them even more fearful and aggressive. Many trainers who have used the technique admit that it is harsh and inhumane. When science proved the process ineffective in canines, they quickly changed to more gentle methods such as counterconditioning and desensitisation.

CHAPTER 10
OPERANT CONDITIONING

While classical conditioning relies on external stimuli to create a reflexive involuntary response, operant conditioning involves voluntary responses, that is, a dog chooses to offer the requested behaviour. Undoubtedly, this process shaped Mila into the Supermutt that she has become since our obedience training with Zoli.

During the late 1800s to early 1900s, American psychologist Edward Lee Thorndike (1874–1949) began to analyse the reaction that different consequences have on behaviour. This study became known as the Law of Effect or Thorndike's Law of Effect and concluded that responses producing rewards tend to increase in frequency. In other words, if someone rewards us for a specific behaviour, we are more likely to repeat it.

Without a doubt, this principle was the essential foundation for the development of operant conditioning. Throughout his lifetime, Thorndike undertook various experiments. In one such prominent study, he placed a cat in a box and recorded how long it took the cat to free itself.

Subsequently, he put some food just outside the box and noted that the cat managed to free itself faster and faster with food incentives. Clearly, with a suitable reward, the responses increased in frequency. Based on Thorndike's research work, dog trainers widely use motivational or treat-based training today.

Thorndike was the first person to outline the concept of operant conditioning in his 1911 work *Animal Intelligence*, but he was also a significant influence on B.F. Skinner's work (1904–1990).

Over time, Skinner discovered that he could methodically change the behaviour of rats when he gave a food reward for pressing a lever. Skinner's most significant achievement was *The Behavior of Organisms*, published in 1938, the first publication to clarify operant conditioning principles. Subsequently, he published numerous books and papers, including his article 'How to Teach Animals', over fifty years ago, in which he described the use of a clicker, referred to as a cricket, which was initially widely used in marine animal training. Incidentally, operant conditioning experts have already used this innovative little device since the 1940s.

Any voluntary behaviour that operates upon the environment to generate a consequence is known as operant conditioning. Our actions and the responses to these actions influence whether or not they will recur in the future. In other words, a dog will more likely choose to sit on command if we reward its actions and is more likely to repeat this in the future. Furthermore, Skinner is well known for his research on small animals in an operant conditioning chamber, also known as the Skinner Box.

During his ongoing studies, he identified two key aspects of operant conditioning: reinforcement and punishment.

Reinforcement increases the likelihood that the behaviour will recur, and punishment decreases the probability that the behaviour will occur. With the incorporation of positive, when we add something, and negative, when we take something away, we have the four operant conditioning principles to obtain the desired response. Significantly, we don't have to limit operant conditioning principles to our animals. We can also apply them with significant effect within a wide-ranging sphere of influence, including the workforce, schools, and husbands and children.

Of course, clicker use on family members is optional. Nevertheless, words of encouragement and gratitude are often enough to reinforce the response we expect.

Positive reinforcement – when we add something to ensure that the behaviour will happen more often. The dog's behaviour makes something good happen. Each time our dog sits on command, and we reward it with a treat, it is likely to repeat the action more often and faster. Consequently, we add some form of reward to ensure that the desired behaviour recurs. Similarly, our children, husbands and employees are more likely to regularly perform well if we add praise and other attractive incentives.

Negative reinforcement – taking away something to increase the likelihood that the behaviour will recur. Inevitably, shock collars stop shocking when the dog voluntarily stops barking. Consequently, the dog learns that when the desired conduct has occurred, and it stops barking, the shock is removed. Furthermore, to avoid additional unpleasant electrical jolts, the desired behaviour is more likely to recur, and the dog is, therefore, less inclined to start barking. Accordingly, we have taken away something (the shock) to ensure the desired behaviour recurs. Similarly, to silence nagging parents, a child will more than likely do its homework, chores, etc., to ensure that the negative stimulus, the nagging, ceases. They will also be more likely to do their homework in the future to avoid any further recurrence of the unpleasant harassment.

Positive punishment – adding something to decrease the likelihood that a specific behaviour will occur. If a dog is in the habit of jumping up, and we regularly knee it in the chest (not something I would advocate), it will learn not to repeat this behaviour. As a consequence of its actions, we add something (knee to chest) to discourage the undesirable behaviour from happening again. Adding a reprimand for unwanted behaviour in our children or increasing extra chores will ensure that the undesirable behaviour will not reoccur.

Negative punishment – taking away something to decrease the likelihood that the unwanted behaviour will occur. If a dog begs at the dinner table, and we ignore it, the dog will learn to stop soliciting for food. Therefore, we take away something (our attention) to ensure that unacceptable behaviour does not reoccur. We can correct inappropriate behaviour in our children by taking away certain privileges, such as TV, pocket money, an outing with friends. These incentives help to ensure that they will behave appropriately in future.

By understanding these fundamental principles, we can shape the behaviour of our dogs. For instance, if a dog jumps up and we pat it, we positively reinforce the behaviour and ensure that the action will recur, and the dog will continue to jump up more often. On the other hand, if we withhold our attention from the same dog when it jumps up, we take away something to change its behaviour, which is negative punishment. When the dog stops leaping up, it regains our attention, and, in future, it will be less inclined to repeat the unfavourable conduct.

Fortunately, as old ideas fade and modern trends evolve, many trainers have embraced and actively advocated positive reinforcement, adding something to ensure that the dog repeats the desired action. Although, some forms of negative reinforcement may seem appropriate in certain circumstances based on each dog's individual needs, taking into consideration the dog's breed as well as its psychological health. On the other hand, studies have shown that pets trained with aversive techniques are fifteen times more likely to exhibit stress symptoms.

Thankfully, training methods popularised in the 1970s by Barbara Woodhouse, and more recently publicised by Cesar Millan, are systematically falling out of favour.

A 2014 French study compared behaviours linked to stress, using different training methods, positive reinforcement and negative reinforcement, at two distinct dog training schools. Interestingly, they concluded that dogs from the school that used the negative reinforcement method demonstrated lowered body postures and signs of stress. In contrast, the dogs from the positive reinforcement method school showed increased attentiveness towards their owner.

In the past, I have reflexively used the tone of my voice to stop unwanted behaviour. At the time, my dog did stop what it was doing when it heard the reprimand. Undoubtedly, we can also consider this an example of positive punishment, as I added something to change the dog's action. However, I immediately asked for the correct behaviour and rewarded my dog copiously when it complied. This is a clear example of positive reinforcement, adding something to ensure the dog reproduces the proper response. Just as I might withhold a treat if it does not present the required behaviour – negative punishment – naturally, the dog will be eager to correct the error and collect its reward.

Moreover, the question remains, does a stern look or a reprimand constitute punishment within operant conditioning terms, bearing in mind that both these actions would indicate that the dog did something that the owner did not want the dog to continue?

Theoretically, as we add something to stop an unwanted activity, both these actions would constitute examples of positive punishment. However, according to behaviour analysts Drs Burch and Bailey, the actual effect the event has on the dog determines whether a punishment was delivered. Therefore, for punishment to have taken place, the behaviour must decrease or stop. Accordingly, if we reprimand or look at our dog sternly and have no effect on its behaviour, we have not punished it.

A stimulus used to deter specific behaviour is a *punisher*.

Facial expressions and a stern tone are conditioned punishers that only function as punishers if we pair them with unconditioned punishers, which are biological, such as heat, cold, pain, loud noises or another conditioned punisher.

For instance, a rebuke on its own may have no effect, but a reproach with a raised voice may stop an unwanted action. This is a form of classical conditioning. For example, if we reprimand (conditioned punisher) our dog and deliver pain or a loud noise (unconditioned punisher), the dog learns to associate the reprimand or harsh sound with discomfort or fear. Therefore, the rebuke becomes a conditioned punisher on its own, even without the noise or pain. Admonitions with raised voices are the most frequently used method of punishment. Consequently, if the dog stopped the undesirable action, the dog was punished. However, if there was no effect, then the reprimand is not a conditioned punisher, and the dog was not punished.

Accordingly, it is virtually impossible to train dogs using only positive reinforcement; consequently, dog trainers frequently use a combination of reinforcement and punishment to achieve the desired results, which Skinner referred to as 'shaping'.

For example, shock collars and most aversive methods rely on positive punishment to attain the expected conduct, providing a consequence for the dog's behaviour, and will decrease the likelihood that the unwanted action will occur again in the future. When the collar shocks the dog, it stops barking = positive punishment; we have added something to stop unwanted behaviour.

Consequently, to avoid any further pain, it is unlikely that the dog will resume barking. As soon as the dog understands that the consequence of not barking removes the shock, it will increase the likelihood that the required behaviour (silence) will recur = negative reinforcement; we take away something to reinforce the desired conduct.

Frequently, various combinations are used, such as negative punishment in tandem with positive reinforcement. For example, during training, when we withhold a treat for the wrong behaviour = negative punishment; however, when we subsequently reward the dog copiously on his next try when he gets the exercise correct = positive reinforcement.

Dog training predominantly relies on operant conditioning, which links a dog's actions to a specific reward, which may also act as an incentive to avoid further punishment. We should determine the inducements by the intensity of motivation based on each dog's preference. Generally, food, play, contact with its owner, or a combination of all three prove to be excellent motivators for most dogs and offer essential rewards for positive reinforcement that ensure the desired behaviour will recur in the future. Subsequently, we reinforce behaviour that we want to encourage by adding something.

Treat-based training uses primary reinforcers, which are biological, and include food, drink and pleasure. Secondary reinforcers relate to social conditions and acquire their effect by association with the primary reinforcer.

Secondary enforcers, also known as conditioned reinforcers, include praise, positive facial expressions and affection. For example, when a dog sits on command, the primary reinforcer would be a treat, followed by a 'good dog'. The dog learns to associate praise with the tasty tidbit, a form of classical conditioning. Eventually, it will perform the required behaviour, even if only praise is given in lieu of a treat, thus becoming the secondary reinforcer.

A clicker can also act as a secondary reinforcer to precisely mark the required behaviour, followed by gastronomic incentives. Ultimately, when the dog has mastered the necessary action, we can phase out the clicker.

As we can see, the more we reinforce a behaviour, the more likely it is to recur. But what happens when we no longer reinforce a behaviour?

When we no longer reinforce a practice that we have previously encouraged, extinction occurs. In his 1938 book *The Behavior of Organisms*, Skinner detailed how extinction works. In the laboratory, technicians trained rats to obtain food by pressing a lever. When the lab assistants no longer reinforced the rodents' behaviour with food rewards, they stopped pressing the lever, and in time the well-engrained behaviour died out.

Similarly, if we feed a dog tidbits at the dinner table and it subsequently starts to beg for food, the only way we can stop this behaviour is if we stop the reinforcement. If we desist from feeding the dog at the table and ignore it, the dog will eventually stop begging, and extinction will occur. When we stop rewarding unwanted behaviour, the behaviour will ultimately fade away. Furthermore, it is essential to remember that extinction takes time, and frequently a dog's conduct gets worse before it gets better, leading to an extinction burst. During this period, new behaviours such as frustration and aggression may appear. It is vital not to give in, otherwise we will be rewarding more unwanted and possibly dangerous behaviours.

However, if the unwanted behaviour is self-rewarding, then extinction would not be recommended. For instance, if a dog barks at the postman, who then leaves, the action is self-rewarding because the dog's behaviour caused something to happen. Similarly, chewing on inappropriate things, digging in the garden, chasing small animals, or sleeping on the couch are self-rewarding behaviours dogs enjoy. Therefore, ignoring these behaviours will not make them go away. Subsequently, it is then up to us to train the practices we want with operant conditioning principles.

For instance, if we'd don't want our dog to sleep on the couch, we can use positive punishment in the form of aversive training, shock collars, shouting, or hitting the dog, none of which I would advocate. Conversely, we can move the dog's bed, a dog cushion or a dog blanket next to the couch and train the dog with positive reinforcement to slumber on its designated day bed rather than on the furniture, rewarding it generously when it complies.

Depending on the breed, some dogs may learn this in a few days, other dogs may take longer to make the connection, but with patience, all dogs will eventually realise that they should sleep on their bed and not on the couch. The more we reinforce this behaviour with rewards, the more they will wish to comply.

While putting operant conditioning into practice with Mila, our sessions continued with Zoli, although under less arctic conditions. As the sun began to warm the earth, snowdrops and crocuses appeared, leading the way for tulips and daffodils, while trees took on a green hue.

During our second shared session with another client, Bernadette, and her dog, Zed, Zoli asked us to swap dogs. Sharing a lesson was a novel experience for the dogs. Although we were all still in training, humans and canines, I was not altogether thrilled that someone else was giving Mila commands at such an early stage of her rehabilitation, and vice versa. Additionally, Mila is fluent in Hunglish, as I used a mixture of both Hungarian and English commands. At the same time, Zed was monolingual and only responded to Hungarian, which made Bernadette and I unsure of each other's appropriate commands.

Furthermore, research has shown that dogs are 25% less likely to respond to a stranger, and I feared that the exercise was not setting our dogs up for success.

Naturally, after the lesson, I aired my views with Zoli, who disagreed with me but respected my wishes, and we did not have to swap dogs again. I was glad Zoli compromised, as we enjoyed the shared lessons, which benefited Mila, taught her impulse control and allowed her to socialise with a different dog. Even though, at the end of each session, Mila still had a free-for-all with Zoli's dogs, whom she no longer wanted to tear apart. Additionally, Mila also remained a firm favourite of Svetlana. The latter adored Mila and always tried to pick her up by her fleecy doggy pullover and carry her around like a puppy.

During this period, John, a client of Zoli's, who was unable to take his black Labrador for a walk, requested urgent assistance. Each time someone approached John for a chat on their daily outings, the dog barked and lunged at the advancing person, regardless of whether they were familiar or not. During a training session with John and his Labrador, Zoli asked Bernadette and me to assist. In turn, Zoli instructed us to approach John, and if his dog responded negatively and lunged or barked, the owner had to hit him with an empty plastic bottle (positive punishment). On the other hand, if on our approach the dog chose to sit calmly and did not react as we drew closer, John rewarded the desired behaviour with copious treats (positive reinforcement), which involuntarily conditioned the dog to strangers and treats (classical conditioning).

The exercise did no physical harm, but each time John hit his dog on the head with the plastic bottle, it did startle the dog and stopped the unwanted action. Unfortunately, these actions may condition a fear response in the dog towards its owner. Alternatively, if the dog associates being hit on the head with people walking up to his owner, it could make the dog react even more severely in future. We know that the limbic system records all emotional interactions, and the more positive interactions we have with our dogs, the more they are likely to cooperate with us. Similarly, the opposite is true for negative experiences, so it is essential to train dogs positively whenever possible and avoid fear-based training. In cases like this, behavioural analysis by a qualified professional can give more in-depth information. If we know the reason for the dog's behaviour, we can specifically tailor a remedial programme to target the cause.

Furthermore, there is an overwhelming mountain of evidence emphasising the complex emotional and cognitive capabilities of dogs. Several canine MRI studies have shown that the emotional intelligence displayed by dogs is comparable with a human two- to three-year-old. Subsequently, would anyone in their right mind consider whacking a three-year-old child on the head with an empty plastic bottle to teach acceptable behaviours? So why would we do it to our dogs?

Alternatively, we could approach John and his dog from a distance, keeping the dog under its threshold while John feeds it high-value treats as we slowly inch closer (classical conditioning). Precisely the way Little Peter was counterconditioned. If the dog reacts at any time, we could withdraw slightly until the dog is once again comfortable with the distance. Eventually, we'd move progressively forward until we'd be able to approach John without the dog reacting. Finally, we'd even be able to feed the dog treats.

Unfortunately, despite various attempts, I could not procure any help with Mila's reactive issues, so I decided to work on her problems independently. Strangely, if she has no anticipation of what another dog might do to her, and a dog gets out of a car directly in front of her, she remains relatively relaxed even when she is on a leash; she does not react at all. Additionally, she can socialise with dogs up close and personal, but as soon as she sees a dog from a distance on our walks and is unsure of its intentions, she becomes very reactive.

When she spots another dog, even from several blocks away, her ears prick up; she tenses, barks, screams, the hair on her neck stands up, and she has an overwhelming urge to rip the other hound to shreds. Mila seems to believe that the best defence is a good offence. She pulls on the leash and lunges like a demented animal. If the other dog barks back or is unrestrained, despite leash laws, the situation escalates dangerously. Mila's reaction to other dogs was consistently violent, totally out of control, and she always took a long time to calm down and recover, even after the other dog disappeared.

After we moved from the family villa to the last house in our cul-de-sac, bordering a forested area, I tried to make the acquaintance of several large dogs, who live two houses from us. Unfortunately, any placatory gestures ignited furious barking and overwhelming rage, so eventually I just ignored them. Gradually they became habituated to me and I mostly learnt to do the same. However, if I don't regularly refresh their memory, the associations they formed with me die out, and they bark with great vehemence once again. Of course, when I added Mila to the mix, all bets were off.

Fortunately, the owners restrain the sizeable mixed-breed Lady and the two well-built St Bernard-type dogs, Lego & Co, behind a wrought iron fence which does not deter them from their constant aggressive barking at passers-by. As there is no vehicle through traffic in our tranquil little street, in the hill district, we have many joggers, dog walkers and families walking with their children, especially on weekends. Lego & Co bark at all of them.

Initially, when we tried to walk past Lego & Co with Mila, it seemed as if all the furies of the world descended upon us. Not only were the three large dogs communicating their confrontational aversion to our presence at full volume, but, additionally, not to be outdone, Mila added her individual blood-curdling screams to the crazed cacophony in our ordinarily peaceful street. In the beginning, we used to have a similar reaction from Mignon the papillon across the road, but he soon made friends with Mila and us. So, naturally, running the gauntlet of Lego & Co not only stressed Mila, but it also left my own nerves jangling. Eventually, after many weeks of repeat performances, despite their indications to the contrary, I realised that even if Lego & Co were willing to call a truce, Mila was not and invariably set up a perpetual chain reaction. Subsequently, I had no other option but to try and change Mila's attitude.

Since our daily obedience practices in the garden were progressing very well, I decided it was time to expand our range and move slightly further afield.

Although we practised during walks over the past few months from the family villa to the new house nearby, our outings did not always go well. Invariably we'd see a dog in the distance or an unleashed dog up close and personal, as often was the case, and Mila would have a total meltdown.

As I knew that while a dog's anxiety is high learning will not occur, we began with various obedience exercises in front of our house, where there is a minimum level of threat stimulus, all the time treating liberally. In time Mila breezed through the various exercises going into sit, down, heel, peek-a-boo and twirling in both directions while I fed her generously with a selection of her favourite treats.

Eventually, we moved closer to Mignon the papillon across the street near the boundary fence with Lego & Co. Fortunately, by then, Mignon was a firm friend who invariably came to greet us with tail wagging and watched our antics in the cul-de-sac with considerable interest. After we entertained Mignon for several days, we moved up the road within range of Lego & Co. As anticipated, Mila became noticeably more nervous and cast worried looks toward the large dogs, who did not respond kindly to our presence and vocalised accordingly.

At this point, as the purpose of the exercise was to keep Mila under her threshold, we did a quick turn and practised our exercises all the way home. Each day we repeated the same course up to Lego & Co's boundary, and a week later, we attempted to run the gauntlet past Lego and his pack. Thankfully, with the continuous food supply, I managed to get Mila past the dogs quickly, thus limiting any extreme reactions on her part.

Gradually, over a few more weeks, we were able to walk past Lego & Co at a more leisurely speed, without Mila reacting, while I shovelled treats into her mouth. Naturally, praise was also high on the agenda. By then, we could do several exercises right in front of the big dogs, and Mila would routinely heel or go into peek-a-boo, then into down, followed by a stay.

Another useful command that I taught Mila was 'look at me', as I found it essential to make eye contact and redirect her focus when it faltered or when she became distracted. Teaching eye contact is the initial step to effective counterconditioning. Moving gradually closer to the big dogs as I dispensed countless treats, while keeping Mila under her threshold, is fundamental classical conditioning. On the other hand, asking Mila to tackle various exercises in front of the dogs voluntarily is based on operant conditioning principles. Behaviour modification often utilises a combination of multiple therapies in tandem.

From the first day we started training in front of our house to applying the same exercises in front of Lego & Co, two houses away, took six to eight weeks, although Mila and I began training walks several months previously. Even when the big dogs reacted to something else down the street and barked while we were in front of them, Mila usually managed to restrain herself. Once I established eye contact with her, she could focus on me and respond to my instructions while disregarding the dogs barking. With an inexhaustible supply of treats, Mila was able to carry out my commands and go into down or peek-a-boo. Even when she did react anxiously, she didn't lose complete control. After a few barks, I could usually attract her attention by asking her to heel, or sit, naturally, with liberal offerings of delicious treats.

Further afield, the neighbourhood held similar challenges, as this shady residential area with large plots is home to many furious front-yard barkers. During the outings, I planned our journey with military precision to avoid needless canine encounters, although unforeseen circumstances tormented us daily. Additionally, I could never relax our training exercises during the walks, which had to be constant. Painfully, bent over double, I dispensed treats to a very low-slung hound as needed, which is incredibly back-breaking work.

Most dogs in the distance still set Mila off. At times, we managed to inch marginally closer without Mila reacting by doing the various exercises with quick turns and non-stop treats. However, the sight of other dogs still concerned her, and she frequently declined to accept any treats while they were in view. If we were fortunate, we could avoid dogs in the distance, but they often popped up behind us or from around corners. Adding to the danger, they were often unleashed, with their owners lagging several blocks away, distracted by their mobile phones.

I realised that Mila's reactive issues were severe, and although they did improve marginally, like her reaction to thunder, they would never completely resolve. It can take years to manage a dog's reactivity and maintain it at acceptable levels. Unfortunately, dogs seldom lose their fear, especially if it is well ingrained. However, with training, we can teach them to manage their anxiety and not react to it. Some days, Mila is more sensitive to stimuli that she doesn't usually respond to, and we don't even make it past the big dogs in our street.

After almost a year, even though our training area had expanded slightly, we could still not go for an ordinary peaceful walk. These were still dominated by treats and training, as counterconditioning leash reactivity is a very long process requiring a lot of patience.

Admittedly, progress would have been more constant if we could have trained in a controlled area and did not have to contend with off-leash dogs, which often set our training back significantly, and stressed Mila unnecessarily. When Mila reacts, she is noisy and over the top. However, we can keep our distance from other dogs because I always restrain her. Thus, she is no danger to anyone.

Unfortunately, unrestricted dogs present an unpreventable risk when they come racing over to Mila. It can be incredibly stressful even for two normal dogs when they meet on-leash, which experts do not recommend. When we remove the advantage of a safe distance, and if stress levels increase, the dogs may feel compelled to react.

For an already reactive dog, it is a perilous situation. When I shout at owners to control their dogs, invariably they do nothing and happily assure me that their pooch is harmless. Even if that is the case, 'friendly' dogs can become instantly unfriendly and react defensively when faced with a reactive dog. Such encounters left us both stressed and tired.

Although we have a lot of work ahead of us, we have made progress. It is true that distant dogs still set her off. However, after a quick turn, I can sometimes re-engage her, and we can watch the other dog move away; if not, then we head off in the opposite direction. Whereas, initially, every day was a disaster, they happen less often. Invariably, when she does react to other dogs, she calms down and recovers a lot quicker than in the past.

Mila is an example of how counterconditioning works to change an animal's response to a trigger by presenting the impulse at a low level and only gradually increasing the intensity of the stimulus while keeping the dog's arousal at a minimum and pairing the fear stimulus with a second stimulus, such as food.

While counterconditioning is a long process requiring a lot of patience, Mila has been able to gradually get closer to other dogs as I simultaneously feed her high-value treats. In this manner, she learns to associate all dogs with tasty treats rather than fear and aggression.

The anticipation of food elicits pleasant emotions and responses, which are incompatible with fear. Hopefully, these responses will replace the fear response in time, or the fear response will become more manageable. This is involuntary learning based on Pavlov's classical conditioning. On the other hand, the obedience exercises I do with Mila are voluntary; she chooses to present the required behaviour, keeping her focus on me instead of reacting to the dogs, which I reward with a treat. Combining classical conditioning with operant conditioning illustrates that behaviour modification programmes often simultaneously utilise Pavlovian and Skinnerian methods.

Further to the above, we know the principle behind operant conditioning is that behaviour is determined by its consequences that are either reinforced or punished, making it more or less likely that the behaviour will occur again. However, the new kid on the block, cognitive training, promotes problem-solving and independent thinking in dogs and treats dogs as partners and students.

This revolutionary reasoning suggests that while operant conditioning has its uses, it churns out dog robots focused on training and conditioned always to obey their owners.

Unlike operant conditioning, cognitive training encourages a partnership of shared emotions and promotes a more liberal approach than the narrower perspective of behaviourism.

Many experts agree that dogs are gifted in reading human social cues and understanding language and human gestures, which encourages a relationship based on an exchange of information and teamwork. Additionally, reward and punishment-based learning does not consider dogs' natural instincts, the driving force behind canines. Although, the concept is still in its infancy and has not filtered down to the grassroots, but perhaps it gives us a tantalising glimpse into the future of dog training. Hopefully, cognitive training will find its niche along with classical and operant conditioning.

CHAPTER 11
NEONATAL-SENSITIVE PERIOD

Several months ago, our former, pretty, blond neighbour, Suzie, a massive fan of Mila's, decided that she would like a dachshund puppy. She resolved that she'd like a puppy that looks like Mila, acts like Mila, is as friendly as Mila and is as well trained as Mila. In essence, she wanted a Mila clone. Naturally, she recognises that Mila is a Supermutt and impossible to replicate; however, she predicted that her puppy will be a genius, born with a PhD, a dachshund Einstein.

Since I'd warned Suzie, in the past, about the seriousness of responsible canine ownership, and as she has no experience with dogs, she asked me to assist her in her search for the perfect canine companion. Sadly, many puppy mills unashamedly masquerade as creditable breeders, so I agreed to guide Suzie through the hazards. It was late in the season, and winter was already knocking on our door when we started our search early in November. I warned Suzie that breeders of repute rarely have available puppies, and she may have to wait up to a year or longer.

After Franky died, I had bookmarked a well-regarded dachshund breeder, who has earned the title of Golden Wreath breeder, by the number of victories and placements in the show ring. Unfortunately, after I contacted her, she confirmed that she was only planning a litter in summer, six months away. A successful and determined lawyer, the prospect of delaying for so long didn't appeal to Suzie, who wanted a puppy as a Christmas present to herself. Undaunted by the challenge, I tried various acquaintances and contacted a few breeders, none of whom had litters, but recommended others.

In the interim, I advised Suzie to make sure that a dachshund was the perfect dog for her and to explore various other breeds. Besides the PhD, she wanted a small, smooth-coated dog with personality that was easy to train, and although she considered multiple options, she assured me that a dachshund was the right breed for her. Ideally, I'd have preferred to do a personality test in tandem with a dog breed selector questionnaire before obtaining a new dog. These tools would give Suzie insight into her strengths and determine the most suitable breed options based on her busy lifestyle. Unfortunately, as it transpired, due to time constraints and her hectic schedule, she could not meet up at the time.

Some weeks later, after several false leads, I discovered a breeder who professed to have two pedigree litters, a black/tan and a red litter that was two weeks younger. As I requested, the breeder sent me pedigree certificates of the black and tan parents and a few photos of both, including the puppies. She also reassured me that she raises all the puppies indoors as part of the household. Naturally, Suzie and I were excited about the visit, although the logistics of organising our excursion proved quite a challenge. Not only did I have to accommodate my schedule and Suzie's busy law practice but the breeder's timetable as well.

Furthermore, I also had to coordinate the appointment according to which litter Suzie wanted to inspect. At that time, the red litter was too young to have visitors for at least another two weeks due to the risk of transmitting dangerous canine diseases and viruses. However, bearing in mind that the breeder only had one unreserved black/tan puppy, Suzie had to make a quick choice. Considering that Mila is also black/tan, I wasn't surprised when Suzie opted for the same colour, and hence, we set a date.

Once we had the address, I realised that the breeder lived in the countryside, which concerned me. At the time, I wondered how well the parent dogs would be socialised and habituated to the usual stimuli that urban dogs must typically adapt to, or whether the breeder had socialised the puppies at all.

Armed with sandwiches Suzie had prepared on the designated date, we made ourselves comfortable in the warm car, while Malcolm, her husband, drove us. During the two-hour uneventful drive, we discussed puppy names and made plans for the Einstein dachshund. Resolved that she would not leave her dog home alone, we made mental lists of the necessary carrier bags, portable enclosures, wee mats and beds that the puppy would need as it commuted everywhere with Suzie.

The bleak rural settlement where the breeder was waiting for us was even more remote than I'd anticipated. Without delay, she kindly invited us in to view the six-week-old puppies after we removed our shoes. As most canine diseases, which can wipe out a litter in forty-eight hours, are transmitted on the soles of shoes, removing ours was a necessary precaution to avoid introducing any contamination.

We can seldom resist the first sight of puppies. The warm and fuzzy feelings generated by these little creatures lower our defences and make it harder to decide with our heads rather than our hearts. Indeed, this was no exception as our eyes automatically locked on the three black/tan and one red puppy that were fast asleep in a large pen, just inside the entrance passage.

The red puppy intrigued me, it seemed such an anomaly amongst the dark puppies, and when I asked the breeder about it, she told me it was a throwback. I was unconvinced. It is possible, however, without getting too technical about the colour genetics of dachshunds and without knowing the full genetic background of the parent dogs, I was unable to validate my doubts. As a rule, one pair of genes controls black/tan dachshunds, which is recessive to red. In this situation, black/tan parents cannot produce red puppies unless both parents have a red gene, which is unlikely, given that the breeder purchased her bitch and dog from different kennels, as confirmed by the pedigree certificates. As a rule, serious breeders do not usually consider a union between black/tan and red dogs, as it can produce colour variations that go against breed standards.

Even though the matter troubled me, I was just as concerned that I hadn't spotted any adult dogs. I was surprised that only a small white fluffy dog ran around inside, yapping excitedly, but there was no trace of any adult dachshunds. As we expected to inspect the parents, I questioned their whereabouts, and the breeder advised that she kept them outside in a container shed, but we could see them later. Despite this, I was curious to know how much time the parents spent with the puppies. The breeder confirmed that the mother 'wanted nothing to do with the puppies since they were weaned', a week ago, and as they tracked too much mud in the house, the adults did not see the puppies often, which raised a red flag. Basically, it meant that the puppies were separated from their parents when they were five weeks old.

It appeared that the small white fluffy dog was the indoor pet, and the dachshunds were her breeding stock that remained outside, mainly in the shed. Even if the mother is no longer feeding the puppies, owners should not separate the litter from their mother at five weeks. Although, with hindsight, both Suzie and I wondered whether the breeder also kept the puppies in the shed. We speculated that she only took them into the house to show prospective owners that she raised them as part of the family.

The puppies were fast asleep and didn't seem as if they wanted to wake up. When we commented on the lethargic state of the puppies, the owner confirmed that the puppies had had a big play session before our arrival. Breeders often use this excuse to explain abnormal inertia and lack of interest in puppies.

As we sat in the warm kitchen just off the passage from where we could see the sleeping puppies, we chatted to our hostess. After asking permission, Suzie picked up her allocated puppy with great tenderness and stroked it affectionately while holding it in her lap. The puppy trembled like a leaf. This behaviour worried me, as shivering or shaking can indicate stress and fear in canines. I pointed out the fear reaction, and the breeder confirmed that the puppy was not used to people and was probably nervous, which raised another red flag.

After some polite small talk about their lives in such a quiet, remote locality, the breeder recounted how she makes a living breeding her dogs, miniature goats and Shetland ponies. With the chit-chat out of the way, Suzie and I proceeded with our questions about the puppies, though Malcolm stayed uncharacteristically quiet. It transpired that the puppies were unfamiliar with household noises, vacuum cleaners, kitchen sounds, etc., which was odd, considering the owner maintained that the puppies were born and raised in the house.

Additionally, it disturbed me to note that since weaning, the puppies' diet consisted solely of dry adult dog food, which the owner showed us, and assured Suzie she'd be happy to give her some if she decided to take the puppy. More red flags. The solid, dry chunks were large and made for adult dogs, and I wondered out loud how the puppies could handle such big pieces of food. In response, the owner reassured us that the puppies managed, contradicting their flat little tummies and slim bodies.

Adult dog food is not formulated to satisfy the nutritional demands for healthy development in growing puppies. Unsuitable food robs them of critical nutrients, which is why puppies need specially balanced food designed for their all-encompassing requirements. More red flags started popping up when the breeder confirmed that she mates her bitch twice a year, which is exceedingly draining for the mother dog. In the meantime, the puppies were still dozing, and exhibited no interest, and made no move to inspect us, not even the one on Suzie's lap, who continued to tremble.

Generally, reputable breeders are proud to display their prize pedigree dogs in the show ring, even if it is only a few times. Showing their dogs allows them to assess their form and quality, which provides the foundations for their professional reputation, including the stability of any future breeding programme. Although our breeder had never exhibited her dogs, this signified nothing *per se*; however, breeders who enter for shows take great care to produce well-balanced, sound animals, both genetically and psychically.

Suzie also asked the breeder's opinion on whether it was all right to leave a puppy at home when she went to work, and the breeder dismissed the matter and advised that it would not be a problem, as dogs get used to being alone very quickly. Another red flag. The only thing in the breeders favour was that she would only allow the puppies to leave at eight weeks according to Hungarian law. Consequently, the puppies would only be ready to go to their new home just before Christmas, in two weeks, although many miniature breeds stay with their mothers for longer.

Before we left, Suzie returned the still shaking puppy to rejoin its siblings. After we retrieved our shoes and coats, we stepped out of the warm house into the grey, frigid wintery day while the breeder went to the rear of the yard and let out the mother and father dog from a shed.

The little black and tan parent dogs approached us with hunched bodies, ears pulled back, tails between their legs in a classic, fearful, submissive attitude. Although both dogs stopped some distance from us, I gently coaxed the mother over after I crouched down. She timidly sniffed my outstretched hand. Even though her mammary glands still looked very pendulous, she seemed healthy. Anxiously she gazed at me, and with her gentle yet frightened demeanour, she kindled my compassion.

Both dogs were the very long elongated dachshund variety, which places excessive stress on the back and results in many genetic spinal health issues, which did not appeal to Suzie. As I hadn't spotted the red breeding pair, I asked our hostess where they might be. I wondered if she also kept them sequestered in the shed, which would corroborate our suspicions that she did not raise the puppies in the house. To my bewilderment, the breeder denied having any other dogs. This revelation was quite surreal, considering the photos she sent of the red mother and puppy. Not to mention the discussion we had about the red litter being too young for visitors to view for another two weeks. The situation made no sense, but as we were already heading towards the gate, and the red litter was not an issue for Suzie, I dropped the subject. As a last word of farewell, the breeder asked Suzie to confirm her decision by the following morning, as someone else was also interested in the puppy.

As we drove off, we sat in silence, listening to the hum of the car, and watched the stark scenery passing by. With Malcolm at the wheel, we tried to assimilate the details of our visit until Suzie asked for my opinion.

During the previous few weeks, Suzie was so excited about getting a puppy and had researched obedience classes, day care centres and an abundance of canine accessories, including clothes and toys. Therefore, I was aware of how much she wanted a puppy. Nevertheless, I knew how discriminating she was and how important it was for her to have a 'bombproof' dog. Moreover, I also realised that, even though Suzie maintained she would only consider an Einstein puppy, by the gentle way she held and cradled the puppy and the warmth in her eyes, her heart would easily sway her.

Even though she felt sorry for the puppy, I was unsure of her feelings, so I tried to be as honest, albeit as tactful as possible. A master of diplomacy, I reminded her that although I had my reservations, it was her decision, and despite my opinion, she was under no obligation to take my advice. Nevertheless, we both realised that there were some shortcomings. The parents were very timid and anxious, which may genetically predispose the puppies to these undesirable traits. Furthermore, the breeder did not socialise or habituate the puppies and possibly raised them in the shed with no stimulation. It also seemed that the breeder separated the litter from the mother at five weeks of age, and they could no longer assimilate valuable lessons from her. Additionally, their diet was inappropriate and unsatisfactory, so it was questionable whether they had received the best start in life.

There were concerns that they may present with long-term behaviour issues. Pedigree dogs are a considerable expense; therefore, breeders have a responsibility to ensure that they meet all the essential needs of their puppies to reach their full potential and grow into well-balanced adult dogs. Of course, Suzie could work on any potential issues the puppy may have.

With appropriate training, socialisation and patience, it is possible to correct and improve many problems in young dogs before the close of the socialisation period and the start of the fear response. In light of the above, I suggested that if Suzie were willing to take on a puppy that may have possible behaviour deficiencies, why didn't she adopt a rescue dog instead? However, since she had her heart set on a puppy, this option did not appeal to her.

As dog parents, the more we can learn about our dogs, the more we will understand their behaviour and provide an environment where they can thrive and become good canine citizens. The initial twelve weeks of a puppy's life is the most crucial period, which defines the essence of the adult dog it will become. Unfortunately, most people do not understand the significance that these early weeks represent.

Neonatal Period: Day 0–Day 12

In his book *Dog Behaviour, Evolution, and Cognition*, Ádám Miklósi explains that a wolf mother occupies a den two to three metres below ground, a few weeks before the birth of her cubs, which provides a stable physical environment. During this time, the cubs rely on tactile and olfactory senses, and the only sources of physical interactions are from siblings and the mother. The male feeds the mother, who rarely leaves the den.

Human selection has interfered with this process in canines by choosing and providing the nesting sites that are usually open and well lit. This involvement has altered the developmental environment of puppies, and because of this, we expose puppies to additional social stimulation during the neonatal period.

In addition, due to the human element, many mother dogs decrease their time with their puppies at an early age. Humans also intervene and often assist with the birth process, clean the puppies and feed the mother, which has resulted in a marked decrease of paternal behaviour in male dogs. According to leading experts, one of the primary reasons for the high infant mortality in feral dogs is that the mother chooses inappropriate nest sites. In addition, because of the lack of help from the male dog that does not provide food, she often leaves her puppies alone when searching for food.

After the birth of the puppies, the mother licks the pups dry, which imprints the puppy into her mind. Unfortunately, because of human interference and breeding practices, some dogs cannot give birth naturally and require a Caesarean section under general anaesthetic. Subsequently, they cannot carry out the imprinting process, which results in some mothers rejecting their puppies.

Puppies enter the world blind and deaf, and for the first two weeks, they cannot regulate various body functions, such as temperature and elimination. These tasks are the responsibility of the mother, who not only stimulates them to urinate and defecate but grooms and feeds her pups. By licking her puppies and her nipples, she imprints on their developing minds that she is their mother and leaves an olfactory scent trail for them to follow, which is vital for the puppies' survival. If we wash a mother's nipples with soap and water, the puppies cannot smell their way back to their food source.

How well a mother cares for and behaves with her offspring will influence their minds and behaviour for the rest of their lives. At this time, there is a negligible difference in brain activity between when a puppy is sleeping or awake. Despite this, the first weeks are the most important in a puppy's life, and every early experience has a long-term impact.

We know that the olfactory senses are highly developed in dogs, even newborn puppies, and the imprinting process between the mother and her puppies forms a powerful bond. Bearing this information in mind, I couldn't help wonder how long the imprinted scent of their mother lasts and whether after separation mothers recognise their adult puppies and vice versa.

Most experts believe that if we leave puppies with their mothers and only separate them after four months, they will recognise each other later on in life. However, the consensus seems that if we remove the puppies at around eight weeks of age, the mother and her adult offspring will not recognise each other later in life.

On the other hand, experiments conducted by Peter Hepper from the School of Psychology at Queen's University Belfast seem to contradict the above view. After collecting several litters of puppies between four and five and a half weeks of age, they carried out various experiments, which left no doubt that both mothers and puppies recognised each other's scent, even after a brief separation. Taking the study one step further, Hepper collected a set of approximately two-year-old dogs that were removed from their mothers when they were eight weeks and had no further contact with each other until the testing. The team repeated the same experiments with these older dogs.

Interestingly, the results showed that 78% of mothers showed far more interest in a cloth impregnated with the scent of her own offspring than in a cloth containing the smell of unrelated, though similar dogs. Subsequently, when they reversed the experiment, the results were very similar: 76% of the grown dogs showed a preference for a cloth infused with the scent of their mother, despite not having had any contact with her since they were puppies. Therefore, we cannot underestimate the bond of maternal imprinting and the effects of early experiences.

Transitional Period: Day 13–Day 21

Puppies are born in a very early stage of development. They call such animals 'altricial'. During the transitional period, a puppy catches up with those animals born in a much more developed state, such as foals or calves that are examples of 'precocial' animals. As the puppy's senses develop, it gains control over thermoregulation, and at the end of the transitional period, it can eliminate spontaneously (and the mother stops eating its stools).

Throughout this period, puppies experience increased cerebral activity as the brain undergoes drastic changes and their motor abilities and senses develop. This period starts with the opening of the eyes and ear canals. It is interesting to note that the opening of the eyes and ears varies from breed to breed.

For example, Scott and Fuller (1965) recorded that cocker spaniels usually open their eyes by day fourteen, whereas only 11% of fox terriers open their eyes by then. On the other hand, puppies' ears open soon after the eyes, when almost all fox terriers showed a startle response to sudden sound, while only 61% of cocker spaniels responded to the same test.

The transitional period is a time of enormous change for puppies. By the time their teeth appear and direct stimulation between the pups and mother decreases, they no longer require guidance to find the mother's nipples. In addition, their temperature-regulating mechanism and motor coordination improves, allowing for a range of complex movements as pups begin to walk, jump and wag their tails. They may even bark and growl for the first time.

During this period, the mother also disciplines her puppies, and amongst other things, teaches them not to bite so hard. If we remove puppies from their mother and littermates too early, they cannot learn essential lessons, including bite inhibition.

As the pup's senses develop, the world around it opens up. During this time, its siblings and environmental stimuli dramatically affect the puppy's mind, which will shape the rest of its life. For example, when the eyes first open at around fourteen days, the puppy's response to light and moving objects is weak; however, its vision will become almost that of an adult within the next two weeks.

Similarly, a pup only shows brainstem auditory evoked response (BAER) around fourteen days; however, within the next two weeks, the BAER activity is equivalent to that of an adult dog. Likewise, after birth, puppies only experience touch reflexes around their head; however, by the age of fourteen days, their front legs have touch reflexes and their hind legs a week later. Additionally, at birth, puppies have a very low pain sensation; however, their pain response is similar to an adult by the transitional period.

Experiments with rats demonstrate that animals raised in a sensory-rich environment develop thicker cerebral cortexes and have more synaptic contacts between neurons. Similarly, a dog's experiences during the transitional phase will affect it for the rest of its life. Most building blocks of the future are laid down during this period.

Socialisation Period to Dogs: 4-6 Weeks

We also often refer to this period as the primary socialisation period.

Many milestones that began during the transitional period continue into the early part of the socialisation period. By this time, the puppy will process information quickly and efficiently, increasing play activity among littermates. During the transitional stage, puppies learn about bite inhibition from their mother, continuing into the socialisation period. They learn to bite and what it feels like to receive bites, which is an essential lesson for dogs. Additionally, bite inhibition teaches them to be gentle, so they don't hurt people or other dogs later on as adults. Mothers also teach them important lessons about manners and discipline, resorting to inhibited bites, growls and mouth threats, when necessary. During these vital lessons, puppies show compromise and respect by rolling onto their backs so their mothers can lick them.

Everything that puppies experience and learn from their mothers during this time will form the basis of their characters as adult dogs. For example, puppies that receive severe and frequent discipline from their mothers become withdrawn and less sociable with humans than puppies with more gentle mothers. On the other hand, mothers who do not teach boundaries or limits and do not provide disciplinary corrections are likely to produce puppies that will become challenging to handle later in life.

Removing a five-week-old puppy from its litter is like removing a three-year-old child from its family unit, sending him off to boarding school and expecting him to cope emotionally and socially.

Although we try not to humanise dogs, the fundamental emotional and social needs of all mammals are similar. If we deprive very young children of their family's guidance and emotional support, they become fearful, prone to phobias and anxieties. They cannot self-soothe, have trouble coping with everyday frustrations and display inappropriate and unreasonable anger. Additionally, they also struggle with peer interactions and suffer from similar behaviour issues to puppies removed from their litter at an early age. Taking a puppy from its siblings and mother at five weeks interrupts its behavioural development and much needed social interaction before it is fully socialised to dogs.

According to thirteen years of research by Scott and Fuller (1965), the socialisation period begins at three weeks and continues until week fourteen. During the time of early socialisation, from three to six weeks, dogs learn to be dogs. If we remove puppies from their littermates and mother before this time, they will be poorly socialised and more likely to grow into fearful adults and find it challenging to fit in with dogs and people.

Researchers at the University of Milan recently studied the effects of separating puppies from their litters between five and six weeks. The study involved seventy adult dogs ranging from eighteen months to seven years old. They published their findings in the scientific journal *Veterinary Record*, which concluded that very young puppies separated from their litter were prone to many behaviour problems as adult dogs. These ranged from destructiveness, excessive barking, reactivity, fearfulness, possessiveness and attention-seeking behaviours.

During the socialisation period, as puppies play with their siblings, they learn to be dogs and develop skills that they will require in the future. While they play-fight, stalk, chase, hunt, catch and learn guarding and sexual behaviours, they form social bonds and learn necessary communication skills to interact with others.

Underrated by most of us, play is a potent medium from which puppies learn about cooperative behaviour, problem-solving, inventiveness and creativity, develop physical fitness, and improve coordination and balance. Through play experiences, they become familiar with specific behaviours that ultimately prepare them to live and communicate with other dogs. As a rule, it is best to avoid puppies from small litters, as there is not enough interaction between littermates for them to learn the necessary doggy social graces or bite inhibition. Orphans or runts who seldom play with other puppies are more attached to humans and may fear other dogs later in life. Puppies learn the ground rules from their mother and littermates and from us, which provides the social structures for the rest of their lives.

Socialisation Period to Humans: 4-16 Weeks

This is also known as the secondary socialisation period. Between three and eight weeks old, breeders should gradually and with care introduce puppies to a profusion of environmental stimuli, including the sounds of household appliances, short car rides, unfamiliar surfaces, other animal species, loud noises, different people, children, bicycles, various forms of transportation.

The two- to sixteen-week 'critical period for social development' derives from the 1930s study by Nobel Prize-winning biologist Konrad Lorenz. The critical period refers to the period when a puppy is most predisposed to, and has the greatest capacity to learn, particular social skills. After sixteen weeks, the social learning window closes. Following this, the dog has limited abilities to develop or change social skills. The original idea conceptualised this period as a rigid time frame of events. However, we now know that there is more flexibility to early learning, and the early learning window of opportunity is often referred to as the 'sensitive period'.

Furthermore, we can better understand the importance of this period if we revisit the subject of development in a dog's brain, which we can compare to the growth of a limb or any other body part. For instance, if a leg does not walk while growing (critical period), it will wither and become useless. We can say the same for the brain, which can grow and change shape, depending on the environmental stimulation during the sensitive period; the first sixteen weeks coincide with the most rapid brain growth.

For instance, a newborn livestock-guarding dog has a brain volume of ten cubic centimetres. In contrast, by the time it is sixteen weeks old, the brain has grown to eighty cubic centimetres, almost full size at just over a hundred cubic centimetres, which illustrates just how much a dog's brain develops over a short period.

A newborn puppy has all the brain cells it will have in its entire life. However, brain growth depends on the connections between the cells. At birth, most are not connected or wired together, which takes place during puppy development. Some nerves make spontaneous connections, and others are motivated by external signals. The more stimuli a puppy receives, the more cell connections it will make.

A puppy raised in a shed or an environment lacking stimulation will have a smaller brain, even though it still has the same number of cells, but fewer cells will be wired. Once a puppy reaches sixteen weeks old, it will have made all the cell connections it is ever going to make. Even if we take an adult to a more stimulating environment, it cannot cope with its environment because it does not have the necessary cell connections. It is essential to keep up the social, environmental stimuli for the dog's life because, just as a limb will wither if not in use, the brain will also atrophy.

Some breeders advocate removing puppies as early as six weeks old to move to their new homes and start socialising with various humans as soon as possible. Conversely, multiple studies have shown that removing them from their mother and littermates at such an early age is, in fact, detrimental to their health and social development.

Therefore, most breeders will allow new owners to take puppies between seven to nine weeks old, which is already within the socialisation period. There is, therefore, a great deal of responsibility on breeders to implement early puppy socialisation, even before they go to their permanent homes. Socialisation refers to a process whereby an animal learns to interact with the living part of the environment, including humans and all other species, even its own.

Prospective owners should ensure that the breeder did not raise the puppies in a kennel or locked away in a laundry or shed, with only the mother and littermates for company, during the first eight weeks, and has also started the socialisation process.

For this reason, it is not advisable to buy puppies from a pet store, as there is no way to determine the circumstances under which the breeder kept and raised the puppies. Another important consideration, after the puppy moves to its permanent home, is whether the new owner will leave the puppy alone all day while they are at work. Under these conditions, the puppy will not have enough stimulation to grow and develop its brain. Therefore, some discerning breeders will not sell puppies to people who are often away from home all day unless they can make provisions for daily dog walkers or doggy day care.

Ian Dunbar, a passionate advocate of early puppy socialisation, suggests that breeders should gently expose puppies to as many environmental stimuli as possible before they are eight weeks old. Additionally, puppies should interact and be handled by at least a hundred people during the first month in their new home. Many canine experts offer a plethora of desensitisation checklists. Although the list is not inclusive, most advise owners to handle the puppy's neck, ears, eye area, tail, paws, mouth, belly and groin.

After we got Mila, I started grooming her every day. Obviously, this was something she was unused to, as she pranced around like a wild horse. First, I wiped her face and body with a damp face cloth, and then I cleaned her feet one by one. Finally, I rubbed her teeth with a wet muslin cloth and brushed her. Now when I groom her, she stands calmly, and after I've finished wiping her, she lifts her feet, one after the other without being asked, just like a well-mannered horse. Mila doesn't care for the teeth cleaning but stoically puts up with it without any fuss. Another matter of contention used to be nail clipping, but with treats after each nail, she is much better and allows me to keep her claws in check, although because she has black nails, I only trim the tip and leave the more thorough manicure to the vet. I've used the same grooming strategy with all my past dogs, whether long or short-haired, as it gets them used to being handled, prodded and poked without reacting.

The lists also include socialising them to babies, children, men, other animals, skateboards, scooters, couriers and other dogs, to name a few. Inappropriately socialised puppies may become fearful, although it is essential to remember that puppies are very impressionable, and meetings and new experiences should not be overwhelming or forced.

We should also habituate puppies to household sounds: noisy tools, playgrounds, street noises, public transport, schools, elevators, escalators, crowds, thunderstorms and fireworks.

Socialisation and habituation aim to ensure that puppies, especially in urban areas, grow up without fears or phobias and enjoy the company of other people and dogs in various settings. Puppies removed from their litter at a later date can also do well in their new homes as long as they have had some exposure to humans. Experimental evidence suggests that puppies socialise to humans rapidly, even with just a few minutes of social contact over a couple days. Only puppies that have had no experience with humans show extreme avoidance. Even exposure to a minimum amount of human socialisation is enough to reduce wariness in dogs, which equips them with the ability to maintain social contact with strangers, even after the end of the sensitive period of three to twelve weeks.

Bearing all this in mind, Suzie decided not to take the puppy and hold out for her PhD Einstein. Now that Suzie is armed with the practical experience gained during our trip, she knows the recipe for the perfect puppy. Take two calm and friendly parent dogs. Add a litter of several healthy and lively puppies with an abundance of curiosity, raised indoors as part of the family. Season well with plentiful socialisation and habituation to many household items and people. Allow to mature with patient and loving owners who can provide ongoing training, consistent discipline and regular outlets for the dog's mental and physical wellbeing, allowing it to reach its full potential. These are all vital ingredients in making stable and bombproof dogs.

CHAPTER 12
ONGOING EARLY LEARNING

A wide range of canine reviews have highlighted the increasing incidence of behaviour disorders, including fear and aggression, in dogs acquired from commercial breeders, puppy farms and pet stores. Based on a questionnaire incorporating information on the number of available litters, age of pup at purchase and the mother's interaction with puppies, a recent study revealed a prevalence of behavioural disorders in dogs obtained from irresponsible breeders. Additional studies have suggested that insufficient maternal care, the lack of appropriate stimulation during early life and negative experiences contribute to an increase in the likelihood of developmental disorders in commercially bred dogs.

Doubtless, some backyard breeders mean no harm; unfortunately, they don't realise the consequences of their actions. Furthermore, a significant majority erroneously believe that keeping their dogs and litters warm and fed with a roof above their heads has catered to all their needs. Pet dogs that will share our homes should be raised in the household hub, either in kitchens or living rooms, and not isolated in sheds. As behaviourist Ian Dunbar points out, prospective owners should avoid puppies raised in kennels and basements. Dogs raised in isolation are not pet-quality dogs and are nothing more than 'livestock', on a par with cattle, pigs and caged poultry. Left to their own devices, with no attention from the breeder, they are neither housetrained nor socialised and do not make good companions.

For the most part, numerous dog owners also believe that their pets only require basic amenities, such as food and shelter. Unfortunately, while more information comes to light daily, it takes years for details of recent canine developments and research to filter through to the grassroots. In the meantime, our collective ignorance often causes canine companions immeasurable misery and avoidable wide-ranging behaviour issues, such as fear and aggression precipitated by poor socialisation.

When confronted with something unfamiliar or what it perceives to be a threat, the first response of a fearful dog is to run away, but it may resort to aggressive behaviour if it is unable to do so. The lack of proper socialisation is the most significant contributor to fear aggression in dogs. Initially, before the onset of fear response, puppies experience very little fearfulness. Therefore, during this time, the more we expose them to various stimuli, including humans, different objects and situations, other animals and dogs, the less afraid they will be as they grow older.

Puppies only have a few weeks to develop positive associations within their environment, after which they become increasingly cautious about objects and situations they have not previously encountered. This genetically inherited trait ensures that dogs are alert to dangers and treat anything unfamiliar as potentially hazardous.

Across the board, fear is not only a threshold response in canines but also an avoidance of anything unknown in all mammals. Before the onset of fear response, dogs do not show fear of unusual shapes or sounds. Everything is novel and exciting for puppies who explore the world around them with great curiosity.

After the onset of fear response, puppies will approach unfamiliar shapes and sounds with intense caution or will fearfully avoid them, depending on each dog's threshold. The appearance of fear response varies between breeds, which may be any time from six to ten weeks depending on the breed and the individual dog's stress limits; some dogs are undoubtedly more sensitive than others.

Similarly, a lack of socialisation to other dogs can lead to various behaviour problems, including aggressive tendencies. Removing a puppy from the litter at an early age interrupts its behaviour development, and the chances are that it will be poorly socialised to other dogs. Furthermore, it will not have the social skills or greeting protocols to interact with other dogs, nor will it be interested in doing so. Consequently, a dog that is unsocialised to conspecifics will be at a disadvantage in social situations. It will not recognise that it is the same as other dogs and because it sees them as an alien species, it is likely to respond aggressively.

The first person to investigate the imprinting process was the Austrian Nobel Prize-winning ethologist Konrad

Lorenz in his study of birds, although research has shown that imprinting takes place in many social animals during the primary socialisation period, including canines.

During imprinting, puppies respond to visual and auditory cues by following their mother and discover what species they belong to, and learn appropriate sexual and social behaviour. If we remove a puppy from the litter before five weeks, it will not have a chance to imprint on dogs and will not realise it is a dog.

As a result, it will not learn how to be a dog or experience appropriate canine behaviour as demonstrated by its mother and siblings. Because these dogs don't know how to read calming signals shown by other dogs, nor do they know how to give them, socially immature dogs are often the culprits involved in altercations at dog parks.

Unfortunately, these dogs don't stand a chance in social situations because they have no idea what appropriate and polite social dog behaviour looks like and are likely to respond aggressively to overtures from other dogs. Furthermore, they are unable to have proper social interactions with other dogs because of crippling fears and phobias, and most encounters end in aggression.

If a mother dog has not learnt these necessary social skills as a puppy, she will be unable to pass them on to her litter, creating another generation of socially inept dogs. Additionally, it can be challenging to housebreak puppies that breeders remove from their mothers too early.

In the long term, they can also face a host of psychological issues because they lack confidence. For example, even when introduced to obedience classes and provided with social opportunities, they may show fear or aggression and become fear biters. Occasionally, we can minimise these issues, but we can seldom eliminate them entirely. Generally, information learnt during the imprinting process and the sensitive period cannot be reversed. Similarly, if we do not socialise puppies to humans of all shapes and sizes, they may react fearfully and aggressively to people later in life. For instance, if we socialise puppies to women and not men or children, they may become wary and fearful or even hostile when encountering men and children as adult dogs.

When researchers introduced a sample of puppies aged between eight, twelve and sixteen weeks of age to a test area with a selection of unfamiliar articles, the younger puppies explored enthusiastically. On the other hand, puppies who were not shown the same stimuli until they were over eight weeks old were more cautious and tended to withdraw rather than explore the test area. The older puppies that had not entered the test area until they were twelve or sixteen weeks old became paralysed by fear.

Undoubtedly, it is imperative to habituate puppies to as many environmental stimuli as possible during the socialisation period, as this will prepare them to cope and survive in our diverse world.

As in all cases, a fearful dog may become an aggressive dog. Unfortunately, behavioural disorders, including aggression, are the primary reasons owners euthanise their dogs or abandon them to shelters. However, in most cases, if breeders and owners had adequately socialised them to a multitude of humans, a wide selection of conspecifics and a variety of environmental stimuli at an early age, they could have avoided much suffering.

Accordingly, we should never underestimate the effects of positive socialisation, including habituation, which create a record of information that the dog can draw on throughout its life and equips the dog to handle future experience. Quite plainly, it is a matter of life or death to adequately socialise puppies as early as possible so that they and their owners can lead long and happy lives together. Shockingly, Ian Dunbar recounts the little-known fact that many puppies suffer from the terminal illness of being unwanted. Unable to live up to their owners' expectations, they do not live past their second birthday.

For over a century, various experts have studied the effects of habituation, which is part of the socialisation process. In their authoritative review, Rankin *et al.* (2009) defined habituation as: "a behavioural response decrement that results from repeated stimulation, which does not involve sensory adaptation, sensory fatigue or motor fatigue." In more general terms, habituation is a type of 'single-stimulus' learning that allows animals to avoid costly responses in situations where there is no benefit from responding to repeated stimulation.

The main difference between conditioning and habituation is the type of learning that takes place. Habituation does not learn from associations; there is no pairing between a trigger and behaviour. Recurrent exposure to a stimulus will result in a reduced response to that stimulus.

While living in Botswana, we were fortunate to have experienced the African bush in all its glory, where we first encountered the term 'habituation', which is the gradual exposure of animals to non-threatening environmental stimuli.

In safari concession areas where wildlife moves unrestricted from one country to the next, it was imperative that game guides recognise animals that were not habituated to the vehicles and subsequently gave those animals a wide berth. These measures were crucial for the safety of their guests and to avoid frightening and spooking the animals, which could have tragic consequences. A panic-stricken wild animal is unpredictable and could easily lash out at the object of its fear.

Over time, the guides gradually exposed animals to the same stimuli. Eventually, elephants, lions, African wild dogs and reclusive leopards became used to the presence of the game drive vehicles. After many such gradual exposures, they stopped responding to the stimulus, allowing the guides to venture closer without causing the animals any anxiety or stress. Once the animals realised that the safari vehicle was not a threat, they learnt to ignore it.

New animals to the area, especially ones from neighbouring countries where hunters or poachers were active, were volatile around unfamiliar objects and required time to become habituated to the safari vehicles. Approaching fearful animals was perilous and reckless and would undoubtedly result in an aggressive and possibly lethal attack. Naturally, habituation does not mean 'tame'. Never letting their guard down, the guides were constantly vigilant and always mindful of each animal's body language, as even habituated animals responded with increased irritation on certain days, depending on physical and environmental factors.

On a family holiday to the Botswana wilderness with our teenage children, Tammy and Lance, we had the first-hand experience of being charged by an elephant. Our guide was searching for African wild dogs in the dense mopane bush, which is a favourite hangout of elephants, partial to the high-protein content of young mopane leaves. I nervously scanned the dense thicket for evidence of any pachyderm activity, and without warning, we happened on a pair of amorous elephants. The five-ton bull elephant took extreme umbrage at being rudely disturbed during his mating rituals and angrily wheeled around to face us with ears flapping. From the way he launched himself at us, there was no mistaking his intent. Quite simply, he wanted to annihilate us. We felt very vulnerable in the open safari vehicle, as the dense bush is no place to encounter a charging, murderous elephant.

As our guide tried to beat a hasty retreat, the motor stalled. Usually, these things only happen in movies, when at the crucial moment, the engine dies. While we were sitting there, completely exposed and paralysed by fear, the bull kept hurtling towards us. Thankfully, due to its limited binocular vision, the elephant mistook the bush between us as an extension of the vehicle, which it viciously tusked with great vehemence, no more than a few feet from us. Finally, the motor roared to life, and our guide accelerated with extreme urgency, and we took off like a shot, slaloming left and right through the overgrowth.

Realising its mistake, the elephant charged after us. As African elephants can run at speeds of 25–40km/h, the vehicle was at a distinct disadvantage careening around in the overgrown thicket. In imminent danger of being thrown from our seats, the Landcruiser jostled us from side to side as it bounced around at breakneck speed on the uneven terrain. We rejoined the track, a euphemism for road, although the thick sand greatly hindered our speed.

Did I fear for our lives?

Africa is rife with stories about elephant encounters and how easily an enraged elephant can overturn a vehicle, and trample the passengers to death. I've seen the round tusk holes in the safari vehicles when frenzied elephants have got too close. So yes, I did fear for our lives.

I turned around to gauge how long we had before the enraged animal got hold of us and to check on how Tammy and Lance were faring, in the back seat behind us, directly in the path of the rampaging elephant. The blood froze in my veins. The rear seat was empty. On closer inspection, I spotted two pairs of petrified eyes staring out from under the back seat. Did I mention that we were terrified?

Contrary to popular belief, my life did not flash before my eyes, as I was too catatonic with fear to have any thoughts at all. The young bull elephant was in superb condition with impressive stamina, and despite our high speed of 30km/h, he kept up the chase barely a metre from the back of the vehicle. After what seemed like hours but was probably only minutes, he eventually gave up the chase, and, greatly relieved, we headed back to camp at a considerably slower pace, more shaken than stirred.

Even though the elephant was accustomed to vehicles, it was obviously not used to being interrupted during mating rituals. A dog may react similarly if unused to specific situations, such as being pounced on by a child or disturbed when eating or sleeping. If not socialised and properly habituated, our pet dogs can be just as unpredictable and dangerous.

Habituation in various situations is vital to ensure that our canine companions don't feel threatened or stressed by every stimulus and learn to ignore environmental elements that are not dangerous. For puppies to share our busy, noisy world, they must learn to filter out irrelevant stimuli that have no consequence for them. The list of environmental factors is extensive and includes household appliances, everyday items such as umbrellas, prams, wheelie bins, traffic, various forms of transport, thunder, etc. Naturally, it is impossible to habituate a puppy to every stimulus it may encounter during its lifetime. However, if we expose them to as many as possible during the socialisation period, it will help them develop skills to deal with things they may encounter in later life. If we habituate dogs to an urban environment from a young age, they will learn to ignore a vast number of non-threatening stimuli that constantly bombard them.

Mila is a perfect example of a dog that was not properly socialised and habituated when she was young. Invariably she is very nervous around many sounds and noises, including thunder, fireworks and previously unencountered objects, including hairdryers, electric nail files, shavers, which I discovered during the last visit to the vet when they tried to shave her leg. Merely opening a drawer unexpectedly startles her, while unfamiliar situations make her exceedingly anxious.

Without a doubt, it takes considerably longer to acclimatise and countercondition an adult dog to various environmental stimuli than to introduce and condition a puppy to these elements before the onset of the fear response. Bearing this in mind, I must carefully choose my battles with Mila, as she fears so many things, it would be impossible to habituate and countercondition her to them all. My experience with thunder therapy has shown that even though it has taken months to reach a point where she can stay under threshold, she will never be completely comfortable with thunder and loud noises. She will always be anxious.

Environmental stimuli are things or events that evoke a specific functional reaction that elicits a physiological or psychological response and result in a profusion of neurons firing off in a dog's brain. Naturally, responding to various stimuli is vital to a dog's survival. However, responding to all of them may cause sensory overload, resulting in stress, anxiety, fear and aggression. If we do not habituate dogs to their environment, they will react to every stimulus, every sound, sight and smell, which is comparable to being continually in a fearful flight or fight mode. The more we expose our dogs to various stimuli, the more stable and reliable their response will be in the future.

On reflection, I recalled our move from Africa to Australia with Franky and Lulu. Due to strict Australian live animal import regulations, we had to quarantine the two dogs for seven months before they were allowed to take up residence in Australia. Initially, they spent half of their sentence at a small quarantine appointed kennels near Johannesburg in South Africa. Here they were prepared for their eventual entry to Australia following numerous, repeated blood tests, various physical examinations, additional vaccinations, and decontamination from any internal and external parasites.

Although there was minimal stimulation for the dogs during their South African kennelling, the staff tried to make their stay as pleasant as possible and incorporated one or two one-hour play sessions in a grassed yard, where an assistant would play with them daily. Unfortunately, after Franky and Lulu flew to Australia, I realised that the largest Australian quarantine centre at Eastern Creek near Sydney did not offer the same services. Instead, the station catered to ninety horses, seventy-two cats, birds, bees, plants and 597 dogs accommodated in long rows of pens, interspersed by large eucalyptus trees. These unhappy animals would lie in their enclosures day after day. Only the non-stop barking of other dogs encroached on their peace and with no mental or physical engagement, as quarantine staff were too busy to exercise or interact with them. Not surprisingly, during their stay, the quarantine staff advised me that Franky seemed depressed. This station was eventually closed in 2016 to make way for state-of-the-art facilities in other parts of the country.

Unfortunately, during their seven long months of enforced incarceration, I was only able to visit Franky and Lulu twice at the Johannesburg kennels and once in Australia. I'm not sure which was more heartbreaking, when the dogs tried to scratch their way through the gate to follow me, or when they gave up even trying.

Eventually, the Eastern Creek quarantine officers gave the dogs a clean bill of health. After the pet travel agency arranged their flight to Brisbane and additional road transport to Bribie Island, we were finally united. Naturally, I was overjoyed at our reunion and couldn't stop hugging and stroking them, and while Lulu bounced around me, equally ecstatic, Franky barely wagged her tail. After a few days of bonding and rest, Franky's tail perked up and the twinkle in her eyes returned.

Subsequently, with the very best of intentions, I decided that we would all enjoy a nice long walk along the esplanade, especially considering Franky's very rotund shape. Dachshunds are infamous for their gluttony, and Franky was no exception. Unfortunately, feeding times were unsupervised at the Australian quarantine facility and being a consummate opportunist, Franky often ate not only her food but also Lulu's.

Consequently, while Lulu was no more than skin and bones, Franky was exceedingly corpulent and needed to work off a few kilos. Bearing in mind that it was a weekend, people thronged the island where we lived. Easily accessible by a one-kilometre-long bridge, the island, a mere fifty-four kilometres from Brisbane, was popular with holidaymakers, sightseers, day-trippers and picnickers. Hordes of joggers, prams, children and cyclists packed the esplanade with a cacophony of noise and constant, unceasing motion. While Lulu pranced along fluidly in true Italian greyhound style with tail wagging, taking it all in her stride, Franky hunched over with 'whale eyes', shaking with her tail between her legs. After seven months of isolation, she was overwhelmed with terror; the outing was just too much for her.

During their seven-month detention, I missed both dogs and our daily walks. In my excitement to reintroduce them to the world, I underestimated Franky's mental state after so many months of sensory deprivation.

Following that disastrous outing, I was more thoughtful of her needs and realised that I had to reintroduce her gradually to habituate and socialise her to the outside world. Initially, I'd take her out for short periods on quiet days during the week when the esplanade was deserted, with fewer distractions to bombard her senses, until she was once again able to ignore non-threatening environmental stimuli.

Our daily walks in Botswana had lain down a solid foundation, and with a gentle and gradual refresher course, her rehabilitation did not take long. Soon Franky enjoyed our long daily walks along the esplanade with a spring in her step, and her head held high. Additionally, she also shed the extra weight. From this experience, I learnt that we cannot underestimate the importance of ongoing socialisation into adulthood.

Furthermore, multiple studies have shown that the effects of puppy socialisation wear off if we do not persevere with the process into adulthood and probably for the dog's life.

According to canine behaviourists, if well socialised three- to four-month-old puppies are subsequently kept in a kennel environment and deprived of stimuli until they are six to eight months of age, they will become shy of strangers. If we socialise a twelve-week-old puppy properly to children, it will require the socialisation to continue until it matures to achieve full benefits. Likewise, if we habituate a puppy to urban traffic in the first weeks of life but subsequently move it to a rural environment, the habituation will wear off without periodic exposure to the urban hustle and bustle. As a result, the dog can become fearful of something that it had previously accepted.

Confirmed research substantiates that in dogs of less than six months of age, the effects of socialisation can wear off if we halt the socialisation and subsequently deprive the dog of exposure to stimuli. A possible explanation for this is that many neural pathways forming in a puppy's brain are still developing, therefore if a channel is unused regularly, it may be overwritten by new experiences. A dog can learn for the length of its life, and even though you can teach old dogs' new tricks, new learning becomes more challenging with age. Therefore, it is crucial to reinforce socialisation skills and introduce new things regularly. Successful socialisation instils confidence in dogs, and a confident dog is a happy, well-adjusted pet.

Further illustrating the significance of habituating puppies to as many items as possible was the incident with Franky. At the time, we lived in Botswana, a very arid part of Africa on the edge of the Kalahari. For a large part of the year, from April to October, the area received no precipitation, and even though we got Franky as an eight-week-old puppy, in April, she was already eight months old when she first saw rain. Fortunately, this did not pose a problem other than a passing curiosity.

As always, I took Franky to work with me and while I drove to the office on a quiet Gaborone back road, millions of fat raindrops splattered on the windshield, obscuring my view, and, naturally, in the circumstances, I turned on the wipers. Unexpectedly, my gentle little dachshund exploded into killer Dobermann mode. Accompanied by furious barking, she snarled and flashed her teeth as she tried to slaughter the offending wipers from inside the car. Although I stopped the car and tried to pacify Franky, she wouldn't calm down if the windscreen wipers were on.

From that day onwards, the windscreen wipers always sent her into a murderous frenzy. Now I know that if I had habituated Franky to the windscreen wipers soon after we got her, I could have avoided her rage and anxiety. At the time, I was also unaware of desensitisation, counterconditioning techniques or how to manage her environment. With new understanding, I realise that there were other alternatives to control her surroundings successfully. Even if I had acclimatised Franky to a travelling box from where she wouldn't have a view of the wipers, she would have travelled much calmer and more comfortably. Merely by managing their environment, we can often quickly correct issues before they become insurmountable problems.

Despite the importance of keeping puppies close to their mothers during the early development period, researchers believe that mild stress, such as brief separation from their mother or daily handling of puppies during the neonatal period, seems to have a positive impact on stress resilience. It also leads to enhanced motor and problem-solving skills, faster maturation of the nervous system, accelerated body growth, and may even boost resistance to various diseases. Additionally, puppies exposed to multiple stimuli from birth to five weeks became more confident, inquisitive and socially dominant than unstimulated puppies. Moreover, puppies handled daily, from three to twenty-one days after birth, were calmer, more prone to explore, and gave fewer distress calls in eight-week-old puppy isolation tests than unhandled littermates. Similar studies on the effects of early stimulation in puppies concluded that introducing short amounts of mild stress, such as being put on cold surfaces, etc., may activate hormonal and neural systems, making the puppy more resistant to stress later in life.

Initially, researchers suggested mild stress may cause an adaptive change in the puppy's hypothalamic pituitary adrenal (HPA) system, which would account for better stress control in adulthood. On the other hand, recent studies indicate that mothers seem to groom and lick puppies who have undergone mild stress more than unstressed puppies. Possibly, the extra attention can suppress a pup's HPA response. The main factors of HPA axis activity are genetic background and early-life environment. How a mother behaves towards her offspring has a lasting effect on the development of physiological and behavioural responses to stress later in life.

Conversely, with specific reference to humans, early life stress is one of the most distinct and unequivocal environmental risk factors for a host of chronic ailments in later life, including metabolic and psychiatric disorders. Unfortunately, we still know very little about the effects of early life stress (ELS) during the neonatal and subsequent periods and their influence on adult domestic dogs.

However, we know that one of the most critical parts of a dog's education is learning about bite inhibition from its mother and littermates. If we remove puppies from their mother and litter at an early age, they fail to learn essential lessons, including bite inhibition. Accordingly, we see some of the worst cases of inadequate bite inhibition in singletons and puppies removed too early from the litter.

Bite inhibition is the foundation of the socialisation process; it is not just a matter of safety but also about acquiring the necessary skills to become polite members of society. A dog that has not learnt to inhibit its bite can cause damage even when playing. On the other hand, a dog with a soft mouth that can control its bite can prevent damage even when it is angry or stressed.

These lessons start during the weaning process when the mother disciplines her puppy if it becomes overzealous with its sharp teeth when nursing. She may growl and bare her teeth at the puppy and may even grab its muzzle in her mouth in a checked bite as a warning of inappropriate or rough behaviour. This discipline usually results in an immediate understanding of the rules, as only a mother can teach them. Eventually, the puppies learn to heed these threats by rolling onto their backs and showing their bellies in a classic submission pose. The mother will usually respond by licking the puppies.

Littermates also provide additional reinforcement if a sibling delivers a painful play-bite and yelp in pain as they move away from the offender. While his littermates shun him, the puppy quickly realises that its unacceptable actions have ended the game. In this way, a puppy soon learns to be more careful.

In addition, these valuable lessons teach the puppy impulse control, so it does not use the full arsenal of its flashing sharp teeth and learns to inhibit its bite. If the puppy learns these lessons well, it will not use the maximum force of its bite potential as an adult, even when stressed or excited. Unfortunately, puppies removed from their mother in the transitional stage of their life will never learn these vital lessons from her and the litter.

Thousands of case studies show that dogs with inadequate, or no bite inhibition have caused exceedingly severe injuries. Fortunately, even though most dogs are likely to experience unpleasant, painful or stressful incidents, they will control their bite with the proper bite inhibition and won't cause any damage.

For example, if we step on a dog by accident, it will probably yelp in pain, but with appropriate bite inhibition, it will not bite the offender. On the other hand, a child might trip over a dog and receive disfiguring injuries if the dog has no bite inhibition. Dog trainers and experts warn about the dangers of dogs with no bite inhibition, with good reasons. Dogs with no bite inhibition are unpredictable and dangerous not just to humans but also to other dogs.

To pre-empt any tragic incidents, dog behaviourists advise us to enrol our pups in bite inhibition and puppy training classes as soon as we receive them to teach them bite inhibition before it is too late. As a result, puppy schools are mushrooming all over the world. Experts like Ian Dunbar believe that one hour of puppy school has much more impact on the puppy, and the force of its bite, than one week of training at home with its owner. Although not all puppy classes are created equal, finding a good one is essential. Additionally, we should bear in mind that the emphasis should be on enjoying human company and not uncontrolled playing between puppies, which may do more harm than good.

Some controversy does exist regarding the effectiveness of such puppy classes, as owners usually enrol their puppies after the age of eight weeks, by which time these interactions typically peak. Although, even after they go to their new homes, puppies are notorious mouthers and nippers, and it is the responsibility of the new owners to guide them towards acceptable behaviour.

Generally, new doggy parents fear exposing a young unvaccinated puppy to certain stimuli due to the risk of contracting various deadly diseases and viruses. Although puppies acquire some immunity from their mother's placenta and milk, which protects them in the early weeks, this usually wears off when they are six weeks old and by the time they receive their first vaccination. Complete immunity will only come into effect a week after their second vaccination, by the age of thirteen weeks.

Before a puppy is fully immunised, doggy carriers, shoulder harnesses or doggy backpacks could come in handy. During this vulnerable period, these devices allow us to take puppies out and about, meet and greet people, and introduce them to a wide range of stimuli and experiences without being on the ground exposed to dangerous infections and viruses.

The consensus seems to be that not socialising a puppy that may grow into a dog with far-reaching behaviour problems far outweighs any minimal risk of the puppy contracting a contagious disease if introduced to people and other dogs responsibly and with care.

During this time, the more significant part of a puppy's socialisation will involve humans, probably in the dog's own home where there is no risk of infection if visitors take off their shoes. When owners introduce puppies to humans in public places, they should carry them and not place them on the ground, minimising any risk of infection. Of course, we can also socialise puppies with healthy, vaccinated dogs in a secure yard, where only vaccinated dogs live. On the other hand, owners should not walk puppies in parks or areas where dogs have urinated or defecated, nor should they allow puppies to mix with dogs of unknown vaccination status until they are fully immunised.

Overwhelmingly, puppies are expected to become familiar with an extensive amount of stimuli as soon as possible to live and cope in our wide-ranging world. There are many socialisation checklists on the internet. Some list as many as 300 items, including a hundred people of all shapes, sizes and colours; a hundred different encounters with dogs; and a hundred different experiences to be fulfilled by the time the puppy is twelve weeks old. If dogs do not become bombproof at an early age, they may become antisocial and challenging to train as they get older. The lack of early socialisation may indeed cause severe fears and phobias towards a wide range of things, including people, conspecifics, children, bikes, prams, basically anything that they have never encountered or been exposed to in the past.

Furthermore, dogs with restricted experiences do not reach their full potential, whereas dogs exposed to a broad range of experiences show improved skills. Limited social exposure during the socialisation period can lead to aggressive behaviour in adult dogs; the extent of deprivation and lack of socialisation a dog suffers from is directly proportional to the magnitude of the maladjustment. If a dog has had no exposure to certain stimuli at the end of the sensitive period, it will always be fearful of it. On the other hand, if it has had some but insufficient exposure, it will be better adjusted but not entirely stable, unlike a dog with adequate exposure during the sensitive period, which will become bombproof.

Because one never gets back the critical socialisation period, some behaviourists encourage new owners to take time off work for a few weeks to socialise their puppies properly. Furthermore, they also argue that although taking time off is inconvenient, it is nothing compared to spending countless hours trying to eliminate behavioural issues later in life. Taking time off work could also prevent the need to hire a dog behaviourist in the future, to stop their dog from running away, chewing up furniture, and acting aggressive and insecure.

Whereas I see the necessity of early learning and a well-socialised dog, I don't believe that one should rush around in a frenzy, trying to tick everything off these lists. Instead, owners should enjoy this time with their new puppy and not become despondent if they cannot introduce their puppy to all the experiences mentioned on these checklists. The process should be fun, gentle and stress-free; after all, they are dogs, not robots.

As you know, good Samaritans found Mila wandering the streets of a country town. Under the circumstances, it was safe to assume that she had never previously encountered an elevator. Initially, Mila was highly dubious about the strange contraption and approached it fearfully. Gradually, I enticed her far enough that she could grab a treat from me before she withdrew to safety. In time she managed to enter and stay in the lift, and, eventually, we could travel between floors.

Mila learnt to associate a ride in the box with treats, outings, including day care, and agility training upstairs. Either way, good things happen after we travel in this contraption, a clear-cut case of classical conditioning. Now I don't even need to give her any treats; she queues up impatiently when I say 'lift'.

Additionally, following our purchase of a new robotic lawnmower, I was curious to see what Mila would make of it. Initially, she barked at it, although the novelty soon wore off when she realised that it was not a threat, and she soon became habituated to it. Now she ignores it. With the right incentive, old/er dogs *can* learn new tricks and become used to new experiences without too much fuss.

If Mila had been subject to an unpleasant experience with a lift or Robomow in the past, training her would have been more difficult. Although, both the lift and the Robomow are silent. Had they been noisy, it is questionable whether Mila would have got used to them, as she has an ingrained fear of loud noises. When rehabilitating fearful dogs that have been deprived of stimulation, we can use counterconditioning, although prevention, as always, is better than the cure.

CHAPTER 13
CHOOSING THE RIGHT BREED

Now that I knew Mila's full genetic background, I had a broader palette of options to choose from, bearing in mind the dominant behaviour characteristics inherited from dachshund and spaniel breeds. Although her ancestors also included Jack Russell terrier, she inherited few physical attributes such as her natural bobtail, some skeletal features, the texture of her fur on her tummy, but no Jack Russell traits.

When feasible, we should find out as much about our dog as we can. If we examine the types of dogs used to create a particular breed, its history and its purpose, we can often explain various inherent behaviour traits. Dogs are not created equal. Although they are all cute as puppies, some breeds will be more energetic when they grow up, while others may be prone to barking or predisposed to copious shedding or genetic diseases. A significant amount will be wary of strangers or other dogs, whereas others will be easier to train.

Without a doubt, it is just as important to select the

right breed of dog as it is to choose the right breeder. Knowing how a particular dog can adapt to different living conditions, how easy it is to train, and how much exercise and grooming it requires all impact our choices. For instance, if we have an aversion to dog hair, we should choose low-shedding breeds like the bichon frise or poodle. Many active breeds like the border collie, vizsla and Jack Russell-type dogs require eighty to ninety minutes of intense exercise a day and make splendid jogging buddies. On the other hand, if we prefer a couch potato, then the bulldog is an excellent choice, but not if we dislike dog drool.

A further consideration is where we intend to house and keep our dog, indoors or outside, in a large yard or small apartment, where we may prefer a smaller dog that is not overly vocal.

Some breeds are notoriously hard to housetrain, while others dislike being left alone and are prone to separation anxiety disorders. Although virtually all dogs can become loving family members if well socialised and trained from an early age, not all may be suitable for families with small children. At the same time, experts do not recommend various breeds for inexperienced owners. There are other variables to consider, especially genetic health issues, the lifespan of the dog and its intelligence.

Stanley Coren's dog intelligence ranking, which he based on how quickly each breed understands a new command and how often they obey the first command, has generated much interest. Ranked in the top tier, the brightest dogs include the border collie, poodle, German shepherd, golden retriever and Dobermann pinscher.

These breeds understand new commands after less than five repetitions and obey the first command 95% of the time or better.

Even though Mila looks like a dachshund, the dominant part of her genetic make-up is the English and cocker spaniel family, which is in the second tier ranked within the top twenty-five and is regarded as an excellent working dog. Based on my own experience with Mila, I can confirm that she understands new commands after five to fifteen repetitions and obeys the first command 85% of the time or better.

At the same time, dachshunds in the third tier rank forty-ninth and are considered an average working and obedience breed. They understand new commands after twenty-five to forty repetitions and obey the first command 50% of the time or better.

In comparison, the Italian greyhound in the fifth tier is ranked sixtieth and is considered a fair working and obedience dog. IGs understand new commands after forty to eighty repetitions and obey the first command 30% of the time or better.

Once again, I believe it is just a matter of motivation. For example, Lulu loved raspberries, and we grew a few bushes in the family villa garden. In summer, Lulu accompanied me on our daily tour of the grounds and helped inspect the crop. Without fail, Lulu would execute a lightning-fast sit in anticipation of her favourite fruit, after only one repetition, 100% of the time. Similarly, she was obsessed with playing ball, and she knew that we'd only throw the ball when she sat. As a result, we never had to repeat the sit command twice.

As I mentioned in an earlier chapter, there was a noticeable difference between how quickly Mila learnt to ring the doggy doorbell compared to Lulu. Lulu was no whizz at obedience or problem-solving, probably because I didn't find the right motivation. I'm sure that had I offered her cooked chicken, she'd have been much more willing to try anything.

In contrast, Lulu's talent lay in understanding speech. Usually, when we spoke to Lulu or asked her something, it would be in a specific tone, like talking to a child. I always believed that dogs understood our intonation rather than our words. Yet when the family conversed normally with each other, Lulu always reacted instantly whenever she recognised specific words or phrases. Often, we had to spell out certain words, when speaking to each other, so Lulu wouldn't understand them.

Over the years, scientists have shown that dogs do respond to familiar words. They were, however, unsure of how dogs organise this information. Recently Hungarian researchers using magnetic resonance imaging (MRI) discovered that dogs process speech in the same order as humans and share the task between both brain hemispheres. First, the right hemisphere recognises and processes tone, and then the left hemisphere processes the meaning of more complex known words and phrases.

Even though many dogs show a tremendous aptitude in distinguishing the relevance of certain words, they do not understand language. However, had I appreciated Lulu's talent at the time, I could have trained her to expand her vocabulary.

Naturally, human nature dictates a curiosity to know how smart our dog is, so the rankings list is hard to resist. Stanley Coren's test assesses adaptive intelligence and measures how quickly a dog can solve new problems and how well it can learn and benefit from these experiences within its environment. It also appraises social awareness, reading facial expressions and recognising frequent visitors, according to Coren. How well a dog performs a job and how easily we can shape its instinctive intelligence into functional skills is directly affected by how quickly the dog picks up social cues and how quickly it learns. These skills become more apparent when combining multiple commands as required in various activities, including agility, obedience course work and guide work. How well we can develop and mould a dog's skills depends mainly on a dog's adaptive intelligence.

As with all things canine, some experts dispute the soundness of Coren's tests. One of the first people to study the intelligence of dogs in the early twentieth century was Edward Thorndike, who primarily concentrated on canine problem-solving abilities. Most of the experiments involved placing dogs in puzzle boxes. Dogs used in the studies could open these from the inside if they could find and release the opening mechanism, usually by unintentionally stepping on a lever, or pawing open a bolt at the top of the door, etc.

Based on these experiments, Thorndike came up with the concept of trial-and-error learning, which is a cornerstone of operant conditioning and requires no insight or problem-solving skills. Even though the variety of problems on the test does acknowledge that intelligence is multi-faceted, some experts believe that scientifically, the test is questionable. Another debatable issue is Coren's theory that dogs scoring low on the IQ test may be stubborn, unwilling to follow orders and more challenging to teach.

However, the well-respected primatologist and ethologist Frans de Waal suggested that dogs with low IQs are independent-minded and are therefore unwilling to follow orders blindly but are just as intelligent as other dogs. Possibly that is the reason people assume that dogs are more intelligent than independent-thinking cats who would score quite dismally on an obedience test.

Based on my experience with an Afghan hound, I'd have to agree with Frans de Waal. When a friend who was relocating from Botswana to another country offered me her eight-month-old Afghan hound, I decided to take her. Despite not knowing anything about the breed, as we still lived in the Dark Ages before the internet, this stunning dog had always fascinated me. Until then, I'd been used to overly effusive lapdogs, whereas Mandy was aloof and mostly ignored me.

She also fulfilled her reputation as an adept escape artist and flew over the waist-high fence that surrounded the rented property we lived in at the time. Once she was out, there was no way to recall her. When I tried to contain her inside the house, she worked out how to open the windows. There was no restraining her, which was getting her into trouble.

Gaborone was a semi-rural settlement at the time, and it was not unusual to see livestock, cows, goats or donkeys roaming the streets. Although our neighbours only kept chickens, they were far from impressed when Mandy jumped over our fence and landed in their yard. They often complained that Mandy chased their poultry. Also, young African children used to the Tswana village dogs were unnerved by Mandy's appearance and threw stones at her when she went absent without leave, which also concerned me.

One day, hoping to find a compromise, I drove Mandy to the office with me several kilometres away. She sat in the passenger seat of my green VW taking in the quiet main road and clean-swept dusty yards; the only splashes of colour were the odd flowering bougainvillea adorning the functional houses we passed. My office was on the first floor of a low-slung, nondescript building where I worked for a cattle farmer, as a Jill of all trades. Although Mandy behaved well, she did not like being cooped up and didn't settle. It is exasperating to keep a high prey drive dog constrained in a small office all day. Bearing this in mind, I did not repeat the exercise and never took her to work with me again.

Several weeks later, buried under a mountain of correspondence, I heard a scratching noise on my office door, which I ignored. When the scratching continued, I started to get annoyed and flung the door open. I expected to find a friend or children playing a prank and had not anticipated that my uninvited guest would be Mandy sitting in the corridor. At the time, I was unaware that Afghan hounds were initially used for hunting and were highly prized for their ability to think and hunt independently, without human supervision. She had another useful attribute, similar to a boomerang or a homing pigeon: she always returned. No matter how far she wandered, she seemed to have had a built-in GPS and never got lost. Without fail, she found her way home.

Mandy repeatedly astonished me with her intelligence and her ability to solve problems. Based on her ability to open windows and locate my office without being trained, I found it hard to believe that Afghans and beagles are only in the seventh tier, in the bottom ten of Coren's dog IQ list. The dubious honour for the lowest ranking, based on working and obedience intelligence and understanding new commands after eighty to one hundred repetitions and obeying the first command 25% of the time or worse, goes to the Afghan hound at number seventy-nine. As a matter of interest, the clever little beagles are ranked seventy-two.

Similarly, as an advocate of dachshunds, I can substantiate that they are brilliant strategists, worthy of a higher ranking on the IQ list than forty-ninth.

One day, Franky had a pressing problem. My lap was not a free-for-all, which Lulu did not seem to understand. Franky had reserved this unique location for her own use as a privilege of seniority, but Lulu always had selective memory when respecting Franky's possessions or wishes. The problem Franky faced was how to unseat Lulu after she impudently occupied my lap without resorting to a bloody battle. Deep in thought, Franky sat down in front of us and pondered the matter. A few minutes later, she jumped up, ran to the toy box and came bounding back with the squeakiest toy she could find. Deliriously happy, Franky bounced and twirled in front of us, having a wonderful time playing with her toy, all the while completely ignoring Lulu. True to her breed characteristics, Lulu refused to be ignored or left out of anything, and not to be outdone, she leapt off my lap to join Franky in her high jinks. No sooner than Lulu's feet touched the ground, Franky sprang up into my lap and left a bewildered Lulu wondering what just happened. I had never seen a dog work out such an elaborate plan before.

Allegedly, dogs do not have a theory of mind, which is an understanding of others' mental states, beliefs and knowledge that differs from their own. Over time researchers have speculated whether an animal can predict the behaviour of others. Seeing this display with my own eyes, I am a firm believer that Franky did have a rudimentary theory of mind to gauge what would motivate Lulu to leave my lap. When comparing puzzle-solving abilities, dogs are not as skilled as wolves, but I think that both Mandy and Franky did very well at resolving their specific, unique issues. Although dachshunds are bred as a badger hound and hunting dog, their remarkable skills required independent thinking and action, not blind obedience.

Furthermore, according to Coren's intelligence test, one of Hungary's national treasures, the corded coated puli, is rated in the third tier, thirty-third amongst the above-average working dogs. Apparently, they learn a new trick after fifteen to twenty-five repetitions and obey at least 70% of the time. Yet, ask any puli owner, and they will attest to the breed's unrivalled intelligence. Puli aficionados unanimously agree that these dogs are not just above average; they are extraordinary.

While the puli's origins are a tad nebulous, the various theories reaching back centuries are hard to prove. However, we do know that the puli came into the Carpathian basin with the nomadic Magyars when they settled there in 895 AD. The very existence of these ancient people depended on their working dogs, on which they relied so heavily. The puli is a natural shepherd and instinctively knows how to herd livestock. It often does the work of three or four men and usually works in tandem with the similar-looking, albeit larger and less well-known komondor. As a team, the puli herds and guards the flock during the day, while the komondor guards and protects during the night. If a puli sounds the alarm, several komondors will run to its aid, ready to defend the herd and deter intruders and predators.

As a herding dog, experts hold the puli in exceedingly high esteem. An authority on the puli, Suk Dezsö, wrote the following:

> *As a sheep herder this little genius is an absolute dream. There is no doubt that it is indispensable, and generally speaking, it is impossible to replace them with humans. There is no other dog in the world that is as intelligent and quick to learn. I've seen a puli guard 400 sheep, independently without a shepherd, on a 27-acre pasture, which was no wider than 150 meters, and was surrounded by wheat fields on all sides. Despite this, the sheep did not even get one mouthful of wheat. One can truly say that the only thing this dog cannot do is talk. It understands everything, not just words, but even the slightest expression on its owner's face.*

It is, therefore, no surprise that people fall in love with the puli. These small-medium, lively dogs make fabulous family pets and are very gentle with children. Although this proud little dog is often reserved with strangers and can be somewhat independent, they fearlessly guard their owner's property. Not only are they good-natured and exuberant, but they are also fiercely dedicated to their family.

Additionally, they can also be sensitive and will not tolerate harsh treatment; they are therefore only recommended for experienced owners. This high-energy dog needs lots of physical and mental stimulation and does very well in agility, and, not surprisingly, at herding. Even border collie enthusiasts are awestruck when watching a puli herd sheep. Typically, border collies are bred to handle a smaller flock of sheep, whereas the puli can handle up to 400 or more. Puppy parents should purchase puli puppies, like all other dogs, from a reputable breeder who will ensure that the parents undergo health clearances for various conditions, including hip dysplasia and PRA. The corded coat does not shed; however, the puli's eye-catching dreadlocks can be challenging to keep clean if left to grow long, and it can take up to two to three days for the locks to dry completely after a bath. Consequently, many owners keep their puli's coat clipped, incurring the wrath of puli purists, who believe that a short coat detracts from the breed's natural characteristics.

During WWI and WWII, enemy soldiers indiscriminately killed dogs on sight lest their barking alerted others to their presence. These actions almost annihilated the puli population as well as the other Hungarian dog breeds. Fortunately, there was already a healthy breeding population outside of Hungary, and due to tireless conservation efforts within Hungary, this breed's future is now secure. This delightful little dog is gaining popularity worldwide. Independent puli clubs have mushroomed in various European countries, the USA, Canada and Australia. Additionally, celebrities like Mark Zuckerberg have also become puli converts, making this little dog even more popular. In 2017, the Hungarian Parliament declared all nine Hungarian dog breeds as 'National Treasures', including the puli, which remains a source of intense national pride.

Based on the above, it is no surprise that some experts dispute whether Coren's assessment measures actual intelligence. Various studies have demonstrated that the discrepancy in intelligence is based on the difference in a dog's motivation, nature, attentiveness and basic sensory capabilities.

For instance, working dogs are highly motivated and are bred for alertness, and are more likely to establish connections between things going on in their surroundings. On the other hand, dogs such as beagles and foxhounds are bred to focus on tracking scents without being distracted, which makes them somewhat inattentive to matters of social interaction. Consequently, scenthounds will be less interested in noticing or rushing to obey their owners.

Some people believe that IQ tests may be another way of humanising our pets, although the scientific community do not consider surveys as conclusive evidence. Even though IQ evaluations are fun and may shed additional light on our dog's abilities, it does seem that the validity of Coren's IQ test may be questionable.

As researchers undertake new intelligence studies at universities worldwide, they realise that just because not all breeds are Skinnerian automatons, they are all equally intelligent in their own right. Each breed has uniquely wired brains with breed-specific behaviour conformations that predispose them to accomplish specific jobs they perform better than other breeds.

After all, the border collie is brilliant at herding sheep, while the Alaskan malamute excels at pulling a sleigh. On the other hand, the German shepherd's talents lie in guarding, and let us not forget the talented little detection dog, the beagle. Each breed is exceptional, a genius in its field. Who can say that one is more intelligent than the other?

Typically, a breed's history defines its genetic predisposition towards certain traits, and we should always bear these in mind when selecting a dog. In addition, over decades, humans have shaped the domestic dog's appearance and behaviour, which breeders often determine. While many dogs are suitable for novices, power breeds are only recommended for experienced owners. Unfortunately, numerous dogs are bred to execute the kill-bite and for impulsive, uncontrolled aggression. The kill-bite and unrestrained ferocity are most certainly genetically determined in several breeds. These include pit bull-type dogs, the American Staffordshire terrier, English bull terrier and American bulldog, all initially bred for bull-baiting and dog fights.

An example of a power breed with its genetics steeped in aggression is the Fila Brasileiro. During the seventeenth century, Portuguese colonists established large sugar, cotton and rubber estates in Brazil. At the time, ranchers were desperate for massive amounts of human labour to run the plantations, which they resolved when they imported over three million African slaves to Brazil. Naturally, most slaves refused to accept their enforced servitude gracefully, and, consequently, countless thousands escaped and disappeared into the jungle. The plantation owners wanted to find an efficient means of tracking the runaway slaves, and with this in mind, some ranchers decided to tailor-make a new dog breed.

They chose various elements from several breeds, including the English mastiff for toughness and size, the English bulldog for ferocity, the bloodhound for its tracking abilities and Portuguese guard dogs, to create a custom-made hound with all the appropriate physical and behavioural characteristics. Subsequently, with the successful crossbreeding of the above dogs, they designed the Fila Brasileiro, which became well known for its distinctive method of capturing slaves by their neck and holding them down till their masters arrived. '*Filar*' in Portuguese means 'hold, arrest, grab', indicating that it is a dog that grabs and holds. Although, some people believe that the Fila Brasileiro were not explicitly intended to catch and return runaway slaves, but rather to rip them apart on the spot, as a lesson to other slaves and to discourage further escapes.

Over the years, the Fila Brasileiro acclimatised to Brazilian conditions and is one of the most heat-tolerant of all mastiff-type dogs. It also gained natural resistance to diseases and parasites in the region. After Princess Isabel officially abolished slavery in 1888, ranchers throughout

Brazil utilised the Fila Brasileiro as guard dogs and even for hunting game, such as jaguar and cougar. The Fila had excellent tracking skills and the size and power to capture any predator that was threatening livestock. The breed has earned a reputation of being highly aggressive, which various factions hotly dispute.

Fila authorities claim that they only became aggressive due to the indiscriminate and reckless breeding practices of the twentieth century. The dog is known for its '*ojeriza*', now a breed standard, which states that Fila Brasileiro should not tolerate the approach or the touch of strangers. Indeed, the Fila Brasileiro despise strangers. With their 45–81kg frame, they are more suited to rural life, where they have space to work off their energy. At present, they are mainly used as guard dogs and are bred for high levels of human aggression, especially in Brazil.

A few breeders began importing Fila Brasileiro to Europe and the USA, where a number of these dogs were involved in severe attacks. Due to its hostile and antagonistic nature, the Fila has been banned in numerous countries, including the UK, Australia, Israel, Denmark, Malta and Cyprus. On the other hand, these dogs can be intensely loyal and affectionate with their family when suitably raised and bred; they become outstanding protectors. Without a doubt, with an experienced owner able to devote a massive amount of time to socialise and train this breed, the Fila Brasileiro can make a superb companion and watchdog.

Besides the Fila Brasileiro, farmers worldwide created several other large, powerful dogs such as the Boerboel in southern Africa, known to defend their homestead against lions, leopards and other dangerous wildlife. Additionally, the striking Dogo Argentino was used as a guard dog and for hunting big game, while ranchers traditionally used the Presa Canario to herd cattle. These breeds, including the Tosa, which the Japanese initially bred for fighting, have high prey drives, distrust strangers and are considered aggressive, which is why professional dogfighters capitalise on and exploit these dogs in fighting pits.

With unethical and indiscriminate breeding practices, lack of socialisation and training, they can all prove deadly, resulting in many governments banning these breeds worldwide. However, studies have shown that one of the results of banning so-called dangerous breeds has been to increase their attractiveness to the wrong people. One of the most common reasons for dangerous breed dog ownership is using dogs as weapons, breeding for financial gain and dogfighting. *The Irish Examiner* described Rottweilers as 'time bombs on legs'. At the same time, the Supreme Court of Kansas designated pit bulls as 'public hazards'; however, the origins contributing to stereotype views on breeds and aggression require a more in-depth inspection.

Without a doubt, breeders hold the highest responsibility, as they decide which dogs will mate to create the next generation. Would-be dog parents should always obtain puppies from reputable breeders. I cannot stress this enough. With power breeds, we have an added responsibility to be even more prudent because of their natural aggression and distrust of strangers. Additionally, it is vital to manage their energy levels. It is not an option but is compulsory to provide these dogs with plenty of mental and physical stimulation. Along with early and ongoing obedience training, including lessons to reinforce bite inhibition and consistent and early socialisation, power breeds can make loyal pets and outstanding guard dogs. These breeds are not for novices and require firm, confident owners to help achieve their full potential as stable and well-adjusted family members. However, some experts believe that regardless of how we raise these dogs, it is impossible to remove the aggressive behaviour traits from their genes, just as we cannot remove the stalk from a border collie.

With global demand for assertive guard dogs, especially where violent crime is rife, competition amongst backyard breeders and puppy mills is fierce. Recently, various UK studies have concluded that gangs keep dangerous dogs as expensive status symbols and to maintain their image as enforcers. Gang members as young as seventeen years old are indiscriminately breeding dangerous breeds and trading them as commodities or selling puppies for £2,000 each, providing a lucrative income. These unscrupulous profiteers disregard responsible breeding practices and cash in on certain violent subcultures where aggressive dogs have become a popular, lethal, albeit legal accessory. On the whole, inexperienced owners often try to exaggerate the already vicious traits of their dogs by training them with physical abuse and exposing them to all manner of cruelties, exacerbating the problem further.

While it is true that certain breeds are undeniably more disposed towards hostile tendencies, these traits can occur in many other domestic pets if they don't have adequate stimulation as well as early and ongoing socialisation, even in dachshunds and Chihuahuas. Similarly, if we train dogs using punishment and negative reinforcement or mistreat them, they may become fearful and more likely to become aggressive.

Remember the limbic system?

As we know, this complicated system plays a vital role in learning and memory. It is responsible for how a dog understands and responds to its experiences and the environment around it. The more negative events, such as punishment, a dog experiences, the more anxious and aggressive it is likely to become. A dog may also become hostile if it is ill and in pain.

New dog parents should remember that the type of dog they choose does make a difference and must fit in with their living arrangements, training abilities and energy levels. For example, it is pointless buying a dachshund just because it is cute, only to find out later that it is prone to very loud barking, which will drive its owners up the wall. My own experiences have taught me not to act on emotion and be very circumspect when choosing a new dog.

While we lived in Gaborone for many years, I fantasised about owning an Irish wolfhound. Their imposing height was a huge attraction. Being the tallest dog, they can easily reach over two metres when standing on their hind legs. Additionally, I admired their natural yet gentle majesty. Wolfhounds are not an everyday breed, and when I heard of a breeder nearby with available puppies, I was overjoyed and booked an appointment to view these noble giants up close and personal. Undoubtedly, this is an incredible breed, and owing to their sweet and gentle disposition, they make good family dogs, although owners should contain them in a large, fenced yard as they have a high prey drive. With early socialisation, they will be courteous towards other household pets and put up with the family cat. However, outside animals will remain fair game.

Coming face to face with these massive, sensitive hounds, I realised that I had not considered several practicalities, including how on earth I would transport a fully grown dog in my VW Beetle. No, it did not have a sunroof. How would I bath it? With a minimum weight of 54kg, how could I lift it if it was sick or hurt?

From experience, I know how stressful and heartbreaking it is to lose a well-beloved family pet after fifteen-odd years, but bearing in mind the Irish wolfhound's life span, we would only have six to eight years together. Even though Irish wolfhounds are considered healthy, because of their size, they can be predisposed to additional health issues such as hip and elbow dysplasia, liver shunt, heart disease, fibrocartilaginous embolic myelopathy, osteochondrosis dissecans, osteosarcoma and progressive retinal atrophy. With the lack of available specialised veterinary care in our area, this was also a concern. Although, a good breeder will test puppies and their parents for specific conditions and provide the necessary health clearances.

Another substantial issue that I had failed to consider, the *pièce de résistance*, was the size of their poop. Forget the pooper scooper; they were shovel size.

Alas, I realised that as much as I admired the dog's dignified bearing and size, there were too many issues that I had not considered. For this reason, it is imperative to make sure we find out as much as possible before we purchase any dogs. Had I been as circumspect before accepting Mandy, the Afghan hound, I might never have agreed to take her, as I could not meet all her needs and did not have the resources to provide a secure environment for her. Alas, I had to rehome her, which has remained a source of remorse ever since.

A further anecdote involved my parents, who lived on a fenced property on a large cattle farm just outside Gaborone at the time. The farm was home to free-ranging cattle and a profusion of game, including impala, kudu, warthog and guinea fowl.

At some point, my parents accepted a honey-coloured puppy of unidentifiable origins, which they believed was a cross between a Great Dane and a retriever. In time, Jacky grew up to be a large, very handsome and incredibly talented snake dog. Although he disliked strangers, he loved to chase game whenever someone left a gate open, for which the owner of the ranch often chastised him. Upon reflection, considering Jacky's prey drive and other characteristics, I cannot help but wonder whether the dog's genetics didn't also include an amount of Rhodesian ridgeback. These dogs are intelligent with a high prey drive and require an experienced owner who can be consistent and firm.

Unaccustomed to large dogs, my father was neither. Always a schemer, my father decided that he wanted to keep free-ranging chickens on the property and ordered one hundred-day-old chickens from neighbouring South Africa, which arrived hale and hearty a few days later. True to his plan, he released the adorable little bundles of fluff that resembled yellow marigolds running in different directions over the green lawn. Due to a previous commitment, my parents had to go out, and on their return, several hours later, they were faced with Jacky amidst one hundred motionless little marigolds. I'm sure he didn't mean to kill the chicks but enjoyed his game of catch and release while it lasted. Alas, my father had not considered Jacky's instinctive urges, including prey drive, nor had he appropriately managed Jacky's or rather the chicks' environment, which could have avoided the massacre.

An additional trait of Jacky's that we found fascinating at the time was that he was racist. He was fine around Europeans, but whenever my parents had African guests, Jacky became uncontrollably aggressive, and they had to restrain him. This behaviour of Jacky's was quite embarrassing, as the visitors were often VIPs with an entourage of security staff, who waited outside while the restrained Jacky continued his aggressive and violent barking.

When I mentioned the matter to various friends, they recounted similar problems with their dogs, yet none of us raised our dogs to be discriminative, so we were quite perplexed. Now, of course, with hindsight, I realise that the reason for the racist problem was that the majority of dogs belonging to Europeans were not adequately socialised to Africans. Before the era of security systems, dogs were purchased from European breeders specifically as guard dogs to deter intruders, and their owners kept them on two-metre-high walled properties. Socialisation was not on the agenda. Therefore, the dogs became accustomed to their European family and their European friends but mixed less with Africans, hence their aggressive reaction to the unfamiliar.

Our understanding of dogs has come a long way. However, I'm still embarrassed by how ignorant we were several decades ago, which reminded me of an incident in Botswana with our black and white bull terrier.

We obtained Brandy as a puppy, and she grew up into a happy, friendly, playful dog who seemed to get on well with our family bunny. Naturally, I introduced them to each other, and they kept in touch daily through the picket fence, where Bunny had her own fenced-off enclosure. The first time Bunny tunnelled under the gate and came hop-hopping onto the veranda where she'd often find us, I nearly had a heart attack, bearing in mind Brandy's reputation with cats and other furry animals. Fortunately, Brandy didn't hurt Bunny and seemed more inclined to play with her. Despite refilling the tunnel, Bunny quickly dug a new one. Eventually, her luck with Brandy ran out, as one fine morning, I found Bunny's dismembered body on the lawn. I'm not sure whether Bunny had a suicidal death wish, but as we can see, Brandy was more than willing to oblige. Unfortunately, we sorely underestimated Brandy's natural prey drive, although when we were present, she was fine with Bunny, until one day, she was not.

During our time in Botswana, everyone who resided in a house kept at least one outside guard dog, mostly Boerboels, Rottweilers, Dobermanns and Staffordshire bull terriers. Because of the high crime rate, their owners did not socialise these dogs precisely because their purpose was to be wary of strangers and aggressively discourage intruders. Nevertheless, most were polite with visitors when their owners were present, which lulled me into a false sense of security. Usually, I have a healthy respect for large dogs, but when I visited my friend Julia, I did not give the Rottweiler sitting in the garden a second glance. Actually, I did give it a few glimpses, but because it did not seem aggressive and calmly sat watching me, I decided to persevere, although admittedly, I was quaking in my boots.

Because Julia had a young child, I assumed that she wouldn't risk keeping a dangerous, aggressive dog around her family. As there was no response when I rang the bell, finding the gate unlocked, I boldly walked up the path to the front door. A locked gate always indicates an aggressive dog. Unfortunately, these were pre-mobile phone days, so I had no option to phone. The Rottweiler had not moved but intently followed my progress along garden path with a fixed expression. When Julia opened the door, she visibly paled. She was incredulous that I made it past the Rottweiler in one piece. They usually locked the gate to keep unescorted visitors out, but, apparently, the gardener had left it unsecured. I also did not know that, like the other power breeds, Rottweilers have a natural instinct to protect their families. If unsocialised, they can be ferociously aggressive in their defence and attack strangers. After that experience, I realised that it is incredibly hazardous and irresponsible to assume anything about an unfamiliar dog. I could very easily have ended up like Bunny.

Of course, we cannot know everything about the several hundred existing dog breeds. However, before buying a new dog, it is our responsibility to research the various breeds of interest. With numerous books and the internet, there is a plethora of readily available information that would-be dog owners can arm themselves with before the prerequisite visit to a reputable breeder.

Companion dogs come in all shapes and sizes, depending on whether we'd prefer a jogging companion or someone to share your couch. While some dogs are born to work, companion dogs, which include many of the toy breeds, make good family lapdogs, including Maltese, papillon, Havanese and the Löwchen, to name a few.

The latter was not a breed I was familiar with until my good friend Margaret in Australia adopted one. The origin of the Löwchen is somewhat nebulous. Most people believe that they originated either from northern Europe as the forerunner of the toy poodle or related to the bichon breeds in the Mediterranean. Regardless, they are intelligent, lively, affectionate, and are considered the embodiment of a well-balanced companion dog. If you prefer something larger, Great Danes, greyhounds, Irish wolfhounds, and Newfoundlands are also incredibly partial to their owner's lap, and their size permitting, are very happy to share the couch.

Whether large or small, lively or lazy, we are spoilt for choice. The onus is on us to choose wisely, as each breed has uniquely different physiological and physical characteristics to consider when selecting a family pet. A puppy is not a dress that we can return after a few days because we dislike the colour or it does not fit. A puppy is for life.

CHAPTER 14
PUNISHMENT

The benefits of dog training are impossible to sum up in a few short sentences, although for me it was not all smooth sailing. I questioned various techniques and strategies because I didn't understand how the course's diverse elements combined to build confidence and reinforce obedience and impulse control. I struggled with one particular exercise for several weeks.

The object was to drop a treat into a small container at Mila's feet, but before she could touch it, I had to draw her away with another tidbit in my hand. Easier said than done. Even before the delicacy landed in the dish, it disappeared into Mila's mouth.

It seemed like an insurmountable task, and I questioned the significance of the exercise. However, after Zoli demonstrated the exercise's anticipated result with one of his dogs, I understood the importance of persevering.

He asked his dog to sit and stay, or alternatively lie down and stay, and placed the container with the treat behind his dog's back, near its tail. After Zoli walked several metres with his back to the patient hound who had not moved a muscle, he turned to face his dog and gave the release word 'yours', allowing the dog to eat the treat behind him. This is an excellent exercise to train impulse control, and we had to go through the preparatory stages leading up to the ultimate outcome.

It took ages to draw Mila away just one step, and I was ready to throw in the towel, but we persevered. Gradually, I enticed her further and further before allowing her back to collect the treat in the dish. Finally, after what seemed like a lifetime, we amassed some distance between us and the tidbit in the container, when I increased the difficulty level and challenged her impulse control even more. Several metres from the treat, I asked Mila to sit or lie down and stay before releasing her back to claim her prize. Eventually, weeks later, I was able to place the container behind Mila, who turned and swallowed the treat before I even turned my back. Obviously, Mila misunderstood the object of the exercise. Finally, with more practice, we succeeded, and I increased the distance by over ten metres, while Mila waited patiently until I turned to face her and released her to claim her treat. To this day, the exercise remains unwaveringly solid and a favourite for practising impulse control.

Zoli never lost his sense of humour. He was always patient and open to discuss any concerns that I had. With his direction I transformed Mila into an absolute treasure. A true Supermutt. She is more relaxed, outgoing, much more confident, as am I, concerning all things canine. Because Mila was a rescue dog, it was essential to understand her needs and strengthen the bonds between us as soon as possible. Dog training offered us that opportunity.

Although it is not an exact science, as each pooch responds differently, we sometimes have to implement specific tailor-made solutions, especially with older dogs. Zoli genuinely loves all his four-legged charges and works tirelessly to ensure they all reach their full potential. Without his help and guidance, Mila and I wouldn't have attained the goals we have achieved. But don't be fooled into thinking that dog training courses are magic. Admittedly it was hard work. Our daily practice and ongoing training require commitment and perseverance. However, the benefits of a happy and balanced dog are immeasurable. In all honesty, observing Mila blossom has been one of the most rewarding experiences in my life, which catapulted me on my journey of discovery into canine behaviour.

In retrospect, I even appreciate the lessons in dominance theory and punishment-based training. By understanding all aspects of dog training and behaviour modification programmes, the good, the bad and the ugly, I have a more balanced insight into dog behaviour and an appreciation of how dogs think and why. With this knowledge, it is easier to train dogs with the appropriate methods tailor-made to their specific requirements. In addition, a comprehensive understanding of what motivates our dogs helps us teach them to fit into our society without extinguishing their essence under our absolute domination.

Even though dogs have the cognitive ability and emotional awareness of a two- to three-year-old infant, and the human–canine relationship is more like parent and child, dogs are not children. By anthropomorphising our pets, we create the fantasy that they possess characteristics and emotions far beyond their actual capabilities. In truth, extremely popular TV shows and films depicting incredible doggy heroes, from Lassie and Rin-Tin-Tin to Old Yeller and Benji, with their skilful organisational abilities, displaying devotion, tenderness and resolve, are in part to blame. In contrast, *White God* portrays dogs as brutes when several hundred dogs revolt en masse and violently terrorise the city as they seek vengeance and kill humans who mistreated or abused them in the past. These films bestow dogs with cognitive thought processes they are incapable of possessing and inadvertently send the wrong message to inexperienced and ignorant humans.

We faced a similar situation at the safari camps in Botswana. As regular returning guests, we became familiar with many animals and learnt to recognise a broken tusk, a scar on the face, different colour patterns, or a missing tail. Over time we bestowed appropriate names on animals we were able to identify, which the guides discouraged. Perceptions are misleading, and giving human names to animals enhances the illusion of tameness, domesticity and implied humanness. There were no fences around the safari camps, where dangerous creatures freely moved day and night. Visitors accustomed to African animals know that they are wild. Unfortunately, tourists fresh out of New York or London might be tempted to approach regular camp visitors, such as Bessie the elephant or Clive the hippo. Even the slightest hint of anthropomorphising a wild animal could mislead tourists and lull them into a false sense of security, with tragic consequences.

Our relationship with dogs is no different. Do you remember the lakes of urine and mountains of poop when we first got Mila? At the time, friends told me that she was testing me and was deliberately defiant, and I must punish her. However, when we removed the perceived human characteristics from the equation and inspected the situation purely from a canine point of view, we soon discovered the problem. Mila was not obstinate or testing her limits; she was just stressed and scared. Similarly, when an owner returns home to find the couch destroyed, they often believe their dog was being vengeful for being left alone and frequently dispense severe punishment.

The truth is that dogs are social creatures, who would not choose to be alone. Long hours of solitude with nothing to do leave dogs stressed and bored, and chewing is an instinctive activity that alleviates anxiety and tension. Instead of humanising the dog with misguided ideas of vengeance, owners should try to manage the dog's environment based on the dog's inherent needs and leave suitable foraging toys and appropriate things to chew.

Dogs do not have the reasoning capabilities to act on premeditation and connivance. They are motivated purely by primaeval behaviour patterns, which we should learn to understand. Sadly, humans tend to overestimate dogs' cognisant abilities and underestimate their emotional needs. When we punish dogs for instinctive behaviour, they are confused and do not comprehend why their most beloved owner has suddenly gone mad and is shouting at and hitting them.

Based on operant conditioning principles, where even a sharp NO is considered punishment, it is evident that most people do use some form of punishment to control, train and discipline their dogs without even being aware of it. Of course, often, more extreme measures are used. Subsequently, the debate rages as to whether it is possible to exist with our dogs using no punishment at all, or if we do use punishment, the question is how much and how often? A further question posed is whether punishment is even a natural part of canine behaviour?

Puppies learn valuable lessons from their mothers during the transitional stage, which continues into the socialisation period. Mothers teach them important lessons about manners and discipline, resorting to inhibited bites, growls, mouth threats and even muzzle-grabbing to warn of inappropriate or rough behaviour. The mothers' disciplinary actions would most certainly equate to positive punishment in operant conditioning terms.

Littermates also provide additional reinforcement when a puppy quickly realises that his unacceptable actions have ended the game, as his siblings shun him for a while, which is a clear example of negative punishment. During the socialisation period, a puppy learns vital social skills, including greeting protocols, interacting with other dogs, reading and giving proper calming signals, which are the fundamentals of communication. Learning how to give and receive calming signals ensures that puppies become polite and responsible canine citizens and prepares them to participate as mature members of the domestic canine social system.

Ethologists believe that calming signals may be hardwired automatic responses for self-preservation and use various parts of the body, including posture, face, ears, tail, sound, movement and expression. Calming signals also coined, 'the language of peace', ensure that dogs have a way to avoid altercations and live together in harmony while maintaining a healthy social hierarchy with conflict resolution. Using the signals, dogs can avoid threats, calm fears, make friends.

If we examine some of these calming signals, such as licking their lips, freezing, sitting down, yawning, our dog adds something to show the other dog that its behaviour is not acceptable. Similarly, when an overenthusiastic puppy pesters a more senior dog, the adult may ignore the youngster until it calms down. This is precisely how we may respond when our dog exuberantly jumps on us, and we withhold our attention by turning away, which is negative punishment.

Dogs also have threatening signals, such as staring, walking straight towards someone, standing over another dog, growling, barking, raising hackles and tail, attacking, and showing their teeth. However, various canine behaviourists have established that aggression is not part of normal canine behaviour and dogs avoid conflict whenever possible. Experts generally believe that dogs who engage in hostility and violence are not products of nature but are a consequence of human artificial manipulations. However, in rare instances, dogs may resort to drastic measures, any of which we can interpret as a form of punishment.

Therefore, we can conclude that canine communication, including a mother's discipline, sibling reprimands, calming and threatening signals, correspond to operant conditioning principles of punishment, which can alter the other dog's behaviour. The position of the tail and ears, a lick of the nose, an expression in the eyes, a yawn, a growl, all add something to communicate to the other dog or person to stop their unwanted actions.

Despite the above, should we, as a non-canine species, punish our dogs?

Should we shout, prod, poke, hit, shake and growl at them?

We are not the dog's mother, sibling, or even another dog, so is it appropriate for us to imitate canine behaviour?

Do dogs understand when we punish them and why?

Bearing in mind that humans often take 'punishment' to extremes and certainly don't apply it at the same level that dogs do. Some aversive training methods include holding a dog's nose in a hole filled with water to stop it from digging, kneeing a dog sharply in the chest if it jumps up and hitting a dog with a leather belt to stop excessive barking. Frequent practices, including the use of choke chains, prong collars, shock collars, sudden loud noises such as a can of coins, electric shocks, beating, hitting, kicking, are among the few methods that actively deliver painful and fearful stimuli to dogs.

Why even use these methods?

In the past, trainers and owners did not know any better, and these methods routinely showed results. Indeed, these methods only worked as avoidance of pain but did not produce long-lasting results. Even Zoli, who was progressive with clicker and treat training, had many ingrained and outdated beliefs. When he felt the need, he did not hesitate to jerk on a leash, stare a dog down, smack it on the nose, poke it in the ribs, or growl at it. Unfortunately, the pack leader and dominance theory mentality lead to many horrific cruelties being practised on animals. A common form of discipline involves hoisting a dog in the air by its choke chain for up to a minute, which can cause brain damage.

Like Zoli, most trainers of the day genuinely loved dogs and didn't intentionally set out to be cruel but were acting on the misguided belief that their training was in their dogs' best interest. For a while, even scientists believed that positive punishment would make an animal learn faster. How many of us regularly used a rolled-up newspaper to chastise our dogs? Although, I must admit that I still advocate its use. I advise all owners to smack themselves over the head with the rolled-up newspaper whenever they think their dog is naughty. Dogs are just dogs, they do not misbehave. If canines have unacceptable manners, the fault lies with their humans, who have not taught them well enough or not at all.

Sadly, many trainers still cling to the old beliefs and inadvertently mislead well-meaning dog parents to use aversive training techniques. Universally utilised prong collars train dogs that pull on the leash with almost immediate results and are successfully employed to teach sit, stay, down and recall.

Unfortunately, if a trainer misuses punishment, it can have adverse consequences. One trainer regretfully admits that he inadvertently trained his dog to be reactive to other dogs. When his dog pulled on the leash in excitement to greet another dog, the trainer pulled back hard on the prong collar. The more the dog pulled, the harsher the trainer responded on the collar. It didn't take the dog long to associate the pain from the collar with another dog's appearance. After that, each time he saw a dog, he reacted severely to its presence. Alas, this is a common fault with many dog owners, who pull their dogs at the wrong time and inadvertently train them to become reactive to other dogs. That is why the 'Hungarian dog whisperer' suggested I was to blame for Mila's reactivity.

In popular terms, according to the Collins English Dictionary, "you can use punishment to refer to severe physical treatment of any kind. Harsh, or injurious treatment." Within operant conditioning principles, where behaviour is controlled by consequence, when we add something to stop unwanted behaviour from recurring, positive punishment occurs. These actions may be as minor as giving the dog a stern look, a reprimand, or a simple 'NO'. Similarly, when we take something away to ensure that the dog does not repeat a particular behaviour, which might be something as insignificant as taking away our attention, we have applied negative punishment. Although, more severe corrections are often administered to stop unwanted behaviour. Broadly speaking, psychologists categorise positive punishment as learning that occurs due to pain or physical discomfort.

With ongoing research in dog training and the psychological effects some methods have on dogs, we now know that punishment interrupts and temporarily suppresses unwanted behaviour but does not change it. Additionally, punishment can lead to anxiety, slower learning and aggression. Punishment without side effects does not exist, and torture always has its price.

Canine behaviourists concur that violence not only breaks our bond with our dogs, but it also damages us. Experts do not recommend positive punishment in clinical behaviour modification because it causes fear and pain; however, punishment may still be applicable if the dog is not frightened or hurt. Studies have shown that fearfulness, aggression and submissive behaviours should never be managed with positive punishment, as these traits may be increased rather than inhibited. Furthermore, there is a positive connection between reward-based training and the degree of obedience, which is the antithesis of aversive training methods and the performance of military dogs.

Not only does punishment not provide a dog with enough information, but it also is not specific to the behaviour we want to achieve. For example, if we smack a dog for barking, it does not teach a dog what behaviour we want. Dogs can also learn to associate punishment with their owners and learn to fear them. The more the owner punishes, the more the dog fears. A fearful dog is more likely to fight back in self-defence, and an assertive dog may become aggressive, setting up a dangerous escalating cycle of conflict. Dog personalities range from compliant to very tough. The very soft dogs are easily damaged mentally by applying positive punishment methods, and it is incredibly challenging to regain their trust and confidence. Furthermore, the very tough dogs are likely to fight back if corrected physically.

Collars, prong collars and choke chains are commonplace tools of punishment. Swedish behaviourist Anders Hallgren conducted a study of 400 dogs and concluded that 252 of the dogs had neck and spinal injuries. Of these, 229 had been pulled and jerked on a leash. Contrary to popular opinion, the canine neck is no sturdier than a human's neck. In fact, the skin on a dog's neck is only three to five cells thick compared to human skin, which is fifteen cells thick. Anatomically canine necks are similar to humans' and contain the trachea, oesophagus, thyroid gland, lymph nodes, jugular vein and spinal column. Many eye and ear issues are exacerbated by increased pressure due to compression from pulling on a leash and collar.

Similarly, the force from the collar can easily injure the delicate thyroid gland that sits just below the larynx and in front of the trachea, which can become severely inflamed, leading to hypothyroidism and immune system deficiencies. Other health issues caused by pulling on collars and leashes include whiplash, spinal cord injuries, paralysis, crushed trachea, dislocation of vertebrae, fracture of the larynx and brain damage.

This research established that 79% of the study's aggressive dogs had painful back injuries, and 69% of the timid dogs were diagnosed with back issues. The study results indicate that the force exerted on the neck and throat could cause severe damage or aggravate existing injuries.

Further research at Nottingham Trent University used pressure sensors on a canine neck model to record the intensity of forces exerted by owners/dogs pulling on various collars. Simulating a medium to large dog on a leash, the pressure exerted on the neck model ranged from a low of 83kPa (light leash pull) to a high of 832kPa (strong leash pull). Frankly, I am not particularly well versed in kPa, so to illustrate comparisons, a tourniquet requires 33kPa pressure to stop blood loss in a human arm while 230kPa pressure is ample to crush a human windpipe.

Even low-pressure canine collar values were much higher than those that cause tissue damage and tissue death in humans at 4.3kPa. The study was unable to verify which was more damaging, the progressive pressure of constant pulling or quick sharp jerks on the leash. In conclusion, the study found that the force generated by collars, even when dogs pull lightly, is far too high to justify their use.

A significant number of veterinary surgeons have also aired their concerns regarding neck injuries after vigorous pulling on collars, prong collars and choke chains. Interestingly, many countries, including Austria, New Zealand, Switzerland, Australia and several others, have banned prong collars. Similarly, according to German and Luxembourg legislation, all devices that cause suffering and pain in animals are prohibited. Most professionals advise that we should only use collars to display identification tags and not as leash restraints.

An avalanche of studies has concluded that there is no consistent benefit to be gained from punishment or aversive-based training compared with positive reward-based training. There is also ample evidence affirming that dogs trained using punishment are no more obedient than those trained by other means. Furthermore, punishment-based training increases the number of potentially problematic behaviours. These behaviours can compromise a dog's welfare, including excess anxiety, which is a leading cause of dog abandonment. Because reward-based methods are associated with higher levels of obedience and fewer problematic behaviours, their use is a more effective alternative to punishment for the average dog owner.

Yet, some trainers/owners still cling to the outdated ideas that correctly applied punishment can effectively resolve certain behaviours. Many believe that punishing events originating from the environment rather than from the owner are most effective, such as mousetraps or mats that deliver mild static shocks for counter-surfing dogs. A torrent of empty cans noisily raining down on unsuspecting dogs is recommended as a deterrent for dogs that sneak into empty rooms to urinate. Automated anti-bark collars deliver immediate punishment and are strong enough to suppress behaviour and are said to leave little or no impact on the dog's stress levels. On the other hand, electric shocks must be momentarily painful; otherwise, they would not affect the dog's behaviour. At worst, it can result in immediate discomfort, while repeated delivery of electric shocks can lead to severe fear and anxiety. Despite the above, the use of electronic devices, such as e-collars and invisible fences, are still hotly debated. While most people are aware of their existence as training aids, besides the manufacturers' biased assurances regarding their safety, very little published information exists either for or against their use.

Electronic collars were initially developed and used by hunters to train their dogs; however, these collars are now widely used in urban settings to correct behavioural problems in pet dogs. Manufacturers, suppliers and indeed many trainers feel that training with e-collars combined with rewards is perfectly humane. They state that modern electric collars do not deliver shocks, like their predecessors, but a gentle stimulation that the dog can barely feel on the lowest setting. Although, at a higher intensity, the stimulus is similar to a static shock. According to manufacturers, this distracts the dog from what it is doing but causes no pain. When we increase the correction level, the electrical output remains constant; only the pulses' duration becomes longer. Additionally, they believe that there is no evidence to support claims that e-collars can cause long-term trauma in dogs. The consensus amongst manufacturers, and many trainers, is that with correct use, these devices are an excellent remedial tool in the hands of professionals, especially for recall work and stopping inappropriate behaviour in working dogs.

The question remains, why have so many countries like Norway, Sweden, Austria, Switzerland, Slovenia and Germany, and some Australian states banned them?

As a form of physical punishment, we cannot challenge a shock's effectiveness, which can quickly suppress unwanted behaviour, even remotely, in the owner's absence. These behaviours range from excessive barking, territorial aggression, chasing objects and people, eating faeces, reactivity and wanderlust. However, collars can discharge and misfire at inappropriate times. An unexpected discharge can result in pain aggression directed towards owners, innocent bystanders, other dogs, or cause fear of the environment. Pain is a stimulus for aggression, and animals will reflexively lash out at whatever is nearest to them.

Similarly, badly timed shocks will not correct unwanted behaviour and can confuse and even traumatise sensitive dogs. Dogs often present avoidance behaviour while wearing the device to evade punishment, but may revert to the unwanted behaviour such as barking when the e-collar is removed. Although e-collars and electric containment systems offer a cheap and quick solution because dogs will avoid anything that causes them pain, aversion is not training. Avoiding discomfort does not teach dogs what behaviour we want, only what conduct we don't want.

A recent study highlighting the consequences of e-collar training of pet dogs found that signs of distress were evident in dogs trained with electronic devices. The study revealed behavioural differences between the dogs wearing e-collars consistent with negative experiences and positively trained dogs. These included tenseness, lowered body posture, yawning, yelping, lip licking, tail between their legs and elevated salivary cortisol levels. There was also no evidence that e-collars are more efficient than positive training methods. The study concluded that the routine use of e-collars presents a risk to the wellbeing of pet dogs.

From personal experience, I must agree with the above. When we moved to Budapest, we lived in temporary accommodation while we were renovating the family villa. The proviso for allowing Franky and Lulu in the apartments, that generally did not allow pets, was that they didn't bark. While neither dog was an excessive barker, if they heard unidentified noises in the building, cleaning or maintenance staff talking in the stairwell, or other tenants coming and going, it was inevitable that they would react to unusual sounds in the unfamiliar surroundings.

At the time, there were no day care centres or kennels in the area, and, unfortunately, there were periods when we had to leave the dogs alone for a few hours at a time. Even had I been familiar with positive training principles, I had no time to implement them. Against my better judgement, I invested in two anti-bark collars. The devices automatically gave off a sharp static sting when the dogs barked and did their job for the few months that Franky and Lulu had to wear them when home alone. Both dogs seemed anxious when I approached them to put the collars on, and Franky often tried to hide under duvets and blankets. From their uneasy behaviour, it was evident that the collar caused them some distress.

I cannot judge how the anti-bark collars affected them in the long term, as they had several stressful experiences during their lifetime. These included international travel to two different continents, moving house several times, being separated from us for the duration of the seven-month quarantine period in Australia, all of which caused lasting anxieties. However, using the collars with the best intentions through sheer ignorance of the consequences is one of my deepest regrets. With hindsight, I would never use or recommend anti-bark collars, especially for sensitive dogs.

Generally, handlers unanimously agree that e-collars are a vital tool for training working dogs. Typically, they do not recommend their use for the pet dog market, only in exceptional circumstances when all other training methods, such as positive reinforcement, have failed and in emergencies when a rapid outcome is vital. Experienced dog trainers agree that the use of the device is beyond the average owner's expertise, who often misuses and abuses them. Pet parents should only consider electronic devices after enlisting the help of a qualified trainer/behaviourist.

Fortunately, times have changed; the trend does seem to be shifting.

An interesting anecdote by Mary R. Burch and Jon S. Bailey (*How Dogs Learn*) refers to internationally recognised businessman William Abernathy. At the time, he was teaching a class on performance management to correctional officers and was demonstrating the difference between positive reinforcement and punishment using two rats. After the experiment, a guard started to play with the positively reinforced rat, which was happy with the attention. Meanwhile, another guard picked up the punished rat, which immediately bit his finger and would not let go. After someone finally managed to dislodge the rat from the guard's bleeding finger, he summarised the lesson of the day.

"You can get someone to do what you want through punishment; you just don't want to be around them afterwards."

Thankfully, aversive training methods seem to be dying a natural death, and most people generally avoid positive punishment. Yet, there is still no consensus on whether it is possible to train dogs using only positive reinforcement without resorting to some form of punishment. Even negative punishment can have consequences, and if we repeatedly remove something pleasant such as a toy, the dog may start to mistrust its owner.

The debate also rages on whether a raised voice barking 'NO', is a punishment, even though a loud verbal command can be an unpleasant stimulus. While some trainers see this as a social signal, which might startle a dog and interrupt an unwanted behaviour, others believe that a loud 'NO' is a verbal reprimand, which can be considered positive punishment. As we learnt in a previous chapter, it is considered punishment if the dog's behaviour decreases or stops.

Mila is well trained, obedient and understands the boundaries. Because of her dachshund spine, we do not allow her to go up or down the stairs; her domain is the ground floor, and she never attempts to follow us. However, in a rare moment of sheer mad exuberance, after an outing when she was impatient to go upstairs to greet Rezső, Mila tried to dash up the stairs. The unexpectedness of a quick 'uh-uh' from me brought her back to earth and interrupted the unwanted behaviour as she wheeled around, still happily wagging her tail, and redirected herself back to the lift, which she knows is the proper method of transport between floors. To let her know that returning to the elevator was the correct behaviour, I rewarded her with lavish praise and copious patting.

This example outlines the use of positive punishment, followed by positive reinforcement. I know that Mila was not hurt or traumatised by my verbal correction, which quickly stopped an unwanted behaviour that may become a habit if left unchecked.

I wouldn't hesitate to issue a loud 'NO' in exceptional circumstances or emergencies to stop any dangerous actions. The verbal correction would certainly surprise Mila and gain her attention. If possible, I'd counter the negative incident with something positive. On the other hand, overused empty reprimands lose the element of surprise and become ineffective as a crisis tool.

We have a rule that Mila does not receive any attention when we are seated at the table, even if we are not eating. When our friends Elizabeth and Barnabas used to come over for a game of canasta, they always tested this rule. Especially Barnabas. Of course, Mila is always excited when we have guests and would invariably try to elicit a pat or a tummy rub from our friends. Because she could rely on Barnabas to oblige, Mila being an opportunist, would take advantage of the situation. I explained that giving Mila attention at the table would quickly teach her bad habits and asked Barnabas to desist. The next time Mila went over to him at the table, he responded with 'NOOOO'. I had to elucidate further why NO does not teach the dog anything, and the best course of action, if Mila did approach him at the table, is to ignore her and not reward her with his attention.

Being from the old school, I don't think that Barnabas understood the reasoning behind my plea. I had to remind him of this on many subsequent visits after he either surreptitiously patted Mila or voiced a 'noooo'. After numerous polite and not so polite requests, he eventually stopped, at least when he knew that I was watching. No offence to our guests, but in all honesty, Mila is much easier to train than humans.

Professional dog trainer Pat Miller is a strong advocate of positive training methods. Yet, she understands that extreme measures have to be applied in dire situations, as illustrated with one of her clients' adopted pit bull mix. Even after being kicked in the head, Happy chased horses. After a series of positive reinforcement lessons, which taught the dog good manners but did nothing to alter his inappropriate horse-chasing behaviour, more forceful measures had to be implemented, as a matter of urgency, before Happy was killed by flying hooves. Pat knew that the dog was gun-shy, which she decided to use to their advantage, and the next time Happy ducked under the electric fence leading to the horse paddock, Pat fired a cap gun into the air. The dog did an about-turn and ran home to the porch.

According to Pat, properly applied positive punishment should work within one or two applications; otherwise, it is not doing the job. Just as after one bee sting, Franky learnt to avoid the little creatures. With Happy, they only had to repeat the exercise one more time, which convinced him to leave all horses alone forever. As with Pat Miller's experience, it may not always be possible to avoid punishment. If the situation had not been so urgent, Pat could have adopted less extreme methods. With patience and time, she would have reaped the rewards of a positively trained dog. Serious behaviour modification should only be used by qualified professionals.

When raising a new puppy, I believe it is possible to use only positive methods. However, with adult dogs, such as Happy, when all other dog-friendly methods have failed, some form of punishment may be the only appropriate solution, although we should always avoid aversive and cruel training, bearing in mind that dogs trained with aversive techniques are fifteen times more likely to exhibit signs of stress than those taught with positive methods. In addition, from recent research, we have learnt that force-based punishment methods can trigger aggressive responses in dogs. Therefore, physical or aversive punishment should only be used as a last resort by professionals when it may be the only suitable alternative to avoid certain death or euthanasia.

Experienced behaviourists can avoid punishment and manage to rehabilitate many aggressive or traumatised dogs using positive training methods. Naturally, raising and training dogs is very personal and depends on many variables. No two people are the same, as no two dogs are the same. Often training has to be tailor-made to each dog, considering breed, the dog's character and the level of the owner's experience, as what works for one may not work for another.

In most cases, inappropriate doggy behaviour can be corrected without punishment, using positive reinforcement. It is pointless punishing a dog for chewing shoes or other unsuitable items if we do not provide them with more appropriate alternatives. If we want the dog off the couch, rather than punishing him, place his bed next to the couch and reward him each time he uses it. Dogs are usually very willing to learn if they know what we want from them. By introducing the behaviour that we expect and rewarding it, we set our dogs up for success each time.

Interestingly, Pippa Mattinson relates that the USA Guide Dog Association reported an increase in their pass rate from 50% to 80% after changing to positive reinforcement methods, including science-based clicker training. Many US bomb disposal dogs are also trained using positive practices with toys, games and food as rewards. Trials and pilot schemes have shown that positive training works faster and is more effective.

In the USA, most service dogs, including medical detection dogs, police K9 units, military dogs and sniffer dogs, are trained with positive rewards. Yet, shockingly, new videos often pop up on YouTube highlighting police atrocities against their K9 partners. A recent disturbing video shows a police officer lifting his dog up by the collar and slinging the still hanging dog over his shoulder exactly how a butcher would handle a slab of meat. After he walked to the car, he slammed the dog into the side of the vehicle. The dog's offence? He jumped out of the car without permission. Another circulating video shows a police officer beating his dog's face with his fists after putting the dog into an alpha roll. The reason for this assault? When the officer tried to take away the dog's reward toy, it retaliated forcefully and tried to bite the officer.

Dogs do not suddenly turn aggressively on their owners and attack them for no reason, not even for taking away a toy. When a strong bond of mutual trust and respect exists between dog and handler, it is unlikely that a dog would react with aggression, unless it is regularly hurt or traumatised. The police chief defended the officer's actions and explained that police dogs are trained differently to pet dogs, and the canine in question was not hurt. Nobody, especially authority figures, should ever condone brutal behaviour by humans against animals.

On a happier note, during my research, I was delighted that studies and expert opinions unanimously agreed that using aversive training methods can jeopardise dogs' physical and mental health. Therefore, it is not surprising that so many trainers, dog owners and organisations are turning away from punishment-based training and are applying force-free or positive methods.

With relevance to the above, Pavlov reminds us of the fundamental principles of classical conditioning, whereby associations are formed between events occurring in the real world and reflexes or emotional responses in the individual.

Additionally, if we recall how Little Albert was classically conditioned to the emotion of fear, we realise how quickly we can shape negative or positive associations. In terms of classical conditioning, positive-based training establishes a stronger bond between the owner and his dog, which sets up a positive sequence of events:

Owner>treat/reward>pleasant feeling

The opposite is true of punishment-based training:

Owner>punishment>fear/distrust

Fear conditioning often has life-long adverse effects on our pets. I believe that therein lies the simple answer as to whether we should punish our dogs.

CHAPTER 15
AGGRESSION

Delving into the subject of all forms of aggression opens up a veritable Pandora's box of ideas, beliefs and theories.

One of the most common forms of aggression is owner-directed aggression, formerly referred to as dominance aggression, which manifests itself as exaggerated behaviours directed towards people when dogs react negatively under certain circumstances. Some of these provocative situations include disturbing a sleeping dog, correcting behaviour by pulling on a dog's leash, reaching over a dog's head, grooming a dog, staring at a dog, hugging a dog, handling a dog's face or muzzle, restraining a dog and punishing a dog.

Significantly, even experts are vague on the subject of aggression and often use dominance aggression to describe the character trait of an individual dog. However, ethologists define dominance as a characteristic of a repeated pattern based on the interaction between two individuals. Therefore, we can describe dominance as the relationship between pairs of individuals rather than aiming to achieve status.

Circumstances and prior experience may explain the outcome of an encounter in social animals; subsequently, the consequences of the first encounter between two individuals will profoundly impact future responses. Two adult animals meeting for the first time will have no expectations of the other's behaviour, and both will be apprehensive and watchful of each other.

For example, a large black dog and a small white dog that have never met will draw on previously learnt information from similar encounters. If in the past a small white dog reacted aggressively towards the large black dog, or the small white dog had a fearful confrontation with a large black dog, based on the consequences of their previous experiences, the risk of an aggressive reaction, in this case, is high. Had the two dogs met without any previous negative experiences, the outcome of the meeting would most likely be cordial. This simple example illustrates the complexities of social interactions, which has nothing to do with dominance and is often based on fear.

Even though many experts still use the concept of dominance to describe aggression, the pattern of interactions and prior experiences between dog and owner determine the resulting response. For instance, when an owner intimidates his dog with specific actions such as aversive punishment, it may initially show appeasement or avoidance to halt the unwanted conduct. If the owner fails to heed these signals, the dog's behaviour will eventually escalate to growling or aggression, which usually stops the undesirable behaviour from its owner. Over subsequent encounters, the dog will become more confident in showing aggression. We can use similar associations to explain how defensive behaviour based on fear will transform into the type of offensive behaviour that experts commonly categorise as 'dominant'.

Furthermore, left to their own devices without interference from humans, there is no evidence to show that dogs adopt dominance-based social structures. Generally, experts propose that instead of referring to contrived fabrications such as 'dominance' to explain canine aggression, we only have to recall the fundamentals of classical conditioning to explain why some dogs escalate into aggression in certain circumstances.

We shouldn't be so quick to classify a dog as dominantly aggressive. Chances are the dog is just confused and anxious when owners, through sheer ignorance, miss submissive signals from their dogs, which may develop into an aggressive response, becoming a learnt behaviour over time. Diagnosed as dominance aggression, a dog may react aggressively to avoid some perceived aversive outcome, when, through association, it has learnt that it can prevent unpleasant experiences by growling. Often problems arise when owners do not understand canine signals and behaviour and fail to comprehend simple acts.

Ordinarily, owner-directed aggression manifests mainly in dogs that have not been taught how to function successfully in a domestic environment and are unsure of their social roles. Subsequently, they use aggressive behaviour to gauge what we expect of them. These dogs often display needy behaviours and respond well to SSRIs (selective serotonin reuptake inhibitors), including well-known medications such as Prozac, Paxil, Zoloft, Luvox and various antidepressants. Additionally, experts also recommend implementing a behaviour modification programme, including desensitisation and counterconditioning.

Additional factors that affect aggression include genetics, gender, hormonal influences, socialisation and owner perceptions, whereby owners anthropomorphise their dogs and don't establish consistent rules. By overindulging their dogs, attending to their every whim, owners raise spoilt brats while they reward the wrong behaviours with affection at the wrong time and inevitably produce aggressive dogs.

Like humans, dogs are social creatures and need to be part of a family. When we recognise how our dogs communicate, learn to observe their body language, accept and meet their canine needs, including early socialisation, and provide them with ample opportunities to be dogs, but at the same time give them boundaries, consistent leadership, guidance and love, we ensure a solid and enduring relationship based on mutual trust, respect and understanding.

Our job, as parents, is to guide and teach our children and be consistent in how we wish them to behave. Similarly, we are responsible for guiding and teaching our dogs the necessary social skills and good behaviour practices to ensure that they become well-behaved members of canine society.

Over the years, my mother has kept a succession of small dogs, her little babies, which she undoubtedly loved very much. However, she overindulged them, catering to their every whim with no rules or boundaries. It was a veritable canine free-for-all. When they wanted food, which was all day, they begged. If my mother did not meet their demands, they pawed her arm until she obliged. The dogs slept wherever they pleased, usually with my mother, and sometimes they were even too lazy to go to the toilet outside, which my mother always overlooked. When my mother took them out for a stroll, she carried them if the dogs refused to walk, which was most of the time. I must add that my mother never bestowed the same leniency on her grandchildren or me. In time, she obtained a small pram for the dogs, which resulted in a plethora of health issues, including weight gain and joint problems from lack of exercise. The little angels became impossible little fiends.

The first time one of the dogs aggressively snapped at someone who ventured too close to my mother, she rewarded it with amused attention and a pat for being a good dog. After all, how cute is it when a Chihuahua acts like a Dobermann!

It did not take them long to repeat the performance. All their behaviour was self-rewarding. With their demands, they received everything that their heart desired: attention, food and their most crucial resource – my mother. What more could a furry monster wish for? Even when she was on the receiving end of snapping teeth, my mother did not mind any of these behaviours.

During the night, she often incurred the wrath of a pampered pooch who took offence at being disturbed when she turned onto her other side. These nocturnal expressions of aggression from either one of her dogs sometimes left my mother and her husband with bite-shaped bruises in the morning. Imagine if the dog in question had been anything larger than a Chihuahua. With no rules, set boundaries or guidance, they were potentially dangerous dogs. None of us had a death wish, so we tried not to provide the little fiends with an excuse to rip us to shreds and always gave my mother and them a wide berth.

By anthropomorphising her furry little demons, my mother suppressed their canine characteristics and instincts and failed to provide adequate mental or physical stimulation. They seldom played or ran around freely, and in time were unable to do so. Their purpose in life was to be lapdogs, to be pampered and loved, but at what cost? Plainly, they were unhappy, frustrated, unsocialised caricatures of what a dog should be, ready to snap at the first person who ignored their demands or crossed them. Unfortunately, this is another example of someone acting with good intentions but in complete ignorance of basic canine needs.

If you allow a dog unrestricted freedom, you must consider the consequences and whether these are behaviours that you will come to regret. Similarly, in tourist destinations, wild animals such as monkeys that well-meaning and indulgent visitors feed become viciously demanding when visitors ignore their expectations of food. Additionally, if we do not set parameters and teach our dogs limits, they will become confrontational when denied something they generally receive on-demand. On the other hand, if we allow our dogs on the couch, they are not spoilt if we teach them that we may dethrone them at any time and they will not react antagonistically but will respect our boundaries.

In a similar vein, the author of several parenting books, Rebecca Eanes, touched upon related issues regarding the lack of discipline in children. According to Eanes, parents coddle, dote on and bend over backwards to shield their children from frustration and protect their self-esteem, which is resulting in a "generation of undisciplined narcissists who expect everything to go their way".

Discipline is not punishment. Discipline teaches our dogs straightforward rules and allows them to understand what acceptable behaviours we would like, which alleviates any misunderstanding and promotes more confident pets.

Just as children need parental guidance, dogs also require guidance from their owners. Without rules, there is confusion and frustration, leading to anxiety, stress and aggression, whereas structure provides sanity. Discipline is not about creating the perfect dog but shaping happy and well-adjusted dogs who trust their owners to guide them and teach them socially acceptable behaviours.

One of the most important lessons for humans is recognising that aggression is a natural response to a perceived threat and misunderstanding canine behaviour can lead to inappropriate training methods, resulting in an escalation of aggressive reactions. If we understand the neurological mechanisms involved in this response, we can decipher the development of the aggression and offer the best treatment methods.

Even though an animal's genetic make-up is not the sole factor in predicting its behaviour, it can influence a dog's neural circuitry and predispose it to aggression.

For instance, dogs bred for guarding may not necessarily be aggressive, but owners should be conscious of this possibility. Additionally, how a dog reacts to a perceived threat is predetermined by past experiences.

A web of neuroreceptors in the amygdala stimulates various pathways based on past experiences. These pathways create a behaviour pattern and generate an emotional response. If past experiences are aversive, then the emotional response will be fear. Expert opinion and studies emphasise and concur that the root of most aggressive dog behaviour is fear. However, if the dog has had many positive experiences, the neurological mechanism will create pleasing emotional reactions and generate positive behaviour patterns for the future. Hunger and testosterone can also stimulate the hypothalamus and exacerbate dogs' responses, as do chemical and hormonal imbalances. With a basic comprehension of the RAGE circuit, we can better understand why confrontational training techniques result in additional aggression.

Once again, experts place great emphasis on the lack of early socialisation in dogs, resulting in hyperactivity and altered fear responses later in life. Early experiences have a pronounced impact on the adult dog. Ongoing research and studies indicate that human selection under domestication has had a marked effect on dogs' expression of social aggression. Furthermore, various reports confirm a significantly higher rate of owner-directed aggression by dogs obtained from pet stores than from non-commercial breeders.

Additional findings infer a higher incidence of owner-directed aggression in dogs that were ill as puppies between zero and sixteen weeks of age. While experts don't have all the answers, these findings clearly indicate that both pre- and postnatal maternal stress and early life stress appear to affect adult dogs negatively regarding owner-directed aggression.

Contributory factors leading to aggression in dogs are, without a doubt, assertive training methods.

A profusion of studies have proved that confrontational training techniques can provoke fear in dogs and lead to defensively aggressive behaviour. So, naturally, if you're aggressive to your dog, your dog will be aggressive too. According to an earlier study, the highest frequency of aggression occurred in response to aversive practices.

- 41% of owners reported aggression when hitting or kicking the dog.
- 41% reported aggression when they growled at the dog.
- 38% reported aggression when forcing the dog to release an item from its mouth.
- 31% reported aggression when forcing the dog onto its back and holding it down, generally referred to as an alpha roll.
- 29% reported aggression when forcing the dog onto its side.
- 26% reported aggression when grabbing the jowls or scruff.
- 30% reported aggression when staring the dog down – staring at the dog until it looks away.
- 20% reported aggression when spraying the dog with a water pistol or spray bottle.

- 15% reported aggression when yelling 'no'.
- 12% reported aggression when forcibly exposing the dog to a stimulus that frightens it.

Specific unwanted behaviour, such as fear aggression, must be tackled directly by a precise individual approach to have the best chance of success. We can achieve behaviour modification by teaching and rewarding a dog for alternate behaviours and not utilising dominance, discipline-based training programmes, which do not address a specific behaviour problem and are psychologically cruel. Additionally, aversive training techniques provoke fear or defensively aggressive behaviour.

There seem to be many considerations and factors that can contribute to owner-directed canine aggression, a term which I prefer, to the more commonly used dominance aggression. These elements include genetics, breeding practices, early maternal and sibling interactions, experiences during the socialisation period, brain development, health, anxiety, lack of training, inconsistent boundaries, and miscommunication between the dog and its owner. Most undesirable behaviour elements are a direct result of associated learning, which may also act in combination with several other variables. Fortunately, almost all experts agree that owner-directed aggression has nothing to do with a dog's desire to obtain status over its owner, and we shouldn't even call it dominance aggression, as it sends the wrong message.

Many owners also report a problem with food aggression. However, there seems to be no conclusive explanation for why some dogs become protective over food. Generally, a combination of elements is usually responsible for any canine behaviour issue, such as genetics or early learning, and in this case, competition for food amongst littermates, which could predispose dogs to food aggression. Additionally, various health issues may also be contributing factors, which is why it is always essential to have a veterinarian do a complete health check on dogs with any aggression issues.

Although, we should also examine this from a canine perspective.

Generally, dogs have a personal zone of anything between two to six feet; however, this distance becomes the distance from their mouth to their front feet when food is involved. Socially skilled dogs and free-living dogs don't usually take anything from each other by force; the respectful rule is that you get to keep whatever you have in your zone. Based on canine etiquette, dogs do not understand why we want to take their food away or invade their personal zone when eating. Our inappropriate anti-social behaviour confuses them, resulting in a loss of trust. If we keep invading their space, they might growl a warning for us to stay away while they are eating. The owner that does not heed these warnings is in danger of escalating the cycle of aggression.

As a family, we've always respected our dogs' personal space when they are eating. Although, I did teach them as puppies not to be concerned if I took away their bowl, as I gave them treats in exchange, and always gave back their bowl. Some owners accept that food aggression is a natural canine instinct and respect their dog's personal zone while eating, thus preserving their trust. On the other hand, others maintain that it is not acceptable for dogs to display any aggression, as this could endanger humans, and they believe that we should train dogs to show restraint and impulse control. Yes, that is true, we could train our dogs, or on the other hand, we could train humans not to go near dogs when they are eating.

Inevitably prevention is always better than cure, and it is much easier to teach a dog than a human. Additionally, it is also easier to teach a puppy than to retrain an older aggressive dog already set in its ways. Despite this, we should also be mindful of canine instincts and learn to respect their space.

Sometimes, it is easier to give advice than heed it, which taught me a valuable lesson many years ago. When Brandy, our several-month-old bull terrier puppy, was chewing on a bone, which was in my way, I tried to pick up the bone and move it to a more suitable location. As I had never had a problem with any of our previous dogs, I did this mindlessly, without even thinking. The next minute I felt several needle-sharp teeth painfully lodged onto my hand. Brandy certainly took offence at my thoughtless behaviour, which I took great care never to repeat. The incident taught me not to take anything for granted; after all, dogs are all unique, and they can all be unpredictable in various situations. While most of my previous dogs were not averse to relinquishing their food, knowing that I would return it, Brandy had no such idea of cooperation. Before taking food from her, I should have made sure she was comfortable with that, and, if not, I should have trained her.

Although I don't routinely take food away from Mila, once she was able to show some impulse control around her food, I did implement a few training exercises. Even if I take anything away, I ask nicely, and I swap it for a very high-value treat; I never grab anything away from her. When asked, she will relinquish her antler even if she is happily chewing on it.

In the past, when we had the memorable incidents with the baby mice, she happily gave them up in lieu of a few very, very high-value treats. Although, for Mila, prey drive is about the stalk and successful capture, not about consuming the catch of the day. After all, who in their right mind wants to eat a smelly mouse when they can have salmon pâté instead?

Based on our ongoing training and the bond we have built over the years, I know that Mila trusts me enough to give up anything if required, especially in an emergency, even if I did not have any treats.

Another form of aggression is idiopathic aggression, which refers to canine violence that is unrelated to fear, dominance, jealousy, and arises spontaneously, for which the cause is unknown. This type of aggression is more prevalent in certain dog breeds, including St Bernards, Rottweilers, Dobermanns, German shepherds, and especially blond English cocker spaniels and English springer spaniels. Usually, dogs who suffer from this type of aggression are very affectionate, obedient, well-mannered canines, who, for no apparent reason, will suddenly and ferociously attack their owners or visitors, which is why we sometimes refer to it as the Jekyll-Hyde syndrome.

This is also often referred to as rage syndrome, a term attributed to animal behaviourist Dr Roger A. Mugford, who found that the syndrome usually manifests in dogs around seven months old. Although, recent research has shown dogs presenting with the syndrome as young as three months and as late as two years. However, bearing in mind that the word 'rage' implies an emotional cause, which should logically respond to counterconditioning modification, which it does not, idiopathic aggression seems to be a more appropriate term.

Undoubtedly the reason for this type of aggression is buried deep within the dog's brain, although clinical examinations rarely reveal any abnormalities, which are undoubtedly genetic. Conversely, other theories suggest that it may also be a form of epilepsy, as some dogs twitch and foam at the mouth during an episode. Some researchers have produced abnormal electroencephalogram readings in dogs suspected of having idiopathic aggression, but experts have not as yet studied many dogs with this syndrome. At present, there seems to be enough evidence to suggest that the phenomenon is inherited, and idiopathic aggression is a clear instance of bad genes getting locked into a breeding population. Screening and selective breeding have been very successful in eliminating the problem in various breeds.

Fortunately, true idiopathic aggression is rare.

Although widely studied in the 1970s and 1980s, over thirty studies and tests have failed to produce a clear cause or diagnosis for idiopathic aggression. Although modern DNA testing is expensive, it can at least examine the spread of inherited diseases, especially by detecting carriers with no outward signs of any defects. Unfortunately, there is no treatment for idiopathic aggression, and even though there has been some minor success in treating dogs with phenobarbital drug therapies, dogs with this syndrome remain volatile. Experts usually recommend euthanising dogs with idiopathic aggression, as they endanger their owners' safety by the violently explosive and totally unpredictable attacks.

Owners should seek expert opinion if they suspect their dog has this syndrome, as extensive testing by a behaviour consultant is required. Additionally, a veterinarian should complete a detailed medical and neurological evaluation before confirming a diagnosis of idiopathic aggression, as other conditions may also cause aggressive outbursts. These behaviour anomalies include brain tumours, head trauma and metabolic disorders such as low blood sugar. Unfortunately, owners often label their dogs with idiopathic aggression when an expert can identify alternate conditions to explain their aggressive behaviours.

Many different circumstances attribute to hostility in dogs, such as inter-dog household aggression, also referred to as 'sibling rivalry', regardless of whether the dogs are related or not. Inter-dog household aggression results in more severe injuries than between dogs from different households, remaining one of the most disturbing situations in a multi-dog home, which is a common reason some owners seek professional help.

Bearing in mind how we control every aspect of our dogs' lives, it is a testament to their flexibility that they are willing to let us select their friends most of the time. When dogs roam freely, they choose which dogs to live with and which to ignore, as some dogs are simply incompatible and incapable of ever being friends.

One of the most thorough studies of inter-dog household aggression reported that, generally, it is the same dog that instigates the fights, usually the younger of the two dogs or the newest addition to the household. However, the study also revealed that habitually the conflict occurs between dogs of the same sex, and surprisingly female dogs are more often involved in these altercations than male dogs. Indeed, injuries resulting in female-to-female aggression were more severe and fights tended to be more prolonged and furious.

There are various reasons for inter-dog household aggression and may include over-excitement causing arguments over resources, such as food, toys, beds; in addition, access to the owner's attention is often the catalyst. Additionally, health issues are also a consideration, although antagonism between intact dogs may be hormone driven. Also, owners inadvertently reinforce aggressive behaviour at times due to lack of control and training, interfering with typical social rituals and encouraging the subordinate dog over the higher ranking. Rank in this instance refers to deference and social status relevant to seniority.

Furthermore, stress can also act as a catalyst and contribute to household aggression when tensions escalate. Any number of triggers may push dogs over their threshold, which is why it is essential to manage and remove as many stressors as possible. Sometimes the addition of a third dog upsets the social balance, causing anxiety, stress and tension. Consequently, one cannot emphasise enough the importance of adequate mental stimulation and physical exercise to alleviate stress in our dogs. Adequately socialised pets are usually well adjusted and tend to get along. However, with all things canine, early learning experiences and socialising will impact a dog's character and its ability to deal with stressful stimuli in the future and throughout its life.

Regarding the above, canine behaviourists indicate that dogs generally work things out for themselves and seldom have altercations in the owner's absence. However, owners can trigger violent fights when they try and impose democracy on the social dog structure by feeling sorry for the subordinate dog, giving him special privileges, and reprimanding the dominant dog for being a bully. The subordinate quickly learns that while his owner is around, he can get away with things that he may be unable to do on his own. This added incentive from the owner motivates him to try even harder, provoking a strong reaction from the dominant dog. Stephen Budiansky, author of *The Truth About Dogs*, compares this to encouraging the downtrodden peasants to revolt with vague promises of trifles. Budiansky further suggests that the only solution is to abandon all notions of democracy in favour of a dictatorship. This tactic maximises society's stability and reinforces the dominant position of the top dog, which we should pat first, feed first and give priority above the other dog. Further insights from Budiansky suggest that the cure for sibling rivalry in humans is to reassure the child that it is getting an equal amount of love and attention. The remedy for sibling rivalry between dogs is to reassure each dog that it is not receiving equal amounts of attention.

We also had a minor sibling rivalry situation between Franky and Lulu. Franky, who was one year old, and spayed when we brought home Lulu, took one look at the interloper and growled in displeasure. Even after this introduction, Lulu, the younger and newer family member, could never accept the status quo. Without fail, Lulu always tried to usurp Franky's senior position regardless of the latter's subtle and not so subtle warnings. Despite having identical beds and toys, Lulu always tried to claim anything and everything in Franky's possession, including my lap, which was exclusively Franky's domain. If Franky played with a specific toy, Lulu didn't rest until she had claimed it for herself, while her own identical toy lay abandoned nearby. Lulu insisted on copying everything that Franky did. While Lulu detested water, she would also venture into the sea if she saw Franky happily chasing waves. Similarly, Lulu hated anything cold and wet but would always join in when she saw Franky leaping around in the snow.

Generally, Franky managed to keep Lulu in check, and when the resource wasn't consequential, she'd often defer to Lulu. However, as far as Franky was concerned, I was the one resource that was not up for debate, and although they did have a few skirmishes over me, with some ongoing management on my part, they usually kept the peace.

When she was a year old, I also had Lulu spayed; however, as their rivalry was not hormonal, it made no difference to their relationship. Even though I gave them equal amounts of my time, I always gave precedence to

Franky, who I fed and greeted first, always giving toys, treats and attention first. Additionally, she had permanent access to my lap, which was her right by way of seniority, being the first dog in the house, while Lulu would lie on the couch right next to me. This strategy and long daily walks certainly worked for me and kept conflicts bloodless and down to a minimum. Admittedly, I can't claim credit for any wisdom at the time, as my plan of action was intuitive rather than based on any real experience.

Experts have barely scratched the surface regarding dog behaviour, and there is still much to learn. Fortunately, with ongoing research, new information comes to light daily. For example, recent studies propose that anxiety in dogs could also be genetic, which indicates that anxiety may be a complex combination of genetics, breeding, nurture and the lack of early socialisation. Similarly, various ethologists and experts in dog cognition and behaviour have shown that so-called owner-directed aggression seems disproportionately present in certain breeds. In fact, aggressive behaviour usually has a solid genetic background. Ongoing breeding studies in Rottweilers have reported that by restricting breeding only for dogs that passed the socially acceptable behaviour test, human-directed aggression decreased in the course of six to seven years.

Then we have 'red-zone dogs', an expression popularised by Cesar Millan to describe the state a dog enters when reacting aggressively to a perceived threat, and which has become synonymous with characterising severely aggressive or reactive dogs. Some people also refer to the term 'red zone' as high-intensity behaviour, which past environmental influences may trigger, with inappropriate training methods also becoming a contributing factor.

Admittedly, I have never been a Cesar Millan fan, but he had several interesting and relevant points in a recent article. Surprisingly, he agreed that dogs engaging in ferocious behaviour are not products of nature and result from artificial manipulation. Furthermore, he mentions that the Romans created mastiffs as war dogs to become veritable killing machines, and, unfortunately, humans are still doing this to dogs, even though they will never see a battlefield. Due to overwhelming evidence, it has become widely accepted that mistreated dogs are very likely to develop red-zone aggression issues.

Invariably, fighting dogs are trained and moulded from puppyhood to attack, using abusive training methods that create aggressive killing automatons. Any dogs that don't succeed are usually abandoned or killed in shelters, as they are considered too dangerous and incurable. Most red-zone dogs come from power breeds that are specifically bred for hostility. On a genetic level, some dogs have a greater propensity to violence and are created to execute the kill-bite for impulsive, uncontrolled aggression, which genetically determines many breeds. Even though experts believe that it is impossible to remove aggressive traits from their genes researchers constantly point out that a dog's personality is a consequence of genetics and experience: nature and nurture.

If a dog has problem behaviours, it is worth exploring how we can modify them, or, better still, train a dog before problems develop. When dogs that are genetically predisposed to aggression receive the necessary outlets for their instinctive behaviour, owners can circumvent undesirable responses. Although, we shouldn't have unrealistic expectations as we cannot extinguish innate instincts. That is like hoping your border collie will become less interested in sheep.

Despite some owners doing everything right with their dogs from day one, over time, their dog may snap at a child, bite the vet, and their boarding kennel may ask them to find another place. While we can mould some elements of dog behaviour by training and with patient, dedicated owners, we cannot change instinctive behaviour by training. These hardwired instincts are usually survival-related and reactive in nature, which no amount of training can change. The best that training can achieve is to modify the threshold at which the instinct is triggered or develop a 'stop' reaction when a dog goes into instinct mode; however, training will never stop the innate response from happening.

Similarly, despite all the correct protocols, including choosing a good breeder, providing excellent early socialisation, enrolling in puppy classes and doing everything that behaviour experts recommend, veterinary dog behaviourist Ilana Reisner was surprised when her four-month-old puppy started showing signs of nervousness. A short while later, an unfortunate incident with an out-of-control dog tipped the nervous puppy into outright fear of other dogs. Regardless of the ongoing work over the years, her dog remains a whirling dervish when he sees unfamiliar dogs.

Following years of training, her dog's fear has not diminished, which raises the question of whether her dog's anxiety was genetically predetermined? In the interaction between genetics and the environment, genetics does, at times, gain the upper hand. However, the question of whether a dog's problem is genetic may not be as meaningful as the question, 'Can we help this dog?' With powerful training methods, thoughtful breeding practices, positive socialisation, loving training and management, we can help our dogs live in our complex human world.

It seems clear that genetics does not necessarily mean a death sentence for dogs bred for aggression, as behaviour is genetic and epigenetic, arising from non-genetic influences such as environmental conditions. Unfortunately, modern dogs have limited or no access to things they once did. Very few sheepdogs ever see sheep, and scenthounds live in apartments, while Labradors no longer swim out to fetch ducks. To fit in with our lifestyles, we expect dogs to become urbanised, and, alas, they don't always receive adequate mental stimulation or a proper outlet for their natural drives. These unfulfilled needs lead to frustration, which can, over time, trigger aggression.

As we know, the lack of early learning and socialisation in puppies can cause behaviour problems and aggression in adult dogs. Although we can rehabilitate a dog with learnt aggression, we cannot eliminate genetic aggression or aggression associated with the lack of early socialisation, which can only be managed and hopefully contained.

Furthermore, inexperienced owners who do not understand dogs take on assertive and aggressive breeds and offer no consistent leadership, rules, discipline or boundaries. Inevitably, dogs unsure of their social roles use aggression to release pent-up frustration and gauge what we expect of them.

Some time ago, I heard about an incident in our area involving two Cane Corso dogs who managed to escape from their fenced yard and savaged a vizsla walking by with its owner. After badly injuring the dog, the two Cane Corsos attacked and then dragged the owner on the ground for many metres and shook him like a rag doll. While their absent owner makes no effort to provide any meaningful outlet for their natural drives and even leaves their feeding to a caretaker, the two dogs live bored and frustrated lives and are neither socialised nor exercised. Assuming they were not socialised as puppies, now as aggressive adults, it may be impossible to rehabilitate them.

Similarly, our neighbours, who own Lego & Co, the two large St Bernard dogs, and a large retriever mix, also had another smaller black rescue dog of an undeterminable breed. This smaller dog was usually locked in a dog pen at the back of the garden, as it could get through the fence and had on several occasions run out and attacked and bit passers-by, with no provocation or apparent reason.

As an outsider, it is difficult to assess the issues and how past environmental influences have moulded the little dog's behaviour. However, the owners have not addressed these. The owners never take the dogs for walks; they receive no training and very little attention. Eventually, because of its aggressive behaviour and history of attacking pedestrians, the owners relocated the small black dog to the country.

In the meantime, the three large dogs, who are bored, confined to the front yard, and never receive mental or physical exercise, continue to bark ferociously at passers-by all day. Yet, the owners are very personable; they love their dogs and believe the dogs are better off with them than in a shelter. Unfortunately, being in total ignorance of their dogs' needs is prevalent, as many dog owners in Hungary believe that providing love, food and shelter is all that dogs require. Yet, these dogs would be much more content if their owners made some effort to meet their physical and psychological needs. Admittedly, because these dogs are undersocialised and untrained, the owners would find it impossible to walk the three dogs simultaneously and don't have the time to either train them or walk them individually. As much as we want to, we cannot rescue every single dog. The cornerstone of responsible dog ownership begins with assessing how many dogs we can realistically accommodate, not just with space but with time for training, play, veterinarian bills and daily walks, bearing in mind the dogs' breed requirements.

These are examples of how dogs can become aggressive when we ignore their most basic needs. Even though the Cane Corso is a dangerous breed, we can mitigate its aggressive tendencies over time with the right genetic and environmental conditions, including careful breeding. Additionally, with early learning, early and ongoing socialisation, an experienced owner, training to modify their threshold, plenty of mental stimulation and an outlet for their natural drives, these dogs can also make loving and well-mannered house pets.

Dogs usually avoid hostility. However, red-zone dogs fuelled by intense frustration and possibly fear vent their aggression and lash out at the first thing that crosses their path. This behaviour often becomes self-rewarding when the hypothalamus releases dopamine into the pleasure centres of the brain.

It is regrettable to see so many urban dogs living under similar circumstances. However, unfortunately, humans globally still believe that their responsibility as pet owners only involves providing their pets with food and shelter.

CHAPTER 16
REACTIVITY, AGILITY, FOXES, GASTRITIS

There are volumes of books, articles, blogs on training reactive dogs, and all work well in a perfect world. Additionally, they often advise keeping a reactive dog calm by choosing the right environment and avoiding areas with off-leash dogs. My repertoire also incorporated behaviour adjustment training (BAT) by Grisha Stewart, offering a more natural spin on counterconditioning. Primarily, the foundations are the same. We set our dog up on a long leash, a reasonable distance from the helper and the trigger dog, ensuring our dog stays under threshold. Unlike counterconditioning, we do not lead our dog but allow it to choose how it wants to proceed. Whether to ignore the trigger in the distance or gradually move closer at its own pace allows our dog to control the outcomes it feels comfortable with.

Like other therapies, the focus is on managing the environment and avoiding dogs other than the trigger. This ensures our dog's safety so the desired behaviour can occur and be reinforced naturally. Even though I followed the rules and started Mila's rehabilitation in a quiet area using a combination of positive reinforcement, classical and operant conditioning, off-leash dogs were everywhere and continually disrupted our training. Unfortunately, it is not a perfect world. Owners are lulled into a sense of false security and don't always perceive the dangers of off-leash dog encounters and their detrimental effects on our canine companions.

One of the best ways to strengthen the bonds between owners and their dogs is a daily walk. This feel-good activity promotes a happy, healthy and well-balanced owner and dog. Secure in the knowledge that with leash laws, we should be able to keep our dogs safe, although that is not always the case.

As a matter of interest, my daughter, Tammy, and I undertook our own survey in various Budapest residential areas. Whereas we found that most small dogs are suitably restrained in our suburban neighbourhoods, in contrast, 30–50% of larger dogs that cause the problems are walked off-leash. Even in Hungary, explicit leash laws state that owners must secure dogs in all public areas to protect their four-legged friends from genuine dangers. Naturally, not all owners agree. Many feel that dogs should be allowed to follow their canine instincts and run free as nature intended.

Indeed, it would be wonderful to see our dogs running unshackled and unhindered. Living in relaxed social structures free of aggression, where each dog respects the others' personal space. Regrettably, domestication comes at a price. Humans have created artificial environments where we and our dogs must adapt to the constraints of urban habitats and their inherent dangers. This is why dogs' off-leash frolics should be limited to securely fenced areas like doggy parks and dog runs. In the words of dog trainer Adrienne Faricelli, "even service dogs are required to be on a leash, so regular pet dogs shouldn't be exempt even if they can do backflips or make you a cup of coffee."

An important consideration is that children and dogs are unable to weigh up the consequences of their actions or foresee impending dangers. Even street-smart dogs can run out onto the road in the blink of an eye, which often ends in tragedy. Therefore, it is up to their owners to ensure their safety and keep them from harming others. I cannot count the times I've been pounced on by 'friendly' unrestrained dogs leaping on me when out walking.

This is a dangerous habit, as large dogs can knock over children or senior citizens and potentially cause serious injuries. As responsible dog owners, we should also consider the emotional harm this practice can have. What might seem like an innocuous incident may traumatise a fearful person or child for life. Additionally, many unrestrained high prey drive dogs run the risk of chasing and killing small animals. Furthermore, large dogs often attack smaller dogs believing they are prey.

Surprisingly, when I registered Lulu and Franky at the local city council in Australia, the council worker cautioned me about walking both of them if I was on my own. Apparently, even in Australia, it is not unusual for large off-leash dogs to attack small breeds. If I was on my own, I could pick up one dog and protect it, but not two. One would not usually have the presence of mind to put a small dog in a rubbish bin to protect it, but that is precisely what a woman did when a large dog charged at them. At least her puppy remained safe until she could see off the large dog, or its owner materialised to restrain it.

All dogs, whether large or small, are susceptible to aggressive dog attacks. Last year, I read about a dog attack not far from us, where an unconstrained pit bull-type dog ran over to a leashed dachshund and killed it before anyone could intervene. As mandated, the authorities removed the killer hound to the pound, where, later that day, the owner paid a fine and collected her dog. The following morning, the owner and her unleashed dog returned to walking on the street. Unfortunately, this was not an isolated incident. Frequently, a dog whose owner is responsibly keeping it on a leash is attacked by an off-leash dog.

Even if an unrestrained 'friendly' dog rushes over to a leashed dog, these rude, unwarranted canine overtures are not always welcome and can be interpreted as a form of aggression. Just like humans, dogs have their own rituals when greeting each other. For example, in certain cultures, when people shake hands, they clamp the left hand over their lower right arm, signifying that the person comes in peace and has no hidden weapons in his left hand. The lack of a reciprocal gesture can be construed as either very rude or even hostile.

Similarly, dogs have their own methods of gauging intentions and weighing each other up by observing the other dog's tail signals and body language. Well-mannered dogs versed in appropriate canine greeting rituals never rush at each other head-on. Instead, they usually approach each other calmly from the side in a curve and move toward each other leisurely. An essential part of the introductory ritual are glandular secretions containing pheromones. These are released by the anal sacs and provide each dog with a plethora of information. When dogs meet, tail-wagging helps spread the pheromones from the anal glands, allowing for a kind of chemical communication. Dogs investigate these pheromone-scented greeting cards with their olfactory organs, which reveal an abundance of information about each dog. The chemical autobiographies are crammed with information about social status, age, sex, genetic relatedness, emotional and physiological state. Similarly, sniffing each other's *derrières* is part of this process, which constitutes a polite form of greeting and introduction, similar to a handshake in humans.

By the time two leashed dogs reach the 'polite handshake' phase of their introductions, often one or other of their human owners may pull their dog away in disgust. Unfortunately, cutting a dog off in mid-sniff can be construed as an impolite gesture, resulting in conflict or even an attack from the other dog. Generally, experts do not recommend introducing unfamiliar dogs to each other on a leash. Contrary to popular belief, these interactions do not qualify as socialisation. When canines sniff each other's *derrière* as a respectful form of social intercourse, they convey important details about each other. This information can influence their immediate behaviour responses, as well as long-term perspectives.

Unfortunately, many domestic dogs cannot read or send proper signals due to various body modifications, or through artificial breeding practices, such as docked tails, or because they lack vital early socialisation to other dogs.

When an unleashed dog bolts over to a restrained dog, it might miss warning signals telling it to back off. The leashed dog, unable to evaluate the mood or the intentions of the dog hurtling towards it, may interpret this as an aggressive gesture. Trapped and hindered by the leash and incapable of running away or weighing up its opponent, it might feel vulnerable to an attack and retaliate with hostility. These sudden encounters can quickly escalate into a fight whether the off-leash dog is aggressive or not. We could avoid all confrontational dog encounters by merely keeping our dogs leashed.

Moreover, when owners regularly allow leashed dogs to greet other leashed dogs, this sets up a precedent of anticipation. On subsequent occasions, if these interactions are denied, the dog will become frustrated, resulting in a reactive reaction of leash-pulling, lunging and jumping.

From experience, I appreciate that numerous owners invest a great deal of time, effort and finances to rehabilitate their dogs with fear, reactivity or aggressive issues. Unfortunately, Mila and I know only too well that all it takes is one encounter with an off-leash dog to undo weeks of training and hard work. No sooner than we manage to progress one step forward, and our efforts are swiftly hijacked. Similarly, it takes many years to produce a service dog and only takes a few seconds for an off-leash dog to leave lasting emotional trauma.

Additionally, unrestrained dogs that roam free also risk eating unsuitable items that can be dangerous or toxic. The undergrowth in parks often acts as a depository for all sorts of waste matter, including dog faeces and human excrement. Ingesting any of these can lead to parasitic infestations such as cryptosporidiosis, and bacterial infections, including salmonellosis and *E. coli*. A further lurking danger to unleashed dogs is human food containing xylitol.

Did you know that one or two pieces of chewing gum or half a discarded muffin containing xylitol can kill a dog?

Furthermore, even though I can safely say that I am a reliable driver, I cannot vouch for other drivers. For this reason, and because it is the law, I always wear my safety belt in the car for my own safety. Similarly, we may know that our dog is dependable, but we cannot vouch for other dogs, so for that reason, and because it is the law, we should always leash our dogs for their own safety.

Canines are genetically programmed to be out and about where nature intended, to forage for scraps, scavenge for food and explore their environment. In their natural state, they have periods of activity and rest throughout the day. Like humans, they are not meant to be locked in a room alone all day and need time to be dogs. They need to explore their territory and neighbourhood to retrieve messages left by other dogs on bushes and lamp posts. We know that daily exercise is essential for our canine companions to stay fit and healthy. An additional benefit is the massive amount of information they process from their daily dose of sniffing, which stimulates their brains. This is not just a need, but a physical and psychological compulsion programmed into a dog's DNA.

We cannot eliminate these instinctive urges that are controlled by the brain, and if we try and suppress them, we will only succeed in making our dogs miserable. If we don't give dogs an outlet for these natural compulsions, their pent-up energy and stress can lead to a host of inappropriate behaviours such as digging, destructive chewing, excess barking, anxiety and even aggression. We can usually eradicate these problems with the right amount of physical and mental stimulation. This can include daily walks with additional training and doggy sports for the more active dogs, all of which restore confidence and mental and emotional balance in dogs.

Without a doubt, walks are vital for dogs, but not if they cause an overload of stress and anxiety. Unfortunately, I can't provide a secure and controlled environment where I can safely walk Mila, because of the many off-leash encounters. Also, in Mila's case, I found that our walks seemed to cause more harm than good, and the long-term effects of stress on her health concerned me. Research has proved that stress reduces a dog's ability to learn and leads to increased levels of the stress hormone cortisol, which disturbs normal functioning. Each time our pooches reactively react to other dogs, their cortisol levels increase, which could take days to normalise. When dogs go over threshold and respond to various fear stimuli daily, elevated cortisol levels may not have enough time to recover. This overload can cause biological responses that disrupt the immune system, leading to multiple illnesses, just as it does in humans.

An additional benefit of a daily walk is sniffing, not for us, but for our dogs. We know that dogs process the world around them via their olfactory senses, which is essential for their mental wellbeing during their daily walks.

Have you noticed how dogs can apparently tell time? Dogs can perceive the difference between older, weaker odours and stronger, more recent ones. This is because scent molecules in the air change during the day, and while our scent might be strong in the morning when we leave for work, it will be weaker in the afternoon when we are about to return. Therefore, dogs can learn to associate that we are due home when odours have weakened to a certain intensity.

Sniffing allows dogs to absorb and organise incredible amounts of information about their environment and the creatures living in it. For example, they glean vital information, including the sex, age, health and diet of the various dogs that have posted wee mails on lamp posts. At the same time, the myriad of other scents and odours is their *Daily Mail* newspaper which keeps them up to date about current events. Although their noses can pick up old events as well and can even smell a human fingerprint a week old. Dogs can even track the scent of a person wearing rubber boots or riding a bicycle.

I noticed that Mila sniffed the ground obsessively on our many training walks, and the more I let her sniff, the more tense she became. However, she was noticeably less apprehensive when I kept her away from the verge and only allowed limited sniffing opportunities. Apparently, when some dogs sniff the ground and ignore everything else around them or present avoidance behaviours, it is an indication that they are anxious. According to canine behaviour expert Patricia McConnell, dogs that cannot stop sniffing where other dogs have been are often reactive and fear other dogs.

Interestingly, smell memories last a lifetime, and, as we know, odours have the power to conjure up both good and bad memories. These odour memories dictate how a dog will react to any given situation. It seemed that even the odour of other dogs was enough to stress Mila, which was confirmed by the incident when we first walked her. Arriving in an area where another pooch had walked a few minutes earlier, she screamed in fear, even though she had not physically seen the other dog. Mila's odour memory indicated she had an intense fear of dogs.

Just as walking and sniffing have many benefits, so does chewing. This is a necessary hardwired canine instinct, which is why we should not even attempt to eliminate this normal canine behaviour. Not only would this be cruel, but it would be virtually impossible. Just as humans use their hands, our curious canines investigate with their mouths. Additionally, chewing is perfectly natural for dogs of all ages. It is nature's way of keeping jaws strong and teeth clean. Dogs love to chew on bones, sticks and just about anything else available. They chew for stimulation, they chew for fun and they chew to relieve anxiety. Chewing on a favourite object is a great way to relax. The act of chewing has a calming and soothing effect on the adrenal-pituitary axis in the brain. This triggers the release of endorphins and is a tool that dogs have at their disposal to 'self-medicate' for anxiety and stress.

At the time, Mila was a fanatical chewer and used to gnaw through antlers in significant quantities and was obviously chewing to relieve anxiety. Eventually, I noticed that she chewed more compulsively on the days we walked. Our dogs' behaviour reveals much information about their wellbeing. Bearing in mind her leash reactivity, the intense sniffing on walks and vigorous chewing, Mila clearly communicated that she was stressed and anxious.

I had considered various options, even walking Mila in a cemetery; alas, dogs are not allowed in graveyards. Unfortunately, if I couldn't manage the environment where we walked and avoid situations detrimental to Mila, she would keep repeating and reinforcing the behaviours I wanted to reshape. Revising the facts, I had to evaluate what was best for Mila, from her perspective and not mine. Despite general recommendations for daily walks, one size does not fit all because dogs are as unique as we are. Not all things are black or white, and we often have to think in shades of grey to resolve individual canine difficulties. There are other ways to provide ample mental and physical stimulation without continually exposing Mila to something that obviously caused her so much anxiety. Therefore, I suspended our daily training walks and looked into other ways of meeting her physical and psychological needs.

On reflection, doggy day care seemed like an obvious choice. This would provide Mila with a safe venue where she could meet and play with other dogs, unrestricted by the physical and emotional shackles of a leash. The benefits of socialisation with Zoli's dogs were invaluable to Mila's rehabilitation, and it needed to remain ongoing. My disheartening search led from centres like Zoli's, located too far away, to backyard businesses with rickety fences and a mud wallow where the lawn should have been. I knew that there were kennels near us, where I took Lulu a few times, but it seemed to have disappeared off the grid.

I remembered the well-appointed small family-run kennels on a large acreage also offered day care facilities. Invisible behind high fences, I regularly passed the forested premises on my way to Pilates lessons, but there were no signs to indicate that the kennels were still functioning, and there was no gate bell. The family had started a petting zoo on the adjacent plot, and I feared that they had closed the dog boarding facilities. It did not bode well that their internet page hadn't been refreshed for years.

After a few dead ends, I managed to contact the owner, András, who assured me that both the kennels and the day care were operational and invited us to inspect the premises. I was delighted that the compact indoor kennel building was still immaculately presented. Since my last visit with Lulu, András had implemented several functional improvements, including a sizeable, enclosed area on the forested grounds where the dogs could securely explore and play. As the facility can only cater to a limited number of dogs, it is always well supported by regular clients. The owners don't have to advertise. Even though Mila was on a leash, she behaved exceptionally and seemed very interested in her surroundings. Although I explained her issues to András, he didn't perceive any problems.

Initially, they release new dogs out into the yard on their own until they relax and feel happy in their new environment. In time, they match the newcomer with a similar-sized dog to assess their response and behaviour and gradually let them join small compatible groups in the grassed yard. I'm delighted to report that Mila took to day care like a seasoned veteran and had absolutely no issues at all. Much to Mila's delight, I continue to take her several times a week. According to the caring staff, she is a firm favourite, not just with them but also with the other dogs. Because of her amiability, they often pair her with more difficult dogs, even unsociable Akitas.

On our arrival in the mornings, Mila excitedly flies into the arms of Szandi, her most beloved human carer. Without a backward glance, she trots off to reunite with her circle of canine friends. The only bone of contention is the owner's young boxer, Happy. Even as a puppy, three times Mila's size, he overstepped the boundaries and annoyed Mila with his clownish exuberance. Being a much heavier dog, his roughhousing distressed Mila, no matter how well intentioned. Happy's *joie de vivre* has not waned with maturity, so the owners usually keep him away from the kennels and day care. On occasions when their paths cross, Mila tolerates him silently with unconcealed apprehension. Since her introduction to day care, Mila is noticeably more relaxed and has stopped aggressively chewing the antler, which I seldom have to replace. When Rezső and I need to go away, Mila is also happy to spend a few nights at the kennels in familiar surroundings.

In the past, I'd already lucked out on finding a trainer for nose work. However, wishing to challenge Mila further, I contacted an agility centre with covered premises, which allows them to hold private and group classes year-round. When I spoke to the owner, I mentioned that Mila learns quickly, but, due to her background, she has specific issues. Because of this, I suggested private lessons, so she wouldn't be disruptive in a class with other dogs. Unfortunately, the centre was only interested in training competition dogs, and other schools were too far for us to contemplate.

Undaunted, I bought a set of agility poles and set about training Mila on my own in the garden. Unfortunately, the poles took ages to master. Not because of any deficit on Mila's part, but because of my own incompetence. Even though Mila eventually conquered the slalom poles, they were never her favourite equipment. Although, now that I am more experienced, I can retrain her at some point, so she learns to enjoy them more.

Following the slalom poles, I purchased a few jumps, which were more Mila's forté, as jumping came naturally to her. With her dachshund genetics, mastering our third piece of equipment, the tunnel, proved effortless. Although, initially, she stared at me blankly, and I had to crawl through the tunnel to show her what I expected her to do. Fortunately, she caught on fast.

I bought a seesaw, which is a challenging piece of equipment. It can be highly daunting for anxious dogs with an aversion to loud noises when the end bangs down. Fortunately, our training went smoothly. Within a short time, with ample rewards, Mila confidently powered up and down the seesaw. Obviously, my agility training skills had improved. Although, Mila's cocker and English spaniel ancestors enjoy dog sports such as hunting, tracking, retrieving, competitive obedience and agility, and perhaps her talents are genetic.

Eventually, I hit on the idea of moving the course inside for year-round use, as some of the equipment like the seesaw was for indoor use only. Our unfurnished, rectangular, open-plan top floor with high cathedral ceilings and large double windows at both ends proved to be the ideal bright space, while glass balustrades protect the central square staircase, which neatly divides the room. I set up the course with the seesaw and slalom, for which I use brightly coloured cones, under the picture windows at the two wide ends, respectively. At the same time, the pink tunnel and multicoloured jumps are positioned along the narrower side portions.

Of course, the vibrant colours are wasted on Mila and are more for my benefit than hers. While humans have three different types of colour receptors or cones in the retina, all tuned to varying wavelengths of light, dogs only have two. Whereas we see rainbow colours as violet, blue, blue-green, green, yellow, orange and red, dogs see dark blue, light blue, grey, yellow, brownish yellow and dark grey. In actual fact, the agility accessories and toys should be in tones of blues and yellows that are the two colours most readily discernible by dogs. Although popular colours for dog toys are red and orange, these are difficult colours for dogs to see and may get lost in the background.

Back to agility, but I had to first cover the teak hardwood floors with bright non-slip mats. Although it is a year-round course, I found that we spend more time in the garden in the warmer months and use this space primarily in winter when we are housebound. As a warm-up, and to encourage focus, we begin our sessions with obedience work followed by agility. We start the course at the near end to the right of the seesaw with the five-metre-long tunnel that Mila races down, opening onto six slalom cones at the far end. Then, turning right over the six brightly coloured jumps along the side brings her onto the seesaw leading back to the tunnel. When I want to stimulate Mila further, I can rearrange the equipment, modify the order, or reverse the direction. I can even add more equipment in time and have my eye on an indoor A-frame and bridge or balance ramp.

Agility is a well-known, powerful confidence-builder which provides mental stimulation for dogs, and which Mila thoroughly enjoys. It also reduces boredom and destructive behaviours and reinforces good behaviour. It is immensely gratifying to watch Mila manoeuvre over the course with ease and emerge at the other end triumphant in her success.

Additionally, our sizeable, sloping property with dual street frontage offers ample exercise opportunities between the back lane and the front cul-de-sac. While our neighbour's dog, Paws, keeps watch and barks at passers-by at the back thoroughfare, Lego & Co do the same on the upper road. With a gradient difference of two storeys between the two streets, Mila races up and down the shaded lawn several times a day. Naturally, this is accompanied by loud vocalising to keep up with the other barking dogs. Although the exercise keeps her fit and trim, the barking dogs do stress Mila. Generally, we are advised to remove stressors that cause anxiety. However, we do not have that option in this instance. From spring till autumn, she is an efficient garden supervisor. I often see her sitting in front of Rezső, watching him intently while he is hard at work, weeding, clipping, digging, planting, fertilising and mowing.

Adept at retrieving, courtesy of her spaniel heritage, we play with the Frisbee on cooler days. Though in the heat of summer, Mila loves to indulge in watermelon, which she happily munches, the juice spilling out of her mouth, dripping onto the lawn. Unwilling to waste a drop, she licks each blade of grass until she is satisfied that they are juice free. However, every now and then, we find watermelon plants growing in the middle of the garden courtesy of the seeds she leaves behind. Sometimes I scatter treats, cubed carrots, and apples all over the garden, and Mila enjoys foraging for them. She seldom misses any.

Under the circumstances, I felt that we had covered most of Mila's basic physical and psychological needs even without daily walks. With foraging sessions, lots of play, day care, the large garden for exercise, agility and obedience training, there was more than enough to keep her active and stimulated. And more importantly, she is happy and less anxious. Of course, I will not give up on our daily walks yet, but at least I know I don't have to force the issue, as we have ample other outlets for her canine instincts.

Additionally, our property is an established access route for nocturnal animals. These include neighbourhood cats, martens and foxes that leave plenty of tracks and provide ample sniffing opportunities for Mila the following day.

Have I mentioned that Mila hates cats? Whenever she glimpses one in the garden, all hell breaks loose as she explodes from the house, barking loudly. Dachshunds are infamous for their vociferous barking. Amused, I watch her as she charges up to where she last saw the cat, only to find that the feline intruder has already escaped. Although, I have seen her get lucky and flush out a cat from the undergrowth. With ears flapping and barking at the top of her voice, she chased the hapless feline across the lawn. Within a millisecond, I noticed that it was a very odd-looking cat and realised that she was actually hot on the heels of a panicked fox. This brave or foolhardy behaviour is unusual, as foxes avoid dogs and tend to visit much later after I have securely locked Mila up for the night.

With the help of a trail camera, I've verified that we have one regular fox visiting our property most of the year. Generally, they are solitary hunters, although they can cover territories of 4–8km^2 with overlapping areas. Throughout January, the fox population explodes in our garden during mating season. On any one night, we have had up to five vulpine visitors searching for their forever partners. Red foxes mate for life, though they seldom remain monogamous. Insomnia often plagues me, and I find myself up at all hours of the night. During the mating season, on my nightly wanderings, I'd often see at least one fox taking a protracted tour of our property while calling to other foxes.

One night I watched our regular vixen with her mate for several hours as she walked all over the garden, and he dutifully followed. Every now and then, he'd try to take liberties, without her permission, when she'd face him, and they'd both rise up on their hind legs with their front paws on each other's shoulders. The 'fox trot' is usually an adversarial stance presented by two rival males trying to push each other over. In this instance, it was a reprimand from the vixen for her mate's unchivalrous behaviour. One hour later, after several tours of the garden and several more fox trots, they curled up on the edge of the lawn and went to sleep, next to but not touching each other. That was my cue to also try and get back to sleep. In the morning, there were two dark green patches on the lawn where the foxes had slept and the frost was unable to make its mark.

These interactions in our urban environment offer an exciting glimpse into vulpine behaviour. The only cause for concern was that several foxes had sarcoptic mange. Over the years that I've observed the local fox population, this is the first time I'd noticed any mangy foxes. Several thousand female *Sarcoptes scabiei* mites may burrow into a single square centimetre of skin, depositing an accumulation of tissue fluids and debris on the fox's skin, which forms an intensely itching crust up to 1.5 centimetres thick. The animal will chew or scratch obsessively at the affected area, causing a loss of hair and skin lesions that often become infected. As the mites burrow, they feed on tissue fluid and lay their eggs. Subsequently, on maturity, they extend their mothers' burrow system. A severely infected animal may be host to several million mites. Sarcoptic mange is highly contagious. Depending on population densities, over 30% of foxes can be infected in specific clusters. Following the 1994 mange outbreak in the Bristol area of UK, the fox population decreased by 95%. While numerous foxes died, mange infestation also reduced the reproductive capabilities of males and females. In subsequent years, similar numbers have been recorded in various European outbreaks.

From my nightly trail camera photos, I identified that three of the five foxes were infected to a greater or lesser degree. Our vixen's mate was also infected, with only a pompom of fur on his otherwise naked tail. Even though the infection can clear up on its own, it will spread all over its body if the animal cannot overcome the infestation. The resulting generalised skin lesions, thick crusts, foul odour, with an increase in bacteria and yeast, will eventually lead to emaciation and death.

In a Swedish study, three red foxes were intentionally infected with *Sarcoptes scabiei*. The first sign of mange appeared in all the foxes thirty-one days after infection. Over the following months, two of the foxes developed severe symptoms, one of which died 121 days after being infected. Sarcoptic mange is also highly contagious to dogs and humans, although they cannot complete their lifecycle in humans and rarely survive more than a few days. Because mites can survive between three and twenty-one days without a host, on the ground, or on vegetation, even in cold weather, we are advised to keep dogs from areas where foxes frequent to prevent infection.

In our case, this was unfeasible; as the foxes roam over every inch of our garden, across the lawn, terraces, under shrubs, it was impossible to keep Mila indoors. Naturally, I was concerned about the mange spreading, not only within the fox population but also to Mila and neighbourhood dogs. Hoping to find some assistance for the foxes, I wrote to the Forestry Department, who informed me that urban areas are not under their jurisdiction. I also contacted our vet, who had no suggestions on the vulpine matter but recommended using Bravecto (fluralaner) or Nexgard Spectra (afoxolaner) for Mila. Both these medications protect dogs against ticks, fleas, as well as demodectic and sarcoptic mange. They are also successfully used to treat infected animals. If you recall, we used Bravecto to cure Mila of the demodectic mange, not to be confused with sarcoptic mange.

Not wasting any time, I quickly put Mila on Bravecto, contacted our neighbour, and suggested they might also wish to consider prevention for Paws. Unfortunately, my letter to our city council also led to another dead end. Although the response was polite, there was nothing they can do. They do not interfere with sick wildlife and leave their fate to nature, especially as red foxes are not a protected species. Similarly, the Noé Animal Shelter that has a small fox refuge was unable to help. Although, they brilliantly suggested that I put Bravecto in small meatballs to treat our visiting foxes.

Before I could tackle Plan Bravecto, Rezső bought a few rolls of wire mesh to reinforce our wrought iron fencing and hamper future fox visitations. Although the fence is Mila proof, the slimmer and more agile foxes cleverly find access. Without even undertaking any work, the fencing materials left in the garden proved to be an efficient deterrent that kept the foxes away for a few nights. Obviously, with similar instincts to dogs, they are wary of anything new or unusual and kept their distance.

Bearing this in mind, my friend Judy suggested periodically moving a couple of mannequins around the garden as a suitable fox deterrent. I can imagine them in various poses, raking, digging, weeding, or standing around in a group mutely chatting to each other. The sight of dummies scattered around the premises would surely intrigue our neighbours. Now that I think about it, the robotic lawnmowers moving silently across the lawn would also be proficient at discouraging fox visitations. The downside is that they are not nocturnal and usually only work during the day when Rezső is on hand to free them if they get stuck. Additionally, they hibernate in winter.

Traditional fox deterrents include motion sensor lights, which lose their effectiveness when the foxes habituate to them. A similar recommendation is a motion sensor water sprinkler system, which freezes and is unusable in sub-zero weather. So back to the dummies, although the foxes would in time also habituate to them. However, I discovered that alpacas hate foxes. In their native South America, alpacas have developed an instinctive aversion to foxes, which often prey on their young. With strong guarding instincts, keen eyesight and sharp hearing, alpacas are alert to dangers and will chase foxes and other small predators. If a fox is unfortunate enough to get cornered, adult alpacas will trample it to death. With these deterrents, we don't even have to foxproof the fence. All we need are several mesh rolls dotted around the garden, add a few alpacas with a sprinkling of dummies, and let the robot mowers loose. Doubtless, not many foxes would be willing to run that gauntlet.

Although, with the end of the mating season, I noticed a sudden decline in fox numbers. The trail camera only captured our regular vixen and a magnificent specimen I named Bushy from his spectacularly bushy tail. Inclement weather also delayed Plan Bravecto, but, eventually, I placed a chewable tablet out on the terrace in front of the trail camera and hoped for the best. Bushy did not disappoint. Although he does not look infected, the Bravecto should clear up any mites within a month, even if he is. On the other hand, if he is not infected, it will protect him from infection for three months. He was back for more the next night, but I withheld the Bravecto in anticipation of his return.

Before Rezső got to work on reinforcing the fence, I was hoping to dose our vixen as well, although she proved unusually elusive. With the arrival of arctic weather conditions, I decided to postpone Plan Bravecto. The trail camera lens often freezes over with snow or ice and can't record any photos. Additionally, the hinge freezes solid, and it is impossible to retrieve the memory card. Although, before I adjourned the trail camera, I had quite a unique sighting. During one of those nights when sleep eluded me, I saw an animal slink up to the low retaining wall that gives access to the terrace in front of my study. Backlit by the garden lights, all I could make out was a foxy silhouette, but I did not see a tail when it jumped from the wall to the terrace. The evidence provided by the trail camera and video footage from our security camera proved me correct. Our nocturnal visitor was a fox without a tail. Other than the missing appendage, it seemed in perfect health.

Foxes are good climbers and there are no guarantees that the mesh will keep them out in the long term. Mesh wire is used to keep chickens in and not to keep foxes out. Naturally, this also depends on what incentives our garden offers. The household rubbish is well contained in a purpose-built cement structure with metal doors, and Mila is always fed indoors. Additionally, the daily menu of resident moles, mice and earthworms provides slim pickings. However, during spring, nesting birds in our hedges are plentiful and offer richer rewards. Only time will tell. As much as I enjoy our vulpine sightings, it is worrying to have contagious foxes in such close proximity to Mila. Even if the odds are very low, we cannot risk Mila's health.

And then, Mila got sick.

One morning she had a bout of bilious vomiting, which happens a few times a year, early in the morning on an empty stomach. Dogs only experience bilious vomiting when the stomach is empty, and bile leaks into the stomach causing irritation and a small amount of foamy, yellow vomit. As long as the condition is not chronic and only produces a small volume of vomit with no other alarming symptoms, there is no cause for concern. But this time, she walked very gingerly with a hunched back, indicating a painful abdomen, and ignored her food, which was totally out of character. In the four years we've had Mila, she has never shunned food.

A trip to the vet, Dr Anna, who we also saw alternatively to Dr Réka, revealed that she had an inflammation somewhere in her digestive system. After a vitamin B12 injection, armed with antibiotics, probiotics and anti-vomiting tablets, we headed home. Dr Anna also instructed me to feed Mila a diet of rice mixed with a small amount of her usual hypoallergenic dog food, which she ate that evening. The following day, she remained stable, but we had some more bilious vomiting with blood swirls on day three. Her stools, which had remained firm throughout, were also bloody. Taking samples with me, we headed back to the vet.

Dr Anna decided to keep Mila for a few hours, while giving her intravenous anti-inflammatories and conducting additional tests, including ultrasound and blood work. When I collected her, there was still no specific diagnosis. Parasitic infestation had been ruled out. Similarly, there was no internal blockage, although an injury to the stomach lining or even some form of toxicity, either chemical or organic, was still a possibility. With additional medication, anti-inflammatories, B12 vitamin tablets, and gastrointestinal protectant granules to sprinkle over Mila's food, we headed home once again.

Fortunately, we didn't have any further cause for alarm, and within a few days, Mila reverted to her usual self. When the lab results arrived, they revealed that Mila had gastritis, an inflammation/infection of the stomach, or pancreatitis. It is difficult to tell the difference, as the symptoms and the treatment for both are similar. The cause also remained a mystery, although it is typically triggered by consuming a large amount of very fatty foods, or poisoning. Mila never has access to human food, and we don't keep poisons on the premises, so we could rule out these causes.

Bacterial infections can develop after eating spoiled or contaminated food. We could not be sure whether the foxes had deposited any such offerings in our garden. Viral infections can also occur. Additionally, there is a higher prevalence of pancreatitis in some breeds, including cocker spaniels and dachshunds. That is a double whammy for Mila, with both breeds represented in her genetic background. Whatever the cause, gastritis and pancreatitis are severe conditions that can become life-threatening if not treated in time.

At times we have found bones in our garden, which were probably brought in by foxes. Therefore, we couldn't overlook the possibility that they may have contributed somehow to Mila's illness. Bearing this in mind and not taking any chances, Rezső wasted no time securing the mesh deterrent to our fence. Hopefully, our vulpine visitors will no longer be able to squeeze through the wrought iron bars, and only time will tell if they learn to climb over it. Alas, this also summarily terminated my attempts to continue with Plan Bravecto.

CHAPTER 17
OUR RELATIONSHIP WITH DOGS

Over the centuries, from ancient civilisations to our modern world, we have in turn either revered or reviled dogs. Although Egyptians had a profound relationship with cats, nevertheless, dogs were highly valued members of the family. Ancient wall paintings depicting Tutankhamun hunting with his dogs are testimony to the connection Egyptians had with canines. While Egyptians regularly shaved their heads and bodies to avoid lice, they even shaved their eyebrows, which was a sign of their exceptional grief when beloved family dogs died.

Even though archaeologists discovered catacombs dedicated to the canine god Anubis in the Saqqara Necropolis during the nineteenth century, it was not until 2015 that a team of Egyptologists and researchers revealed the true extent of the burial site. The team made a spectacular discovery during routine excavations when they uncovered an estimated eight million mummified dogs in the subterranean burial chambers. Some theories suggest pilgrims left mummified puppies in the tombs as religious offerings to Anubis, god of mummification and the afterlife. As canines had a solid affiliation to Anubis, perhaps the mummified gifts ensured safe passage for the souls of the devoted to the Hall of Truth, where Osiris, Lord of the Underworld and Judge of the Dead, awaited them.

From religion to mythology, legends of hell hounds are rife. While the Greek three-headed Cerberus, known as the Hound of Hades, guards the gates of hell and prevents the dead from leaving, dogs are also prominently featured in the heavens. The stellar constellations Canis Major and Canis Minor represent the mythological hunter, Orion's faithful companions and hunting dogs. Like the Romans, the Greeks were devoted to their dogs, and by the time of Hippocrates, they were very experienced in the use of veterinary medicine.

While Roman mythology considered dogs worthy of serving the gods, as depicted by the huntress Diana, often portrayed with dogs at her feet, they also fulfilled more mundane positions as bedwarmers on cold winter nights. Dogs also served as Roman sacrifices to celebrate the heliacal setting of the Dog Star, Sirius, when it sets together with the Sun and remains invisible until mid-July, when the constellation of Canis Major, Latin for Greater Dog, becomes visible in the heavens once again. Because the first visible rising of Sirius occurs during the hottest parts of summer in the northern hemisphere, ancient civilisations attributed the subsequent heatwaves from early July to early September to the brightest star in the Canis Major constellation Sirius.

The Romans and Greeks believed the Dog Star was

responsible for the unbearable summer temperatures and called this time of the year '*hemerai kynades*' in Greek or '*dies caniculares*' in Latin, which means 'dog days'. Often referred to in the diminutive, Sirius was also known as 'Canicula', the small dog within Canis Major, the Greater Dog. While most English-speaking countries know the summer heatwaves as 'dog days', many Latin and European countries still refer to this period as *canicula* in Spanish, *canicule* in French, *canicola* in Italian and even *kánikula* in Hungarian.

Whereas the Greeks and Romans often kept companion dogs, and although the Koran mentioned and approved dogs as hunting aids, Muslim cultures perceive dogs as unclean scavengers and prohibit the handling of dogs. Similarly, even though Jewish law does not forbid dogs, it frowns on keeping dogs in one's home, as most are associated with violence and uncleanliness.

In contrast, Zoroastrianism, the ancient pre-Islamic Persian religion, believes that a dog's gaze has the power to keep demons away, and canines guard the Chinvat Bridge to Heaven. They also advocate severe punishment to those who mistreat dogs, which is a sentiment I vociferously support.

Although many Bible verses condemn dogs as vile, dirty, evil creatures, other sections refer to them as faithful. When St Roch, the Patron Saint of Dogs, caught the plague, a dog befriended and cared for him, licked his wounds and took him food. As a tribute, they celebrate the birthday of all dogs on 16 August in Bolivia, which marks the feast day of St Roch. Many South American cultures believe that dogs are guides to the afterlife.

Mystical Eastern beliefs seem to have had a more significant affiliation to dogs than the monotheistic religions. As the guards of heaven and hell, dogs are a notable feature in Hinduism. In Nepal, during the second day of Kukur Tihar, better known as Diwali, one of the most important Hindu festivals, dogs are celebrated and honoured for their loyalty to humans. Devotees uniformly bless pets and strays alike with the Tika, the holy vermillion dot on the forehead. Additionally, worshippers festoon dogs with marigold garlands and feed them special treats during the day.

Both the Aztecs and Mayans revered the hairless Mexican dog Xoloitzcuintle, believed to have healing powers, who escorted the dead through the underworld. Thus, dogs not only fulfilled a religious requirement but, along with turkeys, were also part of the ancient Mexican diet. Interestingly, from the Guatemalan Highlands originates the legend that after the first dog witnessed the world's creation, it ran around sharing these secrets with anyone who would listen. The creator was so enraged by these actions, he punished the dog by swapping the head for its tail. Since then, instead of broadcasting secrets, the dog can now only wag its tail.

Also worthy of mention is that the dog is one of the twelve animals honoured in Chinese astrology; however, according to folklore, dogs only came eleventh in the Chinese Zodiac great race due to their carefree and playful nature. In commemoration, the second day of the Chinese New Year celebrates the birthday of all dogs, and strays are exceptionally well fed on that day.

Yet, in turn, dogs have also kept humans well fed over the centuries. Although most cultures did not routinely eat dog meat, in times of famine, when meat was scarce, dog meat was not wasted and was considered a delicacy. Even though some countries still offer dog meat for sale, with international pressure, these practices are gradually dying. Despite the Yulin dog meat festival, which the organisers first started in 2009, 75% of Chinese citizens support a ban on eating dog meat. In 2020, Shenzhen became the first Chinese city to ban the sale and consumption of dog meat, which Zhuhai, Beijing and Wuhan shortly followed. Additionally, the Chinese Government has prepared guidelines to reclassify dogs as pets rather than livestock and has released a draft policy that would forbid eating canine meat, signalling an end to the human consumption of dogs.

Whereas the sale and consumption of dog meat still flourish in parts of Asia and various African countries, it is surprising to note that although many Western countries have banned the sale of dog meat, its consumption is not illegal. For example, although there is a ban on the sale of dog meat in the UK, there is no ban on eating it. Similarly, in some Australian states, while the sale of dog meat is illegal, the slaughter and consumption of dogs is not illegal for personal use. In Canada, anyone who owns an animal can legally kill and eat it, including farmed animals and lawfully owned companion animals, such as cats and dogs. Although Swiss authorities have banned the commercial slaughter and sale of dog meat, farmers are allowed to slaughter dogs for personal consumption.

Even though Western cultures are critical regarding dog meat consumption, they perpetuate untold horrors against animals in their own countries in the name of research.

Each year, laboratories use an estimated 115 million or more animals, including amphibians, rodents, pigs, apes, cats and dogs, for research purposes worldwide. According to the combined 2015 statistics of thirty-six countries, research institutes used 112,265 dogs for testing in these nations. By applying the weighted average percentage of the above countries, the scientists estimated that in 2015, a total of 207,724 dogs were used in research procedures globally. The top ten countries using dogs were: China, the United States, Canada, South Korea, Japan, Australia, Brazil, the United Kingdom, Germany and India. Recent statistical estimates indicate that there has been a notable increase in the global use of laboratory animals over ten years, from 115.2 to 192.1 million animals.

Breeders supply purpose-bred research dogs to facilities that mainly utilise beagles because of their intermediate size and friendly and trusting natures. Often these dogs are devocalised, so they cannot bark and disrupt technicians in the research facilities. Despite this, animal testing is an emotive subject, with legitimate arguments favouring animal testing. After all, many human lives are saved daily, which would not be possible without drug research and animal testing. However, it is also true that not all animal experimentation is solely for pharmaceutical testing but is also readily employed in industrial research. During many experiments, dogs are subjected to repeated invasive surgeries, implanted with medical devices, exposed to infectious diseases, used for genetic manipulation, and force-fed drugs and pesticides over months. Once the dogs have served their purpose, technicians euthanise them so researchers can study their tissues and organs. Records show that up to 5% of animals experience severe pain, 26% moderate, 50% mild, 11% sub-threshold, and 7% are non-recovery, which means that the animal was anaesthetised before the procedure and euthanised without ever recovering consciousness.

Further shocking statistics reveal that 92% of drugs tested on animals are ineffective in humans, and 98% of tested drugs never reach consumers. For example, over 93% of cancer drugs were ineffectual in human clinical trials after successful animal testing. Additionally, while 100 HIV vaccines were successful in animal experiments, 100% failed to protect humans adequately. In many countries, two-species mammalian testing is a legal requirement that researchers can successfully implement in basic research. However, experts in the scientific field question the reliability of animal models to predict human responses based on the quantitative and qualitative differences between species.

Regulators largely overlook enforcement of alternatives for basic research, and some scientists continue to use animals. However, they could choose alternatives such as *in vitro* tests, three-dimensional modelling and bioprinting, *in silico* tests, organ-on-chip technologies, computer modelling and human micro-dosing. Unfortunately, there are several obstacles to the replacement of animal testing, including deeply entrenched roots in the scientific establishment, bureaucracy and resistance to change.

Probably, the most famous victim of research in the name of human advancement was Laika, the cosmonaut dog from Russia, destined to become the first living being in space. Officials collected several stray, mixed-breed dogs from the streets of Moscow and prepared them for space flight at the research facility. Firstly, to emulate the confined capsule of the Sputnik 2 cabin, technicians kept the little dogs in compact cages, which severely restricted their movements. Their preparation also included training in a centrifuge that replicated the rocket launch's acceleration and in machines that simulated a spacecraft's noise.

Of the three dogs in training, the three-year-old Laika showed the most promising results in the centrifuge and adapted well to tight spaces, an essential requirement for the confined space capsule. The dogs also underwent surgery to implant cables with sensors to monitor their vital signs after launch, scheduled for the 3rd of November 1957. At the time, nobody knew the effects of space flight on humans and whether they could even survive outside of the earth's atmosphere. However, the space programme scientist knew from the start that Sputnik 2 was a suicide mission, an unrecoverable flight. Sadly, the regrettable circumstances dictated that the canine astronaut would live for several days in space until the oxygen ran out, when a pre-programmed delivery system would gently euthanise it with medication-laced space food.

Several days before the launch, out of the three dogs, the project director chose Laika for the mission, and lift-off for the historic flight took place as scheduled. However, the monitors showed that Laika's heart rate shot up three times faster than usual during take-off, indicating extreme stress. Then, unexpectedly after launch, when the nose cone separated from the rocket, part of the heat shield tore loose, causing irreparable problems with the thermal control system. As a result, the capsule could no longer maintain average temperatures, which gradually rose to above 40°C and became a veritable oven.

After several hours and several orbits around the Earth, Laika's sensors failed to detect any further signs of life. Laika, the little street dog from Moscow, was catapulted to fame yet died alone, in abject terror and stress from hyperthermia, commonly known as heatstroke. Laika's space coffin continued to orbit the Earth for another five months before burning up and disintegrating on re-entry to Earth's atmosphere on the 14th of April 1958. By surviving for several hours, Laika's sacrifice was apparently not in vain, as she proved that life in space was a real possibility. In 2008, Russian officials unveiled a monument to Laika near the Moscow military research facility where her space journey began.

Laika's gruesome and tragic death is a poignant reminder of the thousands of dogs that die annually from heatstroke. Even relatively mild outside temperatures can generate extreme heat in locked cars within minutes. For example, mild outside temperatures of 24°C become 40°C in a closed vehicle within twenty minutes and close to 50°C in thirty minutes. Similarly, while outdoor summer temperatures often reach 30°C and over, they can generate internal vehicle temperatures of 40°C within ten minutes and close to 50°C in twenty minutes. Excessive heat gradually increases a dog's core temperature, as they only sweat through the pads of their feet and cannot lose heat quickly enough from panting. The average body temperature for dogs is 38.3–39.2°C, increasing to over 40°C within fifteen minutes. Once their core body temperature reaches over 41.5°C, enzymes are destroyed, and cells start to break down. As the gut leaks toxins into the body, cells begin to die, and a devastating inflammatory response takes place, causing blood clots that obstruct blood vessels throughout the body. This damage is rapidly followed by multi-organ failure and death.

Naturally, we understand the importance of a daily walk, but not at the expense of their health. Walking dogs in high temperatures is just as dangerous as leaving them unattended in cars and can result in severe and irreversible damage and death. In hot weather, pavements radiate intense heat, especially for dogs low to the ground. A foolproof way to test the temperature of the pavement is to place the back of your hand on the hot surface, and if you cannot hold it there for seven seconds, it is too hot for your dog. Additional good advice is to avoid walking during the canicula of the summer months and remember that the optimum temperature for walking and exercising dogs is around 19°C. Even though most dogs will tolerate temperatures up to 25°C, dogs with underlying health issues, including obesity, are already at risk. Walking dogs in temperatures over 25°C endangers puppies, obese, flat-faced and especially large dogs.

Throughout the summer heat, I'm constantly appalled by the number of people I see walking or jogging with their dog during the hottest part of the day when temperatures are well over 25°C. Exercise triggers ten times as many heat-related incidents as hot cars, and vets warn that it is best to avoid walking our dogs on scorching days.

How can we tell if our dogs are too hot?

The most obvious sign of heat exhaustion is relatively easy to spot and includes rapid excessive panting and drooling. On the other hand, dehydration is more challenging to determine, and we should watch out for a dry nose and lethargy; therefore, we must ensure that we keep our dogs well hydrated, especially on outings.

In the UK, the 2016 research data shows that vets treated almost 400 dogs for heat-related issues, of which 14% died. Circulatory failure, oxygen deficiency, and long-term damage to brains and organs are the typical consequences of owners unaware they are endangering their dogs' lives. Not only are dogs left in overheating cars, exercised in extreme heat, but owners often leave them outside, suffering for days in yards that lack shade, in unrelenting temperatures and humidity. From an earlier chapter, you may recall Franky, our dachshund, who refused to walk in temperatures over 25°C. Unfortunately, not all dogs are as intuitive as Franky, so as pet parents, it is up to us to be responsible and protect our dogs from the summer heat. Heatstroke in dogs is avoidable.

Unfortunately, humans are not infallible, and, occasionally, through sheer ignorance, they fail to protect their dogs. In the past, history has not always painted us in a favourable light. For example, when America declared war on Germany in 1917, the population religiously avoided all things German. Although German shepherds became Alsatians, sauerkraut became liberty cabbage and they referred to dachshunds as liberty dogs, a name change couldn't eliminate the evil connection associated with the German enemy. Restaurant owners even took Wiener schnitzel off their menus. Anything even remotely German suffered the consequences, as did the little dachshunds. Frequent reports detailed angry crowds verbally and physically assaulting dachshunds and even stomping them to death when owners took them out for walks. Apparently, after an enraged mob harassed and tormented a breeder, he went home and shot all the dachshunds in his kennels to avoid further confrontations and reprisals.

In Ohio, residents rounded up and killed a large number of German breeds, including dachshunds, and threw them into a pit. The hysteria was not limited to a few random acts but was fuelled by an overwhelming amount of government-generated anti-German propaganda. Political cartoons depicted dachshunds wearing German helmets and the iron cross, being choked to death by Uncle Sam. Other placards showed dachshunds being killed by bulldogs, the United States Marine Corp symbol, which encouraged the insanity. Naturally, the dachshund population plummeted and went from one of the ten most popular breeds in America to a surviving population of only twelve dogs by 1919. Although there don't seem to be similar documented cases in Britain, suffice it to say that in 1913 there were 217 registered dachshunds in Britain, and by 1919 there were none.

Sadly, in England, the darkest days for pets were still to come. In the summer of 1939, the National Air Raid Precautions Animals Committee prepared a notice to animal owners, which appeared in virtually every newspaper in England. In anticipation of possible food shortages and rationing, which might lead to the starvation of pets, it urged owners that if England declared war on Germany, they should move all city pets to the country. The notice further suggested that if relocation were not an option, it would be kindest to destroy them.

When England did declare war on Germany in September 1939, thousands of pet owners had healthy and cherished family pets euthanised. Within a week, vets and shelters euthanised 400,000 animals. Furthermore, additional records indicate that in total 750,000 pets were destroyed in England during the early days of the war. Naturally, those tragic events weighed heavily on those who had to implement such unimaginable horrors and euthanise perfectly healthy pets. Understandably, many believed that after the introduction of food rationing it was immoral to use food for pets. Although, during the mayhem, there were still voices of sanity who urged caution, and among others, Battersea Dogs and Cats Home managed to feed and save 145,000 dogs during the war.

Over the centuries, historical artefacts and writings show that many civilisations specifically trained dogs to participate in wars. From the ancient worlds, Greeks, Romans, Celts all routinely used dogs as guards, messengers, first aid dogs, patrol dogs, mine dogs and draught dogs to pull carts for food and supplies, including weapons and ammunition. Attila the Hun, who used large Molossian dogs, also implemented these practices, while in the twelfth century, Irishmen took wolfhounds into battle. From the fifteenth to the eighteenth century, mastiffs were a popular choice on the battlefields from England to Spain and France. In 1884, Germany established the first military training school for dogs, and by the start of WWI, all factions had serving military canines. The most suitable breeds for war conditions proved to be Alsatians, Belgian shepherds, Airdale terriers, schnauzers, Dobermann pinschers, boxers and Labrador retrievers.

During WWII, Stalin took the training of war dogs one step further and, using Alsatian dogs, produced anti-tank dog units. Taking advantage of Pavlovian training methods, trainers starved the dogs for several days and then left food for them under a stationary tank. As they formed an association, the dogs soon learnt to run under enemy tanks searching for food. There, they would release an explosive device on a timer, strapped to their back, and then run back to their handlers. In practice, under simulated battlefield conditions, the dogs performed poorly. Distracted by noise, they often became confused and returned to their handlers with the dummy bombs still strapped to their backs. Under actual battle conditions, if a dog returned with a real bomb on a timer, the dogs could blow up their own handlers. The Soviet trainers soon resolved the problem and fitted each dog with a contact bomb, which detonated on contact with the underbelly of the tank. Subsequently, the enemy tank was either destroyed or badly damaged, and the dogs became collateral damage as the force of the explosion blew them to pieces. Stalin's canine suicide missions of 1941–1942 produced debatable results. The lengthy training and the significant turnover of dogs were not cost-effective for just one assignment, which often proved disastrous.

The dogs became accustomed to Russian tanks that used diesel during their training, while German tanks mainly used petrol. As we know, dogs learn by association; however, as they had no experience with the smell of the different fuel, the dogs were unable to process the conflicting information and often returned to their own side with the contact bomb intact. Although they did manage to explode a few enemy tanks, the Germans soon learnt to shoot all dogs on sight in combat areas, neutralising them before reaching their armoured vehicles. Despite the Soviet claims that the anti-tank dogs destroyed up to 500 enemy armoured vehicles, these figures were probably inflated to justify using the suicide dog unit. Because the Soviets only deployed the canine bomb unit for a limited period, we can assume that the experiment was not as successful as alleged. More importantly, no records confirm how many dogs the Soviets exploded during that period.

Sadly, we often treat dogs as disposable commodities. More recently, in 2020, amid false rumours in China that animals could spread the coronavirus, a spate of animal killings shocked the residents of various tower buildings in multiple cities when cats and dogs rained from the sky. In the dawn, shocked residents found the gruesome remnants lying on blood-spattered pavements at the foot of high-rise buildings after their owners disposed of them by throwing them out of windows or off balconies in the dead of night.

Unfortunately, misleading information continually challenges our ability to separate fact from fiction. After notices appeared in various provinces urging owners to dispose of their cats and dogs, many owners abandoned their pets on the streets, where pedigree dogs became the new homeless. With a population of fifty-eight million, the Hubei Province lockdown's biggest tragedy is the undetermined number of pets that perished in their homes. Unfortunate owners, who had intended to be away for a few days over the Chinese Lunar New Year from 25 January 2020, could not return home till 8 April. While some owners managed to contact volunteers to break into their apartments and rescue their animals, it was impossible to save all home-alone pets. Most only had sufficient water and food for a few days and ultimately died of dehydration and starvation.

In the aftermath of the Covid-19 pandemic, canine welfare experts are further concerned about the number of pets purchased globally during the lockdown. During this time, many families jumped at the opportunity to obtain a pet while parents worked from home and schools were closed. Similarly, for others, pets alleviated the feeling of isolation and provided companionship for people living alone. As a result, the demand for puppies boomed, and many rescue centres found their adoption figures skyrocketed. Unfortunately, so did the business of backyard breeders. The general worry is the welfare of lockdown puppies when their owners return to work and school.

Statistics show that 25% of owners did little or no research before buying their puppy, and a similar number believe they may have obtained their pet from a backyard breeder. Almost 50% had not seen the puppy or its breeding environment either in person or via video, and 20% admitted that they had not thought about the long-term responsibilities of pet ownership. Up to 18% are concerned about the consequences of looking after a pet when they return to work, and 15% agree that they are not ready to keep a pet. Unfortunately, impulse purchases exacerbate the future fate of many dogs bought during the lockdown.

Additionally, due to various restrictions, owners could not adequately socialise or train their pets, which may face possible separation anxiety issues when their families return to work and school. As we have seen in previous chapters, dogs purchased on a whim without adequate research, obtained from puppy mills or unscrupulous breeders, lacking vital social skills to humans and other dogs can lead to an assortment of behaviour problems if left unchecked. It is alarming to realise that a whole generation of pandemic puppies may grow up with behaviour issues, which is the principal reason why so many owners relinquish millions of dogs to shelters globally, leading to more abandoned dogs than ever before.

Unfortunately, if something does not appeal or measure up to our expectations in our throwaway society, we discard the old and purchase a new one. This philosophy also applies to our pets, adding to the multitude of homeless dogs. Naturally, abandoned dogs procreate at a phenomenal rate; therefore, the matter of sterilisation is perhaps an acceptable action to curtail more unwanted street dogs, although managing the root of the problem would possibly be more appropriate.

While it may be permissible to neuter street dogs, why are we neutering our own pampered pooches?

As responsible dog owners, how do we ethically justify having bits cut out of them? Many owners and organisations believe that it is irresponsible not to spay/neuter our pets, leading to unwanted pregnancies and increased canine overpopulation. Yet, in Norway, where it was illegal to neuter dogs until recently, there is no canine overpopulation problem simply because people do not allow their dogs to run loose. Surely keeping our dogs safely contained with no opportunity to roam, which also guarantees that they will not get lost or run over, is what responsible dog ownership entails.

Strict Norwegian welfare laws ensure that the authorities fine the owner one week's wages if a dog escapes. The fine is one month's wages for a double offender, and they confiscate the dog for strike three. Similarly, before council workers can issue dog licences in Queensland, Australia, a representative inspects the premises where the owner will keep the dog. This policy is to ensure that the premises are adequately fenced and can keep the dog safely contained. Nevertheless, virtually every veterinary waiting room has posters or pamphlets advertising the benefits of having our pets spayed/neutered, predominantly citing population control, which absolves owners of the responsibility of keeping track of their pets.

Naturally, there are two sides to any argument, and opinions to the contrary believe that spaying/castration is barbaric and belongs in the Middle Ages, when these practices were widespread and performed by people as a sign of victory in tribal conquest or to reinforce dominance in ruling kingdoms. Interestingly, Thomas Jefferson passed a bill in 1778 approving castration as punishment for certain crimes.

It never entered my mind to have any of my previous dogs spayed until we got Franky and later on Lulu. After their first heat, I had both dogs spayed for no other reason than the convenience of avoiding their monthly menses, which is probably why most owners have their dogs neutered without knowing all the pros and cons. Unfortunately, I also knew no better at the time and only began to research the topic after Lulu died of hemangiosarcoma.

Ongoing heated debates for and against neutering question the health advantages and disadvantages of castration/spaying in dogs, which removes the ability to produce sex hormones. Generally, neutering can remove or diminish testosterone-controlled behaviours in dogs. Once testosterone production stops, unwanted behaviour, such as competitive inter-male aggression, is reduced in 60% of cases. However, castration will not help with fear aggression, lack of training, learnt aggression, prey drive, or wandering due to boredom.

With their incredible olfactory senses, a dog can detect the scent of a female in heat from a mile away, and dogs will often wander off in an attempt to mate, frequently putting themselves in danger. According to various surveys, castration reduces this roaming behaviour in 90% of cases. On the other hand, it is the responsibility of every dog owner to always contain their pet safely. To this end, there is an ingenious innovation commonly known as a fence, which reduces roaming behaviour in 100% of cases. Additionally, intact males have a compulsion to mark their territory, whether a lamp post or the dining table leg. Therefore, the higher the spray goes, the better. Across the board, there is unanimous agreement that this is the only behaviour that castration can change and can improve this behaviour in 50% of cases.

Without a doubt, there are valid arguments for sterilisation, such as some behaviour improvements and a few health advantages, which include:

- reduced risk of testicular cancer and non-cancerous prostate conditions

- preventing uterine and breast cancer in females
- reduced risk of perianal fistulas that primarily affect German shepherds.

On the other hand, a plethora of literature is based on numerous studies that resolutely warn about the increased health risks associated with neutering. The lack of sex hormones can cause adverse behaviour in dogs. When we terminate testosterone production, dogs may become anxious and fearful and even show aggressive tendencies. Destroying a dog's ability to manufacture testosterone, especially in young dogs before their bone growth plates have closed, may lead to subsequent disorders. Certain breeds may be more prone to the health risks, such as osteosarcoma (bone cancer), affecting twice as many spayed and castrated dogs.

Additionally, spayed females are 2.2 times more likely to develop hemangiosarcoma in the spleen and are five times more likely to succumb to cardiac hemangiosarcoma than intact dogs. Cardiac hemangiosarcoma is what killed Lulu. Similarly, neutered male dogs are 1.6 times more likely to develop hemangiosarcoma than intact dogs. Furthermore, male dogs castrated at an early age are three times more likely to be diagnosed with lymphosarcoma than intact dogs. Ongoing studies have shown that spayed females up to eight years old are three to four times more likely to acquire one of the above three cancers than intact females. Prostate cancer is four times more likely to occur in castrated males than intact males. There is also more likelihood of sterilised pets developing hypothyroidism, obesity, urinary tract cancers, orthopaedic disorders, geriatric impairment and adverse reactions to vaccinations.

The combined studies of several prominent experts provided data on 15,984 dogs, which established that without sex hormones to stabilise behaviour, a significant number of neutered dogs became anxious, fearful and showed considerably more aggression, from an increase of 20% to more than double the levels of intact dogs.

Comparable to humans, reproductive hormones play a vital role in essential growth processes in dogs, including bone and muscle development, and provide a lasting effect on brain growth and development throughout an animal's life span. However, the brain's delicate chemical balance is severely disrupted by the lack of sex hormones, which negatively impact the structure and the function of the brain, causing severe and chronic changes in brain chemistry. In addition, the lack of sex hormones causes the hippocampus, amygdala and prefrontal cortex to undergo stress-induced remodelling, which alters behavioural and physiological responses.

With ongoing research, more experts agree that the loss of sex hormones creates an imbalance in the endocrine system. This variance alters brain chemistry and function, paving the way for heightened stress, increased fear, and anxiety towards other dogs and people. Therefore, castration may not reduce even testosterone-based aggression. If an intact dog is constantly exposed to the smell of bitches in heat, the unfulfilled urge to mate can cause extreme frustration; however, a testosterone-driven, confident dog may become insecure, fearful, anxious and aggressive after castration.

Until recently, most canine medicine and endocrinology specialists severely underestimated the importance of sex hormones in canines. However, with ongoing research, these hormones are no longer regarded as insignificant and only crucial for reproduction. New studies have shown that neutering acts as an endocrine disruptor and is, therefore, a significant contributor to the development of cancer in dogs.

Although neutering has become the accepted norm in many parts of the world, including Australia, New Zealand and the USA, in most countries, including Hungary, legislation requires mandatory sterilisation of shelter/rescue animals; therefore, Mila is sterilised. However, in the USA, certain states require compulsory sterilisation of all household pet dogs by the time they are four months old. So widespread is the practice that pet parents of intact animals often find their overtures to socialise their dog rejected by owners of neutered dogs and are rebuffed at day care centres and kennels. Unbelievably, as a responsible owner wishing to socialise her dog, my American friend Judy has found no day care centres or kennels willing to enrol or allow her unspayed female on their premises.

Despite a multitude of surveys, some people still argue that nobody has carried out any legitimate scientific studies to confirm the actual disadvantages of castration on a dog's behaviour. In fact, researchers have uncovered mounting evidence that the health problems associated with castration seem to outweigh any advantages. Several recent studies have clearly established that neutered pets are two to four times more likely to develop joint disorders and various cancers than intact animals. Seven per cent of intact males had joint disorders compared to 21% of males that were neutered before one year of age. The studies also revealed that neutered pets are more likely to die of cancer than intact dogs. The percentages of health risks vary significantly between breeds and weigh heavier on larger dogs.

Of further concern is the global trend towards neutering puppies at a younger and younger age. In most breeds, maximum growth takes place from four to eight months of age. By one year of age, most growth plates are fused or closed; large breeds take considerably longer. If we neuter a puppy and remove the hormone-producing organs before the growth plates have fused, young puppies are at risk of developing a myriad of health conditions in their adulthood. These conditions include gastrointestinal issues, Addison's disease, food intolerances, Cushing's disease, thyroid dysfunction, hip dysplasia, various cancers, to name a few, as well as the likelihood of dying at an early age.

Before I had Franky and Lulu spayed, the veterinarian advised me to wait until after their first heat when reaching sexual maturity, and the bone growth plates had fully fused. However, the current trend amongst veterinarians is to carry out the procedure any time between four and eight months or even as young as six to twelve weeks.

Fortunately, leading veterinary scientists are now also questioning the merits of castration/spaying. Alternative methods, such as vasectomies, and tubal ligation, both of which leave the animal sterile and unable to propagate but still able to produce sex hormones, are viable options. Additionally, Italian research teams are working on a noninvasive, hormone-sparing ultrasound treatment for the sterilisation of dogs. Without a doubt, there is compelling data to question the validity of whether there are any health benefits to neutering our dogs. On the contrary, research studies overwhelmingly confirm that there are more negative health risks than positive benefits.

Our dogs' capacity to forgive our limitations and shortcomings never fails to amaze me, despite our ignorance, deliberate cruelty and neglect. Hardly a day goes by that we don't exploit them, sexually alter them, sacrifice them, eat them, abandon them, cull them, blow them up, experiment on them, and yet they still serve us loyally.

Over the millennia, humans have come to rely on our canine assistants, not just as working dogs but also as service and therapy dogs. With diverse research and multiple studies on canine abilities, we appreciate the additional beneficial role our relationship with dogs has played in the past, as well as its continued contributions in the future.

For centuries, man has used shepherd dogs, guard dogs and hunting dogs, but their services to us are expanding daily. Guide dogs and mobility dogs are no longer a novelty as we push the boundaries of the dog–human relationship. Over the years, canines have become invaluable to us in the military, the police force, search and rescue dogs, and banned substance detection dogs. More recently, assistance dogs have become companions to patients afflicted with mobility problems, autistic children and Alzheimer's patients. With further research in the medical field, we also recognise the importance of medical detection canines already employed as seizure and diabetes alert dogs. Bio-detection dogs may well be the diagnostic tools of the future. With ongoing research, specialists are constantly discovering new frontiers as they undertake canine studies in the early detection of various forms of cancer, including prostate, breast, urological and bowel cancer, and other diseases, including malaria and certain viral infections.

During various email correspondences with Judy, the incredible canine olfactory senses came up in conversation. She'd also read that dogs are legendary for their sense of smell and can even perceive odours up to twelve metres underground. Incredibly, they are also able to detect an odour diluted one to two parts per trillion. An expert in dog cognition and author of *Inside of a Dog*, Alexandra Horowitz explains an example of this dilution saying, "We might notice if our coffee's been sweetened with a teaspoon of sugar; a dog can detect a teaspoon of sugar in a million gallons of water: two Olympic-sized pools full."

Similarly, Stanley Coren compared the difference of the canine olfactory senses to humans. For example, if humans can smell one gram of butyric acid (human sweat) in the space of a ten-storey building, in contrast, dogs could detect the same amount of odour in a 135-square-mile city covered by a 300-foot-high enclosure. However, considering all this, Judy couldn't help but wonder, if dogs have such acute smelling ability, why do they have to get one hair width from a pile of poo to sniff it? She has a point. They can detect and recognise a plethora of items, from drugs to underground gas and human illnesses. So why can they not read the journal of other dogs from two metres away?

Whereas humans have five million receptor cells, on average, canines have 220 million receptor cells, depending on the breed. Proficient trackers, bloodhounds have 300 million, German shepherds and beagles have 225 million, and dachshunds have 125 million receptor cells, which is still vastly superior to our own.

In a well-known 1960s experiment, comparing the sense of smell in several dog breeds at Bar Harbour in Maine, John Scott and John Fuller released a mouse into a one-acre field with several beagles. The beagles only took one minute to find the mouse; fox terriers, on the other hand, took fifteen minutes, and the Scotties, despite actually stepping on the mouse, never managed to locate it. The olfactory senses of our dogs are vastly superior to most machines and, based on their portability, canines offer additional benefits. Current research is only the tip of the iceberg, as we fully comprehend the value of our canine companions and realise how much we rely on their services daily and wonder how much more they will be able to offer us in the future.

Consequently, to fill all the above roles, dogs with specific characteristics are in great demand. Before puppies are allowed to begin any training programmes, whether as service or assistance dogs, they undergo a rigorous physical and psychological evaluation. By screening for health issues and only breeding from healthy adult parent dogs with the most desirable traits, breeders lay the foundations for physically fit and well-adjusted offspring. Because working dogs are often responsible for the safety and wellbeing of their owners or handlers, they must calmly stand their ground under various conditions. A fearful dog may become aggressive and dangerous, which is not tolerated in working dogs and is also an undesirable trait in family pets.

Not to be outdone, our family pets provide us with instant comfort, our daily dose of Zen. The health benefits of dog ownership are well documented, as regular dog patting is more likely to keep the doctor away than an apple. Not only does it feel good, but it also lowers blood pressure and relieves stress. Without a doubt, assistance dogs have just as many positive effects and can improve the lives of their disabled owners emotionally and socially.

Additionally, dog walking is a highly social activity. Owners are more motivated to exercise their dogs for thirty minutes a day and are less likely to succumb to depression. Our four-legged furry friends are exceptional people magnets and facilitate reciprocal interaction between passers-by, which alleviates isolation from the community and imparts self-confidence in their owners.

From the dump, dogs inched their way into our lives and homes. While we gave them shelter and food, they gave us their independence, adapting to our every whim. Not only do we constrain them behind fences for their own good, never to run wild, but we also control all their resources. Furthermore, we decide when and where our dogs will walk, poop, socialise, play, eat, bark and be quiet. Additionally, we take them to puppy school, to obedience school, where we teach them a host of commands that will make them well-mannered and well-adjusted canine citizens in our human world, and then we leave them to their own devices all day while we go to work. What's more, we require them to be much better controlled than in the past and expect them to be sociable when we want them to be and inconspicuous when we don't. Frankly, most dogs are more polite and better behaved than the children I know!

In the long term, what does the future hold for our dogs?

Unfortunately, as the restrictions of our modern lifestyles clash with their inherent instincts, our canine companions become the underdog in an equation that does not resolve the needs of the millions of dogs that become increasingly anxious and more stressed by the day. More and more humans spend a significant part of their time interacting on social media networks, where their needs for companionship and instant gratification are satisfied, allowing no time for canine commitments. It is not surprising, therefore, that current predictions indicate that while urbanisation continues, the popularity of dogs may be waning, as they are no longer able to adapt to the stresses and restrictions humans impose on them, especially in cities.

CHAPTER 18
BEHAVIOUR ANALYSIS

One of the essential support professionals we should have on speed dial is a dependable veterinarian, who we can trust with the lives of our most precious pets. Alas, not all vets are created equal. Sometimes it is a process of trial and error before we find the right one who has the professional experience and the necessary empathy, especially when treating anxious and sensitive dogs. Fortunately, we have been quite lucky with the team at the clinic where I take Mila. However, even though she is generally healthy, we still have ongoing anal gland issues.

Additionally, as you may recall, Mila recently had recurring bilious vomiting during the night, and our vet diagnosed her with gastritis. While sucralfate medication protected the stomach from acids by creating a barrier or coating over the stomach lining, omeprazole decreased the amount of acid produced in the stomach, and the bilious vomiting vanished. Unfortunately, a few weeks after we stopped the medication, the night-time bilious vomiting returned several times a week.

The umbrella term gastritis, which includes bilious vomiting, is a condition whereby the stomach lining and other parts of the digestive tract become inflamed from various irritants. The typical reaction for the body is to expel these irritants by vomiting.

At that stage, our vet did not know the cause of Mila's condition, although, during our last visit, she also formulated the idea that perhaps it may be some dietary inefficiency. Generally, vets do not consider the disorder severe. However, ongoing and constant stomach irritation can erode the stomach lining, causing ulcers, lesions or even stomach cancer. Typically, vets recommend reducing the period between meals, feeding the dog several small meals a day, and one late-night snack before bedtime.

As the previous and a more recent ultrasound didn't uncover any anomalies, our vet suggested that we take Mila for gastro-intestinal endoscopy to eliminate conditions such as cancer. Not surprisingly, the short and routine procedure revealed an inflamed stomach lining and a deep duodenal ulcer. Happily, the biopsy did not detect any malignancies. Nonetheless, the report also mentioned signs of several issues, including hyperplastic gastritis, which indicates a marked thickening of the stomach's gastric folds due to the ongoing inflammation. Mila also has pyloric lesions and a possible indication of mild gastro allergy and fibrosis.

Since shortly after we got her, Mila has been on hypoallergenic food. She has never had a runny tummy, and other than the bilious vomiting at night, she's never thrown up her food, so there are no events of sickness other than when this all started a few months ago. Although Mila seems her usual self, this issue with chronic gastritis is a concern. The causes of stomach inflammation in dogs are numerous and include bilious vomiting syndrome, tumours, poisoning, pancreatitis, infections, bacteria and viruses, foreign bodies, dietary indiscretions, food allergies and sensitivities. All these conditions can cause a reaction that weakens the stomach mucus lining, making it vulnerable to erosion from the strong stomach acids, and cause ulcers.

Interestingly, some foods believed to trigger adverse immune responses include milk, oatmeal, eggs, wheat, corn, additives, preservatives, rice and chicken. The latter two are prime ingredients in dog food specifically formulated for gastro-intestinal disorders. In addition, canine immunology research indicates that various commercial dog foods, beef, mutton, pork and rabbit can induce an adverse immune response in dogs. Surprisingly, rabbit is often an ingredient of hypoallergenic dog foods.

Despite our optimism, this was not the end of the story, and while the gastritis improved on medication, night-time vomiting returned once the treatment had finished. Therefore, Dr Anna referred Mila to a canine gastroenterologist at the Veterinary University of Budapest. The specialist is not only an eminent lecturer and examiner but has also written and co-written numerous academic papers. We seemed to be in good hands.

After studying Mila's in-depth medical history, including evaluation reports, blood tests, ultrasound and gastroscopy, her conclusion also agreed with our vet's diagnosis of gastritis. However, her treatment plan was more aggressive and for a longer period than in the past. The specialist explained that because of the ongoing inflammation, Mila's stomach wall is thicker and more rigid than average, with decreased function, causing an imbalance in the gastric system, leading to an overgrowth of microorganisms such as *Helicobacter pylori*. The condition has contributed to the destruction of beneficial stomach flora and caused an adverse immune response whereby the system perceives ordinary nutrition particles as harmful allergens. Therefore, as protocols dictate, the priority is to restore normal gastric balance.

Bearing this in mind, in addition to the medication, the specialist recommended keeping Mila on a strict diet with only hydrolysed hypoallergenic dog food for at least six months to restore normal nutrition absorption. Because hydrolysed food has smaller molecules, nutrients can be absorbed and digested more efficiently. Additionally, the immune system does not react to them, reducing the risk of nutrient intolerances and allergic responses. Armed with parasite meds, antibiotics to control microorganisms, combined probiotics/prebiotics to restore stomach flora, and new dog food to restore optimum nutrition absorption, we left the clinic with a reminder to return in two months for a check-up.

Fortunately, our subsequent check-up revealed that the long-term antibiotic treatment and diet proved effective, and although the condition might recur, Mila is fine for the moment.

Besides a reliable vet, dogs with behaviour problems often require the services of a qualified canine behaviourist trained in functional analysis and behaviour diagnostics. A certified professional is essential, as most standard canine assessments focus on treating a problem without considering the cause or the consequences of the behaviour. As a result, two dogs could display the same behaviours, determined by completely different influences. Consequently, behaviour analysts use functions of behaviour to identify why a behaviour problem is occurring. Identifying the function of a behaviour helps us to decrease the problem behaviours and increase appropriate or desired behaviours. According to the authors of *How Dogs Learn*, Mary R. Burch and Jon S. Bailey, "Functional analysis is a procedure that determines under which conditions a behaviour problem occurs."

On the other hand, functional analysis (FA) provides an in-depth diagnostic technique to evaluate the problem behaviour. Using this system, a behaviourist can recognise why the problem exists, the cause or trigger that precedes a behaviour, and identifies what creates and maintains the problem. In other words, functional analysis helps explain why a dog is acting in a certain way, what happens immediately before the behaviour, and what happens immediately after the behaviour.

In psychology, functional analysis examines how certain stimuli and responses mutually fluctuate. ABC (Antecedent, Behaviour, Consequence) is a behaviour modification programme often utilised in dealing with complex human behaviour issues. This model of applied behaviour analysis is based on the work of B.F. Skinner (1904–1990), possibly the most eminent psychologist of the twentieth century. Acknowledged as the father of operant conditioning, he was greatly influenced by the work of Ernst Mach, who studied the relationship of our sensations to external stimuli. Based on Mach's studies,

Skinner realised that behaviour has consequences and uses a three-term framework to shape behaviour:

- Stimulus
- Response
- Reinforcement

These operant conditioning principles are almost identical to the ABC model, which professionals successfully implement in dog training, including behaviour modification programmes.

I consulted a dog trainer regarding Mila's reactive issues, who came to assess Mila and evaluate our relationship. Even though during the visit she didn't want to see Mila in action with other dogs, being an agility trainer, she was interested in seeing Mila perform on our indoor course. As Mila was about to start on the jumps, she hesitated and seemed reluctant to follow through. Without examining the reason for Mila's hesitation, the trainer suggested that I move the rug at the starting point further back, to give Mila more room to prepare for the low jump. She erroneously assumed that Mila needed more run-up space to launch over the low-set poles, which was not the case.

As the surface of the training area is wood, I have non-slip foam mats covering the course. However, there was a shortage of mats, and I only had a small rug leading up to the jumps. Unfortunately, as Mila came into the jump the day before, the rug slipped on the hardwood floor, and Mila fell on her side, which is why she was wary and hesitant. Subsequently, I remedied the problem and purchased additional non-slip interconnecting mats. Additionally, with some extra encouragement, praise and treats, Mila was soon back on course, sailing over the jumps.

Even a minor incident highlights the importance of exploring what precedes certain behaviours, which dictates the consequences, and how we can remedy the situation. In this context, moving the rug back further from the jump, as suggested by the trainer, would not have resolved the problem.

Similarly, a while ago, Monika, the head of the rescue centre where we adopted Mila, visited us with her diminutive dachshund, Panka. While I went out to greet our visitors, Mila stayed in the house. When Mila spotted Panka through the glass doors, Mila began to bark uncontrollably, running up and down at the French doors with great urgency, wanting to get outside so she could dispatch the intruder. Ordinarily, a dog trainer would assume that Mila was acting territorial. Even though I knew that Mila never behaved like this with visiting dogs, I realised that I had seen this conduct many times before. Based on antecedents of past behaviour, the only times Mila acted like this was when she saw a cat in the garden. Obviously, from indoors, Mila was unable to catch Panka's scent, and from a distance, she erroneously thought that Panka was a cat. As soon as I let Mila outside and she realised that Panka was a dog, she was quite embarrassed by her *faux pas* and became the perfect hostess, welcoming Panka into the house and behaving perfectly during her new friend's visit.

While functional analysis identifies behavioural causes of a problem in terms of operant conditioning principles, it does not consider other anomalies, such as genetics, including breed differences and health issues. Behavioural diagnostics, therefore, examines medical conditions, physical breed characteristics, genetics and environmental issues. Because a significant number of behaviour problems may be attributable to factors other than consequences, including physiological, organic, medication or environmental, a behaviour analyst must be aware of the many factors that affect behaviour.

For instance, a behaviour diagnostic evaluation of a German shorthaired pointer with symptoms of hyperactivity revealed that the dog did not actually have a behaviour problem. For centuries hunters bred pointers to run all day, and therefore the dog behaved in the only way it knew how, as determined by breeding and genetics, and was not, in fact, hyperactive. Similarly, we should also consider environmental and physiological influences when a dog that seems stubborn and unwilling to train is possibly hot and hungry. We often rail at our dogs for raiding the rubbish, but increased hunger may be a symptom of a tapeworm infestation. Additionally, medication and stress can also affect behaviour, which is why a detailed behaviour analysis is vital to rule out all physical variables.

A further valuable analysis tool, this time for humans and not our canine pets, is the Big Five personality test. This test is the most used model of personality in academic psychology and can reveal how we shape our dogs with our temperaments. In addition, researchers use a technique known as factor analysis to assess individual personality traits based on hundreds of personality elements.

These characteristics include:

- **O**penness predisposes to inventiveness and curiosity.
- **C**onscientiousness often predetermines efficiency and organisational skills.
- **E**xtroversion predicts outgoing and energetic personalities.
- **A**greeableness refers to friendliness and compassion.
- **N**euroticism describes sensitive and nervous temperaments.

Diverse roles and tasks are better suited to different personality traits. For instance, scientists and software programmers generally demonstrate intellectual curiosity and openness to experiencing new activities, whereas tennis players are usually more conscientious and agreeable. Prospective employers often assess and evaluate job applicants on the Big Five personality traits.

Apparently, successful leaders display low levels of neuroticism, high scores in openness and balanced results in conscientiousness and extroversion. At the same time, high scores in neuroticism generally result in professional collapse. These principles also apply to dog ownership, and people with certain traits make better owners.

Openness

Openness evaluates a person's aesthetic sensibility, intellectual curiosity and emotional awareness. As a group, they are generally considered to be imaginative, creative, curious and independent. While they may be open to new ideas, they may lose interest and get bored easily. Someone with an extremely high score in openness may be unpredictable, unable to meet goals, lack focus, and may be more likely to take drugs, undertake intense, risky activities, and often prefer chaos and disorder.

Dog owners with high scores are frequently viewed as eccentric and tend to be lax when required to maintain discipline, negatively affecting the behaviour of their dogs. They can alienate other people and may be perceived as non-conformist to society's standards.

In comparison, lower scorers are usually practical, uncreative, incurious and conforming. Owners with lower scores find it challenging to change routines and bad habits and may blame their dog for any behaviour issues rather than themselves. People with extremely low scores often have a narrow range of interests and may be regarded as dogmatic and close-minded; they do not adapt well to change and have a low tolerance for different views and lifestyles.

Conscientiousness

Conscientiousness measures a person's tendency to control impulses, competence, dutifulness, orderliness, striving for achievement. While this group tends to be organised, careful, disciplined and punctual, extremely high scores in this personality often reflect stubbornness. They may take life too seriously and can become obsessive-compulsive, as well as have critical self-judgement. Although they excel at persevering with set tasks and programmes such as dog training, they are less likely to be spontaneous and adaptable. Because of their inflexibility, they cannot accept failure and become frustrated when their dog does not immediately succeed.

Individuals with lower scores are more relaxed and better able to handle unforeseen situations. However, they can be procrastinators and are often seen as disorganised, irresponsible, lazy, and may not follow through on training and dog walking. In addition, low scorers have a higher tendency for substance abuse, smoking, alcoholism and may also be prone to eating disorders, and often have poor impulse control and may seem careless. Very low scorers also exhibit anti-social tendencies and often feel ineffective, with no control over their lives.

Extroversion

Extroversion reflects where a person directs their energy and what they find rewarding. As a group, they are sociable, active, fun-loving and affectionate. However, the trait's extreme high scorers may present as shallow or seem to be attention-seeking and domineering, even tyrannical. Based on their constant need for stimulation, extroverts often become bored when alone and find it hard to stay focused on just one task.

As dog owners, they will probably choose a dog based on the attention it generates rather than suitability and are unlikely to research breeds. In training, they will expect quick results and get frustrated with a low-reactivity breed, as they always need to be doing more and find it difficult to relax.

Sometimes extroversion is a cover-up for the lack of self-worth, making extroverts much more susceptible to adverse effects when they don't receive ample stimulation.

In comparison, low scorers are considered retiring, passive, sober and reserved. Even though they are more likely to research breed requirements, they may believe they know everything and will try DIY methods rather than accept professional help. Furthermore, low scorers can be perceived as self-absorbed or aloof, as they do not enjoy socialisation. As a result, introverts will be overwhelmed by high-energy dogs and are more suited to low-reactivity breeds.

Agreeableness

In psychology, agreeableness measures a person's tendency to be kind, empathetic, trusting, cooperative, and how a person gets along in society. Generally, agreeable people are soft-hearted, trusting, lenient and helpful. In contrast, high scorers are usually perceived as naive, submissive or ingratiating, are often taken advantage of and tend to be less successful in specific fields. Their inability to say 'no' makes them poor leaders, while their excessive friendliness undermines their authority and professionalism. This overindulgence also applies to dog owners who wish to stay in their dog's good graces, and may find it impossible to correct or set down any rules or enforce any forms of discipline. They will try to please their dogs rather than take charge, as they are concerned that their dogs will not like them.

Low scorers are often ruthless, suspicious, critical, paranoid and uncooperative, and may also have narcissistic and anti-social tendencies. They can be highly competitive and critical of others and find it difficult to make friends. In addition, they are often callous and overly aggressive with their dogs, making their dogs fearful.

Neuroticism

Neuroticism describes behaviours that lack emotional stability, although all personality traits are measured on a continuum between two extreme poles. The significance of this is that people can take on adjacent behaviour elements, behave neurotically at times, or be super calm and collected at others. Although a little worry and anxiety are part of the human survival mechanism, anything in excess is detrimental to their wellbeing.

People who score high on neuroticism tend to be anxious, emotionally insecure, self-pitying, and seldom see a silver lining on anything. Consequently, they are often unhappy, easily distressed and overwhelmed by life's challenges that others negotiate with aplomb. Because of this, their negative energies can influence their dogs, leading to a host of behaviour problems, including separation anxiety, guarding behaviours and reactivity. Because they find conflicting behaviours stressful, they may not take their dogs for walks, resulting in a lack of exercise and associated behaviour issues, including anti-social behaviours.

Besides being prone to unpleasant emotions, including anxiety, depression, anger, frustration, envy, neurotics are regarded as emotionally unstable and lacking in impulse control and are likely to be pessimistic, guilt-ridden, with low self-esteem.

On the other hand, low scorers in neuroticism tend to be even-tempered, calm under pressure. They usually feel secure and comfortable in most social situations with a solid control over emotions, although they often present as unconcerned and complacent.

During my canine studies, various practical parts of the syllabus included evaluating dog owners to assess how their personality type may influence any issues they have with their dog. Two of my friends, Vee and Elle, kindly assisted me in this exercise.

CASE STUDY: VEE

In the personality case studies, we did not evaluate the dogs. Instead, we only assessed the owner's personality based on their responses to a questionnaire. The scores achieved indicated the owner's personality strengths and weaknesses, and how these might impact on their dog. Based on the results we were able to suggest positive changes to the dog's regime and proposed a more suitable breed based on the owner's personality.

Vee's personality scores:

LOW on OPENNESS – 8 points
HIGH on CONSCIENTIOUSNESS – 12 points

LOW on EXTROVERSION – 5 points
HIGH on AGREEABLENESS – 13 points
LOW on NEUROTICISM – 7 points

According to Vee's low score in openness, she is practical and conventional. Although she can progressively work her way through challenges and prefers a familiar routine, she may find it hard to change existing bad habits. On the other hand, a high score in conscientiousness suggests that Vee is organised, reliable and hard-working, though she may become frustrated when her dog behaves in contrast to her expectations. While her low scores on extroversion indicate that she is reserved, with a witty sense of humour, she is controlled and good at focusing on a single task. Although, dealing with stress and overstimulation may be a challenge. Introverts can be overwhelmed by high-energy dogs and are more suited to low-reactivity breeds. However, Vee rated high on agreeableness, which makes her dependable, considerate, amicable and popular. Scoring low in neuroticism, she is emotionally secure, flexible, and can use humour to overcome anxiety and cope with adversity.

When asked to describe her boxer dog, Vee reported that he has no default settings, only an 'on' and 'off' switch. When he is not resting on the couch, he is spinning at 200%, which attests to his high energy and high-intensity needs. The dog is well schooled, and when Vee can harness his stamina and focus his active mind, it is an incredible experience working with him. Even though he is an excellent-natured, entertaining dog, he is quite willing to stand his ground and protect his owner when needed. Scoring high on conscientious, Vee is sensible, and, just like her dog, she is very disciplined. Although they both like quiet times at home, her dog seems to be very high energy, compared to Vee's down to earth, practical and somewhat reserved personality, although both have a good sense of humour and a sense of fun. Both seem secure and unflappable.

Issues with Vee's Dog

Being an intact male, he is very dominant on walks and can be aggressive with other male dogs. Or rather, he becomes aggressive if the other dog shows dominant tendencies towards him, to which he reacts. However, when required, he listens and is obedient, which is a testament to Vee's discipline (high on conscientiousness) and ability to work her way through challenges (low on openness) when training her dog.

Vee realises that she should change her bad habits and exercise the dog more intensely several times a day, as he is very excitable and is not working off his pent-up energy. As a result, he pulls on the leash vigorously. The lack of sufficient exercise may contribute to leash-pulling that has now become a habit, and this leash reactivity may also exacerbate the dog's male-on-male aggression. More energetic and extensive daily activities would tire the dog both physically and mentally. Although, dealing with her dog's overstimulation may be a challenge that Vee is unable to deal with (low on extroversion).

Additionally, the dog jumps up on people; more precisely, he is rambunctious with people who indulge him. In truth, Vee feels the problem is not with the dog but with people because they don't listen when she tries to instruct them on the proper way to greet a dog. They also insist on using chirpy, squeaky Mickey Mouse voices when telling the dog how cute he is, and it doesn't matter if he jumps up.

Being high in conscientiousness, Vee is good at sticking to routines and specific tasks, which shows in her exceptionally obedient dog that is well schooled in personal protection training. Although she will eradicate unsociable behaviours in her dog, this high-energy, high-intensity breed that requires a minimum of two hours of exercise per day is difficult to fit into her daily schedule and may be too demanding and draining for Vee. His extroversion, overstimulation and intense exercise needs are stressful and challenging to cope with and may not suit Vee's introverted personality. She may do better with a more manageable, less stressful breed.

Because I know Vee and her dog well, I am aware of various issues that have become a habit through no fault of Vee's. Although it seems that her dog pulls on the leash due to excitement and impulse control issues and an abundance of energy, which is true, I am also aware that during their basic training, they received no help in addressing these problems. Initially, obedience trainers taught Vee to control her dog by jerking him around on the leash (most schools in this part of the world still utilise Cesar Millan-type training methods). Vee believes that she is doing the right thing because that is how the experts taught her, even though it has not resolved the matter and has made the dog more reactive.

Although Vee is somewhat introverted, conventional and down to earth, she has a good sense of humour and is good at sticking to specific tasks and routines. Bearing this in mind, I'd suggest an entertaining dog that is affectionate, intelligent and easy to train, with lower energy and intensity levels than her present dog.

In this instance, I believe that a good choice for her would be a standard poodle that reflects many of Vee's characteristics. Like Vee, they are playful and loyal, with keen intelligence. These dogs are highly trainable and do very well in performance sports, taking care of physical and mental requirements. When owners teach poodles proper canine manners, they have a calm disposition, especially with a regular sixty minutes of exercise per day, to burn off natural energy. The poodle is protective of his home and family, and with lower energy and intensity levels than Vee's current dog, this may be an easier breed for her to manage.

Generally, the prerequisites for the ideal owner will be a high score in conscientiousness. An owner that is too agreeable may lack discipline; therefore, a mid-range score is perfect. Additionally, depending on the dog's energy requirements, both introverts and extroverts can make great owners. In comparison, academics associate most behaviour problems in dogs with high scorers in neuroticism, which is the least desirable trait for dog owners. From this assessment, we can evaluate that Vee would make the perfect dog owner with a lower-energy dog.

CASE STUDY: ELLE

> HIGH on OPENNESS – 12 points
> LOW on CONSCIENTIOUSNESS – 11 points

LOW on EXTROVERSION – 7 points
HIGH on AGREEABLENESS – 14 points
HIGH on NEUROTICISM – 11 points

Elle may be lenient, but she is imaginative and creative, although she can be disorganised at times. Whereas her dog is playful, lively and delights in chasing small animals, they are both reserved with people and are happy to stay at home with a good book lying on the couch. Even though they are curious, enjoy walks and like to explore, Elle and her dog struggle with anxiety and insecurity.

According to Elle, her female dachshund is shy, reserved and dislikes strangers, particularly men. However, although she is a couch potato and a Velcro dog, she has surges of energy and likes walks, exploring the garden and doggy park, although she does not like small dogs. The dog also enjoys chasing cats and birds, likes going in the car and is a good traveller.

There were several issues with Elle's dog. It sometimes obsessively licks the furniture or a blanket, demands food on time and barks a lot outside when owners are at home. The dog also suffers from separation anxiety and dislikes strange objects in the house. Furthermore, it is afraid to retrieve a ball from under a low table and is anxious to find furniture out of its usual place. Although the dog sometimes listens and haphazardly obeys commands, it is usually quite stubborn.

Whereas Elle may be curious and broadminded, her free-spirited ideas concerning discipline may negatively impact her dog. She may not stick to rules or training, which would account for the dog's stubborn streak.

Infamous for their independent thinking, dachshunds like to do things their own way, and, as a breed, they can be headstrong and require lots of positive praise and treats when training. Lacking time, Elle does not walk the dog regularly, leading to boredom, frustration, stress, and may account for the furniture licking. However, it could also be a sign of several physical ailments and should be checked out by the vet. Being quite reserved, Elle may struggle with socialisation, which could be why her dog is under socialised, and has developed issues with other dogs and people.

Additionally, Elle's score on agreeableness is possibly contributing to her dog's lack of discipline and its unwillingness to obey commands, as well as its demanding attitude. The overwhelming problem seems to be the high scores in neuroticism, possibly contributing to her dog's insecurities and anxieties, including separation anxiety. The dog may also view Elle as a source of weak energy, reinforcing the dog's demanding attitude. Her contagious stress could also be instrumental in her dog's guarding behaviours, although dachshunds are notorious for their loud and copious barking. This behaviour is essentially genetically hardwired, and training them takes a lot of patience and consistency, which this dog lacks.

Furthermore, the dog seems to be suffering from an overload of stress and is very anxious, possibly from lack of consistent discipline, training, socialisation, lack of exercise and Elle's insecurities. Naturally, in all things canine, exercise, including daily walks, training, discipline and socialisation, are some of the essential ingredients in moulding a happy and contented dog.

A good workout is also an excellent way to tire dogs with separation anxiety. In addition, giving dogs something appropriate to chew during the day engages their attention and helps to reduce pent-up stress and minimise separation anxiety issues.

I'd also suggest implementing the 'nothing in life is free' or 'say please' programme and ask the dog to perform a task, such as sit or down, before it receives anything at all from the family, whether it be food, play, attention, walks, etc. This programme is a general strategy for dog behaviour control that builds confidence in dogs, teaches their owners to be firm and consistent, and will help tip the discipline scales in Elle's favour.

On the whole, temperament is affected by several factors, including heredity, training and socialisation. In this instance, Elle's dog may lack discipline, consistent and patient training, socialisation, which it requires to overcome some genetic issues. Elle should also consider working with a professional dog behaviourist depending on the severity of the dog's separation anxiety. Additionally, it would benefit from a counterconditioning programme and basic obedience training, building confidence in Elle and her dog.

Even though Elle professes to be a dog person, considering her personality scores, I'd suggest that she may be happier with a cat rather than a dog. A study of over 4,000 participants identified the differences between dog and cat people using the Big Five personality test. The results suggested that dog people scored higher in extroversion, agreeableness and conscientiousness, and lower in neuroticism and openness.

Personality Trait	Dog People	Cat People	Elle
Extroversion	High	Low	Low
Agreeableness	High	Low	High
Conscientiousness	High	Low	Low
Neuroticism	Low	High	High
Openness	Low	High	High

Based on Elle's personality profile, she is an ideal cat candidate.

Despite the above, I searched for an affectionate dog to fit Elle's quirky and imaginative personality. One that would be easy to train and discipline, with low energy to suit Elle's introvert characteristics scores. Additionally, I looked for a dog with low sensitivity to cope with an owner scoring high in neuroticism. Although it was quite tricky finding a dog that fits all the criteria and based on the above, my suggestion for Elle would be a Pekingese, which meets most of the requirements. This low-sensitivity, good-natured companion dog will be a loving and devoted friend. All dogs need early socialisation, and although this breed is not the easiest to train, puppy training classes would be a good start. Furthermore, Pekingese enjoy going for walks and meeting people, which would keep the dog and Elle well socialised.

Although the above tests are not foolproof, I would prefer to have more information about clients, such as functional analyses, as well as in-depth behavioural diagnostics on the dog, which would reveal many so-called 'problem behaviours' based on breed, genetics, or health issues that are unrelated to the owner's character. For example, from experience, I know that even though I socialised Franky and Lulu precisely the same, and while Lulu was outgoing and loved everyone, Franky was always reserved with strangers, which is a typical dachshund trait, nothing to do with owner character. Ideally, I'd prefer to use the Big Five personality test in tandem with a dog breed selector questionnaire before obtaining a new dog. These tools would give the prospective owner insight into their strengths and would also determine the most suitable dog breed for their lifestyle.

In Elle's case, they later found that the dog was going blind, which would account for its dislike of furniture being moved around, and its hesitation about retrieving objects from under tables. Additionally, their vet has diagnosed the dog with canine dementia, a cognitive disorder similar to Alzheimer's in humans. Consequently, we can attribute many of the behaviour issues experienced by the dog, such as anxiety, inappropriate vocalisation and excessive licking, to this degenerative disorder.

We should bear in mind that the Big Five test does not provide any in-depth analysis of dog behaviour or provide a perfect owner assessment. Critics of the Big Five feel that the test is too generalised to be universally relevant, and we cannot condense human personality traits into five categories. Additionally, the test seems unreliable over different social-economic groups, and social psychologists now generally agree that personal and situational variables are needed to account for human behaviour. Various studies have also found that it only works within specific age groups and that most adults become more agreeable, conscientious, and less neurotic as they age. Despite its shortcomings, many researchers still defend the Big Five model, which can give a reasonable indication of personality traits. Undoubtedly, it is a fascinating diagnostic tool owners can use to assess their possible strengths and weaknesses. Based on such insight, they can ultimately make a more informed decision when choosing a dog. Furthermore, all personality traits are a measure ranging between two extreme poles, so it is possible to have both higher and lower characteristics within the same personality trait. Additionally, life experiences can also shape our personality.

Although, various psychological studies have explicitly examined the personality attributes of people who would choose dog breeds with a high risk for aggression, such as the Rottweiler. Accordingly, researchers collected data specifically looking for evidence of criminal convictions. Overall, their findings revealed that high-risk dog owners had nearly ten times more convictions than regular dog owners and were 6.8 times more likely to have been convicted of aggressive crimes.

Additional research findings confirm that ownership of high-risk dog breeds is often associated with a particular personality. As a group, they were more likely to commit violent crimes and were significantly more likely to engage in sensation-seeking and risky behaviours. In addition, high-risk dog owners were more careless, selfish, had strong manipulative tendencies, and engaged in more self-defeating behaviours than low-risk dog owners. Furthermore, the findings also indicate that owners of dangerous canines are not likely to bond with their dogs, and they were much more accepting of mistreatment and abuse of animals.

There seems to be ample evidence that many gangs and drug dealers use dangerous dog breeds as guard dogs. A Leicester University study revealed that high-risk individuals commonly kept aggressive dog breeds to use as weapons, as a status symbol of power, to maintain and enhance their image as enforcers. Additional reasons for ownership were identified, including breeding for financial gain and also for dogfighting. Owners of high-risk dogs had significantly more criminal convictions for aggressive crimes, drugs, alcohol, domestic violence, crimes involving children firearms convictions than owners of low-risk dogs.

Based on the research studies, psychologists have established a link between young people and animal abuse, indicating mental health issues. Generally, problematic behaviour suggested that young animal abusers were a highly troublesome and vulnerable group, who demonstrated more impulsive and risky behaviours, including gang involvement, alcohol and drug consumption, self-harm, with less commitment to schooling. These behaviours closely describe individuals who score extremely low on the personality trait conscientiousness.

The Leicester study also correlated that younger people scoring low on agreeableness are most likely to keep dangerous breeds. These owners are usually unconcerned about the wellbeing of others and can be suspicious, unfriendly and competitive. Various other studies also concluded that owners with aggressive dogs who lack emotional stability usually score low on agreeableness, extroversion and conscientiousness.

Although more and more academics are investigating the reasons for canine aggression, including owner personality, we know that canine behaviour develops through a complex interaction between environment and genetics. In addition, many diverse elements influence these behaviours, including, but not limited to, early nutrition, mother's stress levels during and after pregnancy, housing conditions and social interactions.

With all these variables, it is impossible to pinpoint any specific influence that would account for a dog becoming aggressive. However, early positive experiences, especially socialisation, are considered the key elements in preventing aggressive tendencies. Unfortunately, many dangerous dogs find themselves isolated from positive experiences and are therefore more likely to develop aggressive tendencies. In contrast, dog owners educated and experienced in the finer aspects of canine ownership are more aware of, and are more likely to provide for, the dog's extensive needs. Undoubtedly, responsible dog ownership requires, among other things, a commitment to socialisation, humane training, and a firm, dedicated owner.

CHAPTER 19
ADDRESSING COMMON BEHAVIOUR PROBLEMS

After we finished the course with Zoli, I was concerned that we had not addressed Mila's recall. Although I tried to improve on it, we had little success. Despite being in a low-distraction environment, the garden still offered plenty of stimulation. Usually, my calls went unheeded, and it was hard to get her attention, as Mila was prone to selective hearing, especially when she was in hunting mode.

Some months later, I was happy to hear from Zoli, who had just completed an online fun and games recall course by dog trainer Susan Garrett. Although Zoli was very enthusiastic about this technique and asked us to be his guinea pigs in testing the programme, I was a bit dubious. Although Mila likes to play, games do not motivate her, and even though she loves to run after a Frisbee and enjoys a game of tug, she is not always in the mood to play. When she wants to play, she follows me around the house with a squeaky toy, or she'll put it in my lap until I give in.

Some days when I encourage her with a tug toy or throw her the Frisbee, she is not interested, and on other days she joins in with great gusto and doesn't want to stop. At the time, I'd also just started a project and wasn't sure I'd be able to commit myself fully and contribute as much time as needed to the training that Zoli proposed. But, of course, I was curious and loath to reject anything outright without at least giving it a try, so I agreed to go along for a trial lesson.

Much as I assumed, Mila went through the motions, but she seemed tense and did not enjoy herself, and we could not motivate her to play. When Mila is engaged and interested, she happily bounces along with tail wagging. Instead, her response to the pressure of our contrived play was to switch off. She would have been much happier exploring and sniffing around the yard. Based on Mila's reaction, I thanked Zoli for thinking of us and offering us complimentary first dibs at the course, but declined his kind offer, although I did not give up on recall work.

In time I came across several interesting articles on training recall with a whistle, and I couldn't help wonder whether it would penetrate Mila's selective hearing and capture her attention. Initially, I purchased an ultrasonic whistle that only dogs can hear, but Mila didn't seem to react to it, and because I couldn't hear it, I abandoned the gizmo. Following more research and reading, I bought an Acme 210.5 whistle, which has a sharp tone, and hunters recommend it for certain retrievers, including spaniels. Based on her appearance, it would be easy to forget that Mila is anything other than a dachshund; however, I always keep her spaniel heritage in mind.

Working with the whistle was simple, and, in the beginning, the training was all indoors, while I accustomed

Mila to the whistle's sound and paired it with a reward. To start with, while she was standing in front of me, I blew two long tweets on the whistle, then gave her a treat, and repeated this a few times for a couple of days. Of course, how we decide to blow the whistle is up to us; some people like one or two long tweets or several short pips, which should always be consistent. However, treats should be extraordinary and of high value.

A few days later, I moved a few metres from Mila, and after two long tweets when she came to me, I gave her several treats and repeated this daily for a few days. Soon I had to enlist the help of Rezső to hold Mila while I went into another room to blow the whistle and treated her liberally when she ran to me. Once again, I practised this daily for several days. By then, Mila had made the association of the whistle-sound with some very yummy rewards, and I always had her full attention.

Presently, we moved outside to the garden and practised similarly, keeping the distances short initially and gradually moving further away. Mila's reaction to the sound of the two sharp tweets is instantaneous no matter what she is doing; she races to me on her little legs at full speed, with ears flapping, even if I am out of sight. Because I want to keep her recall strong, we practise this daily.

When Mila is engrossed in the systematic inspection of each blade of grass, I blow the whistle, and immediately she races the sixty metres to wherever I am. Since a solid recall is vital, I always reward her liberally with delicious treats, which I can phase out in time. Had I known the impact the whistle would have on Mila and how easy it was to train with it, I'd have implemented it much sooner.

Additionally, we can even teach commands such as sit, stay and down, with the whistle using different long or short blasts for each exercise. For us, the whistle proved to be a very successful tool, almost on a par with the clicker.

Having made progress on recall, I turned my attention to fireworks.

Fireworks and thunder desensitisation work on the same principle: both introduce the source of the fear stimulus under threshold and gradually increase the intensity without causing any adverse reactions. While we know that we cannot cure fear, we can usually help our dogs manage it with a desensitisation programme. When I undertook the thunder desensitisation programme for Mila, I hoped that it would also positively impact her fear of fireworks, but, alas, it did not. Initially, I chose thunder desensitisation over fireworks because storms are more frequent and have a shorter duration than fireworks; therefore, it is easier to manage Mila's behaviour and keep her interest on other things.

Thankfully the government banned fireworks in Hungary some time ago, and it is illegal for private citizens to buy or sell them at any time, except for New Year's Eve. Unlike storms that pass quickly, the end-of-year fireworks last for hours, from dusk to the wee hours of the morning. Even one or two fireworks is a challenge for Mila, but the non-stop barrage of sound, sometimes closer, sometimes further, but never ceasing for over eight hours, is more than she or I can bear.

After our first New Year's Eve together, when we'd only had her for two months, and she was still anxious and unsure of us, I hoped that she would settle during future fireworks displays, but she didn't. Mila's out-of-control panic, the salivating, the rushing around, the panting, for hours on end, was incredibly distressing to watch. While the lift helped to ground her during severe storms, I did not want to leave her in the lift during fireworks for the whole night. So, the following year, unwilling to watch Mila suffer again for any length of time, I spoke to Dr Réka, our vet at the time, who had a similar problem with her dog.

Bearing in mind the various options, we chose a herbal calming remedy, which I dispensed as recommended, however to no avail. Once again, we were all forced to live through another New Year's Eve with a panic-stricken Mila. As dog owners, one of the hardest things is to watch our beloved pets suffer, unable to help. Alas, the herbal medication had no effect on her whatsoever. The following year, we were back with Dr Réka, who reported a similar experience with her dog and subsequently ditched the herbal remedies and brought out the big guns. While medicating dogs is a controversial topic and not something I'd agree to lightly, I was willing to try anything to provide Mila with some control and comfort. So, naturally, I investigated the pros and cons, and while medication may be a miraculous aid for some dogs, vets must review each case as they will not recommend it for others.

Behavioural medication can be daily, and owners give their dog the proposed dosage every day as part of a long-term treatment plan, including SSRIs like Zoloft and Prozac. On the other hand, vets usually recommend situational medication administered as needed for specific problems, including Xanax and Valium. They generally prescribe these remedies for fireworks, thunder phobias and separation anxiety. Whereas training can improve behaviour issues such as separation anxiety, sometimes the severe underlying stress and nervousness make it impossible for dogs to learn until we can manage their anxiety levels. Although medication on its own will not solve the problem, it can be helpful in tandem with a training plan.

For instance, daily medication can help severely anxious and reactive dogs stay under threshold for longer, react less intensely and be easier to distract when it loses control, making learning and training possible. Similarly, as the medication blocks the panic response in dogs, situational medication keeps dogs calm enough to redirect their attention to play and counterconditioning during storms and fireworks.

Of course, this is not something to undertake lightly, and an essential consideration is whether the drugs are safe. When taken as prescribed, these anti-anxiety medications that have been available for veterinary use since the 1990s have proved to be safe, with few side effects. However, owners have legitimate concerns about drugging and sedating dogs, which were valid for many older medications such as amitriptyline. Vets can adjust the dosage of the newer drugs to circumvent these issues. After all, the goal is to reduce anxiety so the dog can cope without causing sedation.

Sometimes it is difficult to get the dosage spot on, and situational medication, including Xanax, may cause some sedation. However, because they are short-acting and only used occasionally as required, they do not disrupt everyday life, and a vet can monitor the dosage for future use. Having said that, I was pleasantly surprised at the lack of side effects in Mila, who behaved normally with no visible drowsiness. More importantly, she was able to stay under threshold for the duration of the fireworks. After the preceding years' out-of-control panic, it was reassuring to see her calm and coping.

Frankly, I'd rather not have to medicate Mila. However, unfortunately, most of our dogs' behaviour problems relate to our relentless demands on them within the artificial environments we subject them to. Not only do we expect them to continually evolve and manage every situation, no matter how unnatural they are to canine instincts, but, additionally, we seldom consider their needs. After all, fireworks are not a natural phenomenon, yet we are surprised when our dogs cannot cope. Therefore, even though it is distressing to medicate our dogs, I will continue Mila's once a year situational medication unless the government sees fit to ban the New Year's Eve fireworks.

Even though recall and fear of fireworks were not the only issues that I needed to tackle, food aggression was never a potential concern; however, this can be a major concern for many dog owners.

Although most experts find it impossible to explain why some dogs become aggressive over food, general suggestions include genetics or early learning deficits. Competition for food amongst littermates will also predispose dogs to food aggression. In addition, dogs with health issues may also be prone to hostility around food, which is why it is always essential for a veterinarian to do a complete health check on dogs with any aggression issues.

When dealing with food aggression it is important to remember that when food is involved a dog's personal zone is reduced to the distance front their mouth to their front feet. The polite canine rule is that you get to keep what is in your zone, therefore dogs do not understand why we invade their space when they are eating.

Luckily, I've never had a problem with food aggression, but as with everything, prevention is always better than cure. Undoubtedly, it is always easier to teach a puppy the correct behaviour than to retrain an aggressive adult dog. While opinions are divided, some owners believe that food aggression is a natural canine behaviour and manage the situation by respecting their dogs' personal zone at feeding time thus preserving their dogs' trust. Contrarily, others maintain that under no circumstances is it acceptable for dogs to show aggression, which could endanger humans, and believe that we must train dogs to show restraint and impulse control. Naturally, this is a valid point of view. On the other hand, relationships are not just one-sided, and perhaps parents should also teach their children to respect a dog's space in certain circumstances.

Fortunately, we can usually overcome food aggression with a combination of desensitisation (getting the dog used to the presence of people while it is eating) and counterconditioning (creating a positive association between people and food). These methods do work but require patience and time.

Firstly, we can hand-feed the dog all its meals. Some experts suggest that we retire the dog's usual food bowl during the training period and put the dog's food in a completely different dish, mixed with some very high-value treats, which must be out of reach of the dog. Then, while the dog is sitting down, we should hand-feed the dog its whole meal, piece by piece, including the high-value treats at intervals. We should repeat this daily for a few weeks. During this time, the dog becomes accustomed to our presence while eating, which reduces the fear associated with removing its food and establishes trust. Additionally, the high-value treats help the dog associate mealtimes with good things happening when we are around. In due course, we can also include other family members in the exercise.

An alternative method suggested is to repeat the above exercise for a week or two, and, during the subsequent week, put the dog's food bowl on the floor and place its meal in a second dish on the counter. Drop a few pieces of food into the dog's bowl, and when it is happily eating, drop more food into the bowl, so the dog realises that a human hand near the food means it is getting even more food, and it is not going to take the food away. Owners should also repeat this exercise daily for a week or so and may involve the whole family.

Following this, we should place the dog's bowl on the floor with a quarter of the dog's meal already in it. As the dog eats, we continue to add more food, including some very high-value food items, such as pieces of frankfurter, chicken or roast meat. The dog quickly learns that not only does the hand not take away food but it gives food and even bestows the horn of cornucopia with an abundance of gastronomic delicacies.

During the last week, while the dog is eating from its bowl, we should continue dropping food into the bowl while it is eating, and if the dog is relaxed, try and take the food bowl from the dog while dropping very high-value food treats on the floor, in exchange. The dog learns to associate that even though we have removed its meal, we have replaced it with manna from heaven. This high-value exchange reinforces the idea that even if we take the food away, we always replace it with even better edibles.

If the dog in question is likely to bite during the training, it is advisable to seek professional help from a canine behaviourist. Similarly, if the dog seems stressed during the training and refuses to eat, one should seek professional help.

Food aggression should always be a concern for dog owners, but a more concerning type of aggression is that between dogs.

As we learnt from a previous chapter sibling rivalry is one of the most disturbing situations in a multi-dog household which results in more severe injuries than it does between dogs from different households. It is therefore worth remembering that generally, the same dog instigates the fights, usually the younger of the two, or the newest addition to the family. Additionally, these altercations usually occur between dogs of the same sex, and females are more often involved in these fights than males. If owners plan on keeping more than one dog, breeders usually suggest keeping one dog of each sex. Once again experts emphasise the importance of mental stimulation and physical exercise. Bored dogs become frustrated and edgy, which exacerbates the tension between dogs. Highly socialised dogs are usually well adjusted and tend to get along.

Owners are also advised to give the top dog priority who should be acknowledged first and fed first. We should also manage our dogs' environment and limit stressors that may trigger fights, such a toys, food and other coveted resources.

Overall, experts believe that by implementing behavioural techniques, inter-dog household aggression is treatable.

A good strategy is to opt for the nothing-in-life-is-free approach, which requires the dogs to perform simple learnt commands such as sit, down and come, before owners give them access to any assets, including toys, food and attention. The second involves always supporting one of the dogs above the other, which must always have access to resources first. Some owners give precedence to the first dog in the household that has lived with the owner the longest, while others may choose the more active dog.

With modification treatment, we can reduce aggressive behaviour between male-male housemates by 72%, male-female by 75%, and reduce the disputes between female-female pairs by 57%. If hormones cause the aggression, neutering male dogs may alleviate the situation in some dogs, but it is no guarantee that the fights will not continue. On the other hand, vets have successfully treated dogs with anxiety-related aggression using medication, including SSRIs.

In severe cases, if the owner must keep the dogs apart, once health checks reveal nothing untoward, they should consult a professional animal behaviourist. Sadly, in extreme cases, behaviour modification does not have the desired effect, and rehoming one of the dogs is the only solution to ensure that the two dogs don't kill each other.

While the sibling rivalry issues between Franky and Lulu were relatively minor, my strategy of giving priority to Franky the older dog, as well as long daily walks kept their conflicts to a minimum.

One of the leading reasons dogs end up in shelters is due to housetraining issues. Yet, logically, this matter should not create such a huge problem.

After puppies are born, the mother licks them to stimulate elimination and then cleans away the waste, so there is never any odour of urine or faeces in the den. During the transitional period, around three weeks of age, as soon as their temperature-regulating mechanism improves, the puppies can relieve themselves without the mother's stimulation. At that time, their mother encourages and teaches them not to mess in the nest area.

Puppies, therefore, have an inbuilt instinct to avoid relieving themselves in the place where they sleep, which lays the foundation of housetraining. With these foundations and consistency in training, the onus is on us to teach our new pets that the entire house is their 'bed'. As responsible dog parents, we have to teach and show them where they may relieve themselves, whether it be outside or on a puppy pad in a designated area. How well puppies succeed reflects our patience, consistency and how well we teach them.

From the first day, puppies in training should always be under constant supervision. In order to keep their 'nest area' as small as possible, if owners do not restrain them to a crate, it is wise to restrict them to one room or a part of a room. Owners often don't realise that puppies have poor bladder control, and at eight weeks of age, their bladder capacity is around seventy-five minutes, and at twelve weeks, it is ninety minutes.

Generally, a good rule is to take the puppy outside or to the wee pad first thing in the morning and at regular hourly intervals during the day and immediately after playtime, naps and meals. During the night, I used a baby gate to restrict my puppies to a small area of the laundry room or bathroom. Although, we can also use a pen. In addition, I reserved a space in the enclosure away from their bed where they could eliminate on newspapers. Unfortunately, wee pads were not available in Africa at the time. Nevertheless, this method is virtually foolproof and sets them up for success rather than failure. Additionally, if we schedule regular feeding times, we can easily predict when puppies are likely to eliminate.

Although experts advise not to carry puppies to their elimination spot but use a leash, as this forms a physical association with the act of walking outside and eliminating, I found it easier to carry them initially. While they have poor bladder control, it is much quicker and simpler to scoop them up and take them to their potty zone and prevent any accidents on the way. When we carry them, they seem to hold their bladders a little longer. Whilst on a leash, it is much easier to relieve themselves along the way before reaching their designated spot, especially if they are unaccustomed to a leash. Gradually when they have more control, we can introduce a leash. These measures ensure that they learn to eliminate in the preferred designated area and not in the house.

In addition, we can initiate cue words such as toilet or wee-wee, using different words for each action, which we should repeat while the puppy is either urinating or defecating. Owners can use these cue words as prompt words later on. Furthermore, we must always accompany the puppy outside to attach the designated cue words while relieving themselves and offer praise and rewards following the successful elimination. By taking the puppy to the same spot in the garden, through classical conditioning it will learn to associate that spot with going to the toilet, which will trigger it to go in the future.

As the puppy learns not to mess in the restricted area, we can expand this gradually to include more extensive areas of the house. Without fail, I have always used this method in the past with 100% success. So much so that when we moved from Australia to Hungary, Franky and Lulu found the first snowfall of their lives extremely disconcerting. With not a blade of green grass in sight, which was their potty association, they refused to eliminate on the snow. Fortunately, after searching high and low, we found some grass under the eaves, which the snow had not covered, and managed to solve the pressing problem. In a few days, when they caught the scent of other dogs' urine in the snow, Franky and Lulu soon followed.

Bearing in mind the occasional arctic winter conditions, I tried introducing Franky and Lulu to a wee mat with little success. As a result of her training and associations formed as a puppy, Franky, without exception, needed to eliminate outside. Therefore, the concept of relieving herself indoors was abhorrent, even in blizzard conditions. On the other hand, Lulu detested the cold and was more receptive to the idea. While she often used the wee mat at night, she preferred to go outside during the day.

Another method of housetraining a puppy, which I have never used, is initially restricting the puppy to a crate, which becomes the puppy's den. If a puppy wakes up before the one-hour potty break, due to its built-in instinct to keep the den area clean, it is more likely to hold it in for a little longer rather than relieve itself indiscriminately as soon as it wakes up. Left to its own devices, a puppy will usually urinate half a minute after waking up from a nap and may do so randomly if it is unimpeded and if the owner is not on hand to take it outside immediately. This method also requires that owners take the puppy outside every hour to relieve itself. Interestingly, some countries like Sweden believe it is cruel to keep dogs and cats in crates unless used to transport, for hunting, competition or shows.

If restricting the puppy to a pen, or a small part of a room, it should be large enough to house the puppy's crate or den. Additionally, it should have space away from the sleeping area, where the puppy may eliminate on newspaper, puppy pads, turf, or any other surface the owner prefers. Owners who may be absent for periods during the day and cannot take the puppy outside on the hour during the night often use this method. In this way, the puppy learns to relieve itself on the designated surface. Eventually, owners can move this 'potty' closer to the door as the puppy matures. Finally, we can place the 'potty' just outside the door and gradually move it into the garden, where we can phase it out once the puppy makes the required association.

Before deciding on the most suitable method and surface, it is also essential to take the dog's breed into account and environmental conditions where the puppy is likely to live. For example, some small breeds detest the cold and will avoid going outside in wind, rain and sub-zero temperatures at all costs, even if they do wear a coat. For these dogs, puppy pads or doggy toilets may be the solution for those arctic winters, as well as for some apartment dwellers. Naturally, this does not eliminate the need for regular walks, although it does offer a solution to circumvent accidents, especially in bad weather, and for dogs with weaker bladder control.

Certain breeds and 'independent'-thinking dogs are notorious for being very difficult to housetrain. Similarly, toy breeds that owners always carry to the potty area never form an association with walking to their potty zone. If their owner is not on hand to take them outside when they need to go, they will often find a spot in the house. Some large breeds mature later than the average dog; therefore, it takes them longer to grow out of the puppy stage and have the physical and mental capacity to control their potty habits. In particular, scenthounds may relieve themselves indoors if they smell the scent of old urine in the house and will continue to do so if we do not thoroughly clean the area with an enzymatic cleaner. Then, we have the hunting breeds who often get distracted outside and forget about potty time. Additionally, there are the independent terrier breeds who prefer to follow their own rules. However, in all cases, owners must start to train puppies as soon as they move to their new homes. All puppies are trainable with firm consistency, patience, positive reinforcement techniques and the right rewards.

Over the years, I have successfully housetrained all my dogs, despite owning so-called hard-to-train breeds at different times, including an Afghan, an Italian greyhound, dachshund, Maltese, Pomeranian, all of which became bombproof regarding housetraining.

All the issues we have addressed in this chapter are important for all types of dogs. However, if you are housing a rescue dog, then additional care is required.

When going to a new home, all dogs need a period of adjustment, especially rescue dogs that are likely to be anxious and stressed and will require time, patience and a great deal of kindness to adapt to their new surroundings. Some dogs may only need a few weeks or months to adjust fully, but others may need years; each dog is unique.

The new home will be unfamiliar and strange, and, initially, we should allow our new dog to settle into a daily routine and become familiar with the family. During this time, the owner can assess its initial reactions, whether it is anxious, aggressive, nervous around loud noises or people. Bearing in mind that we can attribute some problem behaviours to various medical disorders, if the dog has not had a complete medical check-up, a visit to the vet should be mandatory to rule out any health issues.

Play can be a great form of rehabilitation to help a dog relax, have fun, occupy its mind and build stronger bonds with its new owners. However, we should only attempt to engage the dog gradually and only proceed at the dog's own pace. Some shelter dogs do not know how to or even desire to play; therefore, if the dog doesn't initially show interest, treats can also be a great incentive when teaching dogs new things.

Owners should take nothing for granted during this time and cautiously introduce the dog to all potentially unfamiliar things, be it the vacuum cleaner, the food processor, radio, etc. Even if the dog shows a working knowledge of obedience, I'd still recommend taking the dog to obedience classes. During this extra time spent together, the dog will learn or reinforce basic skills, but more importantly, it allows the owner and the dog to assess each other's strengths and weaknesses. These early foundations help pave the way for positive mutual understanding, which will benefit their long-term relationship.

Furthermore, obedience classes set dogs up for success, which can help anxious dogs build self-esteem and enable them to confidently face the world and learn good manners in the process. Additionally, it is the first step towards socialisation, where the dog can safely learn about new things in its environment and how to interact with other humans and dogs in a controlled setting.

Although friends and family may be impatient to meet the new arrival, we should only introduce them individually, bearing in mind suggestions on meeting and greeting a new dog for the first time. Until the dog is confident around strangers, we should keep all encounters brief and positive, rewarding the dog with lots of praise and treats. Short walks in quiet urban streets with minimum distractions where the dog can gradually get used to its environment without encountering too many potentially stressful objects should also become part of the daily routine.

As the dog becomes familiar with people, dogs, vehicles and other environmental stimuli, the walks can be longer to include additional challenges, including doggy parks and areas where the dog can socialise more broadly with people and with other dogs. Again, however, it is crucial to take things slowly and only proceed within the dog's comfort levels without incurring anxiety or stress.

On the other hand, if the dog shows continued anxiety or aggression, I'd recommend asking for the help of a professional canine behaviourist experienced in socialising very anxious or aggressive dogs.

A study on the 'Prevalence of behaviour problems reported by owners of dogs purchased from an animal rescue shelter' showed that within the first four weeks of being purchased from a rescue shelter, 12.9% of dogs exhibited coprophagy behaviour problems. These findings indicate that the dogs were probably initially relinquished because of this issue. The study also found that considerably more dogs rescued from shelters display problem behaviours than previous owners knowingly admit when they surrender them to the centres.

Mother dogs clean and eat their puppies' bodily waste to keep the nest clean, and it is perfectly natural for dogs to eat the scat of large, hoofed animals, which is an adaptive scavenging behaviour given their nutritional value. On the other hand, eating one's own or other dogs' faeces may result from various issues, including boredom and a host of medical causes that may include parasites, problems with the pancreas, and intestinal disorders, deficiencies and digestive problems. Therefore, in cases of coprophagy, dogs should undergo a complete medical and nutritional check-up to rule out health problems.

Additionally, owners are advised to invest in a good quality dog food that provides all the nutritional requirements for their dogs, including a balanced ratio of vitamins, minerals, proteins, fibre and fat, to avoid deficiencies and digestive problems. Sometimes, unsuccessfully housetrained dogs with house-soiling issues also eat their faeces to hide the evidence of their lapses. In these cases, owners should retrain their dogs starting from the basics.

On the other hand, sometimes coprophagy is also a sign that our dogs are lonely and lack stimulation. Therefore, to avoid boredom in dogs left alone for long periods, we should meet their mental and physical needs with energetic exercise, stimulating, foraging and chew toys, as well as adequate human companionship. Furthermore, a dog walker or doggy day care can also manage signs of both boredom and loneliness.

Often owners give their dogs inappropriate attention at the crucial time, which encourages the behaviour. Instead of reinforcing the behaviour with our attention when we shout at or chase the dog for eating faeces, it is best to ignore these practices. According to the principles of operant conditioning, if we reward undesirable behaviours with our attention, we intensify them, and the dog is more likely to repeat them in future. On the other hand, extinction will occur if the owner no longer reinforces the behaviour and ignores it.

An actual case described by Mary Burch *et al.* in *How Dogs Learn* involved a golden retriever who was found to have no health problems after a complete medical check-up and was also nutritionally well balanced. Yet, the dog continued to eat faeces. On further investigation, it became clear that the owners never cleaned the yard, which is why the dog was helping. In this instance, cleaning up the garden with a shovel and a hose provided the necessary solution to the problem.

Additionally, it is an excellent idea for owners to teach their dogs the 'leave it' command, which is helpful in public areas where other dog owners may not have picked up after their dog. Finally, a dog is a dog and behaves instinctively, as nature intended. Therefore, punishment is never the right solution, especially when a dog 'misbehaves' due to our own failings or oversights.

One common problem with rescue dogs is the desire to 'escape'.

There are several reasons why some dogs regularly try to escape, which include opportunity, prey drive, reproduction, boredom and loneliness. Genetically, canines are active and programmed to curiously explore their environment, although, in our urban settlements, roaming is a dangerous matter.

Escaping is one of the top ten reasons people surrender their dogs to shelters in the USA, and at the same time, owners relinquish up to 16.4% of dogs due to these behaviour problems. Breed characteristics often play a large part in why some hunting breeds with high prey drive are lured away by uncontrollable urges and tantalising odours. A point often overlooked is that prey drive is a primaeval, predatory, instinctive hunting urge motivated by self-preservation to find, pursue and capture prey. The tempting scent of a passing squirrel, or other small animals, including stray cats, offers an enticing invitation that some dogs cannot resist.

Consequently, these behaviours are even more probable if the dog does not receive ample mental and physical stimulation, leading to boredom and stress. If owners do not provide these for him, a bored dog is more likely to look for his own entertainment. Additionally, canines are social animals who rely on their humans for everything. Therefore, most get lonely when their owners leave them alone for hours and may wander off to look for companionship. In addition, male dogs can detect the scent of a female in heat from a mile away, and dogs will often wander away in an attempt to mate. After all, the reproductive drive, a strong genetic urge, can overwhelm even the most well-trained dogs and is one of the leading reasons why intact males will wander off.

Roaming is a self-rewarding behaviour.

Each time a dog gets out to explore the world, its actions are rewarded when it chases small animals, finds companionship or true love. Consequently, preventing roaming behaviour is essential, as once the dog gets into the habit of escaping, it is challenging to extinguish. In this instance, prevention is better than cure, and by managing their environment with a dog-proof fence and providing for all their canine needs, we can and should be able to prevent roaming for their own safety.

When we moved into the cul-de-sac, Mignon, the little papillon from across the road, was the self-appointed guardian of our street. Ordinarily, he was always out and about and greeted Mila through the front gate with a wagging tail and little squeaks of pleasure. However, as he was small enough to fit through their neighbour's fence, he often hung out with Lego & Co in their yard or went for short walks on his own. Happily, he never strayed far, just far enough to find company. Unfortunately, as with many owners, who were always too busy, they never took Mignon for walks or spent much quality time with him at all. Generally, they did not even allow him into the house much, so he amused himself out in the street, and we often herded him home from the end of the road when he ventured too far. Even though he was not our dog, we were concerned that one day he'd expand his area of interest and get lost, or someone would pick him up and take him home, or he'd get run over.

Some time ago, we noticed that Mignon was conspicuous by his absence, and we hadn't seen him for weeks. Of course, we couldn't help but speculate whether someone had dognapped him or whether he was fulfilling stud duties or, bearing in mind the family's lack of attention to Mignon, perhaps they gave him away to a new family. So, naturally, when we next saw his owner, we asked her about Mignon. Sadly, she confirmed that Mignon had died. One morning, he was in the street as usual, and she did not see him as she pulled away from the curb and ran over him. Of course, accidents happen, but one cannot help wonder if the owners could have prevented this tragedy. We all miss Mignon, almost as much as if he'd been our own.

Whenever we move to a new house, our priority is always to make sure it has a secure dog-proof fence. Naturally, therefore, we have no problem keeping Mila in, but it seems we are not as efficient at keeping our foxes out. Yes indeed, Bushy has reappeared despite the mesh fencing. We are happy to see Bushy as long as we only have one fox to contend with, that I can also regularly dose with Bravecto, but we will have to devise a plan for the December vulpine invasion.

As we have already established, canines are social animals and dislike being left alone for hours on end. Not only do dogs rely on their humans for everything in their lives, including shelter, food, exercise, all things great and wonderful, but even their very survival also depends on us.

A solitary dog will not survive for long without human interaction. When we leave them alone and isolated, some pooches become anxious, not knowing if we will return. Each dog reacts differently to solitude depending on various factors, including breed, early maternal care, temperament, what they are used to and how strongly it is bonded to its owner. Although there does not seem to be one distinct reason to explain separation-related disorders, several theories exist.

Due to lack of canine research, the effects of attachment and separation in humans and non-human primates have largely influenced theories concerning the development of separation-related problems in canines. Some dogs form overly intense attachments to their owners and have never learnt to cope with being separated from their primary attachment figure. Similarly, a dog suffering from losing its primary attachment figure may develop an insecure attachment to successive owners, explaining the high incidents of anxiety-related problems in rescue dogs. On the other hand, separation-related problems may be a side effect of unconscious human selection for progressively affectionate, socially dependent, infantilised pets.

Although there has been very little research on how the effects of early experiences could influence separation-related problems, experts emphasise the importance of gradually introducing young puppies to periods of separation in their new homes. While the exact causes of separation anxiety remain undetermined, there are strong indications that disruptions during early developmental stages may be a contributory factor. Some studies suggest that removing puppies at an early age from their mother does have adverse effects on the puppies' overall health, and they are more likely to display a wide range of behaviour problems as adults.

Conversely, others have found that separation-related issues were not more common in dogs taken from their mothers at an early age. Although, there is a higher incidence of separation-related problems in dogs acquired as puppies from pet stores than from breeders. There also seems to be some evidence to suggest that separation anxiety is more prevalent in dogs that have been rehomed one or more times. Various studies have shown that separation-related behaviours affect up to at least 20% of the canine pet population and are more likely to be from shelters, mixed breed or strays. Ongoing research revealed that 40% of the dogs surrendered to shelters due to anxiety-related behaviour spent four or more hours alone, and 20% spent six or more hours alone each day.

Nonetheless, it seems that three- to four-week-old wild canine puppies show no signs of distress due to periodic separation from the mother when she goes hunting. Field studies of wolves have shown that from the age of three to four weeks, the mother often leaves puppies for prolonged periods ranging from two to eighteen hours daily, and pups do not leave the den or follow the adults until they are at least ten to twelve weeks old. Based on the evidence of wild canids, the distress generated by rehoming domestic dogs may be caused by removing puppies from the familiar nest/den rather than separation from their mother. This relocation could accelerate and intensify the bond established with the new owner and negatively impact subsequent separations.

Various theories propose that dogs are more likely to suffer from separation anxiety when they have a hyper-attachment to their owner. In contrast, others believe that the length of time owners leave their dogs alone is a major contributory factor to separation-related behaviours. As canine academics are still undecided about the causes of separation anxiety, it is necessary to examine behaviour-related problems from all angles. Consequently, we have seen from past research that there is no one particular explanation for any one problem but a combination of genetics, breeding, early/life experiences, owner behaviour and training.

Additionally, we cannot overlook the fact that dogs have been so heavily selected and explicitly bred to form strong attachments to humans that technically, they all have a predisposition to developing separation problems. Intelligent, active dogs that have become more strongly bonded to humans over the decades can become incredibly anxious and suffer the effects of separation-related disorders more intensely when left alone. Some of these breeds include toy poodles, German shepherds, Havanese, Labrador retrievers, cocker spaniels, border collies, bichon frises, Australian shepherds, Cavalier King Charles spaniels, vizslas, Italian greyhounds and German shorthaired pointers.

Ongoing research by experts from all over the world provides us with more and more information regarding the canine puzzle, not least of all from distinguished neuroscientist Gregory Berns, who uses MRI scans to study the brains of dogs and how they react to various stimuli. During his studies, Berns found that one of the defining traits of dogs is how they respond to humans and other animals. With the help of MRI imaging, his team managed to map the canine reward responses. When technicians introduced dogs to various smells, they could readily discern the difference between canines and humans. The scent of familiar humans, in particular, evoked reward responses in the brain. No other smell kindled this kind of reaction, not even that of close doggy friends.

Berns emphasises that through this imaging work, scientists have established that dogs love their humans, and not just for food; they love their human company simply for its own sake. Moreover, dogs have similar responses to humans as people have when they see a friend they like. Bearing this in mind, we should remember that for our dogs, separation from us is not voluntary. In general, it is unnatural for dogs to detach and abandon the 'pack'. However, even when they do wander off for short periods, they are aware that they can restore social contact at any time.

Although, some experts prefer to differentiate between separation anxiety and isolation distress, which people often misuse and interchange. Genuine separation anxiety is a clinical term that manifests in dogs that are hyper-bonded to their owners and exhibit uncontrollable panic when they are separated from each other, even if someone else is with them. In comparison, isolation distress describes dogs that are anxious when left entirely alone but don't exhibit signs of stress or anxiety if there is someone with them, which can be a pet sitter, friend, family member or any warm body.

Even though the fundamental roots of separation-related disorders are undetermined, researchers have identified various triggers contributing to emotional trauma. These include distressing events such as birth or death in the family, changes in the family routine, being returned to a shelter after an initial adoption, moving across the country, being removed from the litter too early, emotional trauma. Furthermore, because separation anxiety and isolation distress are panic disorders, we cannot cure them, only manage them to an acceptable degree.

Nevertheless, no dog will ever be happy to be alone for eight to ten hours daily, five times a week. The responsibility of canine ownership dictates that we meet all of their fundamental functional needs, including human companionship.

Unfortunately, recent canine studies confirm that 45% of owners leave their dogs home alone each day, and more than 28% leave them for longer than four hours, and as many as 85% of dogs in the UK are anxious when left alone. In order to circumvent home-alone dog syndrome, some reputable breeders will not sell puppies to prospective buyers who work all day, unless they have a socialisation plan that involves dog sitters or day care centres.

There are many facets to separation anxiety and isolation distress. Unfortunately, there is no one-size-fits-all explanation as to what causes it, whether it is genetic, a breed characteristic, unexpected life changes, rehoming, unforeseen absence of a family member, overdependence on a family member, being left alone for long periods or a combination of any of these factors. Nevertheless, the more we learn about dogs, the more we realise that genetics and breeding have far-reaching effects.

As our society evolves from rural to urban settlements, from one owner to both owners working all day, many dogs are left to their own devices for extended periods regularly and receive very little human companionship. As a result, there has been a great deal of emphasis placed on early puppy socialisation, learning and training, which should include teaching our dogs the skill of being alone for specific periods. Yet, undeniably, our expectations weigh heavily on our dogs' abilities to constantly evolve as we teach them to cope in our fast-paced world. Considering a dog's adaptability as a species, it is incredible that we can even condition them to accept being left alone at all.

Not all dogs with destructive behaviour suffer from separation-related anxiety. Some dogs get bored and need more mental stimulation, while high-energy dogs require lots more physical exercise to work off excess energy. Understimulated dogs will often find ways to amuse themselves and work off extra energy, resulting in destructive chewing, digging, scratching and barking. As with all canine behaviour problems, a qualified professional should thoroughly assess the dog to identify the problem before implementing any behaviour modification programmes.

Canine behaviourists often use video cameras to capture the true nature of what happens in the owner's absence to differentiate whether the behaviour is genuine separation anxiety, boredom or other treatable issues. If the behaviours only occur when the owners are gone, and they occur each time the dog is alone, chances are the problem is separation-related anxiety.

Overcoming separation-related anxiety is possible with various strategies and training programmes, though all require time and patience. Most experts advise a combination of the following:

1. Canine behaviourists often recommend a programme of desensitisation. Owners initially teach their dog to relax and lie calmly on a mat, while they stroke the dog and feed it tasty treats. The dog learns to associate that calmly sitting or lying on the mat means lots of praise and rewards.
2. The next step would be to start gradually moving away from the dog, one step at a time, until the owner can leave the room without the dog moving or showing any signs of anxiety. After that, the next stage is to leave the house for short periods, starting with a few minutes and gradually increasing to a few hours. In time the dog learns that its owner always returns.

3. When owners leave home, they should give the dog something special to keep it occupied and entertained, possibly a stuffed Kong or an IQ toy. They should reserve this toy expressly for when they go out and not use it when they are home with the dog. In this way, the dog associates something good happening when the owner leaves.
4. In addition to the above, owners with dogs that are strongly bonded to them, that suffer from separation-related issues, must train their dogs to be less attached. If the dog is attached to one particular owner, the other owner should take the bulk of responsibility for all the good things in the dog's life, feeding, taking the dog for walks and even training sessions.
5. Other experts suggest a desensitising and counterconditioning programme taking into account the dog's stressors. For example, if the dog becomes agitated in anticipation of our leaving, when we pick up the car keys, handbag, umbrella, briefcase, put on shoes, etc., we should introduce these items one by one during the day when we are at home. Pick up the car keys five times in a row, and if the dog is sitting calmly, give it a treat. Walk away. Owners can randomly repeat these exercises at different times during the day, putting on shoes, taking them off, walking to the door and back, and even walking out the door and back within a few seconds, and reward the dog for calm behaviour each time.

6. We can repeat the exercise with other departure cues, including handbag, umbrella, briefcase, etc., several times a day, between usual at-home activities when we have no plans to leave the house. These practices allow the dog to make different connections with objects that it previously associated with our departure.
7. Furthermore, departures and arrivals should be calm and unemotional. We should only greet our dogs on arrival when they settle down, and we can acknowledge them calmly. Some experts suggest ignoring the dog for up to twenty minutes, but I believe this is excessive, and as soon as the dog can sit or lie down, we should greet it. Even though, as always, we should never reward anxious behaviour. However, punishing a dog by withholding our attention unreasonably does not provide a dog with relevant information about the behaviour we do want.
8. Before leaving for work, we should give our dogs a good exercise workout, bearing in mind the dog's energy requirements. Physical activity can burn off surplus energy, so the dog is more likely to be relaxed and quiet during our absence.
9. As dogs know precisely when we are about to leave, we should try and make the routine as unpredictable as possible and vary our schedules.

10. Additionally, we should leave the dog with things to do and appropriate things to chew on, possibly chew toys, puzzle toys. Hiding treats around the house will also keep the dog busy. These activities will keep a dog mentally stimulated and prevent it from becoming bored.
11. A further option for owners away from home all day is to hire a dog walker or enrol the dog in doggy day care.
12. Some people like to leave on the TV or radio or play classical music, which can also calm an anxious dog. Interestingly, recent studies have found that playing audiobooks to dogs decreases vocalisation and increases resting time more than classical music.
13. Some behaviourists also recommend using medication and anxiety-reducing drugs, such as fluoxetine and clomipramine, on dogs with severe separation anxiety. According to various experts, medication can successfully decrease stress behaviours in dogs over a two-month treatment period. Dogs diagnosed with separation anxiety are increasing daily. With the human market being close to saturation, it is perhaps not surprising that pharmaceutical companies are now exploring the highly lucrative pet market and are pushing SSRIs for dogs. Although, short-term use of medication in tandem with a counterconditioning programme can be highly beneficial.

14. Other considerations are various gadgets, like the AutoTrainer, a reward-based training device, which reportedly solves problem barking and calms dogs while their owners are away. The machine rewards acceptable behaviour and ignores unwanted behaviour. According to the co-inventor, Dr Ian Dunbar, the machine teaches dogs to bark less, provides comfort and companionship, and becomes entertainment for home-alone dogs. Apparently, the device is very effective in rehabilitating dogs with extreme separation anxiety. You can keep track of your pet and communicate with them via two-way audio, using your voice to help them relax. Although, some may argue that this is taking things to the extremes. Instead of leaving our dogs with robots, we should give them more quality human time; that is, after all, why we buy dogs.
15. Bearing in mind that no two dogs are the same, after an in-depth evaluation, a structured treatment plan is usually tailor-made for each dog, considering the severity of the problem, the age and the breed of the dog. I would advise owners to initially implement points 1–3 as the foundation of a structured training programme, making sure to take each step slowly. Furthermore, they can simultaneously work on the additional points to address the issues of breaking bonds to the owner,

desensitising and counterconditioning to departure cues, varying routines, attending to the dog's physical needs, etc. Experts consistently caution owners not to attempt too rapid progression by trying to fix everything at once.

In most cases, owners should consult a certified animal behaviourist who can develop a structured treatment plan customised for each dog.

Consequently, we cannot overlook the human element, which plays a significant part in many canine disorders and health issues. Humans have not only altered their original appearance, but we have also changed their behaviour, as dogs eat, sleep, eliminate, go for walks, sit and roll over, on command. We restrict them behind fences, and they are no longer able to find their own companionship during the day. Pre-programmed machines often feed them, and they 'talk' to their humans remotely via monitors, while robotic devices throw them treats.

We have made dogs utterly reliant on us. As a result, many experts agree that separation-related problems may be a side effect of unconscious human selection for progressively affectionate, socially dependent pets. Thus, unwittingly, we predispose our dogs to disorders such as separation anxiety, when we should be more aware of the adverse effects repeated long-term absence has on them physically and mentally. Yet, we give them less and less of their most basic need, which is human companionship. Therefore, it should not be surprising that these social creatures find it hard to cope with being left alone for long periods daily. Indeed, many studies corroborate that long periods of solitude impact the probability of developing separation anxiety disorders.

CHAPTER 20
FINALE

During the first weeks with Mila, I felt helpless and feared that I had bitten off more than I could chew. Why was she relieving herself in the house when the rescue centre told us she was housetrained? Why was she chewing the carpet? Was she testing me? Was she dominant? Why did she scream and react aggressively to other dogs? At this point, I seriously considered returning her to the rescue centre. Unfortunately, I knew that I did not have the experience to deal with ongoing rescue dog rehabilitation. Although sending back a rescue dog is frowned upon, inevitably, at times, we must accept that various behaviour problems beyond the scope of some owners may only become apparent after adoption. As I wrestled with pangs of guilt, I had no idea that it is almost universal to feel that we have made a mistake after bringing home a rescue dog. It happens to the best of us, even experienced dog trainers, and these feelings do pass in time.

While I struggled with Mila's behaviour issues and my remorse over the possibility of returning her, I was still mourning the loss of our Italian greyhound, Lulu. Unfortunately, an unavoidable certainty is that all pet owners have to face the death of their most beloved companion. Although I've had to say goodbye to several canine friends over the years, their passing never gets easier. Alas, people who have never loved or lost a beloved pet cannot comprehend the profound impact on pet parents, and, in their ignorance, they often try to make light of our grief. Whether we love a person or a pet, the anguish is just as intense when we lose them. Although I felt very confused by the intensity of my pain, I eventually realised that the mourning process does not differentiate between a canine friend and a human. I learnt that overwhelming feelings are normal when we lose a family member, whether two-legged or four-legged.

As my grief eased and I rejoined the land of the living, I began to concentrate on Mila's carpet chewing and toileting habits. While Mila confidently used the doggy door, she persisted in relieving herself indoors. Although well-meaning friends advised me to punish her, I opted to exercise patience, which paid off. When I gave Mila my full attention, I discovered that she was very anxious and feared going into the unfamiliar garden alone. This realisation highlighted the importance of understanding the issues contributing to Mila's various and severe behaviour problems, for which I was unqualified and needed expert help. This assistance came from dog trainer Zoli. Although he was not a canine behaviourist and could not assist with some of Mila's serious behaviour issues, his obedience training helped us with many fundamental problems. Zoli introduced me to the clicker and taught me new training skills, which helped both Mila and I gain confidence and accelerated our bonding process. I also realised that Mila's initial perceived hatred for me was nothing more than a lack of understanding of what I required of her and what she wanted from me. Obedience comes from training and comprehending our expectations of each other and trust built on mutual respect.

When we first started the training course, Zoli constantly emphasised the importance of high-value treats as rewards, but I did not realise how crucial these special incentives were. However, during my ongoing studies, I learnt how the limbic system, a complex loop of neural structures, generates instinctive emotions, including anxiety, fear and happiness, and provides an immediate response to these reactions. This complicated system plays a vital role in learning and memory. If we wish to override the limbic system and instinctive behaviour, we must provide as many positive, feel-good experiences as possible from an early age, utilising whatever activities our dog enjoys. These may be a combination of play, positive training, walks, lots of tactile and verbal interaction, and high-value food rewards. The limbic system records these interactions as enjoyable, emotional experiences. Subsequently, when faced with a choice of following instinctive behaviour or obeying us, our dog is more likely to rule in our favour. With the appropriate rewards, we can override this system, allowing us to control our dog's behaviour.

Understanding how dogs learn by association was a massive breakthrough for me. From then on, I showered Mila with treats, attention, tummy rubs, hugs, games, verbal and tactile interaction. I even considered giving her facials, spa treatments, manicures, although I doubt Mila would have appreciated them, just as she does not enjoy hugs. Although some dogs tolerate hugs generally, most dislike this interaction, and Mila was no exception.

Once I grasped the science behind Pavlov's classical conditioning, I could make sense of how easily we can generate wanted and unwanted behaviours. For example, if we call our dog to us after it has relieved itself in the house, and then we shout at it and smack it, the only thing the dog learns from this incident is that we punished it when it came to us. As a result, the dog associates us with fear and pain, so it will not come when called in the future. Thus, in this instance, not only have we not resolved the house-soiling issue but we have added an additional behaviour problem.

How receptive are dogs to classical conditioning?

One bad experience is enough for some dogs. Subsequently, if we perceive any further reluctance to obey as dominant behaviour and dispense more severe punishment, we start a vicious cycle of punishment and eventual retaliatory aggression from our dog. Fortunately, we can reverse or modify many fear-based behaviour problems with counterconditioning. Based on classical conditioning, this therapy is also applied to rehabilitate leash-reactive dogs and treat thunder sensitivity, which I successfully implemented on Mila.

On the other hand, operant conditioning is widely used in dog training and is undoubtedly the process that shaped Mila into the Supermutt she is today. While classical conditioning relies on external stimuli to create a reflexive involuntary response, operant conditioning involves voluntary responses, i.e. a dog chooses to offer the requested behaviour. In other words, a dog will more likely choose to sit on command if we reward its actions and is more likely to repeat this in the future. While we can reinforce the behaviour we want with treats, play, attention, we can also punish behaviours we don't want.

Unfortunately, punishment may condition a fear response in dogs, which they often direct towards their owners. Furthermore, there is an overwhelming mountain of evidence emphasising the complex emotional and cognitive capabilities of dogs. We now understand that the emotional intelligence displayed by dogs is comparable with a human two- to three-year-old.

So why would we shout, prod, poke, hit, shake and growl at our dogs?

Why even use these methods?

In the past, trainers and owners did not know any better, and these methods routinely showed results. Additionally, a misguided belief in the pack leader and dominance theory has led to many horrific cruelties being practised on animals.

Although I never subscribed to the dominance and alpha pack theories, I was shocked by how widespread these beliefs are, especially when we realise they are based on unfortunate misconceptions about wolves and their relationship to dogs. For decades our dogs were subject to a list of rules reminiscent of medieval serfdoms, or the US slave codes with strict instructions to owners on the appropriate ways to dominate and punish their dogs. Unfortunately, these beliefs became the holy grail of many dog owners.

Additionally, for decades the unsuspecting global public was bombarded with the alpha and dominance myths perpetuated by celebrity dog trainers such as Barbara Woodhouse and Cesar Millan. As they flooded the market with programmes, books and documentaries, their harsh training methods brainwashed unsuspecting dog owners who, in their ignorance, perpetuated a cycle of aggressive training methods on their undeserving dogs. Unfortunately, these outdated views set dog training back by at least twenty years. While the self-proclaimed Dog Whisperer claimed expertise he was unentitled to, newer scientific methods got bogged down in the global Millan popularity quagmire, so successfully marketed and popularised by leading and respected TV channels. Although constant research into canine cognition has proved the benefits of training with positive reinforcement, it has been challenging to break the cycle of the pack theory and alpha dog myths.

While it is true that dogs and wolves are closely related, sharing 99.9% of their DNA, archaeological evidence of dogs as a separate species from wolves dates to at least 15,000–20,000 years ago when dogs took a different evolutionary path. Even though the wolf and dog are very close genetically, we can gain additional insight and form a more precise picture if we examine the overall ecology of wolves and dogs and not just the sequencing of their nucleic acids. The wolf remains a wild animal, a hunter and a carnivore with an entirely different survival strategy from our domestic companions that do not hunt or kill their food. When the canid tree split, wolves and dogs went along separate branches, and while wolves avoid humans, dogs rely on them and have been part of our lives for centuries.

Various studies on free-ranging dogs have conclusively documented how evolution in canines has extinguished wolf behaviour, and there are no advantages for dogs that wander freely to form packs. Although dogs and modern wolves share the same ancestor, dogs are not descendants of modern wolves. Trying to learn canine behaviour by studying modern wolves is like looking for lifestyle tips from chimpanzees.

During my studies, I also discovered that many canine behaviour problems exist because owners choose inappropriate breeds and cannot meet their mental and physical needs. Before selecting a new dog, we should ask ourselves three questions: Why do I want a dog? Why should I have a dog? Why should I not have a dog? If we answer these questions satisfactorily and are convinced that we can look after a dog, there are many other factors to consider. Most importantly, we must remember that canine behaviour relies on an intricate interaction of genetics, breeding, early learning, socialisation and training. Although, genetics usually predetermines basic instincts, such as prey drive, sociability, adaptability and trainability. Knowing how a particular dog can adapt to different living conditions, how easy it is to train, and how much exercise and grooming it requires will impact our choices. It is important to remember that the type of dog we choose does make a difference and must fit in with our living arrangements, training abilities and energy levels. For example, some dogs with high prey drive require up to ninety minutes of intense exercise a day. Other dogs are prone to barking, while various breeds are heavy droolers or shedders, and not all dogs are suitable for families with small children.

All puppies are cute, but we must be discriminating. It is important to choose with our head, not our heart, and take the time to research the best breed for us. Bearing in mind that each breed is unique it is our responsibility to choose wisely when selecting a family pet. A puppy is not a disposable commodity that we can return if we find the requirements of responsible pet ownership too demanding.

Another significant milestone for me was recognising the consequences of socialisation. In common with many dog owners, I did not realise the importance of early and ongoing socialisation, the lack of which often leads to behaviour problems in dogs. With current research, we understand how insufficient maternal care, the lack of appropriate stimulation during early life and negative experiences increase the likelihood of developmental disorders in adult dogs.

Puppies only have a few weeks to develop positive associations within their environment, after which they become increasingly cautious about objects and situations they have not previously encountered. Undoubtedly, breeders have a huge responsibility in providing early care and socialisation, but the buck does not stop there. Unfortunately, many owners believe that their pets only require basic amenities such as food and shelter.

However, studies have shown that the lack of proper socialisation is the most significant contributor to fear aggression in dogs. The extent of deprivation and lack of socialisation a dog suffers from is directly proportional to the magnitude of the maladjustment. Furthermore, dogs with restricted experiences are often timid and do not reach their full potential, whereas dogs exposed to a broad range of experiences are more confident, with improved skills. Unfortunately, while more information comes to light daily, it takes years for details of recent canine developments and research to filter through to the grassroots. In the meantime, our collective ignorance often causes canine companions immeasurable misery and avoidable wide-ranging behaviour issues, such as fear and aggression precipitated by poor socialisation.

Although, we can often prevent many canine behaviour problems simply by managing their environment. It is not the dog's fault if it rearranges the household rubbish in our absence, chews the furniture or relieves itself in our house. The household rubbish holds tantalising odours for our dogs. If we remove the temptation before leaving home, we avoid having our dwellings decorated by canine interior designers. Additionally, dogs are not born knowing that the roast joint on the counter is not a doggy takeaway. Just as we keep things out of the reach of children, we must also remember to keep things out of the reach of our four-legged family members. Furthermore, dogs usually chew because they are bored and frustrated. By meeting their daily mental and physical needs, we can keep our dogs from getting bored and chewing inappropriate objects. Finally, most dogs relieve themselves in the house because we have not trained them adequately or they don't want to go outside for various reasons, as was the case with Mila. With patience and the correct training, we can efficiently teach dogs where to relieve themselves.

Often overlooked, companionship is frequently lacking in our dogs' lives, yet it is one of their most basic needs. If we need to leave them alone, providing lots of interactive toys, treat-filled Kongs and suitable chew toys will keep them engaged and occupied. However, we should never regularly leave dogs home alone for long hours. Bearing this in mind, we should remember that separation from us is not voluntary for our dogs. Therefore, it should not be surprising that these social creatures find it hard to cope with being left alone for long periods daily.

Naturally, it is always best to train the correct behaviour from the start, although we can overcome many behaviour problems with counterconditioning. Inevitably, some dogs with behaviour problems may require the services of a qualified canine behaviourist trained in functional analysis and behaviour diagnostics. Although many dog trainers claim to be dog behaviourists, there is a difference between the two. A dog trainer can teach a range of tasks, including basic obedience, such as sit, down, stay, whereas a behaviourist is an expert in canine behaviour modification. A certified professional is essential, as most standard canine assessments focus on treating a problem without considering the cause or the consequences of the behaviour. As a result, two dogs could display the same behaviours, determined by completely different influences. In other words, functional analysis helps explain why a dog is acting in a certain way, what happens immediately before the behaviour and what happens immediately after the behaviour. Identifying the function of a behaviour helps us to decrease the problem behaviours and increase appropriate or desired behaviours.

While functional analysis identifies behavioural causes of a problem in terms of operant conditioning principles, it does not consider other anomalies, such as genetics, including breed differences and health issues. Behavioural diagnostics, therefore, examines medical conditions, physical breed characteristics, genetics and environmental issues. Because a significant number of behaviour problems may be attributable to factors other than consequences, including physiological, organic, medication or environmental, a behaviour analyst must be aware of the many factors that affect behaviour. Similarly, we should also consider environmental and physiological influences when a dog that seems stubborn and unwilling to train is possibly hot and hungry.

As owners, we don't always consider why our dogs act in a certain way or how we influence their behaviour without realising it. Based on the Big Five personality test, there are indications that our personalities can affect how we interact with our dogs. However, we should remember that the Big Five model does not provide any in-depth analysis of dog behaviour or provide a perfect owner assessment. Although it gives a reasonable indication of personality traits, we should use it as a guideline rather than a scientific tool. Despite its shortcomings, many researchers still defend the Big Five model, which can provide us with the means to assess our possible strengths and weaknesses. Based on such insight, we can ultimately make a more informed decision when choosing a dog.

Generally, the prerequisite for the ideal dog owner will be a high score in conscientiousness. An owner that is too agreeable may lack discipline; therefore, a mid-range score is perfect. Depending on the dog's energy requirements, both introverts and extroverts can make great owners. In comparison, academics associate most behaviour problems in dogs with owners scoring high in neuroticism, the least desirable trait for dog owners.

Usually, most dog owners do their utmost for their canine family members, although over the centuries, humans have in turn loved and loathed dogs. Although many ancient cultures perceived dogs as unclean scavengers and prohibited the handling of dogs, others were devoted to their dogs and considered them worthy of serving the gods. Even today, in some countries, dogs are celebrated and honoured for their loyalty to humans, while in other countries, they are eaten and treated as disposable commodities. Unfortunately, if something does not appeal or measure up to our expectations in our throwaway society, we discard the old and purchase a new one.

Our dogs' capacity to forgive our limitations and shortcomings never fails to amaze me. Despite our ignorance, deliberate cruelty and neglect, they still serve us loyally. Over the millennia, humans have come to rely on our canine assistants, not just as working dogs but also as service and therapy dogs. With diverse research and multiple studies on canine abilities, we recognise and value the additional benefits our relationship with dogs has offered in the past, as well as their continued contributions in the future.

In the long term, what does the future hold for our dogs?

Experts agree that the popularity of dogs may be decreasing due to the difficulties they face in adapting to the stresses of urbanisation and the restrictions humans imposed on them.

According to authors of *Through a Dog's Ear*, Joshua Leeds and Susan Wagner, "Research has shown that dogs are among the most adaptable of animals. Most dog guardians have thus assumed that it is the dog's job to adjust to whatever environment we offer them – no matter how stressful. In this case, perhaps our dogs' willingness to do anything for us has become their Achilles' heel – the result of their total compliance is that canines are more stressed than ever before."

Yet, the best feeling in the world is when our dog greets us with unrestrained exuberance after five minutes of absence. I've never experienced anything like that from either my friends or family, even after five years' absence.

Dogs are social creatures, eager to please, and love being part of a human family. Therefore, we are responsible for keeping their best interests in mind and learning to compromise when necessary. Additionally, if we understand how our dogs communicate, accept and meet their canine needs, including early socialisation, and provide them with ample opportunities to be dogs, but at the same time give them boundaries, consistent leadership, guidance and love, we ensure a stable and enduring relationship based on mutual trust, respect and understanding.

Adopting Mila and running the gauntlet of her behaviour issues inspired my canine studies, which revolutionised my outlook on canine behaviour and training. Thanks to her, I have experienced and learnt an immeasurable amount on the subject of all things canine. In addition, with my new understanding, we were able to forge unbreakable bonds by reciprocally enriching each other's lives through innumerable hours spent learning, training, playing, grooming and just enjoying each other.

Although I am utterly embarrassed by my initial ignorance of rescue dogs and canine behaviour, with my new insight, I realise that although adopting dogs with behaviour issues can be highly challenging, you do reap the rewards you sow. Mila has rewarded us with boundless enthusiasm, unconditional love and immense happiness. To me, she truly is unique in all the world.

> "You become responsible, forever, for what you have tamed. But if you tame me, then we shall need each other. To me, you will be unique in all the world. To you, I shall be unique in all the world."
>
> ANTOINE DE SAINT-EXUPERY

REFERENCES

BOOKS

Ainsworth, M., Blehar, M.C., Waters, E., Wall, S. (2015) *Patterns of Attachment: A Psychological Study of the Strange Situation.* Taylor & Francis Ltd. ISBN 1848726821 (ISBN 13: 9781848726826).

Arany, C. (1998) *The History of the Puli.* ISBN 963 550 395 4.

Arnold, J. (2010) *Through a Dog's Eyes.* Spiegel & Grau. ISBN 1400068886 (ISBN 13: 9781400068883).

Askew, H.R. (1996) *Treatment of Behavior Problems in Dogs and Cats: A Guide for the Small Animal Veterinarian.* ISBN 0632041080.

Berns, G. (2013) *How Dogs Love Us.* New Harvest. ISBN 0544114515 (ISBN 13: 9780544114517).

Bradshaw, J. (2011) *Dog Sense.* Tantor Media. ISBN 1452652031 (ISBN 13: 9781452652030).

Bradshaw, J. (2012) *In Defence of Dogs.* Penguin Books Ltd. ISBN 014104649X (ISBN 13: 9780141046495).

Brown, A. (2009) *Scaredy Dog! Understanding and Rehabilitating Your Reactive Dog.* Dogwise Publishing. ISBN 0976641402 (ISBN 13: 9780976641407).

Budiansky, S. (2001) *The Truth About Dogs: An Inquiry into the Ancestry, Social Conventions, Mental Habits, and Moral Fiber of Canis familiaris.* Penguin Books. ISBN 014100228X (ISBN 13: 9780141002286).

Burch, M.R. and Bailey, J.S. (1999) *How Dogs Learn*. Howell Books. ISBN 1630260398 (ISBN 13: 9781630260392).

Caswell, K. (2018) *Laika's Window*. Trinity University Press. ISBN 159534862X (ISBN 13: 9781595348623).

Coppinger, R. and Coppinger, L. (2002) *A Startling New Understanding of Canine Origin, Behavior & Evolution*. University of Chicago Press. ISBN 0226115631 (ISBN 13: 9780226115634).

Coren, S. (2000) *How to Speak Dog*. Atria Books. ISBN 13: 9780684865348.

Csányi, V. (2005) *If Dogs Could Talk*. North Point Press. ISBN 0865477299 (ISBN 13: 9780865477292).

De Waal, F. (2017) *Are We Smart Enough to Know How Smart Animals Are?* W.W. Norton Company. ISBN 0393353664 (ISBN 13: 9780393353662).

Dugatkin, L.A., Trut, L. (2016) *How to Tame a Fox: (and Build a Dog)*. The University of Chicago Press. ISBN 13: 9780226444215 (e-book).

Eaton, B. (2008) *Dominance in Dogs: Fact or Fiction?* Dogwise Publishing. ISBN 9781929242801.

Fennel, J. (2006) *The Practical Dog Listener*. Harper Collins Publishers. ISBN 13: 9780007145706.

Fisher, J. (1995) *Think Dog*. Octopus Publishing Group Ltd. ISBN 9781844039098.

Fogle, B. (1992) *The Dog's Mind: Understanding Your Dog's Behaviour*. Howell Book House Inc., US. ISBN 0876055137 (ISBN 13: 9780876055137).

Hare, B. and Woods, V. (2013) *The Genius of Dogs: How Dogs Are Smarter Than You Think*. Dutton Adult. ISBN 0525953191 (ISBN 13: 9780525953197).

Hart, B., Hart, L., Bain, M. (2006) *Canine and Feline Behavior Therapy*. John Wiley and Sons Ltd. ISBN 0683039121 (ISBN 13: 9780683039122).

Horowitz, A. (2009) *Inside of a Dog: What Dogs See, Smell, and Know*. Scribner. ISBN 1416583408 (ISBN 13: 9781416583400).

Kean, H. (2018) *The Great Cat and Dog Massacre*. University of Chicago Press. ISBN 13: 9780226573946.

Koehler, W.R. (1962) *The Koehler Method of Dog Training*. ISBN 0876056575.

Mattinson, P. (2012) *Total Recall*. Quiller Publishing Ltd. ISBN 1846891493 (ISBN 13: 9781846891496).

McConnell, P.B. *The Other End of the Leash*. eISBN: 978-0-307-48918-0

McConnell Phd, Patricia. The Other End of the Leash . Random House Publishing Group. Kindle Edition.

McConnell, P.B. (2003) *Feisty Fido*. McConnell Publishin Limited. ISBN 1891767070 (ISBN 13: 9781891767074).

McConnell, P.B. (2005) *The Cautious Canine: How to Help Dogs Conquer Their Fears*. McConnell Publishing Limited. ISBN 1891767003 (ISBN 13: 9781891767005).

McConnell, P.B. (2006) *For the Love of a Dog*. Ballantine Books. ISBN 0345477146 (ISBN 13: 9780345477149).

McConnell, P.B. and London K.B. (2011) *Love Has No Age Limit*. McConnell Publishing Limited. ISBN 1891767143 (ISBN 13: 9781891767142).

McDevitt, L. (2007) *Control Unleashed*. Clean Run Productions LLC. ISBN 13: 9781892694171.

McHugh, S. (2004) *Dog*. Reaktion Books. ISBN 1861892039 (ISBN 13: 9781861892034).

McSoley, R. (1989) *Dog Tales: How to Solve the Most Troublesome Behavior Problems of Man's Best Friend*. Warner Books (NY). ISBN 0446355666.

Miklósi, A. (2007) *Dog Behaviour, Evolution, and Cognition*. Oxford University Press. ISBN 13: 978019964661; ISBN 13: 9780198787778.

Miklósi, A. (2018) *The Dog: A Natural History*. The Ivy Press. ISBN 1782405623 (ISBN 13: 9781782405627).

Miller, P. (2008) *The Power of Positive Dog Training*. Turner Publishing Company. ISBN 0470241845 (ISBN 13: 9780470241844).

Miller, P. (2017) *Beware of the Dog*. Dogwise Publishing. ISBN 9781617811937.

Overall, K.L. (2013) *Clinical Behavioral Medicine for Small Animals*. Mosby. eBook ISBN 978032324065.

Parsons, E. (2005) *Click to Calm*. Sunshine Book Inc. ISBN 9781890948207.

Rugaas, T. (2005) *On Talking Terms with Dogs*. Dogwise Publishing. ISBN 1929242360 (ISBN 13: 9781929242368).

Ryan, T. and Mortensen, K. (2005) *Outwitting Dogs*. Rowman & Littlefield. ISBN 1592282431 (ISBN 13: 9781592282432).

Scott, J.P. and Fuller, J.L. (1998) *Genetics and the Social Behaviour of the Dog*. The University of Chicago Press. ISBN 0226743381 (ISBN 13: 9780226743387).

Semyonova, A. (2009) *The 100 Silliest Things People Say About Dogs*. Hastings Press. ISBN 1904109187 (ISBN 13: 9781904109181).

Serpell, J. (2002*) In the Company of Animals: A Study of Human-Animal Relationships*. Cambridge University Press. ISBN 0521577799 (ISBN 13: 9780521577793).

Serpell, J. (Ed.) (2017) *The Domestic Dog: Its Evolution, Behavior and Interactions with People*. Cambridge University Press. ISBN 1107699347 (ISBN 13: 9781107699342).

Sheldrake, R. (2000) *Dogs That Know When Their Owners Are Coming Home: And Other Unexplained Powers of Animals*. Cornerstone. ISBN 0099255871 (ISBN 13: 9780099255871).

Stewart, G. (2012) *Behaviour Adjustment Training*. Dogwise Publishing. ISBN 1617810509 (ISBN 13: 9781617810503).

VanArendonk Baugh, L. (2013) *Fired Up, Frantic and Freaked Out: Training Crazy Dogs from Over-the-Top to Under Control*. Aeclipse Press. ISBN 9780985934927.

SCIENTIFIC STUDIES

Amat, M., Le Brech, S., Camps, T. *et al.* (2013) 'Differences in serotonin serum concentration between aggressive English cocker spaniels and aggressive dogs of other breeds', *Journal of Veterinary Behavior*, Volume 8, Issue 1, pp. 19-25. ISSN 1558-7878. Available at: https://doi.org/10.1016/j.jveb.2012.04.003

Amaya, V., Paterson, M. and Phillips, C. (2020) 'Effects of Olfactory and Auditory Enrichment on the Behaviour of Shelter Dogs', *Animals:*

an open access journal from MDPI, 10(4), p. 581. Available at: https://doi.org/10.3390/ani10040581

Andenaes, A.G. (2013) 'The Occurance of Behavioural Problems in Re-Homed Dogs with Unknown Backgrounds'. Available at: https://www.semanticscholar.org/paper/The-Occurance-of-Behavioural-Problems-in-Re-Homed-Andenaes/0cb29cf2a14feda6335faa9cec6b95dc0743e805

Angle, T.C., Passler, T., Waggoner, P.L. *et al.* (2015) 'Real-Time Detection of a Virus Using Detection Dogs', *Frontiers in Veterinary Science*, 2, p. 79. doi: 10.3389/fvets.2015.00079. Available at: https://doi.org/10.3389/fvets.2015.00079

Applied Animal Behaviour Science (2008), pp. 294-304. ISSN 0168-1591.

Arhant *et al.* (2010) 'Behaviour of smaller and larger dogs: Effects of training methods, inconsistency of owner behaviour and level of engagement in activities with the dog', *Applied Animal Behaviour Science*, 123(3), pp. 131-142. doi: 10.1016/j.applanim.2010.01.003.

Bailey, J.S. and Pyles, D.A. (1989) 'Behavioral diagnostics', *Monogr. Am. Assoc. Ment. Retard*, 12, pp. 85-107. PMID: 2747444. Available at: https://pubmed.ncbi.nlm.nih.gov/2747444/

Ballard, J.L., Khoury, J.C., Wedig, K., Wang, L., Eilers-Walsman, B.L., Lipp, R. (1991) 'New Ballard Score, expanded to include extremely premature infants', *The Journal of Pediatrics*, Volume 119, Issue 3. ISSN 0022-3476. Available at: https://doi.org/10.1016/S0022-3476(05)82056-6

Basoglu, M., Jaranson, J.M., Mollica, R., Kastrup, M. (2001) 'Torture and Mental Health', in Gerrity, E., Tuma, F., Keane, T.M. (eds), *The Mental Health Consequences of Torture (Plenum Series on Stress and Coping)*. Boston, MA: Springer. Available at: https://doi.org/10.1007/978-1-4615-1295-0_3

Beidler, D., Walker, D. *et al.* (2006) 'Naturalistic quantification of canine olfactory sensitivity', *Applied Animal Behaviour Science*. ISSN 0168-1591. Available at: https://doi.org/10.1016/j.applanim.2005.07.009

Bierne, P. (2004) 'From Animal Abuse to Interhuman Violence? A Critical Review of the Progression Thesis', *Society & Animals*, 12(1), pp. 39-65. doi: 10.1163/156853004323029531.

Blackwell, E.J., Twells, C., Seawright, A., Casey, R.A. (2008) 'The relationship between training methods and the occurrence of behavior problems, as reported by owners, in a population of domestic dogs', *Journal of Veterinary Behavior*, Volume 3, Issue 5, pp. 207-217. ISSN 1558-7878. Available at: https://doi.org/10.1016/j.jveb.2007.10.008

Blackwell, E.J., Bolster, C., Richards, G. *et al.* (2012) 'The use of electronic collars for training domestic dogs: estimated prevalence, reasons and risk factors for use, and owner perceived success as compared to other training methods', *BMC Vet. Res.*, 8, p. 93. Available at: https://doi.org/10.1186/1746-6148-8-93

Bloom, P. (2004) 'Can a Dog Learn a Word?', *Science*, 11 Jun 2004, Volume 304, Issue 5677, pp. 1605-1606. doi: 10.1126/science.1099899.

Blois, S.L. DVM, DVSc, DACVIM (2003) 'Gastro-intestinal Ulcers in Small Animals', Full review/revision, Jun 2020. doi: 10.1016/s0195-5616(03)00052-4. PMID: 14552157; PMCID: PMC7124327.

Blumstein, D. (2016) 'Habituation and sensitization: New thoughts about old ideas', *Animal Behaviour*, 120(1618), Jun 2016. doi: 10.1016/j.anbehav.2016.05.012. Available at: https://www.researchgate.net/publication/303815995_Habituation_and_sensitization_New_thoughts_about_old_ideas

Boitani, L. and Ciucci, P. (1995) 'Comparative social ecology of feral dogs and wolves', *Ethology Ecology and Evolution*, Jan 1995(1), pp. 49-72. doi: 10.1080/08927014.1995.9522969.

Bondar *et al.* (2018) 'Effects of Early-Life Stress on Social and Anxiety-Like Behaviors in Adult Mice: Sex-Specific Effects', Behavioural Neurology, Volume 2018, Article ID 1538931. Available at: https://doi.org/10.1155/2018/1538931

Borchelt, P.L., Voith, V.L. (1982) 'Diagnosis and treatment of separation-related behavior problems in dogs', *Vet. Clin. North Am. Small Anim. Pract.*, Nov 1982, 12(4), pp. 625-35. doi: 10.1016/s0195-5616(82)50106-4. PMID: 6984556.

Bornstein, S., Zakrisson, G., Thebo, P. (1995) 'Clinical picture and antibody response to experimental *Sarcoptes scabiei* var. vulpes infection in red foxes (*Vulpes vulpes*)', *Acta. Vet. Scand.* 36(4), pp. 509-19. PMID: 8669378. doi: 10.1186/BF03547665.

Botigué, L., Song, S., Scheu, A. *et al.* (2017) 'Ancient European dog genomes reveal continuity since the Early Neolithic', *Nat. Commun.*, 8, p. 16082. Available at: https://doi.org/10.1038/ncomms16082

Bradshaw, J.W.S., Blackwell, E-J. and Casey, R.A. (2015) 'Dominance in domestic dogs: A response to Schilder *et al.* (2014)', *Journal of Veterinary Behavior: Clinical Applications and Research*, 11, pp. 102-108. Available at: https://doi.org/10.1016/j.jveb.2015.11.008

Bray, E.E., Sammel, M.D., Cheney, D.L., Serpell, J.A., Seyfarth, R.M. (2017) 'Characterizing Early Maternal Style in a Population of Guide Dogs', *Frontiers in Psychology*, Volume 8. doi: 10.3389/fpsyg.2017.00175.

Brayley, C.V., Montrose, T. (2016) 'The effects of audiobooks on the behaviour of dogs at a rehoming kennels', *Applied Animal Behaviour Science.* ISSN 0168-1591. Available at: https://doi.org/10.1016/j.applanim.2015.11.008

Broom, D.M. (2015) 'New research relevant to companion animal welfare'. doi: 10.12968/coan.2015.20.10.548.

Bruchim, Y., Horowitz, M., Aroch, I. (2017) 'Pathophysiology of heatstroke in dogs – revisited', *Temperature (Austin)*, 9 Oct 2017, 4(4), pp. 356-370. doi: 10.1080/23328940.2017.1367457. PMID: 29435477; PMCID: PMC5800390.

Caldji, C., Tannenbaum, B., Sharma, S., Francis, D., Plotsky, P.M., Meaney, M.J. (1998) 'Maternal care during infancy regulates the development of neural systems mediating the expression of fearfulness in the rat', *Proc. Natl. Acad. Sci. USA*, 95, pp. 5335-5340. Available at: https://doi.org/10.1073/pnas.95.9.5335

Carter, A.J., Roshier, A.L. and McNally, D.S. (2020) 'Canine collars: an investigation of collar type and the forces applied to a simulated neck model', *Veterinary Record.* Available at: https://doi.org/10.1136/vr.105681

Casey, R.A., Loftus, B., Bolster, C. *et al.* (2014) 'Human directed aggression in domestic dogs (*Canis familiaris*): Occurrence in different contexts and risk factors', *Applied Animal Behaviour*

Science, Volume 152, pp. 52-63. ISSN 0168-1591. Available at: https://doi.org/10.1016/j.applanim.2013.12.003

Chaikin, P., Welihozkiy, A. (2017) 'Hemangiosarcoma in a Dog: Unusual Presentation and Increased Survival Using a Complementary/Holistic Approach Combined with Metronomic Chemotherapy', *Case Reports in Veterinary Medicine*, Volume 2018, Article ID 6160980, 6 pages, 2018. Available at: https://doi.org/10.1155/2018/6160980

Champagne, D.L., Bagot, R.C., van Hasselt, F., Ramakers, G., Meaney, M.J., de Kloet, E.R., Joëls, M., Krugers, H. (2008) 'Maternal care and hippocampal plasticity: evidence for experience-dependent structural plasticity, altered synaptic functioning, and differential responsiveness to glucocorticoids and stress', *J. Neurosci.*, 4 Jun 2008, 28(23), pp. 6037-45. doi: 10.1523/JNEUROSCI.0526-08.2008. PMID: 18524909; PMCID: PMC6670331.

Champagne, F., Diorio, J., Sharma, S., Meaney, M.J. (2001) 'Naturally occurring variations in maternal behavior in the rat are associated with differences in estrogen-inducible central oxytocin receptors', *Proc. Natl. Acad. Sci. USA*, 98, pp. 12736-12741. Available at: https://doi.org/10.1073/pnas.221224598

Champagne, F.A., Francis, D.D., Mar, A. and Meaney, M.J. (2003) 'Variations in maternal care in the rat as a mediating influence for the effects of environment on development'. PMID: 12954431; doi: 10.1016/s0031-9384(03)00149-5.

China, L., Mills, D.S., Cooper, J.J. (2020) 'Efficacy of Dog Training With and Without Remote Electronic Collars vs. a Focus on Positive Reinforcement Frontiers in Veterinary Science'. doi: 10.3389/fvets.2020.00508.

Cohn, J. (1997) 'How wild wolves became domestic dogs', *BioScience*, Volume 47, Issue 11, pp. 725-728. Available at: https://doi.org/10.2307/1313093

Col, R., Day, C., Phillips, C.J.C. (2016) 'An epidemiological analysis of dog behavior problems presented to an Australian behavior clinic, with associated risk factors', *Journal of Veterinary Behavior*. doi: 10.1016/j.jveb.2016.07.001.

Cooley, D.M., Beranek, B.C., Schlittler, D.L., Glickman, N.W., Glickman, L.T., Waters, D.J. (2002) 'Endogenous gonadal hormone exposure and bone sarcoma risk', *Cancer Epidemiol. Biomarkers Prev*. Nov 2002, 11(11), pp. 1434-40. PMID: 12433723. Available at: https://pubmed.ncbi.nlm.nih.gov/12433723/

Cooper, J.J., Cracknell, N., Hardiman, J., Wright, H., Mills, D. (2014) 'The Welfare Consequences and Efficacy of Training Pet Dogs with Remote Electronic Training Collars in Comparison to Reward Based Training', *PLOS One*, 9(9), p. e102722. Available at: https://doi.org/10.1371/journal.pone.0102722

Coppola, C., Grandin, T., Enns, R. (2006) 'Noise in the Animal Shelter Environment: Building Design and the Effects of Daily Noise Exposure', *Journal of Applied Animal Welfare Science*, 9(1), pp. 1-7. doi: 10.1207/s15327604jaws0901_1.

Cottam, N., Dodman, N.H., Ha, J.C. (2013) 'The effectiveness of the Anxiety Wrap in the treatment of canine thunderstorm phobia: An open-label trial', *Journal of Veterinary Behavior*. ISSN 1558-787. Available at: https://doi.org/10.1016/j.jveb.2012.09.001

Curley, J.P., Jensen, C.L., Mashoodh, R., Champagne, F.A. (2011) 'Social influences on neurobiology and behavior: Epigenetic effects during development', *Psychoneuroendocrinology*, 36, pp. 352-371. doi: 10.1016/j.psyneuen.2010.06.005.

Czerwinski, V.H, Smith, B.P., Hynd, P.I., Hazel, S.J. (2016) 'The influence of maternal care on stress-related behaviors in domestic dogs: What can we learn from the rodent literature?' *Journal of Veterinary Behavior*, Volume 14, pp. 52-59. ISSN 1558-7878. Available at: https://doi.org/10.1016/j.jveb.2016.05.003

Dale, A.R., Walker, J.K., Farnworth, M.J., Morrissey, S.V. and Waran, N.K. (2010) 'A survey of owners' perceptions of fear of fireworks in a sample of dogs and cats in New Zealand', *New Zealand Veterinary Journal*, 58:6, pp. 286-291. doi: 10.1080/00480169.2010.69403. Available at: https://doi.org/10.1080/00480169.2010.69403

Dawson, J.K., Howell, T.J., Ruby, M.B. and Bennett, P.C. (2019) 'Throwing the Baby Out With the Bath Water: Could Widespread Neutering of Companion Dogs Cause Problems at a Population

Level?' *Front. Vet. Sci.* Available at: https://doi.org/10.3389/fvets.2019.00241

Deldalle, S., Gaunet, F. (2014) 'Effects of 2 training methods on stress-related behaviors of the dog (*Canis familiaris*) and on the dog-owner relationship', *Journal of Veterinary Behavior*, Volume 9, Issue 2, pp. 58-65. ISSN 1558-7878. Available at: https://doi.org/10.1016/j.jveb.2013.11.004

De Meester, R.H., Pluijmakers, J., Vermeire, S., Laevens, H. (2011) 'The use of the socially acceptable behavior test in the study of temperament of dogs', *Journal of Veterinary Behavior*, Volume 6, Issue 4, pp. 211-224. ISSN 1558-7878. Available at: https://doi.org/10.1016/j.jveb.2011.01.003

Denenberg, V.H., Whimbey, A.E. (2002) 'Behavior of Adult Rats Is Modified by the Experiences Their Mothers Had as Infants', *Science*, 29 Nov 1963, Volume 142, Issue 3596, pp. 1192-1193. doi: 10.1126/science.142.3596.1192.

deSandes-Moyer, K. (2013) 'The Dog in Roman Peasant Life', *Anthropology Senior Theses*, Paper 148. Available at: https://repository.upenn.edu/cgi/viewcontent.cgi?article=1029&context=anthro_seniortheses

Diesel, G., Brodbelt, D. and Pfeiffer, D.U. (2010) 'Characteristics of relinquished dogs and their owners at 14 rehoming centers in the United Kingdom', *Journal of Applied Animal Welfare Science*, 13, pp. 15-30. Available at: https://doi.org/10.1080/10888700903369255

Diesel, G., Pfeiffer, D.U. and Brodbelt, D. (2008) 'Factors affecting the success of rehoming dogs in the UK during 2005', *Preventive Veterinary Medicine*, 84, pp. 228-241. Available at: https://doi.org/10.1016/j.pre-vetmed.2007.12.004

Dietz, L., Arnold, A.K., Goerlich-Jansson, V.C. and Vinke, C.M. (2018) 'The importance of early life experiences for the development of behavioural disorders in domestic dogs', *Behaviour*, 155(2-3), pp. 83-114. Available at: https://doi.org/10.1163/1568539X-00003486

Dixon, D.R., Vogel, T. (2012) 'A Brief History of Functional Analysis and Applied Behavior Analysis'. doi: 10.1007/978-1-4614-3037-7_2.

Dodman, N.H., Brown, D.C., Serpell, J.A. (2018) 'Associations between owner personality and psychological status and the prevalence of canine behavior problems', *PLOS One*. 14 Feb 2018, 13(2), pp. e0192846. doi: 10.1371/journal.pone.0192846. PMID: 29444154. PMCID: PMC5812720.

Dorey, N.R., Tobias, J.S., Udell, M.A., Wynne, C.D. (2012) 'Decreasing dog problem behavior with functional analysis: Linking diagnoses to treatment', *Journal of Veterinary Behavior*, Volume 7, Issue 5, pp. 276-282. ISSN 1558-7878. Available at: https://doi.org/10.1016/j.jveb.2011.10.002

Draper, D.D. (1976) 'Improper Puppy Socialization and Subsequent Behavior', *Iowa State University Veterinarian*, Volume 38, Issue 2, Article 1. Available at: https://lib.dr.iastate.edu/iowastate_veterinarian/vol38/iss2/1

Dreschel, N. (2007) 'Behavioral Effects of Stress Related to Fear and Anxiety in Domestic Canines: A Thesis in Biobehavioral Health'. The Pennsylvania State University, The Graduate School Department of Biobehavioral Health. Available at: https://etda.libraries.psu.edu/files/final_submissions/4575

Driscoll, C.A., Macdonald, D.W. (2010) 'Top dogs: wolf domestication and wealth', *J. Biol.* 9, p. 10. Available at: https://doi.org/10.1186/jbiol226

Driscoll, C.A., Macdonald, D.W. and O'Brien, S.J. (2009) 'From wild animals to domestic pets, an evolutionary view of domestication', *PNAS*, 16 Jun 2009, 106 (Supplement 1), pp. 9971-9978. Available at: https://doi.org/10.1073/pnas.0901586106

Duffy *et al.* (2008) 'Breed differences in canine aggression', *Applied Animal Behaviour Science*, 114(3-4), pp. 441-460. doi: 10.1016/j.applanim.2008.04.006.

Duffy, D.L, Serpell, J.A. 'Non-reproductive Effects of Spaying and Neutering on Behavior in Dogs'. Center for the Interaction of Animals and Society, School of Veterinary Medicine, University of Pennsylvania. Available at: https://www.naiaonline.org/uploads/WhitePapers/EarlySNAndBehaviorDuffySerpell.pdf

Dugatkin, L.A. (2018) 'The silver fox domestication experiment', *Evo.*

Edu. Outreach, 11, p. 16. Available at: https://doi.org/10.1186/s12052-018-0090-x

Farhoody, P., Mallawaarachchi, I. *et al.* (2018) 'Aggression Toward Familiar People, Strangers, and Conspecifics in Gonadectomized and Intact Dogs', *Front. Vet. Sci.*, 26 Feb 2018, 5, pp. 18. doi: 10.3389/fvets.2018.00018. PMID: 29536014. PMCID: PMC5834763.

Fan, Z., Silva, P., Gronau, I., Wang, S., Armero, A.S., Schweizer, R.M., Ramirez, O., Pollinger, J., Galaverni, M., Ortega Del-Vecchyo, D., Du, L., Zhang, W., Zhang, Z., Xing, J., Vilà, C., Marques-Bonet, T., Godinho, R., Yue, B., Wayne, R.K. 'Worldwide patterns of genomic variation and admixture in gray wolves', *Genome Res.* Feb 2016, 26(2), pp. 163-73. doi: 10.1101/gr.197517.115. Epub 17 Dec 2015. PMID: 26680994. PMCID: PMC4728369.

Flannigan, G., Dodman, N.H. (2001) 'Risk factors and behaviors associated with separation anxiety in dogs', *J. Am. Vet. Med. Assoc.*, 15 Aug 2001, 219(4), pp. 460-6. doi: 10.2460/javma.2001.219.460. PMID: 11518171.

Foyer, P. (2015) 'Early Experiences, Maternal Care and Behavioural Test Design'. IFM Biology, Division of Zoology. Dissertation No. 1703. ISBN 987-91-7685-945-2, ISSN 0345-7524. Available at: https://www.diva-portal.org/smash/get/diva2:873512/FULLTEXT01.pdf

Foyer, P., Wilsson, E. and Jensen, P. (2016) 'Levels of maternal care in dogs affect adult offspring temperament', *Sci. Rep.*, 6, p. 19253. Available at: https://doi.org/10.1038/srep19253

Froelich, N. (2013) 'A review of canine aggression & treatment options for the territorially aggressive dog'. Available at: https://www.researchgate.net/publication/257652188_A_review_of_canine_aggression_and_treatment_options_for_the_territorially_aggressive_dog

Fugazza, C., Pogány, Á., Miklósi, Á. (2016) 'Do as I … Did! Long-term memory of imitative actions in dogs (*Canis familiaris*)', *Anim. Cogn*, Mar 2016, 19(2), pp. 263-9. doi: 10.1007/s10071-015-0931-8. Epub 25 Oct 2015. PMID: 26498155.

Gábor, A., Gácsi, M., Szabó, D., Milósi, Á., Kubiniyi, E., Andics, A. (2020) 'Multilevel fMRI adaptation for spoken word processing in the awake dog brain', *MTMT*: 31409169; WoS ID: 000556393000001; Scopus ID: 85088982033; PubMed ID: 32747731; doi: 10.1038/s41598-020-68821-6.

Gazzano et al. (2008) 'Survey of undesirable behaviors displayed by potential guide dogs with puppy walkers', *Journal of Veterinary Behavior Clinical Applications and Research*, 3(3), pp. 104-113. doi: 10.1016/j.jveb.2008.04.002.

Gazzano, A., Mariti, C., Notari, L. *et al.* (2007) 'Effects of early gentling and early environment on emotional development of puppies', *Applied Animal Behaviour Science*, Volume 110, Issues 3-4, 2008, pp. 294-304. ISSN 0168-1591. Available at: https://doi.org/10.1016/j.applanim.2007.05.007

Galibert, F., Quignon, P., Hitte, C., André, C. (2011) 'Toward understanding dog evolutionary and domestication history', *Comptes Rendus Biologies*, Volume 334, Issue 3, pp. 190-196. ISSN 1631-0691. Available at: https://doi.org/10.1016/j.crvi.2010.12.011

Gomes, J., Eduardo, C. (2016) 'Personality and aggression: A contribution of the General Aggression Model'. Available at: https://doi.org/10.1590/1982027520160003000008

Gosling, S.D., Kwan, V.S., John, O.P. (2003) 'A dog's got personality: a cross-species comparative approach to personality judgments in dogs and humans', *J. Pers. Soc. Psychol.* Dec 2003, 85(6), pp. 1161-9. doi: 10.1037/0022-3514.85.6.1161. PMID: 14674821.

Gosling, S.D., Sandy, C.J. and Potter, J. (2010) 'Personalities of Self-Identified "Dog People" and "Cat People"', *Anthrozoos: A Multidisciplinary Journal of the Interactions of People & Animals*, 23, Sep 2010, pp. 213-222. Available at: https://doi.org/10.2752/175303710X12750451258850

Grohmann, K., Dickomeit, M.J., Schmidt, M.J., Kramer, M. (2013) 'Severe brain damage after punitive training technique with a choke chain collar in a German shepherd dog'. ISSN 1558-7878. Available at: https://doi.org/10.1016/j.jveb.2013.01.002

Groothuis, T.G. and Taborsky, B. (2015) 'Introducing biological realism into the study of developmental plasticity in behaviour', *Frontiers in Zoology*, 12(Suppl 1):S6. doi: 10.1186/1742-9994-12-S1-S6

Grumbach, M.M. (2000) 'Estrogen, bone, growth and sex: a sea change in conventional wisdom', *J. Pediatr. Endocrinol. Metab.*, 13 Suppl 6, pp. 1439-55. doi: 10.1515/jpem-2000-s619. PMID: 11202221. Available at: https://pubmed.ncbi.nlm.nih.gov/11202221/

Guagnin, M., Perri, A.R., Petraglia, M.D. (2018) 'Pre-Neolithic evidence for dog-assisted hunting strategies in Arabia', *Journal of Anthropological Archaeology*, Volume 49, pp. 225-236. ISSN 0278-4165. Available at: https://doi.org/10.1016/j.jaa.2017.10.003

Gudsnuk, K. and Champagne, F.A. (2012) 'Epigenetic Influence of Stress and the Social Environment', *ILAR J.*, Dec 2012, 53(3-4), pp. 279-288. doi: 10.1093/ilar.53.3-4.279.

Haggbloom *et al.* (2002) 'The 100 most eminent psychologists of the 20th century'. doi: 10.1037/1089-2680.7.1.37.

Hailer, F., Kutschera, V.E., Hallström, B.M. *et al.* (2012) 'Nuclear genomic sequences reveal that polar bears are an old and distinct bear lineage', *Science*, 336(6079), pp. 344-347. doi: 10.1126/science.1216424.

Harlow, H.F., Harlow, M.K., Dodsworth, R.O. and Arling, G.L. (1966) 'Maternal behavior of rhesus monkeys deprived of mothering and peer associations in infancy', *Proceedings of the American Philosophical Society*, 110(1), pp. 58-66; *Journal of Comparative and Physiological Psychology*, 64(3), pp. 371-377. Available at: https://doi.org/10.1037/h0025221

Hart, B.L., Hart, L.A., Thigpen, A.P., Willits, N.H. (2016) 'Neutering of German Shepherd Dogs: associated joint disorders, cancers and urinary incontinence', *Vet. Med. Sci.*, 16 May 2016, 2(3), pp. 191-199. doi: 10.1002/vms3.34. PMID: 29067194. PMCID: PMC5645870. Available at: https://doi.org/10.1002/vms3.34

Hart, B.L., Hart, L.A., Thigpen, A.P., Willits, N.H. (2020) 'Assisting Decision-Making on Age of Neutering for 35 Breeds of Dogs: Associated Joint Disorders, Cancers, and Urinary Incontinence Frontiers', *Veterinary Science*. doi: 10.3389/fvets.2020.00388. ISSN 2297-1769.

Haug, L.I. (2008) 'Canine Aggression Toward Unfamiliar People and Dog', *Veterinary Clinics of North America Small Animal Practice*, 38(5), Oct 2008, pp. 1023-41, vi. doi: 10.1016/j.cvsm.2008.04.005.

Haverbeke, A., Diederich, C., Depiereux, E., Giffroy, J.M. (2008) 'Cortisol and behavioral responses of working dogs to environmental challenges', *Physiol. Behav.*, 93(1-2), pp. 59-67. doi: 10.1016/j.physbeh.2007.07.014.

Heldström, P., Bearman, P. (2017) 'The Oxford Handbook of Analytical Sociology'. ISBN 9780199215362. doi: 10.1093/oxfordhb/9780199215362.001.0001.

Herron *et al.* (2009) 'Survey of the use and outcome of confrontational and non-confrontational training methods in client-owned dogs showing undesired behaviors', *Applied Animal Behaviour Science*, 117 (1-2), p. 47. doi: 10.1016/j.applanim.2008.12.011d.

Hiby, E.F., Rooney, N.J., Bradshaw, J.W.S. (2004) 'Dog training methods: their use, effectiveness and interaction with behaviour and welfare', *Animal Welfare*, 13, pp. 63-69. Available at: https://www.researchgate.net/publication/261106650_Dog_training_methods_Their_use_effectiveness_and_interaction_with_behaviour_and_welfare

Horowitz, A. (2011) 'Theory of mind in dogs? Examining method and concept', *Learn. Behav.*, 39, pp. 314-317. Available at: https://doi.org/10.3758/s13420-011-0041-7

Houpt, K., Bamberger, M. (2006) 'Signalment factors, comorbidity, and trends in behavior diagnoses in dogs: 1,644 Cases (1991-2001)', *Journal of the American Veterinary Medical Association*, 229(10), pp. 1591-601. doi: 10.2460/javma.229.10.1591.

Hsu, Y. (2010) 'Factors associated with aggressive responses in pet dogs', *Applied Animal Behaviour Science*, 123(3), pp. 108-123. doi: 10.1016/j.applanim.2010.01.013.

Hsu, Y. and Serpell, J. (2003) 'Development and validation of a questionnaire for measuring behavior and temperament traits in pet dogs', *Journal of the American Veterinary Medical Association*, 223, pp. 1293-300. doi: 10.2460/javma.2003.223.1293.

Jagoe, A. and Serpell, J. (1996) 'Owner characteristics and interactions and the prevalence of canine behaviour problems', *Appl. Anim. Behav. Sci.*, 47, pp. 31-42. ISSN 0168-1591. Available at: https://doi.org/10.1016/0168-1591(95)01008-4

Kim, J.-H., Graef, A.J., Dickerson, E.B., Modiano, J.F. (2015) 'Pathobiology of Hemangiosarcoma in Dogs: Research Advances and Future Perspectives', *Vet. Sci.* 2, pp. 388-405. Available at: https://doi.org/10.3390/vetsci2040388

Kirchhofer, K.C., Zimmermann, F., Kaminski, J., Tomasello, M. (2012) 'Dogs (*Canis familiaris*), but Not Chimpanzees (*Pan troglodytes*), Understand Imperative Pointing'. Available at: https://doi.org/10.1371/journal.pone.0030913

Kogan, L.R., Schoenfeld-Tacher, R. and Simon, A.A. (2012) 'Behavioral effects of auditory stimulation on kenneled dogs', *Journal of Veterinary Behavior: Clinical Applications and Research*, 7, pp. 268-275. Available at: https://doi.org/10.1016/j.jveb.2011.11.002

Kubinyi, E., Virányi, Z. and Miklósi, Á. (2007) 'Comparative social cognition: From wolf and dog to humans', *Comparative Cognition & Behavior Reviews*, Volume 2(1), pp. 26-46. Available at: http://etologia.elte.hu/file/publikaciok/2007/kubinyiVM2007.pdf

Landsberg, G., Nichol, J., Araujo, J.A. (2012) 'Cognitive Dysfunction Syndrome A Disease of Canine and Feline Brain Aging', *Veterinary Clinics of North America Small Animal Practice*, 42(4), pp. 749-68, vii. doi: 10.1016/j.cvsm.2012.04.003.

Landsberg, G.M., Melese, P., Sherman, B.L., Neilson, J.C., Zimmerman, A., Clarke, T.P. (2008) 'Effectiveness of fluoxetine chewable tablets in the treatment of canine separation anxiety', *Journal of Veterinary Behavior*, Volume 3, Issue 1, pp. 12-19. ISSN 1558-7878. Available at: https://doi.org/10.1016/j.jveb.2007.09.001

Larson, G., Perri, A., Karisson, E., Webster, M. (2012) 'Rethinking dog domestication by integrating genetics, archeology, and biogeography', *Proceedings of the National Academy of Sciences*, 109(23), pp. 8878-83. doi: 10.1073/pnas.1203005109.

Laurent *et al.* (2016) 'Genomic and archaeological evidence suggest a dual origin of domestic dogs'. doi: 10.1126/science.aaf3161.

Leblanc, B., Fox, J.G., Le Net, J.L. (1993) 'Hyperplastic Gastritis with Intraepithelial Campylobacter-like Organisms in a Beagle Dog'. First published 1 July 1993, Brief Report. Available at: https://doi.org/10.1177/030098589303000413

Lindquist, B., Chase, I. (2011) 'Relationships, Dominance Hierarchies, and the Structural Form of Hierarchies in Animals', *The Oxford Handbook of Analytical Sociology*. doi: 10.1093/oxfordhb/9780199215362.013.24.

Lines, J.A., van Driel, K., Cooper, J.J. (2013) 'Characteristics of electronic training collars for dogs', *Vet. Rec.*, 172(9), pp. 243-244. doi: 10.1136/vr.f1333. Available at: http://eprints.lincoln.ac.uk/id/eprint/7827/

Lupien, S., McEwen, B., Gunnar, M. *et al.* (2009) 'Effects of stress throughout the lifespan on the brain, behaviour and cognition', *Nat. Rev. Neurosci.*, 10, Apr 2009, pp. 434-445. Available at: https://doi.org/10.1038/nrn2639

Lyons *et al.* (2010) 'Animal Models of Early Life Stress: Implications for Understanding Resilience', *Dev. Psychobiol.*, Jul 2010, 52(5), pp. 402-410. doi: 10.1002/dev.20429.

Lyons, D.M., Buckmaster, P.S., Lee, A.G. *et al.* (2010) 'Stress coping stimulates hippocampal neurogenesis in adult monkeys', 17 Aug 2010, 107(33), pp. 14823-27. doi: 10.1073/pnas.0914568107. Epub 30 July 2010. Available at: https://doi.org/10.1073/pnas.0914568107

Macri *et al.* (2004) 'Dissociation in the effects of neonatal maternal separations on maternal care and the offspring's HPA and fear responses in rats, September 2004', *European Journal of Neuroscience*, 20(4), pp. 1017-24. doi: 10.1111/j.1460-9568.2004.03541.x.

Manimanis, V. *et al.* (2011) 'Sirius in Ancient Greek and Roman Literature: From the Orphic Argonautics to the Astronomical Tables of Georgios Chrysococca', *Journal of Astronomical History and Heritage* (ISSN 1440-2807), Volume 14, Number 3, pp. 180-189. Bibcode: 2011JAHH...14..180T. Available at: https://ui.adsabs.harvard.edu/abs/2011JAHH...14.180T/abstract

Mariti, C., Falaschi, C., Zilocchi, M. *et al.* (2017) 'Analysis of the intraspecific visual communication in the domestic dog (*Canis familiaris*): A pilot study on the case of calming signals', *Journal of Veterinary Behavior*, Volume 18, pp. 49-55. ISSN 1558-7878.

Available at: https://doi.org/10.1016/j.jveb.2016.12.009

Marshall-Pescini, S. and Kaminski, J. (2014) 'The Social Dog: History and Evolution', *The Social Dog: Behavior and Cognition*, pp. 3-33. doi: 10.1016/B978-0-12-407818-5.00001-2.

Masson, S., Nigron, I., Gaultier, E. (2018) 'Questionnaire survey on the use of different e-collar types in France in everyday life with a view to providing recommendations for possible future regulations', *Journal of Veterinary Behavior*, Volume 26, pp. 48-60. ISSN 1558-7878. Available at: https://doi.org/10.1016/j.jveb.2018.05.004

McCord, M.A., Joseph, D.L., Grijalva, E. (2014) 'Blinded By the Light: The Dark Side of Traditionally Desirable Personality Traits'. Available at: https://doi.org/10.1111/iops.12121

McCrave, E.A. (1991) 'Diagnostic criteria for separation anxiety in the dog', *Vet. Clin. North Am. Small Anim. Pract.*, Mar 1991, 21(2), pp. 247-55. doi: 10.1016/s0195-5616(91)50030-9. PMID: 2053248.

McMillan, F.D. (2017) 'Behavioral and psychological outcomes for dogs sold as puppies through pet stores and/or born in commercial breeding establishments: current knowledge and putative causes', *J. Vet. Behav. Clin. Appl. Res.*, 19, pp. 14-26. ISSN 1558-7878. Available at: https://doi.org/10.1016/j.jveb.2017.01.001

McMillan, F.D., Serpell, J.A., Duffy, D.L., Masaoud, E., Dohoo, I.R. (2013) 'Differences in behavioral characteristics between dogs obtained as puppies from pet stores and those obtained from non-commercial breeders', *J. Am. Vet. Med. Assoc.*, 15, 242(10), pp. 1359-63. doi: 10.2460/javma.242.10.1359. PMID: 23634679.

Meaney, M.J. (2001) 'Maternal Care, Gene Expression, and the Transmission of Individual Differences in Stress Reactivity Across Generations', 24(1), pp. 1161-92. doi: 10.1146/annurev.neuro.24.1.1161.

Menache, S. (1997) 'Dogs: God's worst enemy?', *Society and Animals*, 5 (1), pp. 23-44. doi: 10.1163/156853097x00204.

Miklin, S. (2012) 'Cujo in the Family: Owning an Aggressive Dog in the Contemporary United States' (thesis). Available at: https://www.academia.edu/6862542/Cujo_in_the_Family_Owning_an_Aggressive_Dog_in_the_Contemporary_United_States

Mills, D., Karagiannis, C., Zulch, H. 'Stress: its effects on health and behavior: a guide for practitioners', *Vet. Clin. North Am. Small Anim. Pract.*, May 2014, 44(3), pp. 525-41. doi: 10.1016/j.cvsm.2014.01.005. Epub 12 Mar 2014. PMID: 24766698. Available at: https://pubmed.ncbi.nlm.nih.gov/24766698/

Modiano, J.F., Ritt, M.G., Breen, M., Breen, T. 'Canine Hemangiosarcoma: The Road from Despair to Hope'. University of Colorado Health Sciences Center, Denver, CO (JFM), Animal Hospital Center, Highlands Ranch, CO (MGR), and North Carolina State University (MB, TB); University of Minnesota. Available at: http://www.modianolab.org/cancer/HSA%202014%20update.shtml

Nicholson, P.T., Ikram, S. and Mills, S.F. (2015) 'The Catacombs of Anubis at North Saqqara', *Antiquity*, 89 (345), pp. 645-661. 10.15184/aqy.2014.53 file. Available at: http://dx.doi.org/10.15184/aqy.2014.53

Nimmervoll, H., Hoby, S., Robert, N., Lommano, E., Welle, M., Ryser-Degiorgis, M.P. (2013) 'Pathology of sarcoptic mange in red foxes (*Vulpes vulpes*): macroscopic and histologic characterisation of three disease stages', *J. Wildl. Dis.*, Jan 2013, 49(1), pp. 91-102. doi: 10.7589/2010-11-316.

O'Donahue, W.T., Fisher, J.E. (2008) 'Cognitive Behavior Therapy: Applying Empirically Supported Techniques In Your Practice'. ISBN 978-0-470-22778-7. Available at: https://www.semanticscholar.org/paper/Cognitive-behavior-therapy-%3A-applying-empirically-O%27donohue-Fisher/17681367b6feed9dc9c4814c6109980c8bfe0649

Oetjens, M.T. *et al.* (2018) 'Analysis of the canid Y-chromosome phylogeny using short-read sequencing data reveals the presence of distinct haplogroups among Neolithic European dogs,' *BMC Genomics*, Volume 19, 350, 10 May 2018. doi: 10.1186/s12864-018-4749-z.

Overall, K.L., Dunham, A.E. 'Clinical features and outcome in dogs and cats with obsessive-compulsive disorder: 126 cases (1989-2000)', *J. Am. Vet. Med. Assoc.*, 15 Nov 2002, 221(10), pp. 1445-52. doi: 10.2460/javma.2002.221.1445. PMID: 12458615.

Overall, K.L., Hamilton, S.P., Chang, M.L. (2006) 'Understanding the genetic basis of canine anxiety: phenotyping dogs for behavioral, neurochemical, and genetic assessment', *Journal of Veterinary Behavior*, Volume 1, Issue 3, pp. 124-141. ISSN 1558-7878. Available at: https://doi.org/10.1016/j.jveb.2006.09.004

Overall, K.L., Love, M. 'Dog bites to humans: demography, epidemiology, injury, and risk', *J. Am. Vet. Med. Assoc.*, 15 Jun 2001, 15, 218(12), pp. 1923-34. doi: 10.2460/javma.2001.218.1923; PMID: 11417736.

Panksepp, J. (2010) 'Affective neuroscience of the emotional BrainMind: evolutionary perspectives and implications for understanding depression', *Dialogues in Clinical Neuroscience*, 12(4), pp. 533-545. Available at: https://doi.org/10.31887/DCNS.2010.12.4/jpanksepp

Parry, N.M.A. (2020) 'COVID-19 and pets: When pandemic meets panic', *Forensic Science International: Reports*, Volume 2 (2020) 100090 ISSN 2665-9107. Available at: https://doi.org/10.1016/j.fsir.2020.100090

Patronek, G.J., Bradley, J., Arps, E. (2019) 'What is the evidence for reliability and validity of behavior evaluations for shelter dogs? A prequel to "No better than flipping a coin"', *Journal of Veterinary Behavior*, Volume 31, pp. 43-58. ISSN 1558-7878. Available at: https://doi.org/10.1016/j.jveb.2019.03.001

Paulovics, A. (2018) 'Legal Rules on the Protection of Animals in Hungary'. doi: 10.2478/danb-2013-0011.

Pierantoni, L., Albertini, M. and Pirrone, F. (2011) 'Prevalence of owner-reported behaviours in dogs separated from the litter at two different ages'. doi: 10.1136/vr.d4967.

Polsky, R. (2000) 'Can aggression in dogs be elicited through the use of electronic pet containment systems?', *Journal of Applied Animal Welfare Science*, 3, pp. 345-358. Available at: https://doi.org/10.1207/S15327604JAWS0304_6

Protopopova, A. and Gunter, L.M. (2017) 'Adoption and relinquishment interventions at the animal shelter: a review', *Animal Welfare*, 26, pp. 35-48. ISSN 0962-7286. doi: 10.7120/09627286.26.1.

Prüfer, K., Munch, K., Pääbo, S. *et al.* (2012) 'The bonobo genome compared with the chimpanzee and human genomes', *Nature*, 486, pp. 527-531. Available at: https://doi.org/10.1038/nature11128

Rankin *et al.* (2009) 'Habituation revisited: an updated and revised description of the behavioral characteristics of habituation', *Neurobiol. Learn. Mem.*, Sep 2009, 92(2), pp. 135-138. doi: 10.1016/j.nlm.2008.09.012.

Rehn, T., Keeling, L.J. (2011) 'The effect of time left alone at home on dog welfare', *Applied Animal Behaviour Science*. ISSN 0168-1591. Available at: https://doi.org/10.1016/j.applanim.2010.11.015

Report from the Commission to the European Parliament and Council (2019) 'Report on the statistics on the use of animals for scientific purposes in the Member States of the European Union in 2015-2017'. Available at: https://op.europa.eu/en/publication-detail/

Riemer, S. (2020) 'Effectiveness of treatments for firework fears in dogs', *Journal of Veterinary Behavior*, Volume 37, pp. 61-70. ISSN 1558-7878. Available at: https://doi.org/10.1016/j.jveb.2020.04.005

Rilling, J.K., Scholz, J., Behrens, T.E. (2012) 'Differences between chimpanzees and bonobos in neural systems supporting social cognition', *Soc. Cogn. Affect. Neurosci.*, Apr 2012, 7(4), pp. 369-379. doi: 10.1093/scan/nsr017.

Romanucci, M., Salda, L.D. (2013) 'Pathophysiology and pathological findings of heatstroke in dogs', *Vet. Med. (Auckl.).* 9 Jan 2013, 4, pp. 1-9. doi: 10.2147/VMRR.S29978. PMID: 32670838. PMCID: PMC7337213.

Rooney, N.J., Cowan, S. (2011) 'Training methods and owner–dog interactions: Links with dog behaviour and learning ability', *Applied Animal Behaviour Science*, Volume 132, Issues 3-4, pp. 169-177. ISSN 0168-1591. Available at: https://doi.org/10.1016/j.applanim.2011.03.007

Ru, G., Terracini, B., Glickman, L.T. (1998) 'Host related risk factors for canine osteosarcoma', *Vet. J.*, Jul 1998, 156(1), pp. 31-9. doi: 10.1016/s1090-0233(98)80059-2. PMID: 9691849.

Salman, M., Hutchinson, J., Ruch-Gallie, R., Kogan, L., New Jr, J., Kass, P., Scarlett, J. (2000) 'Behavioral Reasons for Relinquishment of

Dogs and Cats to 12 Shelters' Apr 2000, *Journal of Applied Animal Welfare Science*, 3(2). doi: 10.1207/S15327604JAWS0302_2.

Sapolsky, R. (2004) 'Social Status and Health in Humans and Other Animals', *Annual Review of Anthropology*, 33(1), pp. 393-418. doi: 10.1146/annurev.anthro.33.070203.144000.

Sargisson, R. (2014) 'Canine separation anxiety: strategies for treatment and management', Vet Med Volume 5, pp. 143-151. Available at: https://doi.org/10.2147/VMRR.S60424

Schalke, E., Stichnoth, J., Ott, S. and Jones-Baade, R. (2007) 'Clinical signs caused by the use of electric training collars on dogs in everyday life situations', *Applied Animal Behaviour Science*, 105 (4), pp. 369-380. Available at: https://doi.org/10.1016/j.applanim.2006.11.002

Schilder, M., van der Borg, J. (2004) 'Training dogs with help of the shock collar: short and long term behavioural effects', *Applied Animal Behaviour Science*, 85(3-4), pp. 319-334. doi: 10.1016/j.applanim.2003.10.004.

Schwartz, S. (2003) 'Separation anxiety syndrome in dogs and cats', *J. Am. Vet. Med. Assoc.*, 1 Jun 2003, 222(11), pp. 1526-32. doi: 10.2460/javma.2003.222.1526; PMID: 12784957.

Scott, D.M., Baker, R., Tomlinson, A. *et al.* (2020) 'Spatial distribution of sarcoptic mange (*Sarcoptes scabiei*) in urban foxes (*Vulpes vulpes*) in Great Britain as determined by citizen science', *Urban Ecosyst.*, 23, pp. 1127-1140. Available at: https://doi.org/10.1007/s11252-020-00985-5

Sechi, S., Di Cerbo, A., Canello, S., Guidetti, G., Chiavolelli, F., Fiore, F., Cocco, R. (2017) 'Effects in dogs with behavioural disorders of a commercial nutraceutical diet on stress and neuroendocrine parameters', *Vet. Rec.*, 7 Jan 2017, 180(1), p. 18. doi: 10.1136/vr.103865. Epub 24 Nov 2016. PMID: 27885066. PMCID: PMC5284471.

Serpell, J.A. (1996) 'Evidence for an association between pet behavior and owner attachment levels', *Applied Animal Behaviour Science*, Volume 47, Issues 1–2, pp. 49-60. ISSN 0168-1591. Available at: https://doi.org/10.1016/0168-1591(95)01010-6

Serpell, J.A. and Jagoe, A. (1996) 'Owner characteristics and interactions and the prevalence of canine behavior problems', *Applied Animal Behaviour Science*, 47(s 1–2), Apr 1996, pp. 31-42. doi: 10.1016/0168-1591(95)01008-4.

Shanks, N., Greek, R., Greek, J. (2009) 'Are animal models predictive for humans?', *Philos. Ethics Humanit. Med.*, 15 Jan 2009, 4, p. 2. doi: 10.1186/1747-5341-4-2. PMID: 19146696. PMCID: PMC2642860.

Sherman, C.K., Reisner, I.R., Taliaferro, L.A., Houpt, K.A. (1996) 'Characteristics, treatment, and outcome of 99 cases of aggression between dogs', *Applied Animal Behaviour Science*, Volume 47, Issues 1-2, pp. 91-108. ISSN 0168-1591. Available at: https://doi.org/10.1016/0168-1591(95)010130

Simone, M.S. (2017) 'Neonatal corticosterone administration in rodents as a tool to investigate the maternal programming of emotional and immune domains'. doi: 10.1016/j.ynstr.2016.12.001. PMCID: PMC5314439. PMID: 28229106.

Sonoda, H., Kohnoe, S., Yamazato, T., Satoh, Y., Morizono, G., Shikata, K. *et al.* (2010) 'Colorectal cancer screening with odour material by canine scent detection'. doi: 10.1136/gut.2010.218305.

Soulsbury, C.D., Iossa, G., Baker, P.J. *et al.* (2007) 'The impact of sarcoptic mange *Sarcoptes scabiei* on the British fox *Vulpes vulpes* population, *Mammal Rev.*, Volume 37, No. 4, pp. 278-296. Printed in Singapore. School of Biological Sciences, University of Bristol, Woodland Road, Bristol BS8 1UG. doi: 10.1111/j.1365-2907.2007.00101.x.

Srithunyarat, T., Höglund, O.V., Hagman, R. *et al.* (2016) 'Catestatin, vasostatin, cortisol, temperature, heart rate, respiratory rate, scores of the short form of the Glasgow composite measure pain scale and visual analog scale for stress and pain behavior in dogs before and after ovariohysterectomy', *BMC Res Notes*, 9, p. 381. Available at: https://doi.org/10.1186/s13104-016-2193-1

Stewart, L., MacLean, E.L., Ivy, D., Woods, V., Cohen, E., Rodriguez, K., McIntyre, M., Mukherjee, S., Call, J., Kaminski, J., Miklósi, Á., Wrangham, W.R., Hare, B. (2015) 'Citizen Science as a New Tool in Dog Cognition Research'. Available at: https://doi.org/10.1371/journal.pone.0135176

Svartberg, K. (2007) 'Individual Differences in Behaviour-Dog Personality'. doi: 10.1079/9781845931872.0182.

Taylor, K. and Rego Alvares, L. (2019) 'An Estimate of the Number of Animals Used for Scientific Purposes Worldwide in 2015'. Available at: https://doi.org/10.1177/0261192919899853

Taylor, K. (2019) 'Recent Developments in Alternatives to Animal Testing'. doi: 10.1163/9789004391192_025.

'The Dog Star', in *Sirius*. New York, NY: Springer Praxis Books. ISBN 978-0-387-48941-4. Available at: https://doi.org/10.1007/978-0-387-48942-1_2

The PLOS One Staff (2014) 'Correction: The Welfare Consequences and Efficacy of Training Pet Dogs with Remote Electronic Training Collars in Comparison to Reward Based Training', *PLOS One*, 9(10), p. e110931. Available at: https://doi.org/10.1371/journal.pone.0110931

Theodossiou, E., Vassilios, N.M., Dimitrijevi, S., Mantarakis, P. (2011) 'Sirius in Ancient Greek and Roman Literature', *Journal of Astronomical History and Heritage*, 14(3), pp. 180-189. Available at: https://www.academia.edu/25764133/Sirius_in_Ancient_Greek_and_Roman_Literature_From_the_Orphic_Argonautics_to_the_Astronomical_Tables_of_Georgios_Chrysococca

Tiira, K., Sulkama, S., Lohi, H. (2016) 'Prevalence, comorbidity, and behavioral variation in canine anxiety', *Journal of Veterinary Behavior*, Volume 16, pp. 36-44. ISSN 1558-7878. Available at: https://doi.org/10.1016/j.jveb.2016.06.008

Topál, J., Gácsi, M., Miklósi, A., Virányi, Z., Kubinyi, E., Csányi, V. (2005) 'Attachment to humans: a comparative study on hand-reared wolves and differently socialized dog puppies', *Animal Behaviour*, Volume 70, Issue 6, pp. 1367-1375. Available at: https://www.researchgate.net/publication/222419926_Attachment_to_humans_A_comparative_study_on_hand-reared_wolves_and_differently_socialized_dog_puppies

Torres de la Riva, G., Hart, B.L., Farver, T.B., Oberbauer, A.M., Messam, L.L.M., Willits, N. *et al.* (2013) 'Neutering Dogs: Effects on Joint Disorders and Cancers in Golden Retrievers', *PLOS One*,

8(2), p. e55937. Available at: https://doi.org/10.1371/journal.pone.0055937

Toth, Z., Gaspar, K. (2012) 'Animal Protection and Animal "Rights" in Hungary University', *Budapest Jogelméleti Szemle*, 4, 14 Dec 2012, pp. 166-175. Available at: https://papers.ssrn.com/sol3/papers.cfm?abstract_id=2645712

Twedt, D.C. DVM, DACVIM 'Is it vomiting or regurgitation?' *Gastroenterology*. Available at: http://vetfolio.s3.amazonaws.com/13/06/b90ee9954a39bc207105f32efcb5/is-it-vomiting-or-regurgitation-pdf.pdf

Udell, M.A., Dorey, N.R., Wynne, C.D. (2010) 'What did domestication do to dogs? A new account of dogs' sensitivity to human actions', *Biol. Rev. Camb. Philos. Soc.*, May 2010, 85(2), pp. 327-45. doi: 10.1111/j.1469-185X.2009.00104.x. Epub 24 Nov 2009. PMID: 19961472.

University of Leicester (2012) 'University of Leicester study finds low agreeableness linked to a preference for aggressive dogs'. Available at: https://www2.le.ac.uk/offices/press/press-releases/university-of-leicester-study-finds-low-agreeableness-linked-to-a-preference-for-aggressive-dogs

Valsecchi, P., Barnard, S. *et al.* (2011) 'Temperament test for re-homed dogs validated through direct behavioral observation in shelter and home environment', *Journal of Veterinary Behavior*, Volume 6, Issue 3. ISSN 1558-7878. Available at: https://doi.org/10.1016/j.jveb.2011.01.002

van der Worp, H.B., Howells, D.W., Sena, E.S., Porritt, M.J., Rewell, S., O'Collins, V. *et al.* (2010) 'Can Animal Models of Disease Reliably Inform Human Studies?', *PLOS Med*, (3), p. e1000245. Available at: https://doi.org/10.1371/journal.pmed.1000245

Van Norman, G.A. (2019) 'Limitations of Animal Studies for Predicting Toxicity in Clinical Trials: Is it Time to Rethink Our Current Approach?', *JACC: Basic to Translational Science*, Volume 4, Issue 7, pp. 845-854. ISSN 2452-302X. Available at: https://doi.org/10.1016/j.jacbts.2019.10.008

Vendramini, T., Amaral, A. *et al.* (2020) 'Neutering in dogs and cats:

Current scientific evidence and importance of adequate nutritional management', *Nutrition Research Reviews*, 33(1), pp. 134-144. doi: 10.1017/S0954422419000271. Available at: https://pubmed.ncbi.nlm.nih.gov/31931899/

'Veterinary Clinics of North America: Small Animal Practice', Volume 21, Issue 2, 1991, pp. 247-255. ISSN 0195-5616. Available at: https://doi.org/10.1016/S0195-5616(91)50030-9

Vilá *et al.* (1997) 'Multiple and Ancient Origins of the Domestic Dog', *Science*, 276(5319), pp. 1687-89. doi: 10.1126/science.276.5319.1687.

Vonholdt, B.M., Pollinger, J.P., Lohmueller, K.E. *et al.* (2012) 'Genome-wide SNP and haplotype analyses reveal a rich history underlying dog domestication'. doi: 10.1038/nature08837.

Waelchli, J., Draper, D. (1997) 'Canine Dominance Aggression', *Iowa State University Veterinarian*, Volume 59, Issue 2, Article 10. Available at: https://lib.dr.iastate.edu/iowastate_veterinarian/vol59/iss2/10

Ware, W.A., Hopper, D.L. (1999) 'Cardiac tumors in dogs: 1982-1995', *J. Vet. Intern. Med.*, Mar-Apr 1999, 13(2), pp. 95-103. doi: 10.1892/0891-6640(1999)013<0095:ctid>2.3.co;2; PMID:10225598.

Waters, D.J., Kengeri, S.S., Clever, B., Booth, J.A. *et al.* (2009) 'Mechanisms of sex differences in longevity: lifetime ovary exposure and exceptional longevity in dogs', *Ageing Cell.*, 8(6), pp. 752-5. doi: 10.1111/j.1474-9726.2009.00513.x. Epub 2 Sep 2009. PMID: 19732047. PMCID: PMC2805875.

Weaver *et al.* (2004) 'Epigenetic Programming by Maternal Behavior', *Nature Neuroscience*, 7(8), pp. 847-54. doi: 10.1038/nn1276.

Weaver, I.C., Cervoni, N., Champagne, F.A., D'Alessio, A.C., Sharma, S., Seckl, J.R., Dymov, S., Szyf, M., Meaney, M.J. (2004) 'Epigenetic programming by maternal behavior', *Nat. Neurosci.*, 7, pp. 847-854. PMID: 15220929. doi: 10.1038/nn1276.

Weaver, I.C., Diorio, J., Seckle, J. *et al.* (2004) 'Early environmental regulation of hippocampal glucocorticoid receptor gene expression: characterization of intracellular mediators and potential genomic target sites', *PMID*, p. 15265782. doi: 10.1196/annals.1321.099.

Wells, D.L., Graham, L. and Hepper, P.G. (2002) 'The influence of auditory stimulation on the behaviour of dogs housed in a rescue shelter', *Animal Welfare*, 11, pp. 385-393. Available at: https://www.ncbi.nlm.nih.gov/pmc/articles/PMC7222336/

Wells, D.L., Hepper, P.G. (2002) 'Prevalence of behaviour problems reported by owners of dogs purchased from an animal rescue shelter'. Canine Behaviour Centre, School of Psychology, The Queen's University of Belfast, Belfast, BT7 1NN, Northern Ireland, UK. Accepted 28 Feb 2000. Available at: https://doi.org/10.1016/S0168-1591(00)00118-0

Wilson, K.G., Murrel, A.R. (2002) 'Functional Analysis of Behaviour'. doi: 10.1016/B0-12-343010-0/00101-X. Available at: https://doi.org/10.1016/B0-12-343010-0/00101-X

Wilson, P., Norris, G. (2003) 'Relationship between criminal behaviour and mental illness in young adults: conduct disorder, cruelty to animals and young adult serious violence'. doi: 10.1375/pplt.2003.10.1.239.

Wilson, M., Boesch, C., Fruth, B. *et al.* (2014) 'Lethal aggression in Pan is better explained by adaptive strategies than human impacts', *Nature*, 513, pp. 414-417. Available at: https://doi.org/10.1038/nature13727

Yoman, J. (2008) 'A Primer on Functional Analysis'. doi: 10.1016/j.cbpra.2008.01.002.

Zapata, I., Serpell, J.A. and Alvarez, C.E. (2016) 'Genetic mapping of canine fear and aggression', *BMC Genomics*, 17, p. 572. Available at: https://doi.org/10.1186/s12864-016-2936-3

Zhenxin, F. *et al.* (2016) 'Worldwide patterns of genomic variation and admixture in gray wolves'. doi: 10.1101/gr.197517.115. PMCID: PMC4728369.

Ziv, G. (2017) 'The effects of using aversive training methods in dogs: A review', *Journal of Veterinary Behavior*, Volume 19, pp. 50-60. ISSN 1558-7878. Available at: https://doi.org/10.1016/j.jveb.2017.02.004

Zupan, G.E.M. (2020) 'Dogs' Sociability, Owners' Neuroticism and

Attachment Style to Pets as Predictors of Dog Aggression', *Animals (Basel)*, 10(2), p. 315. doi: 10.3390/ani10020315.

ARTICLES

Abrantes, R. (2017) *Critical Reasoning – on Aggression and Dominance.* Available at: https//ethology.eu/tag/dominant-behavior/

Ackerman, C. (2021) *Big Five Personality Traits: The OCEAN Model Explained.* Available at: https://positivepsychology.com/big-five-personality-theory/

Ancic, M. (2018) *Drive and Instinct: Harness the benefits for training your dog and you!* Available at: https://www.training-your-dog-and-you.com/drive.html

Anderson, E. (2017) *What's a Functional Assessment in Dog Training? (And Why You Should Care).* Available at: https://eileenanddogs.com/blog/2017/09/18/functional-behavioral-assessment-dog-training/

Angel, L. (2018) *Is the domestic dog a true pack animal?* Canine Mind. Available at: http://www.caninemind.co.uk/pack.html

Arnold, C. (2017) *Why Are Some Dogs More Aggressive?* Available at: https://www.nationalgeographic.com/animals/article/why-are-some-dogs-aggressive-hormones

ASPCA. *Separation Anxiety.* Available at: https://www.aspca.org/pet-care/dog-care/common-dog-behavior-issues/separation-anxiety

Bailey, G. (2017) *America's Complicated Relationship With the 'Hot Dog'.* Available at: https://www.realclearhistory.com/articles/2017/10/02/americas_complicated_relationship_with_the_hot_dog_dog.html

Balance Behaviour. *The Dog's Amazing Nose!* Available at: http://www.balancebehaviour.org/blah-1/

Bates, A. (6 August 2021) *Cretan Hound.* Available at: https://www.dogbreedplus.com/dog_breeds/cretan_hound.php

BBC (6 Nov 2018) *Nepal festival celebrates 'day of the dogs'.* Available at: https://www.bbc.com/news/world-46111525

Bekoff, M. (2017) *Dogs Smell Human Fear and Mirror Our Mood When They Do.* Available at: https://www.psychologytoday.com/intl/blog/animal-emotions/201711/dogs-smell-human-fear-and-mirror-our-mood-when-they-do

Bernsdorf, C. *University of Queensland Poodle.* Available at: https://www.dogzone.com/breeds/poodle/

Best Friends Animal Society. *Rehabilitate Dogs from Puppy Mill or Hoarding Case.* Available at: https://resources.bestfriends.org/article/rehabilitate-dogs-puppy-mill-or-hoarding-case#Training

Biology LibreTexts (August 2020) *Stabilizing, Directional, and Diversifying Selection.* Available at: https://bio.libretexts.org/Bookshelves/Introductory_and_General_Biology/Book%3A_General_Biology_(Boundless)/19%3A_The_Evolution_of_Populations/19.3%3A_Adaptive_Evolution/19.3B%3A_Stabilizing%2C_Directional%2C_and_Diversifying_Selection

Blue, A. (2017) *Hormones Could Be Making Your Dog Aggressive.* Available at: https://news.arizona.edu/story/hormone-could-be-making-your-dog-aggressive

Blue Cross for Pets, UK (2017) *Socialising puppies and dogs.* Available at: https://www.bluecross.org.uk/pet-advice/socialising-your-puppy

Boeree, G.C. (2006) *Famous Psychologists: B.F. Skinner.* Available at: http://webspace.ship.edu/cgboer/skinner.html

Border Collie Museum (2018) *Sydenham Edwards.* Available at: http://www.bordercolliemuseum.org/SydenhamEdwards/Edwards.html

Boyle, J. (2017) *Sorry, but some dog breeds are dangerous.* Available at: https://eu.citizen-times.com/story/news/local/2017/05/13/boyle-sorry-but-some-dog-breeds-dangerous/101592002/

Brackman, J. (2008) *The Making of a Guide Dog.* Available at: https://thebark.com/content/making-guide-dog

Brady, C. (2018) *Dog Neutering.* Available at: https://dogsfirst.ie/health-issues/dog-neutering/

Breeden, P. *Are dogs and wolves the same species?* Available at: https://biologyofbehavior.wordpress.com/2014/02/09/are-dogs-and-wolves-the-same-species/

Breitner, J. (2017) *Leash Reactivity: How to Relieve Your Dogs Anxiety.* Available at: https://www.dogdecoder.com/leash-reactivity-relieve-dogs-anxiety/

Briffa, M. (2010) *Territoriality and Aggression.* Available at: https://www.nature.com/scitable/knowledge/library/territoriality-and-aggression-13240908/

British College of Canine Studies. Course Notes. Available at: https://www.britishcollegeofcaninestudies.com

Brooks, W. (revised 2020) *Hemangiosarcoma is Blood or Skin Cancer in Dogs and Cats.* Available at: https://veterinarypartner.vin.com/default.aspx?pid=19239&id=4951909

Brunette, M., Jane Goodall Institute of Canada. *Are chimpanzees more aggressive than humans?* Available at: https://janegoodall.ca/our-stories/are-chimpanzees-more-aggressive-than-humans/

Cabral, R. (2017) *Drives of Dogs.* Available at: https://robertcabral.com/drives-of-dogs/

Campbell, C. (2020) *'They Are Overwhelmed.' China's Animal Shelters Can't Cope With the Number of Pets Abandoned Due to COVID-19.* Available at: https://time.com/5793363/china-coronavirus-covid19-abandoned-pets-wuhan/'

Carter, M.R. (2017) *Remembering the British 'pet holocaust': WW2's slaughtered cats and dogs.* Available at: https://www.independent.co.uk/news/long_reads/world-war-two-pet-slaughter-death-cats-dogs-a8042026.html

Cat – Cruelty Free International (2019) *Shocking new statistics show big rise in dog, monkey and rabbit tests as government ignores public outcry.* Available at: https://www.crueltyfreeinternational.org/what-we-do/breaking-news/uk-dog-experiments-16-despite-public-opposition

Centre for Canine Behaviour studies. President and CEO Dr Nicholas Dodman – Various past and ongoing canine studies. Available at: https://www.centerforcaninebehaviorstudies.org/in-the-news

Charlton, R. (2018) *Can Dogs Understand Punishment?* Available at: https://wagwalking.com/sense/can-dogs-understand-punishment

Chavez, R. *What is the 'Big Five' and How Can It Help You?* Available

at: http://thinkgrowprosper.com/blog/big-five-personality-traits
Cherry, K. (2020) *Taste Aversion: Avoidance of Certain Foods and Classical Conditioning.* Available at: https://www.verywellmind.com/what-is-a-taste-aversion-2794991
Chewy Editorial (2010) *Rescued Dog Won't Play.* Available at: https://petcentral.chewy.com/rescued-dog-wont-play/
Coates, J. (2013) *Hemangiosarcoma in Dogs.* Available at: https://www.petmd.com/blogs/fullyvetted/2012/july/hemangiosarcoma_in_dogs-26511
Colman, S. (2019) *Training Police Dogs and Military Dogs Using Positive Methods.* Available at: https://www.whole-dog-journal.com/training/training-police-dogs-and-military-dogs-using-positive-methods/
Coren, S. (2008) *Can Dogs See Colors?* Available at: https://www.psychologytoday.com/us/blog/canine-corner/200810/can-dogs-see-colors
Coren, S. (2017) *Compared to Humans, How Good Is a Dog's Visual Acuity?* Available at: https://www.psychologytoday.com/intl/blog/canine-corner/201712/compared-humans-how-good-is-dogs-visual-acuity
Coren, S., Canine Corner (2009) *Canine Intelligence: Breed Does Matter.* Available at: https://www.psychologytoday.com/intl/blog/canine-corner/200907/canine-intelligence-breed-does-matter
Coren, S., Canine Corner (2009) *Psychological Characteristics of Owners of Aggressive Dog Breeds.* Available at: https://www.psychologytoday.com/intl/blog/canine-corner/200903/psychological-characteristics-owners-aggressive-dog-breeds
Coren, S., Canine Corner (2010) *Canine Dominance: Is the Concept of the Alpha Dog Valid?* Available at: https://www.psychologytoday.com/us/blog/canine-corner/201007/canine-dominance-is-the-concept-the-alpha-dog-valid
Coren, S., Canine Corner (2010) *Reward Training vs. Discipline-Based Dog Training.* Available at: https://www.psychologytoday.com/intl/blog/canine-corner/201012/reward-training-vs-discipline-based-dog-training)

Coren, S., Canine Corner (2011) *Why Do Dogs Have Whiskers?* Available at: https://www.psychologytoday.com/intl/blog/canine-corner/201109/why-do-dogs-have-whiskers

Coren S., Canine Corner (2012) *Is Punishment an Effective Way to Change the Behavior of Dogs? Use of punishment during dog training leads to increased aggression.* Available at: https://www.psychologytoday.com/gb/blog/canine-corner/201205/is-punishment-effective-way-change-the-behavior-dogs

Coren, S., Canine Corner (2013) *Does Punishing a Dog After a Transgression Really Work?* Available at: https://www.psychologytoday.com/us/blog/canine-corner/201305/does-punishing-dog-after-transgression-really-work

Coren, S., Canine Corner (2014) *Aggression Between Dogs in the Same Household.* Available at: https://www.psychologytoday.com/us/blog/canine-corner/201404/aggression-between-dogs-in-the-same-household)

Coren, S., Canine Corner (2014) *An Easy Way to Prevent Food Aggression in Dogs: Food bowl guarding in dogs can be stopped before it ever appears.* Available at: https://www.psychologytoday.com/us/blog/canine-corner/201411/easy-way-prevent-food-aggression-in-dogs

Coren, S., Canine Corner (2016) *A Punished Dog is an Aggressive Dog: Physically punishing a dog for misbehaviors is apt to make it more aggressive.* Available at: https://www.psychologytoday.com/intl/blog/canine-corner/201508/punished-dog-is-aggressive-dog

Coren, S., Canine Corner (2016) *At What Age Should Puppies Be Brought to Their New Homes?* Available at: https://www.psychologytoday.com/us/blog/canine-corner/201601/what-age-should-puppies-be-brought-their-new-homes

Coren, S., Canine Corner (2016) *Does 'Mother Love' Play a Role in Rearing Better Dogs?* Available at: https://www.psychologytoday.com/intl/blog/canine-corner/201605/does-mother-love-play-role-in-rearing-better-dogs

Coren, S., Canine Corner (2017) *Do Adult Dogs Still Recognize Their Mothers?* Available at: https://www.psychologytoday.com/us/

blog/canine-corner/201708/do-adult-dogs-still-recognize-their-mothers

Coren, S., Modern Dog Magazine. *Pill-Popping Pups*. Available at: https://moderndogmagazine.com/articles/pill-popping-pups/753

Courtney, B. *Digging, Chewing, Chasing, Barking: Instinctive Drives You Love or Hate*. Available at: https://positively.com/contributors/digging-chewing-chasing-barking-instinctive-drives-you-love-or-hate/

Crisley, K. (2020) *Canine Corner*. Available at: www.balanceddog.co.nz /

Cullen's Archangel Rescue Prey Drive. Available at: https://www.caretoadopt.org/info/display?PageID=2275

D'Abruzzo, M. (2016) *'Dominance in Dog Training Debunked' or is it?* Available at: https://dogtraining.world/dominance-in-dog-training-debunked-or-is-it/

Daily Dog Discoveries (2016) *How Puppies Learn the ABCs of Bite Inhibition*. Available at: https://www.dailydogdiscoveries.com/how-puppies-learn-the-abcs-of-bite-inhibition/

Dell'Amore, C. (2011) *Ancient Dog Skull Shows Early Pet Domestication*. Available at: https://www.nationalgeographic.com/animals/article/110819-dogs-wolves-russia-domestication-animals-science-evolution

Dobbins, B. (2020) *To Neuter, or Not to Neuter Your Dog: That is the Question*. Available at: https://www.whole-dog-journal.com/health/neuter-or-not-to-neuter-your-dog-that-is-the-question/

Dog First. *Dog Neutering is an Emotive Subject*. Available at: https://dogsfirst.ie/health-issues/dog-neutering/

Dogedit (2019) *7 Amazing Facts About Your Dog's Sense of Smell*. Available at: https://www.dogster.com/lifestyle/dogs-sense-of-smell-facts

Dog Peer (19 Jun 2021) *Is Crate Training Cruel? Finland and Sweden Seem to Think So…* Available at: https://blog.dogpeer.com.au/dog-training-guides/is-crate-training-cruel-finland-and-sweden-seem-to-think-so/

Dog Secrets (2011) *Who is a Positive Dog Trainer? Not Me!* Available at: https://www.dog-secrets.co.uk/who-is-a-positive-dog-trainer-not-me/

Dogs in Ancient Greece and Rome. Available at: https://penelope.uchicago.edu/~grout/encyclopaedia_romana/miscellanea/canes/canes.html

Dogs Pet Care (2020) *Preventing Trouble*. Available at: https://www.rspcaqld.org.au/blog/trending-now/off-leash-dogs Off-Leash Dogs

Dogtime. *Italian Greyhound*. Available at: https://dogtime.com/dog-breeds/italian-greyhound#/slide/10

Dog Training Excellence. *Operant Conditioning: 'Using positive vs. negative dog training methods correctly'*. Available at: https://www.dog-training-excellence.com/operant-conditioning.html

Donaldson, L. (2017) *The Cognitive Revolution and Everyday Dog Training: The Case of 'Look at That'*. Available at: https://spring2017.iaabcjournal.org/cognitive-revolution-dog-training-lat/

Douglas, G.R., Butler, C.S. and Serpell, J. (2016) *Do puppies from 'puppy farms' show more temperament and behavioural problems than if acquired from other sources – using CBARQ to assess.* Presented at British Society of Animal Science Annual Conference, Chester, UK. Available at: http://www.ufaw.org.uk/downloads/york-2016---programme-and-abstracts-23-june.pdf

Douglas, M. (2009) *Food Aggression*. Available at: https://www.dogstardaily.com/blogs/food-aggression

Dunbar, I. *AFTER You Get Your Puppy*. Available at: https://www.dogstardaily.com/storefront/after-you-get-your-puppy

Dunbar, I. (2001) *Before You Get Your Puppy – Handbook*. Available at: https://www.siriuspup.com/files/pdfs/BEFORE_You_Get_Your_Puppy_SIRIUS.pdf

Dunbar, I. (2015) *Why Don't We Adequately Socialize Young Puppies With People?* Available at: https://www.dogstardaily.com/blogs/dr-ian-dunbar/why-don't-we-adequately-socialize-young-puppies-people

Dunbar, I. (2016) *An exciting new cure for separation anxiety*. Available at: https://www.dogstardaily.com/blogs/dr-ian-dunbar/exciting-new-cure-separation-anxiety

Dvorsky, G. (2016) *Why Are Dogs So Insanely Happy To See Us When We*

Get Home? Available at: https://www.gizmodo.com.au/2016/03/why-are-dogs-so-insanely-happy-to-see-us-when-we-get-home/

Easy PetMD. *Alopekis*. Available at: http://www.easypetmd.com/doginfo/alopekis

EasyPetMD. *Anti-dachshund propaganda*. Available at: https://www.easypetmd.com/doginfo/anti-dachshund-propaganda

El-Hai, J. (2016) *The Chicken-hearted Origins of the 'Pecking Order'*. Available at: https://www.discovermagazine.com/planet-earth/the-chicken-hearted-origins-of-the-pecking-order#.W1ciXy2B1o4

Elliot, P. (2018) *Guide to Raising a Puppy When You Work Full Time*. Available at: https://blog.petcube.com/raising-a-puppy/

Emmalee (2016) *Socialising Your Adult Rescue Dog*. http://www.woofliketomeet.com/2016/05/socialising-your-adult-rescue-dog/

Emmalee (2016) *The Dominance Myth: Why it has no place in modern training*. Available at: http://www.woofliketomeet.com/2016/04/the-dominance-myth/

Explore Italian Culture (2018) *Ancient Roman Animals: the history of animals in Italy*. Available at: https://www.explore-italian-culture.com/ancient-roman-animals.html

Falconer-Taylor, R. (2015) *Shock Collars: What Manufacturers Don't Want You to Know*. Available at: https://www.petcpd.com/behaviour/shock-collars-what-manufacturers-dont-want-you-to-know/

Farricelli, A. (2016) *I Am Your Dog's Hippocampus*. Available at: https://dogdiscoveries.com/health/dogs-hippocampus

Farricelli, A. (2018) *Dog Brain Chemistry and the Use of Medications and Behavior Modification*. Available at: https://pethelpful.com/dogs/Dog-BehaviorThe-Role-of-Brain-Chemistry

Farricelli, A. (2018) *Using Functional Analysis for Dog Behavior Problems*. Available at: https://pethelpful.com/dogs/Using-Functional-Analysis-For-Dog-Behavior-Problems

Farricelli, A. (2020) *Dangers of Keeping Dogs Off-Leash*. Available at: https://pethelpful.com/pet-ownership/Dangers-of-Keeping-Dogs-Off-Leash

Farricelli, A. (2020) *David Mech's Theory on the Wolf Alpha Role.* Available at: https://pethelpful.com/dogs/David-Mechs-Theory-on-the-Alpha-Role

Farricelli, A. (2021) *A Guide to Dog Behavior Modification Techniques and Terms.* Available at: https://pethelpful.com/dogs/Dog-Behavior-A-Guide-to-Behavior-Modification-Terms

Farricelli, A. (2021) *Is Sensory Overstimulation Stressing Your Dog?* Available at: https://pethelpful.com/dogs/Understanding-Sensory-Overstumulation-in-Dogs

Farricelli, A. (2021) *Should Male Dogs Be Neutered? Pros and Cons to Consider.* Available at: https://pethelpful.com/dogs/Should-Male-Dogs-be-Neutered-To-Neuter-or-not-to-Neuter-Some-Considerations-About-this-Debate

Farricelli, A. (2021) *What Is a Conditioned Emotional Response (CER) in Dogs?* Available at: https://pethelpful.com/dogs/Conditioned-Emotional-Responses-in-Dog-Training-and-Behavior-Modification

Feeney-Hart, A. *The little-told story of the massive WWII pet cull.* Available at: https://www.bbc.com/news/magazine-24478532

Fila Brasileiro. Available at: http://www.vetstreet.com/dogs/fila-brasileiro

Finke, B. (2012) *What Colors Do Dogs See?* Available at: https://thebark.com/content/what-colors-do-dogs-see

Finlay, J. (2018) *Living with the high prey drive dog.* Available at: http://www.canismajor.com/dog/hidrive.html

Flank, L. (2015) *Chicken Politics: Life in the Flock.* Available at: https://lflank.wordpress.com/2015/01/27/chicken-politics-life-in-the-flock/

Friedman, S. (2009) *Functional Assessment: Hypothesizing Predictors and Purposes of Problem Behavior to Improve Behavior-Change Plans.* Available at: https://www.semanticscholar.org/paper/FUNCTIONAL-ASSESSMENT%3A-HYPOTHESIZING-PREDICTORS-AND-Friedman/2694edd0ddac368861df232f3e6eae15aed7967e; https://www.behaviorworks.org/files/articles/Functional%20Assessment.pdf

Fricke, I. (2017) *'Return' is not a dirty word*. Available at: https://www.animalsheltering.org/blog/return-not-dirty-word

Gary, M. (2018) *Landsberg Behavior Modification in Dogs*. Available at: https://www.msdvetmanual.com/dog-owners/behavior-of-dogs/behavior-modification-in-dogs

Geeson, H. (2012) *The Genetics of Dachshund Coats and Colours*. Available at: https://dachshundbreedcouncil.files.wordpress.com/2012/02/coat-and-colour.pdf

Geier, E. *5 Frighteningly Common Reasons Dogs Run Away*. Available at: https://www.rover.com/blog/why-dogs-run-away/

Geier, E. *How Much Do Dogs Really Remember?* Available at: https://www.rover.com/blog/how-much-do-dogs-really-remember/#

Godtfredsen, A., Anouska, G. (2013) *The Occurance of Behavioural Problems in Re-Homed Dogs with Unknown Backgrounds*. Available at: http://www.huveta.hu/handle/10832/879

Gray, A. (2019) *Why Not to Be Ashamed If You Have to Return a Shelter Pet*. Available at: https://www.petful.com/animal-welfare/ashamed-to-return-shelter-pet/

Gray, J. (1918) *A Brief Overview of Canine Reactivity: Frustrated Greeting, Fear Based Reactivity and True Canine Aggression (FG, FR and TA)*. Available at: http://ajcs.org.uk/uncategorized/a-brief-overview-of-canine-reactivity-frustrated-greeting-fear-based-reactivity-and-true-canine-aggression-fg-fr-and-ta/

Gray-Nelson, C. (2016) *Might He Bite? 3 Genetic Factors That Explain Why Some Dogs Bite*. Available at: http://www.dogtalkdiva.com/2016/05/25/bite-me/

Greer, S. (2017) *Stop walking your dog*. Available at: https://stacythetrainer.blogspot.com/2017/04/stop-walking-your-dog.html

Grice, H. *Stress in dogs – what we can't see*. Available at: https://www.doglistener.tv/2015/05/stress-in-dogs-what-we-cant-see/

Guise, L. (2013) *The Untold Story of Laika: The First Astronaut Dog In Space & The Communist Sputnik 2 Mission*. Available at: https://fluentwoof.com/laika-the-first-dog-in-space/

Hall, E., British Veterinary Association (2020) *'Dogs die in hot cars and on hot walks' – new evidence on heat-related illness in UK dog.* Available at: https://www.bva.co.uk/news-and-blog/blog-article/dogs-die-in-hot-cars-and-on-hot-walks-new-evidence-on-heat-related-illness-in-uk-dogs/

Haller, F. (2016) *Why dog breeds aren't considered separate species.* Available at: https://theconversation.com/why-dog-breeds-arent-considered-separate-species-56113

Halpenny, B. *The Origin of the Domestic Dog.* Available at: https://citeseerx.ist.psu.edu/viewdoc/download?doi=10.1.1.504.6011&rep=rep1&type=pdf

Hare, B., Woods, V. (2016) *Pit Bulls Are Chiller Than Chihuahua.* Available at: https://www.theatlantic.com/science/archive/2016/09/pit-bulls-are-chiller-than-chihuahuas/500558/

Healy, D. (2017) *Dogs and Serotonin.* Available at: https://davidhealy.org/dogs-and-serotonin/

Heeds, C. (2019) *RSPCA issues advice on how long dogs should be left home alone for.* Available at: https://www.lancs.live/news/lancashire-news/rspca-issues-advice-how-long-17345591

Hekman, J. (2019) *Is Our Dogs' Behavior Genetic? Or is it all in how you raise them? Nature vs. nurture and raising a well-adjusted dog.* Available at: https://www.whole-dog-journal.com/issues/19_9/features/Is-Our-Dogs-Behavior-Genetic_21514-1.html

Hibby, E., Roonery, N., Bradshaw, I. (2004) *Dog training methods: Their use, effectiveness and interaction with behaviour and welfare.* Available at: https://www.researchgate.net/publication/261106650_Dog_training_methods_Their_use_effectiveness_and_interaction_with_behaviour_and_welfare

Higgons, K. (2018) *An Open Letter to People Who Walk Their Dog Without a Leash.* Available at: https://thebark.com/content/open-letter-people-who-walk-their-dog-without-leash

Ho, S. (2020) *Pets Are Being Killed in China Due to Coronavirus Misinformation.* Available at: https://www.greenqueen.com.hk/pets-are-being-killed-in-china-due-to-coronavirus-misinformation/

Hodges, D. (2019) *One is the loneliest number: How to recognize and treat separation anxiety in dogs according to an expert.* Available at: https://www.cbc.ca/life/pets/one-is-the-loneliest-number-how-to-recognize-and-treat-separation-anxiety-in-dogs-according-to-an-expert-1.5039538

Hodgson, S. (2017) *Think Twice Before You Cut Off Your Dog's Balls.* Available at: https://www.huffpost.com/entry/think-twice-before-you-cu_b_8002116

Hogle, P. (2018) *Cognitive Dog Training.* Available at: https://www.courteouscanine.com/cognitive-dog-training/

Hole, F. (1968) *Prehistory and Human Ecology of the Deh Luran Plain: An Early Village Sequence from Khuzistan, Iran.* Available at: https://www.academia.edu/8238552Prehistory_and_Human_Ecology_of_the_Deh_Luran_Plain_An_Early_Village_Sequence_from_Khuzistan_Iran?auto=download

Hole, F., Wyllie, C. (2007) *The Oldest Depictions of Canines and a Possible Early Breed of Dog in Iran.* Available at: https://www.persee.frdocAsPDFpaleo_0153-9345_2007_num_33_1_5213.pdf

Horowitz, A. (2019) *Dogs Are Not Here for Our Convenience: Spaying and neutering puppies shouldn't be standard policy – and it isn't automatically the 'responsible' choice either.* Available at: https://www.nytimes.com/2019/09/03/opinion/dogs-spaying-neutering.html

Horwitz, D. *Disobedient, Unruly and Excitable Dogs.* Available at: https://vcahospitals.com/know-your-pet/disobedient-unruly-and-excitable-dogs

Horwitz, D. (2012) *Interdog Aggression: Managing Problems Between Household Dogs.* Available at: https://aztecanimalclinic.com/interdog-aggression-managing-problems-household-dogs/

Hughes, G., Prof. Maher, J. and Lawson, C. (2011) Submitted to the Royal Society for the Prevention of Cruelty to Animals by the Cardiff Centre for Crime, Law and Justice, Cardiff University. Available at: https://orca.cardiff.ac.uk/78197/1/wp139.pdf

Humane Society of United States. *Dogs used in experiments.* Available at: https://www.humanesociety.org/resources/dogs-used-experiments-faq

Humane Society International. (2019) *UK animal experiment statistics indicate reluctance to embrace modern tools to advance British labs into the 21st century.* Available at: https://www.hsi.org/news-media/uk-animal-experiment-statistics-2018/

Hungarian Puli Club. Available at: http://www.puli.hu/hu/fajtaleiras/tortenete

Hurt, C. (2013) *The Melitan Miniature Dog: The most popular lapdog in antiquity.* Available at: https://foundinantiquity.com/2013/11/15/the-melitan-miniature-dog/

Jaratz, L. *Off-Leash Dogs Pose Real Threat.* Available at: https://www.embracepetinsurance.com/waterbowl/article/off-leash-dogs-pose-real-threat

Jones, B., Sirius Dog, *Your Dog's Instincts: A Modern Day Pet or Primal Beast?* Available at: http://siriusdog.com/dog-instincts-behavior/

Jones, L. (2016) *Soviet Scientists Created the Only Tame Foxes in the World.* Available at: http://www.bbc.com/earth/story/20160912-a-soviet-scientist-created-the-only-tame-foxes-in-the-world

Kaiser K9 (2016) *Forging Favourable Correlations Between Emotion and Work.* Available at: https://www.kaisercanine.com/blog/2016/1/8/the-conditioned-emotional-response

Kaspersson, M. (2008) *On treating the symptoms and not the causes: Reflections on the Dangerous Dogs Act.* Papers from the British Criminology Conference, Volume 8. Available at: https://www.academia.edu/13022544/On_Treating_the_Symptoms_and_Not_the_Cause

Kaszás, F. (2020) *Coronavirus and Pets: What Should You Do Now?* Available at: https://hungarytoday.hu/coronavirus-and-pets-what-should-you-do-now/

Katrin (2017) *Dog Has Sensory Overload on Walks.* Available at: https://maplewoodblog.wordpress.com/2017/09/17/dog-has-sensory-overload-on-walks/

Kay, N. (2017) *Canine Vasectomies.* Available at: http://speakingforspot.com/blog/2017/02/19/canine-vasectomies/

Keim, B. (2012) *The Hidden Power of Whale Poop.* Available at: https://www.wired.com/2012/08/blue-whale-poop/

Kendra, C. (2017) *Big Five Personality Traits: The Five Factor Model*. Available at: https://www.explorepsychology.com/big-five-personality-traits/

Khan, H. (Updated 15 Jan 2019) *The places around the world you can still eat dog meat*. Available at: https://www.sbs.com.au/news/dateline/the-places-around-the-world-you-can-still-eat-dog-meat

Kidd, R. (Updated 2019) *Use Corticosteroids On Your Canine With Caution*. Available at: https://www.whole-dog-journal.com/health/use-corticosteroids-on-your-canine-with-caution/

Kidd, R. (2019) *The Canine Sense of Smell*. Available at: https://www.whole-dog-journal.com/health/the-canine-sense-of-smell/

Kim, A. (2020) *Cats and dogs abandoned at the start of the coronavirus outbreak are now starving or being killed*. Available at: https://edition.cnn.com/2020/03/15/asia/coronavirus-animals-pets-trnd/index.html

Klein, C. (Updated 2019) *The Ancient Greek Origins of the 'Dog Days of Summer'*. Available at: https://www.history.com/news/why-are-they-called-the-dog-days-of-summer

Kloeppel, J. (2006) *Constant din of barking causes stress: behavior changes in dogs in shelters*. Available at: https://news.illinois.edu/view/6367/206908

K9 Aggression. *Causes of Dog Aggression*. Available at: https://k9aggression.com/dog-aggression-overview/causes-of-of-dog-aggression/?v=f24485ae434a

Korneliussen, I. (2011) *Should dogs be neutered?* Available at: https://sciencenorway.no/animal-welfare-forskningno-norway/should-dogs-be-neutered/1419580

Labrador Training (2019) *Dog Instincts and Drives*. Available at: https://www.labradortraininghq.com/labrador-behavior/dog-instincts-and-drives/

Landesmuseum Württemberg, Stuttgart (2018) *The Sites of Geißenklösterle, Hohle Fels, and Middle Paleolithic sites in the Swabian Alb near the city of Ulm*. Available at: https://www.donsmaps.com/hohlefelssite.html

Landsberg, G. (2018) *Behavior Modification in Dogs*. Available at:

https://www.msdvetmanual.com/dog-owners/behavior-of-dogs/behavior-modification-in-dogs

Leerburg. *The Problem with All-Positive Dog Training*. Available at: https://leerburg.com/allpositive.htm

Lees-Smith, G. *Dogs Are Not Pack*. Available at: http://www.simplybehaviour.com/dogs-do-not-view-their-family-as-pack/

Lee-St. John, J. (2010) *Dog Training and the Myth of Alpha-Male Dominance*. Available at: http://content.time.com/time/printout/0,8816,2007250,00.html

Lehr, M. (2016) *The Big Five Personality Traits*. Available at: https://omegazadvisors.com/2016/12/26/openness-personality-trait/

Lenz, N. (2017) *Bilious Vomiting Syndrome in Dogs, aka 'Hunger Pukes'*. Available at: https://nomorevetbills.com/2017/bilious-vomiting-syndrome-aka-hunger-pukes/

Let's Get Pet (2020) *Stanley Coren's dog intelligence ranking*. Available at: https://www.letsgetpet.com/dogs/all-about-dogs/stanley-corens-dog-intelligence-ranking/

Levine, J. (2013) *The Education of a Bomb Dog*. Available at: https://www.smithsonianmag.com/innovation/the-education-of-a-bomb-dog-4945104/?no-ist)

Lindley, P. (Updated 2021) *The Canine Prey Drive Instinct*. Available at: https://www.dogways.info/the-canine-prey-drive-instinct

Lim, A. (15 Jun 2020) *The big five personality traits*. Available at: https://www.simplypsychology.org/big-five-personality.html

Lishishwar, L. and Jordan, I.K. (2020) *What are Haplogroups? Living DNA explain*. Available at: https://livingdna.com/blog/haplogroups-explained

London, K. (2012) *Prey Drive in Dogs: Fact or Fiction?* Available at: https://thebark.com/content/prey-drive-fact-or-fiction

London, K. (2017) *Dog Behavior: Bite Inhibition Matters*. Available at: https://thebark.com/content/dog-behavior-bite-inhibition-matters

Luescher, U. (2012) *Canine Behavioral Development*. Available at: https://docplayer.net/18590970-Canine-behavioral-development-urs-a-luescher.html

Mark, J.J. (14 Jan 2019) *Dogs in the Ancient World*. Available at: https://www.ancient.eu/article/184/dogs-in-the-ancient-world/

Marshal, L. (2018) *Annual Statistics of Scientific Procedures on Living Animals, Great Britain 2018*. ISBN 978-1-5286-1336-1. Available at: https://assets.publishing.service.gov.uk/government/uploads/system/uploads/attachment_data/file/835935/annual-statistics-scientific-procedures-living-animals-2018.pdf

Mattinson, P. (2015) *Punishment in Dog Training*. Available at: https://thehappypuppysite.com/punishment-in-dog-training/

Mattinson, P. (2016) *Dog Training: What To Do When Treats Don't Work*. Available at: https://thehappypuppysite.com/dog-training-when-treats-dont-work/

Mattinson, P. (2016) *Over Excited Dog: How Understanding Behavior Thresholds Can Help You*. Available at: https://thehappypuppysite.com/over-excited-dog/

Mattinson, P. (2018) *The Evidence for Positive Reinforcement Training in Dogs*. Available at: https://thehappypuppysite.com/the-evidence-for-positive-reinforcement-training-in-dogs/#comments

Mattinson, P. (2020) *Dog Training With Treats – Is Food Really Necessary?* Available at: https://thehappypuppysite.com/dog-training-with-treats/

Mattinson, P. (2020) *How Force-Free Dog Trainers Use Reinforcement to Get Great Results*. Available at: https://thehappypuppysite.com/reinforcement-in-dog-training/

Mattinson, T. (2018) *Suprelorin Implants For Dogs*. Available at: https://www.thelabradorsite.com/suprelorin-implants-for-dogs/

McConnell, P. (2009) *Dog-Dog Aggression, Puppies and 'Intensive Sniffing'*. Available at: https://www.patriciamcconnell.com/theotherendoftheleash/dog-dog-aggression-puppies-and-intensive-sniffing

McConnell, P. (2009) *Let's Talk: Treating Separation Anxiety*. Available at: https://www.patriciamcconnell.com/lets-talk-treating-separation-anxiety

McConnell, P. (2011) *One is the loneliest number: How to recognize and treat separation anxiety in dogs according to an expert*. Available at:

https://www.cbc.ca/life/pets/one-is-the-loneliest-number-how-to-recognize-and-treat-separation-anxiety-in-dogs-according-to-an-expert-1.5039538

McConnell, P. (2017) *What Was I Thinking? (Rescue Regrets are Usually Temporary)*. Available at: https://www.patriciamcconnell.com/theotherendoftheleash/what-was-i-thinking-rescue-regrets-are-usually-temporary

McLeod, S. (2021) *Systematic Desensitization as a Counterconditioning Process*. Available at: https://www.simplypsychology.org/Systematic-Desensitisation.html

Miller, L. (2015) *Positive Dog Training Doesn't Mean Ignoring 'Bad' Behavior*. Available at: https://www.thedodo.com/positive-dog-training-doesnt-mean-ignoring-bad-behavior-1316442910.html

Miller, P. (2003, updated 2019) *Is Your Dog Spoiled?* Available at: https://www.whole-dog-journal.com/behavior/demand-behavior/is-your-dog-spoiled/

Miller, P. (2003) *Think Your Dog Has ADHD?* Available at: https://www.whole-dog-journal.com/behavior/think-your-dog-has-adhd/

Miller, P. (2006) *Understanding Dog Appeasement Signals. These canine gestures are intended to do more than just 'calm' others*. Available at: https://www.whole-dog-journal.com/behavior/understanding-dog-appeasement-signals/

Miller, P. (2007, updated 2019) *The 5 Most Common Dog Training Mistakes. The top five errors committed when training your dog with positive techniques and positive dog training methods*. Available at: https://www.whole-dog-journal.com/training/the-5-most-common-dog-training-mistakes/

Miller, P. (2008, updated 2019) *How to Help With Separation Anxiety in Dogs*. Available at: https://www.whole-dog-journal.com/behavior/how-to-help-a-dog-with-separation-anxiety/

Miller, P. (2009) *Demand Behaviors in Dogs: How to eliminate your dog's demand behaviors (such as begging)*. Available at: https://www.whole-dog-journal.com/behavior/demand-behavior/demand-behaviors-in-dogs/

Moore, L. (4 March 2014) *Sausage Dogs Persecuted: the Fall of*

Dachshund during WW1. Available at: https://blog.maryevans.com/2014/03/sausage-dogs-persecuted-the-fall-of-dachshund-during-ww1.html

Morell, V. (2016) *Your dog remembers more than you think.* Available at: https://www.sciencemag.org/news/2016/11/your-dog-remembers-more-you-think

National Museum Scotland. *Neolithic dog skull.* Available at: https://www.nms.ac.uk/explore-our-collections/stories/scottish-history-and-archaeology/neolithic-dog-skull/

Nelson, J. (2017) *Fear Aggression in Dogs and How To Help.* Available at: https://iheartdogs.com/fear-aggression-in-dogs-and-how-to-help/

Nicholas, J. (2021) *When to Start Socializing Your New Puppy.* Available at: https://www.preventivevet.com/dogs/when-to-start-socializing-your-new-puppy

Norton, A. (2020) *Why Some Dogs Are at Higher Odds of Dying From Heat.* Available at: https://www.usnews.com/news/health-news/articles/2020-06-18/why-some-dogs-are-at-higher-odds-of-dying-from-heat

Oliveria, A., University of Lisbon. *Doberman.* Available at: http://www.dogzone.com/breeds/doberman/

Olson, L. (2011) *Adopting a Dog With Issues.* Available at: https://www.dogsnaturallymagazine.com/adopting-a-dog-with-issues/

Overall, K. (2014) *Separation Anxiety in Dogs.* American Kennel Club Canine Health Foundation. Available at: https://www.akcchf.org/educational-resources/podcasts/podcast-transcripts/Dr-Karen-Overall-Separation-Anxiety.pdf

Pack Leader Dog Care Services (2017) *The Positive Reinforcement Only Propaganda.* Available at: https://packleaderdogs.com/the-positive-reinforcement-only-propaganda/

Pappas, S. (2013) *Dogs Domesticated 33,000 Years Ago, Skull Suggests.* Available at: https://www.livescience.com/27691-dogs-domesticated-oldest-skull.html

Park, G. (2015) *Intestinal Obstruction in Dogs.* Available at: https://wagwalking.com/condition/intestinal-obstruction

Penelope (2018) *Dogs in Ancient Greece and Rome.* Available at: http://penelope.uchicago.edu/~grout/encyclopaedia_romana/miscellanea/canes/canes.html

PETA. *11 Shocking Animal Testing Statistics That Are Hard to Swallow.* Available at: https://www.peta.org/features/animal-experimentation-statistics/

PETA. *Animal Rights Uncompromised: Crating Dogs and Puppies.* Available at: https://www.peta.org/about-peta/why-peta/crating-dogs/

PETA. *International Animal Testing Programs.* Available at: https://www.peta.org/issues/animals-used-for-experimentation/us-government-animal-testing-programs/international-animal-testing-programs/

PetMD Editorial (Updated 2021) *Dog Dementia: Symptoms, Causes, Treatment and Life Expectancy.* Available at: https://www.petmd.com/dog/conditions/neurological/c_dg_cognitive_dysfunction_syndrome

Pryor, K. (2006) *Operant Conditioning and the Traditional Trainer.* Available at: https://clickertraining.com/node/87

Pryor, K. (2013) *Don't Socialize the Dog!* Available at: https://www.clickertraining.com/dont-socialize-the-dog

Pryor, K. (2013) *History of Clicker Training.* Available at: https://www.clickertraining.com/node/153

Psychologist World. *Pavlov's Dogs and Classical Conditioning.* Available at: https://www.psychologistworld.com/behavior/pavlov-dogs-classical-conditioning

Pultarova, T. (2017) *Why Do Dogs Chew Everything?* Available at: https://www.livescience.com/61096-why-dogs-chew-everything.html

Radermacher, A. (2018) *Big Dog, Little Dog: How IGF and humans influenced dog size.* Available at: https://genetics.thetech.org/original_news/news52

Rawlinson, S. (2001) *Dogs and the Alpha Myth.* Available at: https://www.doglistener.co.uk/alpha/thealphamyth.shtml

Rawlinson, S. (2003, updated March 2019) *Different Types of*

Dog Aggression. Available at: https://www.doglistener.co.uk/aggression/types.shtml

Rawlinson, S. (2006) *Dominance and Dog Behaviour.* Available at: https://www.doglistener.co.uk/aggression/dominant_behaviour.shtml

Rawlinson, S. (2008) *RSPCA Admit Spaying and Castrating Puppies at Six Weeks.* Available at: https://www.doglistener.co.uk/neutering/rspca.shtml

Rawlinson, S. (2015) *Understanding Instinct and Drive of Dogs.* Available at: https://www.doglistener.co.uk/instinct-and-drive-controls-our-dogs

Rawlinson, S. (2018) *Neutering Dogs. In Depth.* Available at: https://www.doglistener.co.uk/neutering_definitive

Reading Museum (2020) *Sacred animals of ancient Egypt.* Available at: https://www.readingmuseum.org.uk/blog/sacred-animals-ancient-egypt

Ross, V. (2012) *Look at This: Enormous Whales Have Enormous (and Interesting) Poop.* Available at: https://www.discovermagazine.com/environment/look-at-this-enormous-whales-have-enormous-and-interesting-poop

Rottweiler. Available at: https://dogtime.com/dog-breeds/rottweiler

Rowles, D. (2009) *Pack theory: Is the domestic dog still a pack animal?* Available at: https://www.streetdogrescue.com/aboutus/Pack_theory.pdf

Rütten and Fleissner (2004) *On the function of the greeting ceremony in social canids – exemplified by African wild dogs Lycaon pictus.* Available at: http://www.canids.org/canidnews/7/Greeting_ceremony_in_canids.pdf.

Sandolu, A. (2019) *Punishment could make your dog more pessimistic.* Fact checked by Gianna D'Emilio. Available at: https://www.medicalnewstoday.com/articles/326954

Schenkel, R. (1946) *Expression Studies on Wolves.* Available at: http://davemech.org/wolf-news-and-information/schenkels-classic-wolf-behavior-study-available-in-english/

Semyonova, A. (2003, updated Nov 2017) *The Social Organization of the*

Domestic Dog. Available at: https://nonlineardogs.com/analytical-papers/social-organization-domesticated-dog/

Sewanee, The University of the South. *Home Front, War Front: Sewanee and Fort Oglethorpe in World War I.* Available at: https://library.sewanee.edu/c.php?g=118671&p=773217

Seward, A., Ryan Veterinary Hospital, University of Pennsylvania School of Veterinary Medicine. *Fear of Thunderstorms and Fireworks.* Available at: https://www.vet.upenn.edu/docs/default-source/ryan/ryan-behavior-medicine/fear-of-thunderstorms-amp-fireworks-(pdf).pdf?sfvrsn=c15e17ba_2

Sexton, C., Smithsonian Mag (2020) *Why Fireworks Scare Some Dogs But Not Others.* Available at: https://www.smithsonianmag.com/science-nature/firework-fear-why-your-dog-does-or-doesnt-react-and-how-you-should-180975182/

Shaw Becker, K. (2018) *How Long Is Too Long to Leave Your Dog Alone?* Available at: https://healthypets.mercola.com/sites/healthypets/archive/2018/06/27/how-long-can-you-leave-a-dog-alone.aspx

Simon, L., University College Dublin. *Dogo Argentina.* Available at: http://www.dogzone.com/breeds/dogo-argentino/

Snowdog Guru (2015) *Early removal of puppy from mother.* Available at: https://www.snowdog.guru/early-removal-of-puppy-mother/

Speilman, B. (2015) *Structure and Function of the Endocrine System in Dogs.* Available at: https://www.petplace.com/article/dogs/pet-health/structure-and-function-of-the-endocrine-system-in-dogs/

Staff, A.K.C. (2020) *Bowel Obstruction in Dogs: Symptoms, Treatment, and Prevention.* Available at: https://www.akc.org/expert-advice/health/bowel-obstruction-in-dogs/

Staub, A. (2013) *What Is the Oldest Breed of Dog? 14 Ancient Dog Breeds.* Available at: https://www.mypawsitivelypets.com/2013/07/what-is-oldest-breed-of-dog-14-ancient.html

Stefanovic, S. (2015) *In the dog house: when does crating your canine become pet abuse?* Available at: https://www.theguardian.com/lifeandstyle/2015/jun/25/dogs-crating-pet-abuse

Stephens, T. (2013) *DNA study clarifies relationship between polar bears and brown bears*. Available at: https://news.ucsc.edu/2013/03/polar-bear-genomics.

Stillwell V., Positively Victoria. *Why I'm not (and never have been) a purely positive dog trainer*. Available at: https://positively.com/victorias-blog/why-im-not-and-never-have-been-a-purely-positive-dog-trainer/

Stilwell V., Positively Victoria (2013) *Why are dogs aggressive?* Available at: https://positively.com/victorias-blog/why-are-dogs-aggressive/

Stilwell, V., Positively Victoria (2014) *What is Positive Training?* Available at: https://positively.com/dog-training/positive-training/what-is-positive-training/

Summerfield, J. (2015) *Behaviour Medication: First-line therapy or last resort*. Available at: http://www.drjensdogblog.com/behavior-medication-first-line-therapy-or-last-resort/

Sundman, A-S. (2017) PhD student essay: *On how dogs behave themselves: The why and how of testing dog behaviour.*

Taazakhabar News Bureau. *15 countries where people eat dogs and cats*. Available at: https://taazakhabarnews.com/dogs-in-the-pot/

Tabor, B. (2019) *Heat Stroke in Dogs*. Available at: https://www.vetfolio.com/learn/article/heatstroke-in-dogs

Taylor, H. (2018) *Why not just punish my dog for behaviours I don't like?* Available at: http://www.helentaylordorset.co.uk/Punishmen

Tennenhouse, E. (2018) *Let's Journey Through the Mind of a Dog*. Available at: https://www.discovermagazine.com/planet-earth/lets-journey-through-the-mind-of-a-dog

Tenzin-Dolma, L. (2017) *Thesis: Creating a Dog Centred Care Approach*. Available at: https://theiscp.com/2017/08/thesis-creating-dog-centred-care-approach-must-stop-always-trying-fix-things/

The Association of Professional Dog Trainers (accessed 2018) *Dominance and Dog Training*. Available at: https://apdt.com/resource-center/dominance-and-dog-training/

The Big Five Super Trait: Neuroticism. Available at: https://www.theworldcounts.com/happiness/define-neuroticism-personality

Tóth, Z.J., Károli Gáspár University, Budapest, Hungary (2012). Available at: https://www.law.muni.cz/sborniky/dny_prava_2011/

files/prispevky/03%20ZVIREToth_Zoltan.pdf

Training Your Dog and You. *Dog Training Corrections are controversial, but what do we know of them?* Available at: https://www.training-your-dog-and-you.com/Dog-Training-Corrections.html

Twedt, D.C. *Is it Vomiting or Regurgitation?* Available at: http://vetfolio.s3.amazonaws.com/13/06/b90ee9954a39bc207105f32efcb5/is-it-vomiting-or-regurgitation-pdf.pdf

UK Wolf Conservation Trust. *Domestication: the Evolution of the Dog.* Available at: http://ukwct.org/files/domestication.pdf

Uller, C. (2017) *Your dog can remember more than you think.* Available at: https://phys.org/news/2017-02-dog.html

UNESCO (2015) *Susa.* Available at: https://whc.unesco.org/en/list/1455/

Valente, S. *Countering the Effects of Neuter.* Healthy and Happy Dog. Available at: https://healthyandhappydog.com/countering-the-effects-of-neuter/

Valente, S. *Physical Effects of Spay.* Happy Healthy Dog. Available at: https://healthyandhappydog.com/physical-effects-of-spay/

Vesna, M. (2019) *Origin of the Dachshund Breed.* Available at: https://www.sausagedogworld.com/history-and-origin-of-dachshund-breed/

Vets Now. *When is it too hot to walk a dog?* Available at: https://www.vets-now.com/summer/when-is-it-too-hot-to-walk-a-dog/

Victoria, T. *Canine Heat Stroke.* Available at: https://www.iowaveterinaryspecialties.com/student-scholars/canine-heat-stroke-literature-review

Vilá, C., Leonard, J.A. (2012) *Canid phylogeny and origin of the domestic dog.* Available at: https://www.researchgate.net/publication/287355173_Canid_phylogeny_and_origin_of_the_domestic_dog

Villalobos Rescue Centre. *Pitbull Facts.* Available at: http://www.vrcpitbull.com/pit-bull-facts/

Webster, J. (Updated 2020) *ABC: Antecedent, Behavior, Consequence.* Available at: https://www.thoughtco.com/abc-antecedent-behavior-and-consequence-3111263

Welton, M. *Neutering Your Male Dog: Pros and Cons.* Available at: https://www.yourpurebredpuppy.com/health/articles/neutering-male-dog.html

Welton, M. *Spaying Your Female Dog: Pros and Cons.* Available at: https://www.yourpurebredpuppy.com/health/articles/spaying-female-dog.html

Western Wildlife Outreach. Wolf Ecology and Behavior. Available at: http://westernwildlife.org/gray-wolf-outreach-project/biology-behavior-4/

White, C. (2019) *Stalin's Kamikaze Canines: Soviets Trained Dogs to Blow up Tanks.* Available at: https://www.warhistoryonline.com/instant-articles/soviets-during-ww2-used-dogs.html

What are endorphins and why are they relevant to highly active dogs? Available at: http://www.balancebehaviour.org/endorphins/

Wilde, N. (2009) *The Man Who Cried Alpha.* Available at: https://www.dogstardaily.com/blogs/man-who-cried-alpha

Wildlife Online. *Mange in Red Fox.* Available at: https://www.wildlifeonline.me.uk/articles/view/mange-in-the-red-fox

Wilkes, G. (2015) *10 Problems with positive reinforcement.* Available at: https://clickandtreat.com/wordpress/?p=1524

Williams, S. (29 Feb 2020) *Coronavirus: Rescuing China's animals during the outbreak.* Available at: https://www.bbc.com/news/world-asia-china-51614957

Wilson, C. (2019) *Animal testing: Which ones are used in UK experiments?* Available at: https://www.bbc.com/news/newsbeat-47800019

Wolf Centre (2008) *The Quarterly Publication of the International Wolf Centre*, Volume 18, Number 4, Winter 2008. Available at: https://wolf.org/wpcontent/uploads/2013/12/winter2008.pdf

Woods, J. (2018) *14 Dog Shelters Speak Out: What You Should Know BEFORE Adopting a Dog.* Available at: https://www.allthingsdogs.com/adopting-a-dog/

Wooten, S. (2018) *5 things you need to know about food aggression.* Available at: https://www.dvm360.com/view/5-things-you-need-know-about-food-aggression

Yin, S. (2009) *Handling Dominance Aggression in Dogs.* Available at:

https://drsophiayin.com/blog/entry/handling_dominance_aggression_in_dogs/)

Yin, S. (2012) *How Technology from 30 Years Ago is Helping Military Dogs Perform Better Now.* Available at: https://drsophiayin.com/blog/entry/how-technology-from-30-years-ago-is-helping-military-dogs-perform-better-no/

Yin, S. (2018) *The Dominance Controversy.* Available at: https://drsophiayin.com/philosophy/dominance/

Zolfagharifard, E. for DailyMail.com (2015) *Man's best friend has not been around as long as we thought: 30,000-year-old fossil of the oldest dog turns out to be a WOLF.* Available at: https://www.dailymail.co.uk/sciencetech/article-2941736/Man-s-best-friend-not-long-thought-30-000-year-old-fossil-oldest-dog-turns-WOLF.html

Zurlo, J. et al. (2011) *Clearly, some testing and research is done in dogs for historical reasons [existence of benchmark data] rather than because they are the best models.* Available at: https://navs.org/learn-more/dogs-in-research/